Blockchain Applications for Smart Contract Technologies

Abdelkader Mohamed Sghaier Derbali
Taibah University, Saudi Arabia

A volume in the Advances in Information Security, Privacy, and Ethics (AISPE) Book Series

IGI Global
PUBLISHER of TIMELY KNOWLEDGE

Published in the United States of America by
IGI Global
Engineering Science Reference (an imprint of IGI Global)
701 E. Chocolate Avenue
Hershey PA, USA 17033
Tel: 717-533-8845
Fax: 717-533-8661
E-mail: cust@igi-global.com
Web site: http://www.igi-global.com

Library of Congress Cataloging-in-Publication Data

CIP DATA IN PROCESS

Blockchain Applications for Smart Contract Technologies
Abdelkader Mohamed Sghaier Derbali
2024 Engineering Science Reference

ISBN: 9798369315118 (h/c) | ISBN:: 9798369345153 (s/c) | eISBN: 9798369315125

This book is published in the IGI Global book series Advances in Information Security, Privacy, and Ethics (AISPE) (ISSN: 1948-9730; eISSN: 1948-9749)

British Cataloguing in Publication Data
A Cataloguing in Publication record for this book is available from the British Library.

For electronic access to this publication, please contact: eresources@igi-global.com.

Advances in Information Security, Privacy, and Ethics (AISPE) Book Series

ISSN:1948-9730
EISSN:1948-9749

MISSION

As digital technologies become more pervasive in everyday life and the Internet is utilized in ever increasing ways by both private and public entities, concern over digital threats becomes more prevalent.

The **Advances in Information Security, Privacy, & Ethics (AISPE) Book Series** provides cutting-edge research on the protection and misuse of information and technology across various industries and settings. Comprised of scholarly research on topics such as identity management, cryptography, system security, authentication, and data protection, this book series is ideal for reference by IT professionals, academicians, and upper-level students.

COVERAGE

- Electronic Mail Security
- IT Risk
- CIA Triad of Information Security
- Computer ethics
- Technoethics
- Security Information Management
- Global Privacy Concerns
- Device Fingerprinting
- Tracking Cookies
- Cookies

The Advances in Information Security, Privacy, and Ethics (AISPE) Book Series (ISSN 1948-9730) is published by IGI Global, 701 E. Chocolate Avenue, Hershey, PA 17033-1240, USA, www.igi-global.com. This series is composed of titles available for purchase individually; each title is edited to be contextually exclusive from any other title within the series. For pricing and ordering information please visit http://www.igi-global.com/book-series/advances-information-security-privacy-ethics/37157. Postmaster: Send all address changes to above address.

Titles in this Series

For a list of additional titles in this series, please visit:
http://www.igi-global.com/book-series/advances-information-security-privacy-ethics/37157

Investigating and Combating Gender-Related Victimization
Gabriela Mesquita Borges (University of Lusíada, Portugal) Ana Guerreiro (University of Maia, Portugal & School of Criminology, Faculty of Law, University of Porto, Portugal) and Miriam Pina (School of Criminology, Faculty of Law, University of Porto, Portugal & Faculté de Droit, des Sciences Criminelles et d'administration Publique, Université de Lausanne, Switzerland)
Information Science Reference • copyright 2024 • 279pp • H/C (ISBN: 9798369354360) • US $265.00 (our price)

Navigating Cyber Threats and Cybersecurity in the Logistics Industry
Noor Zaman Jhanjhi (School of Computing Science, Taylor's University, Malaysia) and Imdad Ali Shah (School of Computing Science, Taylor's University, Malaysia)
Information Science Reference • copyright 2024 • 448pp • H/C (ISBN: 9798369338162) • US $295.00 (our price)

Analyzing and Mitigating Security Risks in Cloud Computing
Pawan Kumar Goel (Raj Kumar Goel Institute of Technology, India) Hari Mohan Pandey (Bournemouth University, UK) Amit Singhal (Raj Kumar Goel Institute of Technology, India) and Sanyam Agarwal (ACE Group of Colleges, India)
Engineering Science Reference • copyright 2024 • 270pp • H/C (ISBN: 9798369332498) • US $290.00 (our price)

Cybersecurity Issues and Challenges in the Drone Industry
Imdad Ali Shah (School of Computing Science, Taylor's University, Malaysia) and Noor Zaman Jhanjhi (School of Computing Science, Taylor's University, Malaysia)
Information Science Reference • copyright 2024 • 573pp • H/C (ISBN: 9798369307748) • US $275.00 (our price)

Emerging Technologies and Security in Cloud Computing

For an entire list of titles in this series, please visit:
http://www.igi-global.com/book-series/advances-information-security-privacy-ethics/37157

IGI Global
PUBLISHER of TIMELY KNOWLEDGE

701 East Chocolate Avenue, Hershey, PA 17033, USA
Tel: 717-533-8845 x100 • Fax: 717-533-8661
E-Mail: cust@igi-global.com • www.igi-global.com

Table of Contents

Detailed Table of Contents

growth due to the development of smart homes and smart cities. Smart devices are more prone to attacks and the low processing power, storage capacity, and network capacity make current security or cryptography techniques unusable. Blockchain has acquired huge attention since its use in Bitcoin, due to the numerous prospects it raises. Blockchain offers several advantages in addressing security and privacy challenges associated with IoT nodes and networks. This chapter provides insights into incorporating blockchain into IoT networks to achieve confidentiality and safety. The chapter covers details of IoT, smart home applications, and security concerns. The various blockchain solutions to protect IoT and smart home systems are also covered in the study.

This chapter investigates the safe haven property and hedge of gold especially during GFC and COVID-19 for G7 stock markets by using DCC-GARCH and wavelet coherence analysis. The findings reveal that the dynamic conditional correlation between gold and each G7 stock market decreased significantly during extreme market conditions, especially during GFC and COVID-19. The results show that gold served as a strong safe haven asset for all G7 stock markets except Nikkei225 during GFC. However, gold has maintained this traditional role as a safe haven only for CAC40, S&PTSX, FTSE/MIB, and FTSE100 during the COVID-19 pandemic. The optimal portfolio weights of gold in each G7 stock market significantly increased during GFG and COVID-19 pandemic, meaning that investors should invest more in the gold as a 'flight-to-safety asset' during market turmoil. The decomposition of the coherence between gold and each G7 stock market into three investment horizons demonstrates a weak correlation in both the short term and the long term for the normal and extreme conditions market.

stock indexes in the financial market of Saudi Arabia exhibit significant peaks, particularly during the first quarter of 2020 when the COVID-19 pandemic was most widespread. Interestingly, they observe that the announcements of death cases related to COVID-19 in the United States have a substantial impact on the stock market index in Saudi Arabia. This study is the first of its kind to examine the effect of unexpected events in financial markets, specifically those related to new cases, confirmed cases, and death cases of COVID-19 on the volatility of the financial market in Saudi Arabia.

As of the publication of Bowen's masterpiece Social Responsibilities of the Businessman in 1953, it can be claimed that people have started to think that corporations have responsibilities to their societies in addition to their principal task of maximising shareholders' value. Corporate social responsibility owes its existence to this paradigm shift. Currently, there are a bunch of notions that are closely related to or somehow intertwined with the concept of corporate social responsibility. This review has been written to discuss the similarities and differences between these terms—triple bottom line, sustainability, corporate social performance, business ethics, corporate social responsiveness, corporate citizenship, corporate governance, corporate philanthropy, socially responsible investment, environmental, social and governance—and corporate social responsibility, as well as to provide frequently cited definitions of this concept.

Economic growth is reflected in SDG8 of the Sustainable Development Goals. Financial stability has been identified as a factor promoting economic growth. However, there is little evidence on the effect of financial stability on economic growth in Nigeria. This study empirically examines the effect of financial stability on economic growth in Nigeria from 1993 to 2017. The results show a positive relationship between financial stability and economic growth in Nigeria. Specifically, the result shows that a high ZSCORE, which reflects low insolvency risk, has a positive effect on economic growth. Similarly, fewer nonperforming loans improve economic growth in Nigeria. In contrast, capital adequacy was found to have a negative effect on economic growth in Nigeria.

Amazon is a world leader in e-commerce and robotization. Its robotic mobile fulfillment systems (RMFS) aim to speed up product delivery by using robots to move shelves. In terms of speed, precision, and profitability, the RMFS solution seems to guarantee economic and commercial success. Nevertheless, the integration of robotization is accompanied by an increase in workload, daily tasks, and accident risks. The aim of the present study is to provide an in-depth analysis of Amazon RFMS employees' perceptions of current robotization. Through a netnographic study of the comments and opinions of Amazon employees working in robotized warehouses, the empirical study will gather argumentative thinking around the effect of digital transformation in RFMS in terms of employability, working conditions, and quality of work life. The results of the study show a consolidation of working conditions accompanied by stress and a risk of job loss. Certain risks and doubts are also present, notably around the possibility of work-related accidents and the man-machine interactions.

This chapter examines the effect of surprises from financial markets announcements relating to new, confirmed, and death cases of COVID-19 in USA on the volatility of financial markets in Tunisia. The authors use GARCH(1.1) specification by incorporation the surprise component in the estimated model during the period from January 1, 2019 until December 31, 2020. The empirical findings show that the evolution of the daily returns and volatilities of the stock market index in Tunisia show very significant peaks in their evolutions in particular during the first three months of 2020 during the most significant spread of the COVID-19 pandemic. The authors show that the announcements of the new cases of COVID-19 in the United States have a significant impact on the volatility of financial markets in Tunisia. This chapter is the first paper that examines the effect of surprises from financial markets announcements relating to new, confirmed, and death cases of COVID-19 on the volatility of financial markets in Tunisia.

alarm systems, and so on. It also highlights the benefits and difficulties that AI-driven financial apps provide. In summary, artificial intelligence (AI) has enormous promise in banking, but it also confronts several obstacles that, if correctly recognized and overcome, might broaden its use. This chapter is an invaluable tool for researchers, lawmakers, and bank officials who want to learn more about the unrealized potential of artificial intelligence in banking.

Preface

Welcome to *Blockchain Applications for Smart Contract Technologies*, a comprehensive reference book edited by Abdelkader Mohamed Sghaier Derbali from Applied College, Taibah University, Saudi Arabia. In recent years, the integration of blockchain technology and smart contracts has become a focal point for both research and business endeavors. This technology has empowered the deployment of smart contracts, automating, and executing agreements among users, thus revolutionizing various industries.

Blockchain, as a distributed and secure ledger, ensures transparent and immutable data storage. It enables users to perform transactions without the need for a trusted third party. Smart contracts, which are self-executing software applications, streamline processes such as the sale of goods, contract execution, and currency exchange. Stored on the blockchain, these contracts are accessible to all users.

The potential applications of blockchain and smart contracts are vast and varied, spanning digital identity management, product traceability, document certification, supply chain management, e-voting, intellectual property, asset transfers, online payments, medical records management, insurance management, and more. The advantages of blockchain are manifold, offering complete transparency, heightened security, and resistance to tampering. Smart contracts further reduce costs and delays associated with manual processes, providing immutable and automatically executable agreements.

This book aims to present a comprehensive overview of academic and industrial works proposing applications based on blockchain and/or smart contracts across diverse sectors. From healthcare and finance to e-government, e-voting, Internet of Things, energy, identity, telecommunications, Metaverse/NFT, and notary services, each part of the book is dedicated to exploring applications in a specific area. The content will cover fundamental concepts, theories, protocols, architectures, and delve into specific research topics related to blockchains and smart contracts.

In addition to focusing on applications, the book includes parts dedicated to blockchain and smart contract fundamentals, as well as surveys in these domains.

Each chapter has undergone careful review by academic and industry researchers, ensuring the quality and relevance of the content.

We hope this edited reference book serves as a valuable resource for researchers, professionals, and enthusiasts interested in exploring the multifaceted world of blockchain applications and smart contract technologies. The diverse range of topics covered reflects the dynamic and evolving nature of this field, providing readers with insights into the latest advancements and potential future directions.

CHAPTER OVERVIEW

Chapter 1: COVID-19 or Russia-Ukraine Conflict, Which Is Informative in Defining the Dynamic Relationship Between Bitcoin and Major Energy Commodities?

This chapter delves into the intricate dynamics between Bitcoin and major energy commodities, evaluating the impact of COVID-19 and the Russia-Ukraine conflict on the correlation between returns and volatilities. Utilizing the GARCH-DCC(1,1) model with a dummy variable, the authors find substantial and noteworthy dynamic conditional correlation between energy commodities indices and Bitcoin, particularly when incorporating shocks from the specified geopolitical events. The results shed light on the financialization of both energy commodities indices and Bitcoin, emphasizing the varying responses in dynamic conditional correlation during different shocks.

Chapter 2: Internet of Things Security Using Blockchain: A Study on Smart Home-Based Applications

Examining the intersection of the Internet of Things (IoT) and Blockchain, this chapter investigates the security challenges posed by smart home applications. Authored by researchers from Vellore Institute of Technology, India, the chapter provides insights into integrating Blockchain technology to enhance confidentiality and safety in IoT networks. Covering IoT fundamentals, smart home applications, and security concerns, the chapter also explores various Blockchain solutions to safeguard IoT and smart home systems.

Chapter 3: Does Gold React as a Safe Haven and Hedge for G7 Stock Markets? Comparative Assessment Among COVID-19 Pandemic Versus Global Financial Crisis

This paper, authored by researchers from Tunisia and Saudi Arabia, explores the safe haven properties of gold during the COVID-19 pandemic and the Global Financial Crisis (GFC) for G7 stock markets. Utilizing DCC-GARCH and wavelet coherence analysis, the authors reveal that gold served as a strong safe haven asset for G7 stock markets, with variations in its effectiveness during GFC and the COVID-19 pandemic. The findings emphasize the significance of gold as a 'flight-to-safety asset' and its role in optimizing portfolio weights during market turmoil.

Chapter 4: Metaverse and NFT

Authored by researchers from PES Modern Institute of Business Studies, India, this chapter explores the rise of Non-Fungible Tokens (NFTs) and the emergence of the Metaverse. It provides an in-depth look at how NFTs are transforming digital ownership, the role of art in the digital age, and their impact on the economy, commerce, and social structures within the Metaverse.

Chapter 5: The Development of ChatGPT and Its Implications for the Future of Customer Service in the Hospitality Industry

This chapter, co-authored by researchers from Bangladesh and India, examines the transformative role of artificial intelligence, particularly ChatGPT, in revolutionizing customer service in the hospitality industry. Highlighting the integration of AI-driven solutions, the chapter explores how chatbots, powered by models like ChatGPT, have reshaped communication in the hotel business, providing personalized recommendations, support, and continuous interaction.

Chapter 6: The impact of COVID-19 on Financial Market Volatility in Saudi Arabia

Saudi Arabian researchers investigate the impact of unexpected events related to COVID-19 on financial market volatility in Saudi Arabia. Using a GARCH(1,1) model, the authors analyze daily returns and volatilities of stock indexes, revealing significant peaks during the initial months of the COVID-19 epidemic. The study emphasizes the influence of global events on the financial markets of Saudi Arabia, providing valuable insights into the connection between the pandemic and market volatility.

Chapter 7: A Semantical Approach to the Concept of CSR: Its Definitional Evolution and Nearly Identical Notions

Authored by researchers from Turkey, this chapter delves into the semantic nuances of Corporate Social Responsibility (CSR) and its related concepts. It provides a comprehensive review, comparing CSR with terms like triple bottom line, sustainability, business ethics, and more. This chapter aims to enhance understanding by exploring the similarities and differences, offering frequently cited definitions, and contributing to the ongoing discourse surrounding corporate responsibility.

Chapter 8: Impact of Financial Stability on Economic Growth in Nigeria

Coming from a researcher at the Central Bank of Nigeria, this chapter explores the relationship between financial stability and economic growth in Nigeria from 1993 to 2017. Employing the ordinary least square (OLS) regression method, the author identifies a positive relationship between financial stability indicators and economic growth, shedding light on the specific factors such as ZSCORE and nonperforming loans that influence economic development in the Nigerian context.

Chapter 9: Employees and Robots in Amazon's Robotic Mobile Fulfillment Systems: A Netnographic Analysis of a Supply Chain Transformation

Conducted by a researcher from Morocco, this chapter presents a netnographic analysis of Amazon's Robotic Mobile Fulfillment Systems (RMFS). It explores the perceptions of employees working in robotized warehouses, examining the impact of robotic integration on employability, working conditions, and quality of work life. The study uncovers both positive and negative aspects of the digital transformation within the context of Amazon's supply chain.

Chapter 10: Does COVID-19 News Influence Financial Market Volatility in Tunisia?

Authored by a Tunisian researcher, this chapter investigates the influence of COVID-19-related announcements on the volatility of financial markets in Tunisia. Utilizing the GARCH(1,1) model, the study analyzes surprises from announcements related to new, confirmed, and death cases of COVID-19. The findings highlight significant peaks in the evolution of daily returns and volatilities of the stock market index in Tunisia during the early months of the COVID-19 pandemic.

Chapter 11: Nigeria cNGN Stablecoin: Everything You Need to Know About cNGN and eNaira CBDC

This chapter, written by a researcher from the Central Bank of Nigeria based in the United Kingdom, explores the features, benefits, and challenges of the Nigeria cNGN stablecoin. The study compares the cNGN with the eNaira central bank digital currency, providing insights into the potential advantages of the cNGN, such as faster payments and increased participation in the financial system.

Chapter 12: Leveraging Transparency and Privacy Through Blockchain Technology

Authored by researchers from Christ (Deemed to be University) in Delhi, India, this chapter explores the role of Blockchain technology in maintaining transparency and privacy. Discussing various approaches to address data privacy challenges in blockchain, the chapter emphasizes the intricate balance between data consistency, transparency, and privacy. It aims to contribute to the understanding of how blockchain can be applied in different applications and industries to address security concerns.

Chapter 13: Blockchain Health: Smart Contracts Transforming Healthcare Operations

Authored by researchers from India, this chapter explores the transformative potential of blockchain-powered smart contracts in healthcare operations. The authors discuss the role of smart contracts in enhancing transparency, security, and efficiency in managing complex healthcare workflows. By leveraging blockchain's decentralized and tamper-resistant nature, the chapter addresses concerns related to data breaches and unauthorized access, offering a comprehensive overview of the evolving landscape of healthcare operations.

Chapter 14: Applications of Artificial Intelligence Techniques in Modern Banking Sectors

Collaboratively written by researchers from various institutions in India, this chapter provides a comprehensive overview of the use of artificial intelligence (AI) techniques in modern banking sectors. The authors discuss the application of AI in diverse banking domains, including loan approval, customer lifecycle management, and customer services. The chapter offers insights into the benefits and challenges associated with AI-driven financial applications, making it a valuable resource for researchers, policymakers, and banking professionals interested in the potential of AI in the banking industry.

In the realm of *Blockchain Applications for Smart Contract Technologies*, the collaborative efforts of esteemed contributors have woven a tapestry that captures the dynamic landscape of blockchain technology and smart contracts. Under the guidance of Abdelkader Mohamed Sghaier Derbali, the editor of this comprehensive reference book, each chapter stands as a testament to the evolving synergy between academia and industry in exploring the vast applications of blockchain.

The preface sets the stage, defining the transformative nature of blockchain and smart contracts. These technologies have not only automated and streamlined agreements but have also ushered in an era of transparency, security, and efficiency. As we delve into the specific chapters, the diverse range of applications unfolds, reflecting the multifaceted potential of blockchain across sectors such as healthcare, finance, Metaverse/NFT, and more.

Chapter 1 initiates a profound examination of the interplay between Bitcoin and major energy commodities, contextualizing this dynamic against the backdrops of the COVID-19 pandemic and the Russia-Ukraine conflict. The subsequent chapters journey through the intricacies of IoT security, the safe haven properties of gold in G7 stock markets, the rise of NFTs and the Metaverse, and the revolutionary impact of artificial intelligence, notably ChatGPT, in the hospitality industry.

We traverse continents, exploring the impact of unexpected events on financial market volatility in Saudi Arabia, examining the semantic evolution of Corporate Social Responsibility in Turkey, and investigating the symbiotic relationship between financial stability and economic growth in Nigeria. The netnographic analysis of Amazon's Robotic Mobile Fulfillment Systems sheds light on the human experience amidst automation, while Tunisia's financial markets navigate the ripples caused by COVID-19-related news.

The exploration extends to the financial realm with a detailed investigation into Nigeria's cNGN stablecoin and a critical analysis of the implications of artificial intelligence in modern banking sectors. The journey concludes with an insightful exploration of blockchain's role in preserving transparency and privacy, and an in-depth analysis of the transformative potential of blockchain-powered smart contracts in healthcare operations.

This edited reference book, with its meticulously reviewed chapters, is a valuable repository of knowledge. It is not merely a collection of individual insights but a cohesive narrative that paints a comprehensive picture of the ever-evolving landscape of blockchain applications and smart contract technologies. We extend our gratitude to the authors for their dedicated contributions and hope this compilation serves as an enduring resource for researchers, professionals, and enthusiasts alike, sparking further innovations and advancements in this rapidly evolving field.

Editor:

Abdelkader Mohamed Sghaier Derbali
Taibah University, Saudi Arabia

Chapter 1
COVID-19 or Russia-Ukraine Conflict, Which Is Informative in Defining the Dynamic Relationship Between Bitcoin and Major Energy Commodities?

Abdelkader Mohamed Sghaier Derbali
https://orcid.org/0000-0003-4098-3120
Applied College, Taibah University, Saudi Arabia

ABSTRACT

This chapter examines an essential methodology to evaluate the influence of the COVID-19 and Russia-Ukraine conflict surprises and conception statements employed for the dynamic conditional correlation between returns and volatilities of energy commodity indices and Bitcoin. To assess analytically the unexpected component of COVID-19 and Russia-Ukraine conflict surprises, the authors use GARCH-DCC(1,1) model by incorporating a dummy variable which measures the surprise factor during the period of study from January 4, 2016, to April 4, 2022. The results suggest significant and considerable dynamic conditional correlation between energy commodities indices and Bitcoin if COVID-19 pandemic and Russia-Ukraine conflict shocks are incorporated in variance assessments. Additionally, these outcomes demonstrate the financialization phenomena of energy commodities indices and Bitcoin. The authors find that the dynamic conditional correlation between energy commodities indices and Bitcoin start to respond considerably more in the situation of Russia-Ukraine conflict shocks than COVID-19 surprises.

DOI: 10.4018/979-8-3693-1511-8.ch001

1. INTRODUCTION

Financial markets are strongly feeling the effects of global crises, and this is nothing new. Climate disasters, pandemics, political unrest, and military conflicts can compromise our security, health, infrastructure and international relations. These sweeping changes are also hurting businesses and the global economy. They cause considerable uncertainty, which poses a significant threat to investments in financial markets.

The COVID-19 pandemic, unfortunately, fits this picture, harming countries' economies and threatening entire stock markets. In Canada and the United States, stock markets quickly lost more than 30%, erasing most of the gains made in recent years. As the progression of the COVID-19 outbreak in these two countries has not yet peaked, it is unclear what is likely to happen in the coming weeks. The COVID-19 pandemic has thrown financial markets into a whirlwind, the uniqueness of this crisis and how business leaders and government officials can support the economy during this particularly intense time.

The COVID-19 pandemic is unprecedented in its scope and global impact, posing challenges to policy makers and the empirical analysis of its direct and indirect effects within the interconnected global economy. The outbreak of COVID-19 in December 2019, the global economy began to feel the pressure of the outbreak of violence that gripped the planet without any immunization for a year or more, organizations, governments and businesses are wondering how best to prepare for likely business and operational disruptions, as are expanding business and the legitimate ramifications of overseeing such a wellness emergency.

With the invasion of Ukraine by Russia on Thursday, February 24, the conflict between the two nations turned into a real war. This could also have serious economic consequences.

11th world power in terms of gross domestic product (GDP), Russia is one of the world's leading exporters of natural gas. It also supplies petroleum, cereals, such as wheat and rapeseed, and industrial metals, such as nickel and aluminum. In this context, one of the first consequences of the war in Ukraine should be an increase in the price of energy and certain raw materials.

On 24 February alone, the price of natural gas rose by more than 25% on the TTF market, a platform located in the Netherlands and considered a benchmark in Europe.

Several factors explain these pressures on energy and commodity prices. First, Russia could voluntarily reduce its offer, in order to exert pressure on the countries, in particular European, likely to impose the heaviest economic sanctions on it. According to a classic market mechanism, with unchanged demand, the price of a good increases when the quantities supplied decrease. On the other hand, in the face of sanctions taken by the United States and Europe, Russia could find itself increasingly isolated and reduce its participation in trade, which would lead other countries to seek alternative sources of energy and therefore more expensive. Finally, the war unleashed in Ukraine could lead to the deterioration of the infrastructures necessary for the export of goods: ports, gas pipelines, oil pipelines, etc.

In France, as in many countries, the mechanisms for setting gas and gasoline prices are complex and only partly depend on natural gas and oil prices. Rising prices on international energy and commodity markets should, however, cause the acceleration of inflation which made a comeback in the United States and Europe last year.

This acceleration in inflation could have two major consequences:

- First, it should weigh on purchasing power, i.e., the ability of households to buy goods and services with their income. If inflation is higher than the increase in household income, then purchasing power declines. This is also the scenario forecast by the National Institute of Statistics and Economic Studies (INSEE) for the year 2022. According to forecasts by the Institute published last December, the purchasing power of households should fall in France by 0.2% in 2022. The "additional" inflation generated by the war in Ukraine should aggravate this phenomenon.
- The acceleration of inflation could then encourage central banks, including the European Central Bank (ECB) for the euro zone and the Federal Reserve (FED) in the United States, to further tighten monetary policies. To limit inflation, they have already announced the forthcoming end of the quantitative easing programs implemented at the start of the Covid-19 crisis, such as the PEPP in Europe, and increases interest rate futures. Due to the war in Ukraine, central banks could accelerate the implementation of these strategies to the detriment of economic activity.

Finally, Russia's invasion of Ukraine has caused turbulence in international financial markets. Most stock markets in the United States and Europe closed lower. Unsurprisingly, the stocks most affected are those most exposed to the Russian market. For France, it is, for example, banking establishments.

On the Paris Stock Exchange, the CAC 40 index fell by nearly 3.8% during the session on Thursday, February 24.

In recent years, Russia, for its part, has tried to reduce its exposure to the international financial system, by considerably reducing the amount of its public debt and by building up foreign exchange reserves. If the United States and European countries were to completely exclude Russia from the international financial system through their sanctions, Russia's economy could collapse.

This paper is very directly connected to the recent financial and economic literature in the response of the correlation among the returns of Bitcoin and the energy commodities (Crude Oil West Texas Intermediate, Brent Oil, and Natural Gas) to the COVID-19 surprises and Russia-Ukraine conflict through the used period of study since January 04, 2016, to April 04, 2022. Therefore, it is crucial to consider a fundamental connection amongst the heathy crisis and the war conflict surprises and the volatility of financial stock market indices returns, particularly, energy commodities and Bitcoin returns.

Therefore, we study in our article the coronavirus and Russia-Ukraine conflict as a possible factor of the volatility of energy commodities and Bitcoin returns is significant specified used period of rapid catastrophe of the international financial stock market indices and the main role of the healthy and war crises actions on the financial asset values. In this research, we investigate empirically the moment-varying connections amongst strategic commodities including segment of energy (Crude Oil West Texas Intermediate, Brent Oil, and Natural Gas) and Bitcoin, through the period of study since January 04, 2016, to April 04, 2022. Econometrically, we employ the GARCH-DCC (1.1) approach with integrating of the coronavirus and Russia-Ukraine conflict which measured by the dummy variables.

The empirical findings of this paper validate a considerable correlation among Bitcoin and energy commodity indices if coronavirus and Russia-Ukraine conflict surprises are included in variance estimations. These findings demonstrate the existence of the financialization of energy commodity markets and Bitcoin and external factors especially, in the case of health, politic and social. Additionally, the empirical findings associated to the degree of the tenacity of the volatility, are susceptible in the existence of healthy crisis and Russia-Ukraine conflict shocks into the employed GARCH-DCC (1,1) methodology. The dynamic conditional correlation (DCC) among Bitcoin and selected energy commodity indices emerge to react significantly additional in the case of coronavirus surprises than the Russia-Ukraine conflict surprises.

Finally, this research is structured as follows: in the second section, we present a literature review. Section 3 describes the econometric procedure employed in this paper. In the section 4, we present the dataset utilized in our investigation. The section 5 exposes the empirical outcomes relative to the influence of coronavirus confirmed cases in USA and in China on the association amongst energy commodity and Bitcoin. Finally, in section 6, we conclude, and we present some important policy implications of this study.

2. INTRODUCTION

For the sudden incidents, comprising the terrorist assaults, wars, financial coverage news, and wholesome crisis, will result surprise, panic and worry among the worldwide traders and outcome withinside the short panic-promoting response (Burch et al., 2016; Derbali et al., 2020a; Derbali et al., 2020b; Derbali et al., 2012a, Derbali et al., 2021b). A growing grouping of monetary and economic framework, along with the research of Carter and Simkins (2004), Chen and Siems (2004), Nikkinen et al. (2008), Kollias et al. (2011), Derbali and Jamel (2019), and Papakyriakou et al. (2019), which has forwarded the effect of the terrorist attacks on the worldwide economic inventory marketplace indices.

Guidolin and La Ferrara (2010), Hudson and Urquhart (2015) and Gu et al. (2012) study the impact of each violent and non-violent international activities on worldwide inventory markets. Jamel and Derbali (2019) display that terrorism elements is a giant and vital aspect in clarifying the estimate volatilities of the inventory marketplace returns withinside the situation of the DSEWI (Damascus Securities Exchange Weighted Index), which ought to be accredited into rationalization after assessing volatility.

Also, Ye and Karali (2016) hire an intraday dataset to analyze the response of the crude oil returns and volatilities to deliver bulletins via the Energy Information Administration (EIA) and the American Petroleum Institute (API) at some point of the use of duration of observe from August 01, 2012, to December 31, 2013. From their empirical findings, they expect that deliver surprises in collectively API and EIA bulletins have a right of way inverted affect at the returns and a giant and wonderful affect at the volatility.

Similarly, Halova et al. (2014) reveal at an intraday dataset to evaluate the impact of the unanticipated aspect withinside the EIA's crude oil accounting bulletins on collectively the go back and the volatility. Halova et al. (2014) display that the electricity returns react similarly appreciably to unanticipated changes withinside the deliver levels at some point of the insertion duration than throughout the elimination progression. The pandemic propagation will genuinely have the same affect.

Nippani and Washer (2004) deal with the inventory marketplace indices of eight truly encouraged economies via the SARS epidemic propagation and finish that the SARS pandemic had no unwanted and awful impact at the economic inventory markets of the encouraged international locations with the exemption of China and Vietnam. In the identical context, Chen et al. (2007) study the impact of the SARS epidemic at the profitability of the lodge shares in exchanges of Taiwan and the Chinese mainland and finish sizable and terrible affect.

He et al. (2020) attempt to research and examine the direct affects and spillovers of the COVID-19 at the economic inventory markets of eight nations. By using a traditional t-exams and a non-parametric Mann–Whitney assessments, He et al. (2020) inspect empirically each day go back dataset from the economic inventory marketplace in China, Japan, South Korea, Germany, Spain, Italy, France, and USA. Their empirical findings reveal that the COVID-19 pandemic has a poor and sizeable however in short-time period have an impact on at the economic inventory markets of the prompted nations. Also, they discover that the impact of the COVID-19 pandemic at the economic inventory marketplace indices of decided on nations has bidirectional spillover affects amongst Asian economies and European and American economies.

Sansa (2020) commences to look at the have an impact on of the propagation of the COVID-19 at the economic inventory markets in China and in USA thru the duration of look at since March 01, 2020, to March 25, 2020. Additionally, Sansa (2020) shows the lifestyles of effective and large connection among the unfold of the COVID-19 pandemic instances and complete the used global economic inventory marketplace indices (Such as, New York Dow Jones and Shanghai inventory exchange) at some point of the duration of look at because March 01, 2020, to March 25, 2020, in USA and in China. Then, those findings mean that the COVID-19 pandemic had a large have an impact on global economic inventory marketplace indices since March 01, 2020, to March 25, 2020, in China and in USA.

3. METHODS

The econometric method applied in our studies which is going to evaluate returns and volatilities of the power commodities and Bitcoin responses to the COVID-19 epidemic shocks and Russia-Ukraine conflict surprises the DCC multivariate specification (Engle, 2002).

The Dynamic Conditional Correlation (DCC) method has the pliancy of univariate specification of GARCH model (generalized autoregressive conditional heteroskedasticity) but does now no longer allow in view that the 'expletive of dimensionality' of a multivariate GARCH representations (generalized autoregressive conditional heteroskedasticity). The evaluation of GARCH-DCC specs calls for of steps. We evaluate, withinside the initial moment, the conditional suggests of returns and the conditional suggest of variance of all indices hired in our studies. In the section 2, we hire a reliable regression residual hooked up withinside the section 1 to assess the conditional connections amongst power commodity indices and Bitcoin during the COVID-19 epidemic shocks and Russia-Ukraine conflict surprises.

Then, to gain the response of major energy commodities returns associated with bitcoin simply at the surprise element, we make use of the following model:

GARCH(1,1) model (generalized autoregressive conditional heteroskedasticity) is conducted with the assistance of using the equivalent (1):

$$h_t = \omega + \alpha\varepsilon_{t-1}^2 + \beta h_{t-1} \tag{1}$$

Where, the measurements *ω, α and β co*rrelate to the factors that require to will be measured. The estimate conditional relationship matrix Rt o_f the consistent disruptions εt wh_ich is recommended with the following equal:

$$R_t = \begin{bmatrix} 1 & q_{12t} \\ q_{21t} & 1 \end{bmatrix} \tag{2}$$

Where, $\varepsilon_t = D_t^{-1} r_t$ and the estimate matrix R_t can be attained in the following equation:

$$R_t = Q_t^{*-1} Q_t Q_t^{*-1} \tag{3}$$

Where, Q_t symbolizes the time-varying covariance matrix of *εt*and Q_t^{*-1} signifies the upturned diagonal matrix along through the square root of the diagonal basics of Q_t. Besides, by showing that Q_t^{*-1} is equivalent to the subsequent equation:

$$Q_t^{*-1} = \begin{bmatrix} 1/\sqrt{q_{11t}} & 0 \\ 0 & 1/\sqrt{q_{22t}} \end{bmatrix} \tag{4}$$

Consequently, the arrangement GARCH-DCC (1,1) is attained by the subsequent equation:

$$Q_t = \omega + \alpha\varepsilon_{t-1}\varepsilon_{t-1}^{'} + \beta Q_{t-1} \tag{5}$$

With, $\omega = (1-\alpha-\beta)\overline{Q}$, where $\overline{Q}$ signifies the unconditional covariance of the standardized disturbances mentioned by *εt ω, α, and β co*rrespond to the determined measurements. Furthermore, this article provides some contributions to the economic and financial literature by the incorporating of a supplementary value in the arrangement GARCH-DCC (1,1) which assess the COVID-19 epidemic shocks and

Russia-Ukraine conflict surprises. Consequently, our estimated models are presented by the subsequent equations:

$$Q_t = \omega + \alpha \varepsilon_{t-1} \varepsilon_{t-1}^{'} + \beta Q_{t-1} + \gamma COVID-19_t \quad (6)$$

$$Q_t = \omega + \alpha \varepsilon_{t-1} \varepsilon_{t-1}^{'} + \beta Q_{t-1} + \theta RUC_t \quad (7)$$

With, COVID-19$_t$ indicates the unexpected COVID-19 surprise pronouncements at moment t. This variable is a dummy variable which takes 0 before December 18, 2019 and takes 1 for each day beginning to this date. RUC_t indicates the unexpected Russia-Ukraine conflict surprise pronouncements at moment t. This variable is a dummy variable which takes 0 before February 21, 2022 and takes 1 for each day beginning to this date.

4. DATA ANALYSIS

The database utilized in our research consist of everyday period collection at the returns and the conditional volatilities of Bitcoin and decided on energy commodities. Therefore, to research the immediate effect of the COVID-19 pandemic and Russia-Ukraine conflict surprises, we targeted withinside the expected and surprise factors withinside the COVID-19 instances alternate and Russia-Ukraine conflict surprises. Our facts pattern covers the duration of examine since January 04, 2016, to April 04, 2022. The dataset utilized on this article is collected from website such as, https://www.investing.com.

We notice that whole utilized stock price indices of Bitcoin and energy commodities are converted by the logarithm construction. We assess the logarithmic return formulation as $r_t = \ln(p_t/p_{t-1})$, with the indicator P_t symbolizes the stock market index at the period *t* and the indicator p_{t-1} corresponds to the stock market index at the period *t-1*.

In Table 1, we represent extremely significant descriptive statistics for the employed everyday returns of energy commodity indices and Bitcoin. We reveal that straight possible mean of daily return is equal to 0.000220 for the BRENT OIL but the higher probable mean of quotidian returns is equal to 0.000347 for the CRUDE OIL WTI escorted by BITCOIN with a daily return which equal to 0.000251 and the NATURAL GAS with a daily return which equal to 0.000280.

For the volatility of daily return of energy commodity indices and Bitcoin, which measured by the standard deviation, we can show that Natural Gas represents a high daily volatility equal to 0.014180 followed respectively by CRUDE OIL WTI with a quotidian volatility of 0.055769, Bitcoin with a daily volatility of 0.013363 and Brent Oil with a daily volatility of 0.013261.

Therefore, the coefficients of skewness statistic have a negative sign for the BRENT OIL variable. The distribution of the BRENT OIL index is asymmetrical in the left. Also, BITCOIN, CRUDE OIL WTI, and NATURAL GAS present a coefficient of skewness statistic with a positive sign. This outcome suggests that the distribution of BITCOIN, CRUDE OIL WTI, and NATURAL GAS are asymmetrical in the right. The presence of the identical make signs for these indicators supports the presence of a correlations amongst them.

Additionally, our outcomes prove that the assessed coefficients of the kurtosis indicator are greater than the 0. This result encourages the existence of a leptokurtic distribution. Furthermore, the leptokurticity is employed in the economic and financial information, especially with the stronger expansions than the standard distribution, requiring accompanying various abnormal assessments. Moreover, the approximate positive sign of the Jarque-Bera coefficient indicates that the null hypothesis of normal distribution of the indicators employed in our investigation can be reduced. Additionally, the higher-intensity significance of the Jarque-Bera measurement demonstrates that the employed financial period cycle is non-normally distributed.

Definitively, the assessed quantities of skewness, kurtosis and Jarque-Bera measurements of the numerous indices employed in this study suggest that the distribution of the assessed measurement of each indicator are not normally distributed. Consequently, we can eliminate the null assumption of the normality of the financial period cycle of the outputs at a degree of 1%.

Moreover, an examination of the causal association between Bitcoin and energy commodities necessitates stationarity tests to validate the request of integration of each indicator. The results of the Levin-Lin-Chu assessment, the Im-Pesaran-Shin assessment, the Augmented Dickey-Fuller assessment, and the Phillips Perron assessment utilized to the applied indicators are demonstrated in Table 2. Consequently, the recognition or elimination of the null hypothesis of the test is established on the significance of the probabilities and statistics concerning to the suggested assessments. These probabilities are matched to a level of 10%. If these probabilities are lesser to 10%, so we eliminate the null hypothesis which indicates that the utilized indicators are non-stationary and if these probabilities are superior to 10%, so we acknowledge the null hypothesis. In our case and based on Table 2, we observe that all utilized indicators are stationary in concentration corresponding to the Lin-Chu test, the Im-Pesaran-Shin test, the Augmented Dickey-Fuller test and the Phillips Perron test.

Table 3 summarizes major statistical attributes for the unconditional correlation matrix amongst Bitcoin and energy commodities. Founded on the unconditional correlation demonstrated in the table 3, we find that Bitcoin have a negative relationship with the BRENT OIL. Furthermore, we show that Bitcoin have a positive association with CRUDE OIL WTI and NATURAL GAS. This outcome confirms that COVID-19 pandemic and Russia-Ukraine conflict surprises can describes the spillover impacts of Bitcoin in energy commodities indices.

Figure 1 provides the progress of daily returns of employed stock market indices such as Bitcoin and energy commodities. For BRENT OIL, we notice that higher variability is observed in the first quarter of 2020. This period corresponds to the first important propagation of the COVID-19 cases in the world. Also, it can be noted that Bitcoin time series reveal numerous breaks in their projected return evolution across the period of study especially in January/March 2020 (first important propagation of COVID-19 pandemic) and January/March 2022 (Russia-Ukraine conflict). For the CRUDE OIL WTI, we find that their returns exhibit some important breaks in their progressions mostly, in two period such as, January to March 2020 in which the spread of COVID-19 epidemic is started in all countries in the world and throughout the Russia-Ukraine conflict in the first quarter of 2022. The NATURAL GAS index offers numerous significant break downs in their return progressions particularly in the third and fourth quarter of three years 2016, 2017, and 2018 (before the COVID-19) and in the third and fourth quarter of two years 2020 and 2021 (during the COVID-19) in which numerous countries have acknowledged that they have an significant total of COVID-19 confirmed cases and during the first quarter of 2022 which is coincided with the Russia-Ukraine conflict. Then, the pics detected in returns progressions of the chosen energy commodities can be justified by the significance of the impact of COVID-19 and Russia-Ukraine conflict shocks on the measured returns and volatilities of these indices.

Bitcoin presents many substantial pics in their return progressions mainly in the third and fourth quarter of three years 2016, 2017, and 2018 (before the COVID-19) and in the third and fourth quarter of two years 2020 and 2021 (during the COVID-19) in which several countries have recognized that they have an important total of COVID-19 confirmed cases and throughout the first quarter of 2022 which is coincided with the Russia-Ukraine conflict. Then, we can justify the impact of COVID-19 and Russia-Ukraine conflict shocks on the returns and volatilities of the Bitcoin.

Figures 2, 3, 4, and 5 present the progress of the conditional volatilities of returns for the energy commodities indices and Bitcoin. It can be noticed that Crude Oil WTI and Brent Oil accomplish the highest of their conditional volatility evolutions in two periods such as: the first quarter of 2020 which be consistent to the pronouncement of the COVID-19 confirmed incidents in all regions in the world and the first quarter of 2022 which coincided with the Russia-Ukraine conflict. For Bitcoin, we see that the conditional volatility of this asset achieves its highest in the first and the second quarter of all used years; 2016, 2017, 2018, 2019, 2020, 2021, and 2022. Then, we can presume that COVID-19 and Russia-Ukraine conflict surprises show an important influence on Bitcoin. Finally, For Natural Gas, we remark that their conditional volatility attains its greatest value in the third and the fourth quarter of all employed years; 2016, 2017, 2018, 2019, 2020, and 2021, and the first quarter of 2022. Then, we can presume that COVID-19 and Russia-Ukraine conflict surprises show an important influence on Bitcoin. The principal finding validates that COVID-19 and Russia-Ukraine conflict (RUC) shocks have a fundamental and significant impact on the energy commodities indices and Bitcoin.

5. EMPIRICAL RESULTS

In our empirical examination of this study, we investigate the influence of the COVID-19 pronouncements and the Russia-Ukraine conflict surprises on the dynamic relationship amongst the returns of energy commodities indices and Bitcoin. The econometric approach utilized in our research is the GARCH-DCC (1,1) model introduced by Engle (2002). The data sample passes across the period of analysis through January 04, 2016, to April 04, 2022. Furthermore, the chosen energy commodity indices are the Crude Oil West Texas Intermediate, the Brent Oil, and the Natural Gas. Additionally, we integrate a dummy variable in the GARCH-

Table 1. The descriptive statistics

	BITCOIN	BRENT OIL	CRUDE OIL WTI	NATURAL GAS	COVID-19	RUC
Mean	0.000251	0.000220	0.000347	0.000280	0.380827	0.021668
Median	0.000000	0.001017	0.000944	0.000000	0.000000	0.000000
Max	0.085984	0.082852	0.138815	0.085984	1.000000	1.000000
Min	-0.078410	-0.121499	-0.122561	-0.078410	0.000000	0.000000
Std. Dev.	0.013261	0.011310	0.013363	0.014180	0.485750	0.145644
Skewness	0.308453	-1.443906	0.082833	0.175982	0.490836	6.570667
Kurtosis	7.648065	25.35915	32.02592	7.257419	1.240920	44.17366
Jarque-Bera	1395.136	32254.04	53465.65	1158.082	257.5166	118538.0
Prob.	0.000000*	0.000000*	0.000000*	0.000000*	0.000000*	0.000000*
Obs.	1523	1523	1523	1523	1523	1523

Note: Table recaps descriptive statistics of quotidian returns for Energy commodities indices and Bitcoin, such as Crude Oil West Texas Intermediate, Brent Oil, and Natural Gas. The period of study is since January 04, 2016, to April 04, 2022. The significance at the 1% threshold is denoted by *.

Source: Elaborated by authors

Figure 1. Daily returns of energy commodity indices and Bitcoin over the period of study since January 4, 2016, to April 4, 2022
Source: Elaborated by authors

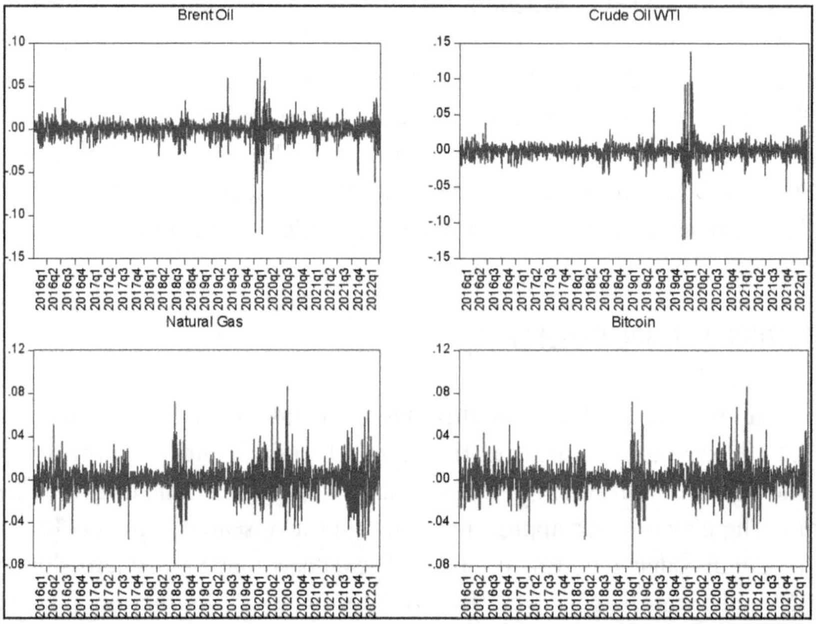

Table 2. The unit root test

Procedure	Statistic	Prob.**	Cross-Sections	Obs
Null assumption: presumes common unit root method				
Levin, Lin & Chu (LLC) t* test	-38.1165	0.0000	4	1520
Null assumption: presumes individual unit root method				
Im, Pesaran and Shin (IPS) W-stat test	-35.0082	0.0000	4	1520
ADF – Fisher Chi-square test	571.380	0.0000	4	1520
PP – Fisher Chi-square test	573.091	0.0000	4	1521

Note: Table 2 recaps unit root test of daily returns of Bitcoin and energy commodity indices. The data period is from January 04, 2016, to April 04, 2022

Source: Elaborated by authors

DCC (1,1) specification which measure the COVID-19 pronouncements and the Russia-Ukraine conflict shocks.

Figures 6, 7, and 8 indicate the evolution of the dynamic conditional correlation between energy commodities indices and Bitcoin. It can be observed that the DCC

Table 3. Unconditional correlation between Bitcoin and energy commodities

	BRENT OIL	CRUDE OIL WTI	NATURAL GAS	BITCOIN	COVID-19	RUC
BRENT OIL	1.0000	0.0434	-0.0089	-0.0098	0.0102	0.0108
CRUDE OIL WTI	0.0434	1.0000	0.0837	0.0069	0.0285	0.0052
NATURAL GAS	-0.0089	0.0837	1.0000	0.0062	0.0375	0.0438
BITCOIN	-0.0098	0.0069	0.0062	1.0000	0.0274	0.0498
COVID-19	0.0102	0.0285	0.0375	0.0274	1.0000	0.1898
RUC	0.0108	0.0052	0.0438	0.0498	0.1898	1.0000

Note: Table 3 recaps unconditional correlation matrix between quotidian returns of energy commodity indices and Bitcoin. The data period is from January 04, 2016, to April 04, 2022.

Source: Elaborated by authors

Figure 2. The daily conditional volatility of Bitcoin over the period of study since January 4, 2016, to April 4, 2022
Source: Elaborated by authors

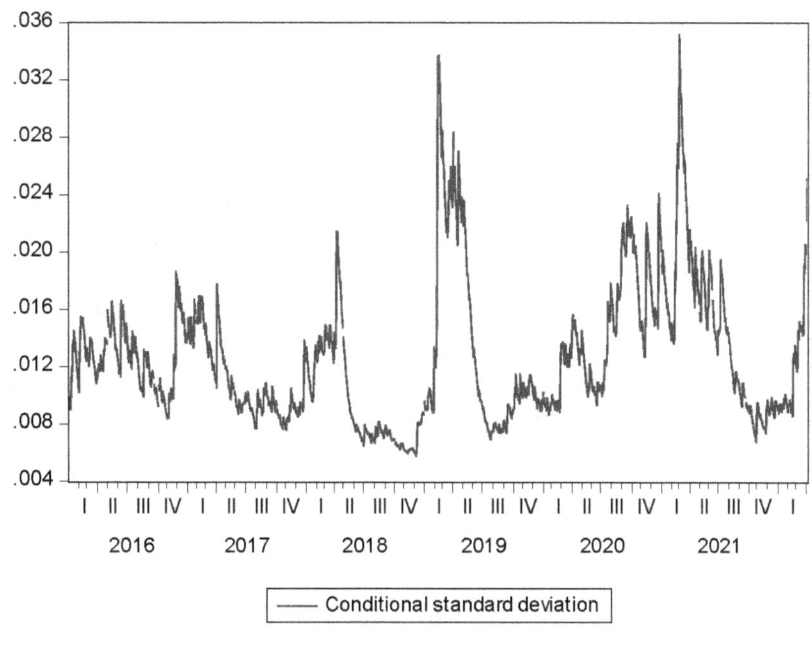

among Bitcoin and Natural Gas and between Bitcoin and Brent Oil accomplish the maximum of their dynamic conditional correlation in two periods such as: in 2020 which be consistent to the pronouncement of the COVID-19 confirmed cases in all

Figure 3. The daily conditional volatility of brent oil over the period of study since January 4, 2016, to April 4, 2022
Source: Elaborated by authors

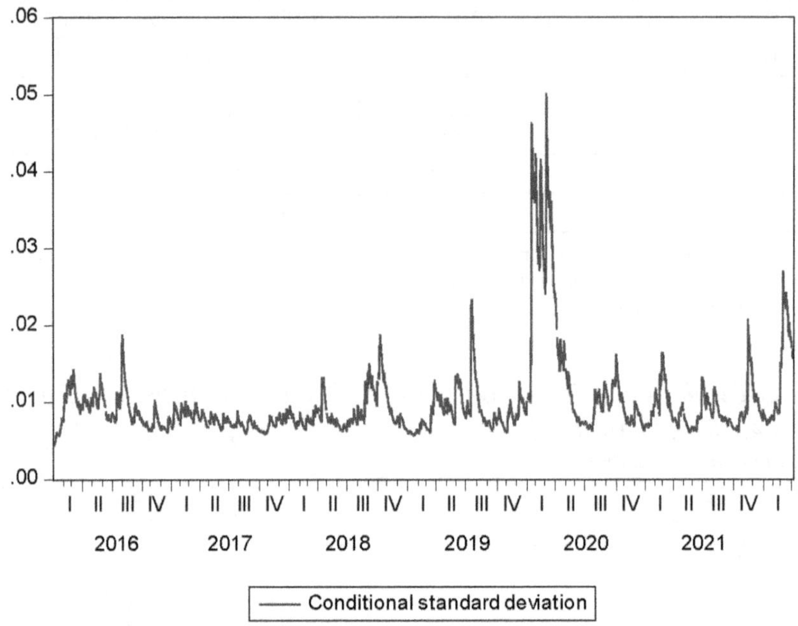

regions in the world and the first quarter of 2022 which coincided with the Russia-Ukraine conflict. It can be observed that the DCC among Bitcoin and Natural Gas and between Bitcoin and Brent Oil accomplish the maximum of their dynamic conditional correlation in two periods such as: in 2020 which be consistent to the pronouncement of the COVID-19 confirmed cases in all regions in the world and the first quarter of 2022 which coincided with the Russia-Ukraine conflict. Then, we can presume that COVID-19 and Russia-Ukraine conflict surprises show an important influence on the dynamic conditional correlation between energy commodities indices and Bitcoin. This result corroborates that COVID-19 and Russia-Ukraine conflict surprises have an important and considerable influence on the dynamic conditional correlation between energy commodities indices and Bitcoin.

The Table 4 describes the most important descriptive statistics relative to the estimated dynamic conditional correlation between energy commodities indices and Bitcoin in without integration of the COVID-19 pronouncements and the Russia-Ukraine conflict surprises in the estimated model. Based on this table, we find that in the maximum the bigger DCC is between Bitcoin and NATURAL GAS (0.70243) and among Bitcoin and BRENT OIL (0.716724). Therefore, these outcomes suggest the significant implication of the two energy commodity indices such as Natural Gas

Figure 4. The daily conditional volatility of crude oil WTI over the period of study since January 4, 2016, to April 4, 2022
Source: Elaborated by authors

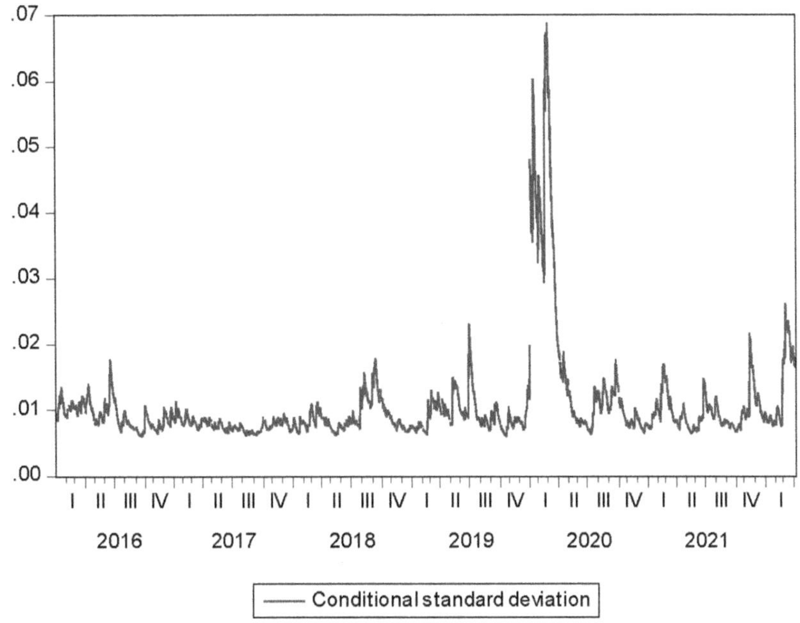

and Brent Oil in the financial stock markets. Furthermore, these findings validate a significant dynamic conditional correlation between energy commodities indices and Bitcoin principally during the period with the presence of unanticipated shocks. Also, we remark the importance impact of the unanticipated surprises in financial stock markets particularly, for the return and volatility of the energy commodity classes.

In addition, Table 5 recap the descriptive statistics for the estimated DCC among energy commodities indices and Bitcoin in the presence of COVID-19 shocks. Based on this Table, we demonstrate that in the maximum, the larger dynamic conditional correlation is between Bitcoin and NATURAL GAS (0.679185) and amongst BRENT OIL and Bitcoin (0.794847). These findings suggest the importance of the two energy commodity indices such as Natural Gas and Brent Oil in the international financial markets. Additionally, this outcome explains the great implication of the dynamic conditional correlation among energy commodities indices and Bitcoin mainly throughout the existence of the COVID-19 shocks.

Finally, based on the Table 6 which summarizes the descriptive statistics for the estimated dynamic conditional correlation between energy commodities indices and Bitcoin in the existence of Russia-Ukraine conflict surprises, we assume that this conflict in is more important than COVID-19 shocks, principally in operation of

Figure 5. The daily conditional volatility of natural gas over the period of study since January 4, 2016, to April 4, 2022
Source: Elaborated by authors

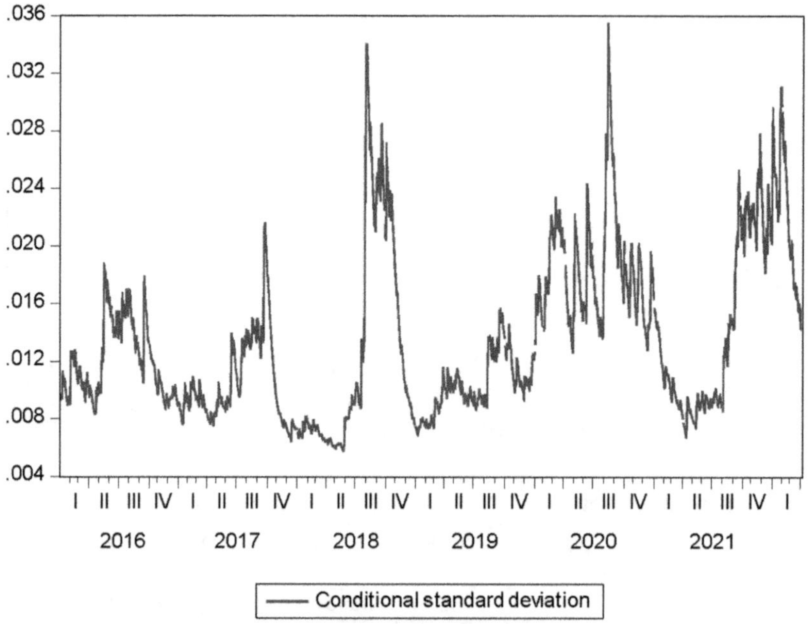

Figure 6. The dynamic conditional correlation between Bitcoin and brent oil over the period of study since January 4, 2016, to April 4, 2022
Source: Elaborated by authors

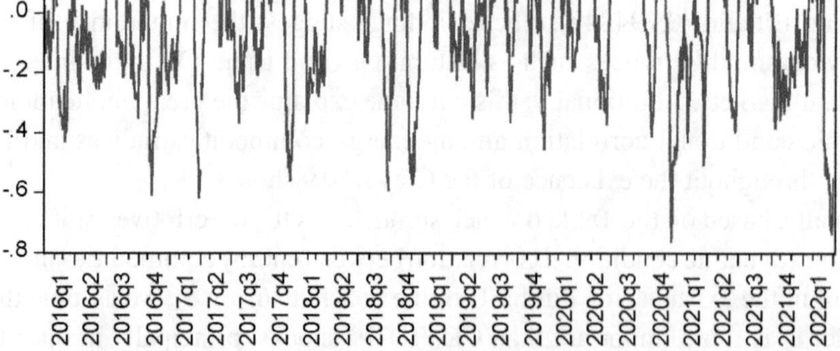

financial stock markets. Furthermore, we observe the presence of a significant linkage between the Russia-Ukraine conflict surprises and the international financial market indices, principally in the case of energy commodities and cryptocurrencies assets.

Moreover, and seeing at the daily moment, we can corroborate that surprise elements in Russia-Ukraine conflict shocks have accomplished a fundamental purpose in the enhancements of the volatility of extremely crucial energy commodities assets. These outcomes are not surprising. The unique possible explanation and probable is to offer the indispensable consequence of the Russia-Ukraine conflict shocks and financial market on the international financial markets and the worldwide economy, and the declarations associated to the fluctuations in Russia-Ukraine conflict shocks may noticeably influence the outside economic fundamentals and subsequently the significant volatility of the energy commodity indices and cryptocurrencies assets such as Bitcoin. Additionally, the considerable influence of Russia-Ukraine conflict surprises in financial stock market can be justified by the role of Russia in exportation of oil and natural gas.

Consequently, the effect of COVID-19 surprises is encouraged by the importance of this epidemic to dominate the global financial stock market indices and the worldwide economic organization. Furthermore, COVID-19 surprises have a significant impact on the uncertainties of the extremely significant and highly uncertain energy commodities.

Table 7 presents the empirical results relative to the Estimation of GARCH-DCC (1,1) model amongst energy commodity indices and Bitcoin in existence of the COVID-19 shocks and Russia-Ukraine conflict shocks and without these factors. Several significant conclusions appear from this empirical examination. First, we exhibit that COVID-19 surprises and Russia-Ukraine conflict shocks influence the dynamic conditional correlation between energy commodity indices and Bitcoin. The negative sign of the coefficients of the COVID-19 surprises and Russia-Ukraine conflict shocks indicates that the fluctuations on health and war crisis decrease the average concentration of volatility of energy commodities indices and the cryptocurrencies assets (Bitcoin).

According to the influence of COVID-19 surprises and Russia-Ukraine conflict shocks on the dynamic conditional correlation amongst Bitcoin and selected energy commodities indices in our study, the experimental results presented in the Table 7 signify that the 1% growth in COVID-19 shocks entrains a reduction of 0.0524688 percent in the dynamic conditional correlation amongst returns of BRENT OIL and Bitcoin, and similarly, 0.0254351 and 0.0635542 for the dynamic conditional correlation between the returns of Bitcoin and CRUDE OIL WTI and NATURAL GAS.

Besides, we show that 1 percent elevation in Russia-Ukraine conflict shocks causes a diminution of 0.0152623 percent in the dynamic conditional correlation

Figure 7. The dynamic conditional correlation between Bitcoin and natural gas over the period of study since January 4, 2016, to April 4, 2022
Source: Elaborated by authors

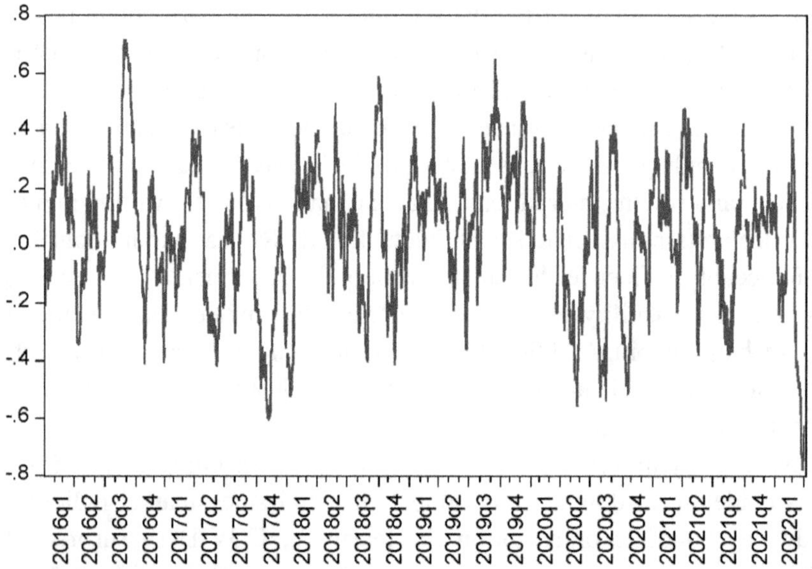

Figure 8. The dynamic conditional correlation between bitcoin and crude oil WTI over the period of study since January 4, 2016, to April 4, 2022
Source: Elaborated by authors

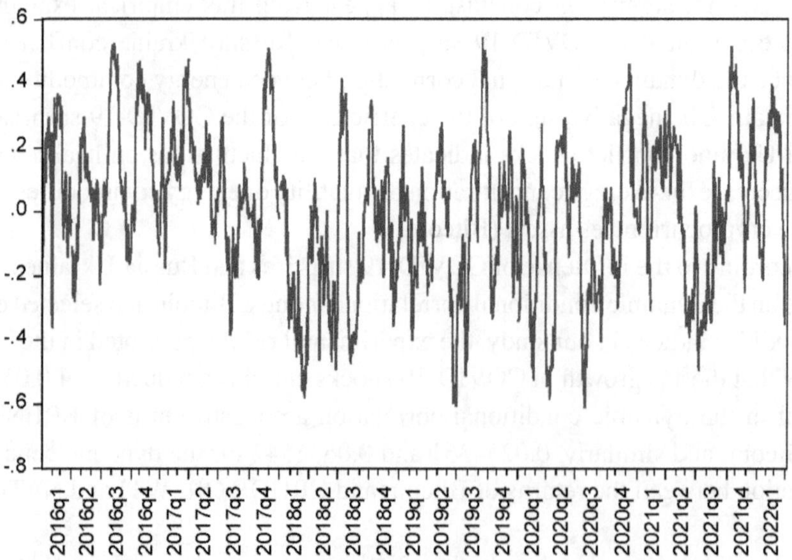

Table 4. Descriptive statistics for DCC among Energy commodity indices and Bitcoin without COVID-19 and RUC shocks

	Dynamic Correlation Among Bitcoin and		
	BRENT OIL	NATURAL GAS	CRUDE OIL WTI
Mean	3.63E-05	0.041963	0.008375
Median	-0.01145	0.068923	0.024053
Max	0.70243	0.716724	0.543701
Min	-0.76363	-0.7805	-0.60983
Std. Dev.	0.258854	0.245634	0.236122
Skewness	-0.00317	-0.29286	-0.18399
Kurtosis	2.673652	3.026085	2.545567
Jarque-Bera	6.672273	21.52758	21.41275
Prob.	0.035574	0.000021	0.000022
Obs.	1503	1503	1503

Notes: The table 5 gives brief statistics of correlation among Energy commodity indices and Bitcoin, specifically the Crude Oil West Texas Intermediate, the Brent Oil, and the Natural Gas in existence of the COVID-19 shocks in China. The used period is from January 04, 2016, to April 04, 2022. The variable significant at the (1%) threshold is characterized by (*).

Source: Elaborated by authors

Table 5. Descriptive statistics for DCC among Energy commodity indices and Bitcoin with COVID-19 shocks

	Dynamic Correlation Among Bitcoin and		
	BRENT OIL	NATURAL GAS	CRUDE OIL WTI
Mean	4.03E-05	0.046537	0.009288
Median	-0.01269	0.076436	0.026675
Max	0.679185	0.794847	0.602964
Min	-0.84687	-0.86557	-0.6763
Std. Dev.	0.287069	0.272408	0.261859
Skewness	-0.00351	-0.32478	-0.20405
Kurtosis	2.96508	3.355928	2.823034
Jarque-Bera	7.399551	23.87409	23.74674
Prob.	0.039452	2.33E-05	2.44E-05
Obs.	1503	1503	1503

Notes: The table 5 gives brief statistics of correlation among Energy commodity indices and Bitcoin, specifically the Crude Oil West Texas Intermediate, the Brent Oil, and the Natural Gas in existence of the COVID-19 shocks in China. The used period is from January 04, 2016, to April 04, 2022. The variable significant at the (1%) threshold is characterized by (*).

Source: Elaborated by authors

Table 6. Descriptive statistics for DCC among energy commodity indices and Bitcoin with RUC shocks

	Dynamic Correlation Among Bitcoin and		
	BRENT OIL	**NATURAL GAS**	**CRUDE OIL WTI**
Mean	4.14E-05	0.047838	0.009548
Median	-0.01305	0.078572	0.02742
Max	0.69817	0.817065	0.619819
Min	-0.87054	-0.88977	-0.69521
Std. Dev.	0.295094	0.280023	0.269179
Skewness	-0.00361	-0.33386	-0.20975
Kurtosis	3.047963	3.449737	2.901946
Jarque-Bera	7.606391	24.54144	24.41054
Prob.	0.040554	2.39E-05	2.51E-05
Obs.	1503	1503	1503

Notes: The table 5 gives brief statistics of correlation among Energy commodity indices and Bitcoin, specifically the Crude Oil West Texas Intermediate, the Brent Oil, and the Natural Gas in existence of the COVID-19 shocks in China. The used period is from January 04, 2016, to April 04, 2022. The variable significant at the (1%) threshold is characterized by (*).

Source: Elaborated by authors

amongst the returns of BRENT OIL and Bitcoin, and consistently, 0.0536263 and 0.0637212 for the dynamic conditional correlation between the returns of Bitcoin and with CRUDE OIL WTI and NATURAL GAS. In the identical framework, we observe that the considerable difference among COVID-19 surprises and Russia-Ukraine conflict shocks and their influence on the dynamic conditional correlation amongst energy commodity indices and Bitcoin. Our experimental outcomes explain that Russia-Ukraine conflict shocks and COVID-19 surprises has a significant and negative but short-term impact on the international financial stock markets. Additionally, we discover that the influence of the Russia-Ukraine conflict shocks and COVID-19 surprises on the stock market indices has a bidirectional spillover impacts amongst energy commodity indices and Bitcoin.

Furthermore, we confirm an explanation that the sum of the assessed volatility coefficients ($\alpha+\beta$) is very contiguous to the unity (1). For the state of the assessed dynamic conditional correlation between energy commodity indices and Bitcoin as showing, we show a preeminent tenacity and persistence of the volatility amongst COVID-19 surprises and Russia-Ukraine conflict shocks and energy commodity markets and cryptocurrencies assets. Formerly, we can validate the presence of one possible clarification which establishes that a significant perseverance drives laterally through the phenomena of financialization of the international financial stock market indices, the cryptocurrencies assets, political crisis and conflicts, war, and health epidemic spread, such as energy commodity indices, Bitcoin, COVID-19 epidemic, and Russia-Ukraine conflict (Creti et al., 2013; Chebbi and Derbali, 2015; Chebbi and Derbali, 2016a; Chebbi and Derbali, 2016b; Derbali and Jouini, 2019; Derbali and Bouzgarrou, 2020; Derbali et al., 2020a; Derbali et al., 2020b; Derbali et al., 2021a; Derbali et al., 2021b). The empirical outcomes of our study emphasize the implication of employing the GARCH-DCC (1,1) measurement in determining the crucial time-varying of the dynamic conditional correlations amongst energy commodity indices and Bitcoin in the existence of the health epidemic (COVID-19) and political crisis and war (Russia-Ukraine conflict).

6. CONCLUSION

Commonly, the associations between energy commodity indices and Bitcoin have understood important literature through the preceding two decades. Various significant developments have been produced to improve the estimated outcomes. Among these improvements, we perceive a presence of the monetary policy surprises in the

Table 7. Estimation results of GARCH-DCC (1,1) among energy commodity indices and Bitcoin

Coefficients	ωi	α_1	β_1	Without Shocks	With COVID-19 Shocks	With RUC Shocks
BITCOIN and BRENT OIL	0.0488971 (2.14)**	0.1193374 (9.89)*	0.8726311 (82.13)*	-		
	0.0611273 (2.13)**	0.1073621 (9.91)*	0.8836282 (67.09)*		-0.0328112 (-6.78)*	
	0.0218734 (2.01)**	0.0911263 (9.78)*	0.9022872 (81.08)*			-0.0152623 (-9.71)*
BITCOIN and CRUDE OIL WTI	0.0585273 (2.09)**	0.0926312 (9.45)*	0.9028372 (63.12)*	-		
	0.0429576 (2.14)**	0.1023643 (9.07)*	0.8812535 (83.44)*		-0.0254351 (-7.88)*	
	0.0418478 (2.18)**	0.1102934 (8.48)*	0.8836452 (71.32)*			-0.0536263 (-9.65)*
BITCOIN and NATURAL GAS	0.0477238 (2.90)*	0.1293993 (8.92)*	0.8635423 (82.09)*	-		
	0.0319450 (2.83)*	0.1023645 (8.83)*	0.8825361 (51.87)*		-0.0635542 (-7.94)*	
	0.0482564 (2.04)**	0.0922442 (9.17)*	0.8836421 (83.12)*			-0.0637212 (-9.32)*

Notes: Table 7 summarizes the estimated parameters from the GARCH-DCC (1,1) specification. To estimate this specification, the authors employ the daily volatility series of the returns for Energy commodity indices and Bitcoin, specifically the Crude Oil WTI, the Brent Oil, and the Natural Gas during the period used in our study since January 04, 2016, to April 04, 2022. The variable significant at the 1%, 5% and 10% points are characterized by *, ** and ***, correspondingly. The statistics in parentheses expose the estimated t-Student.

estimated volatility specifications, the political instabilities surprises, war shocks (Russia-Ukraine conflict), and the health crisis surprises (COVID-19). These groups of surprises in the volatility probably will be influenced by the country-detailed financial and economic proceedings, regional and global financial and economic influences (for example, the 2007-2008 financial crisis surprises, the European sovereign-debt crisis surprises in 2010, the 2011 Arab Spring surprises, the FOMC monetary policy surprises, the ECB monetary policy surprises, COVID-19 pandemic surprises, and Russia-Ukraine conflict surprises).

In our paper, we investigate the dynamic conditional correlations amongst Bitcoin and crucial commodities which covering the sector of energy (Crude Oil WTI, Brent Oil, and Natural Gas), during the period of examination since January 04, 2016, to April 04, 2022. Then, we utilize the GARCH-DCC(1.1) methodology with incorporating of COVID-19 surprises and Russia-Ukraine conflict shocks as a dummy variables. Our experimental outcomes in this research paper suggest fantastic significant dynamic conditional correlations between energy commodity indices and Bitcoin if COVID-19 and Russia-Ukraine conflict shocks are incorporated in the expected variance equivalence. Our conclusions prove the existence of the financialization phenomena of energy commodity indices and Bitcoin. Furthermore, our assessment outcomes correlated with the concentration of the persistence of the volatility, are susceptible in the presence of the COVID-19 and Russia-Ukraine conflict shocks in GARCH-DCC(1,1) model. The dynamic conditional correlations amongst energy commodity indices and Bitcoin emerge to react considerably additional in the existence of the Russia-Ukraine conflict shocks in China than the COVID-19 shocks. Additionally, our outcomes suppose that the performance of the energy commodity indices incorporating Bitcoin elasticities, recommend the suggestion that the energy commodity indices cannot generate a consistent and homogeneous portfolio class.

Completely, the impact of the COVID-19 and war (Russia-Ukraine conflict) shocks on the global financial stock markets exhibit a bidirectional spillover influence among energy commodity indices and Bitcoin. Also, the significant propagation of the coronavirus in the world and Russia-Ukraine conflict shocks negatively affected the connection amongst energy commodity indices and Bitcoin.

Our findings contribute and add to the investigation in financial and economic consequences of the recent epidemic and Russia-Ukraine conflict with providing an experimental confirmation that COVID-19 and recent war between Russia and Ukraine cause a bidirectional spillover influence on energy commodities and cryptocurrencies assets. Our investigation has a significant and considerable concern for the policymakers and the portfolio risk directors and supervisors. Additionally, and from a policy-making viewpoint, receiving straightforward an investigational explanation of the approximation volatility spillovers between worldwide financial stock markets is an imperative and vital phase in creating convenient monetary policy pronouncements and decisions and healthy strategies and policies, and political decisions and plans. For the viewpoint of portfolio risk managers and administrators, the consequences of our study are consistent to the suggestion of the cross-market hedging.

ACKNOWLEDGMENT

The authors would think the editor and the anonymous reviewers for their exceptionally helpful recommendations to enhance the value of our paper.

Declaration of Conflict Interests: The authors proclaim no possible conflicts of interest regarding the investigation, authorship and/or publication of this paper.

Funding: The authors do not receive any financial funding for this study, authorship and/or publication of this research.

REFERENCES

Burch, T. R., Douglas, R. E., & Michael, R. F. (2016). Who Moves Markets in a Sudden Marketwide Crisis? Evidence from 9/11. *Journal of Financial and Quantitative Analysis*, *51*(2), 463–487. doi:10.1017/S0022109016000211

Carter, D. A., & Betty, J. S. (2004). The Market's Reaction to Unexpected, Catastrophic Events: The Case of Airline Stock Returns and the September 11th Attacks. *The Quarterly Review of Economics and Finance*, *44*(4), 539–558. doi:10.1016/j.qref.2003.10.001

Chebbi, T., & Derbali, A. (2015). The dynamic correlation between energy commodities and Islamic stock market: Analysis and forecasting. *International Journal of Trade and Global Markets*, *8*(2), 112–126. doi:10.1504/IJTGM.2015.069425

Chebbi, T., & Derbali, A. (2016a). A Dynamic Conditional Correlation between Commodities and the Islamic Stock Market. *Journal of Energy Markets*, *9*(1), 65–90. doi:10.21314/JEM.2016.137

Chebbi, T., & Derbali, A. (2016b). On the role of structural breaks in identifying the dynamic conditional linkages between stock and commodity markets. *Journal of Energy Markets*, *9*(4), 71–81. doi:10.21314/JEM.2016.152

Chen, A. H., & Siems, T. F. (2004). The Effects of Terrorism on Global Capital Markets. *European Journal of Political Economy*, *20*(2), 349–366. doi:10.1016/j.ejpoleco.2003.12.005

Chen, M. H., Soo, C. S. J., & Woo, G. K. (2007). The Impact of the SARS Outbreak on Taiwanese Hotel Stock Performance: An Event-study Approach. *International Journal of Hospitality Management*, *26*(1), 200–212. doi:10.1016/j.ijhm.2005.11.004 PMID:32287849

Creti, A., Joëts, M., & Mignon, V. (2013). On the links between stock and commodity markets' volatility. *Energy Economics*, *37*, 16–28. doi:10.1016/j.eneco.2013.01.005

Derbali, A., & Bouzgarrou, H. (2020). The dynamic dependence between the major US indices and the meat commodities indices. *PSU Research Review*, *4*(2), 149–168. doi:10.1108/PRR-09-2018-0027

Derbali, A., Jamel, L., Ben Ltaifa, M., Elnagar, A. K., & Lamouchi, A. (2020a). Fed and ECB: Which is informative in determining the DCC between bitcoin and energy commodities? *Journal of Capital Markets Studies*, *4*(1), 77–102. doi:10.1108/JCMS-07-2020-0022

Derbali, A., & Jouini, F. (2019). Analyzing the Dynamic Equicorrelation Between Shanghai Composite (SSEC) and Austral African Stock Market Indices. *Chinese Economy*, *52*(1), 83–106.

Derbali, A., Naoui, K., Ben Sassi, M., & Amiri, M. M. (2021b). Do COVID-19 Epidemic Explains the Dynamic Conditional Correlation between China's Stock Market Index and International Stock Market Indices? *Chinese Economy*, *55*(3), 227–242. doi:10.1080/10971475.2021.1958453

Derbali, A., Naoui, K., & Jamel, L. (2021a). COVID-19 news in USA and in China: Which is suitable in explaining the nexus among Bitcoin and Gold? *Pacific Accounting Review*, *33*(5), 578–595. doi:10.1108/PAR-09-2020-0170

Derbali, A., Wu, S., & Jamel, L. (2020b). OPEC news and predictability of energy futures returns and volatility: Evidence from a conditional quantile regression. *Journal of Economics, Finance and Administrative Science*, *25*(50), 239–25. doi:10.1108/JEFAS-05-2019-0063

Engle, R. (2002). Dynamic conditional correlation: A simple class of multivariate generalized autoregressive conditional heteroskedasticity models. *Journal of Business & Economic Statistics*, *20*(3), 339–350. doi:10.1198/073500102288618487

Gu, X., Zhang, W., & Cheng, S. (2021). How do investors in Chinese stock marketreact to external uncertainty? An event study to the Sino-US disputes. *Pacific-Basin Finance Journal*, *68*(1), 101–614.

Guiolin, M., & La Ferrara, L. (2010). The economic effect of violent conflict: Evidence from asset market reactions. *Journal of Peace Research*, *47*(6), 671–684. doi:10.1177/0022343310381853

Halova, M. W., Kurov, A., & Kucher, O. (2014). Noisy inventory announcements and energy prices. *Journal of Futures Markets*, *34*(10), 911–933. doi:10.1002/fut.21633

He, Q., Liu, J., Wang, S. & Yu, J. (2020). The impact of COVID-19 on stock markets. *Journal of Economic and Political Studies.* doi:10.1080/20954816.2020.1757570

Hudson, R., & Urquhart, A. (2015). War and stock markets: The effect of World War Two on the British stock market. *International Review of Financial Analysis*, *40*(1), 166–177. doi:10.1016/j.irfa.2015.05.015

Jamel, L., & Derbali, A. (2019). Damascus Securities Exchange Weighted Index volatilities and Terrorist attacks in Syria. *International Journal of Business and Risk Management*, *2*(1), 9–15.

Kollias, C., Efthalia, M., Stephanos, P., & Apostolos, S. (2011). Stock Markets and Terrorist Attacks: Comparative Evidence from a Large and a Small Capitalization Market. *European Journal of Political Economy*, *27*(No. S1), S64–S77. doi:10.1016/j.ejpoleco.2011.05.002

Kuttner, K. N. (2001). Monetary policy surprises and interest rates: Evidence from the fed funds futures market. *Journal of Monetary Economics*, *47*(3), 523–544. doi:10.1016/S0304-3932(01)00055-1

Nikkinen, J., Mohammad, M. O., Petri, S., & Janne, A. (2008). Stock Returns and Volatility Following the September 11 Attacks: Evidence from 53 Equity Markets. *International Review of Financial Analysis*, *17*(1), 27–46. doi:10.1016/j.irfa.2006.12.002

Nippani, S., & Washer, K. M. (2004). SARS: A Non-event for Affected Countries' Stock Markets? *Applied Financial Economics*, *14*(15), 1105–1110. doi:10.1080/0960310042000310579

Papakyriakou, P., Athanasios, S., & Zenon, T. (2019). The Impact of Terrorist Attacks in G7 Countries on International Stock Markets and the Role of Investor Sentiment. *Journal of International Financial Markets, Institutions and Money*, *6*, 143–160. doi:10.1016/j.intfin.2019.03.001

Sansa, N. A. (2020). The Impact of the COVID - 19 on the Financial Markets: Evidence from China and USA. *Electronic Research Journal of Social Sciences and Humanities*, *2*(2), 29–39.

Ye, S., & Karali, B. (2016). The informational content of inventory announcements: Intraday evidence from crude oil futures market. *Energy Economics*, *59*, 349–364. doi:10.1016/j.eneco.2016.08.011

Chapter 2
Internet of Things Security Using Blockchain:
A Study on Smart Home-Based Applications

L. Mary Shamala
Vellore Institute of Technology, Chennai, India

V. R. Balasaraswathi
Vellore Institute of Technology, Chennai, India

Anushka Sharma
Vellore Institute of Technology, Chennai, India

ABSTRACT

Integrating blockchain technology into the internet of things is a topic of significant interest and research. The internet of things is an evolving field with incredible growth due to the development of smart homes and smart cities. Smart devices are more prone to attacks and the low processing power, storage capacity, and network capacity make current security or cryptography techniques unusable. Blockchain has acquired huge attention since its use in Bitcoin, due to the numerous prospects it raises. Blockchain offers several advantages in addressing security and privacy challenges associated with IoT nodes and networks. This chapter provides insights into incorporating blockchain into IoT networks to achieve confidentiality and safety. The chapter covers details of IoT, smart home applications, and security concerns. The various blockchain solutions to protect IoT and smart home systems are also covered in the study.

DOI: 10.4018/979-8-3693-1511-8.ch002

There are billions of smart devices around the world that are now linked to the internet, all gathering data, passing on information, and further extracting important insights out of it. The Internet of Things (IoT) (Atzori et al., 2010) constitutes a network of interrelated things, facilitating communication among smart gadgets and other Internet-enabled devices. A growing number of industries and enterprises are leveraging IoT to enhance operational efficiency, provide superior customer service, optimize decision-making processes, and elevate overall business value. A sector of the Internet of Things called "Smart Homes" connects and automates household systems and appliances (Mocrii et al, 2018).

IoT devices such as cameras, mobile phones, sensors, and several home automation equipment handle vast amounts of data, which is sensitive and when transmitted in a network is vulnerable to attacks from cybercriminals. Unfortunately, due to their constrained resources, IoT devices are more vulnerable to attacks and incapable of defending themselves (Gasmi, 2023). Moreover, traditional security techniques frequently cost more in terms of processing time and energy use. Due to the large-scale complexity and single point of failure inherent in contemporary security solutions, they may not be always appropriate for IoT applications (Sicari et al, 2015; Mohamad Noor et al, 2019; Roman et al, 2013). Current approaches to preserve user privacy frequently expose inaccurate or inadequate data, hindering certain IoT applications from providing customized services (Chakravorty,2013). Consequently, IoT needs delicate security and privacy protection solutions that are distributed in nature.

Gartner identifies the IoT and Blockchain as key enabling technologies that shape the smart spaces in coming years (Gartner, 2023). This chapter explores the potential of blockchain for global IoT-based smart homes to address these challenges. The recognition of blockchain technology emerged alongside the inception of cryptocurrency mining, as it serves as its fundamental technology. Blockchain is a decentralized, immutable, and transparent ledger that securely records transactions in a tamper-resistant manner. It is possible to leverage the structure of Blockchain to authenticate, standardize, and secure the adoption of data managed by devices. Since Smart home systems frequently handle private data, strong security measures are needed to preserve user privacy.

INTERNET OF THINGS AND ITS GROWTH

The Internet of Things pertains to a spectrum of distinctly addressable things and devices communicating and exchanging data with each other to establish a global dynamic network. It encompasses a diverse array of applications, including smart homes, smart cities, industrial automation, healthcare, and beyond (Borgia, 2014).

The Internet of Things is one of the current technology innovations that has witnessed remarkable growth due to the proliferation of smart devices. IoT Analytics (2021) predicts that by 2025, it is expected to be more than 27 billion connected devices worldwide. Cisco in its Annual Internet Report (Cisco, 2020) says, by 2023 there will be more IP-connected devices than there are people on the planet. In addition, by the end of 2025, there will be 55.7 billion linked devices, up from 29.3 billion in 2023. Figure 1. depicts the worldwide trend of devices and connections growth outpacing both population and Internet users growth.

These smart gadgets have proliferated greatly, making it extremely difficult to manage networks using conventional techniques like client-server connections. On the other hand, IoT devices often have limited processing power, storage capacity, and network bandwidth. This makes them susceptible to a range of security threats, including unauthorized access, data breaches, and malware attacks. As such, traditional security and cryptography techniques may not be suitable for these resource-constrained devices.

BLOCKCHAIN AND ITS SIGNIFICANCE

Blockchain technology first gained widespread attention with the advent of Bitcoin. (Nakamoto, 2008). Blockchain-based solutions have become more popular in recent years, due to their significant influence on numerous businesses and industries. The global blockchain market was estimated to be worth $2.89 billion in 2019 and is expected to rise to $137.29 billion by 2027, with a CAGR of 62.7% between 2020 and 2027 (Allied Market Research, 2022). Beyond cryptocurrencies, blockchain has various applications, and one of the promising areas is its use in IoT.

Figure 1. Global trend of devices and connections

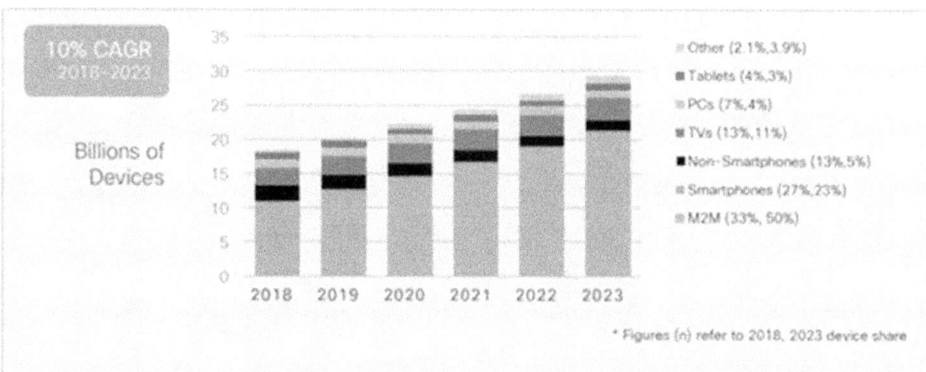

What Is Blockchain?

Blockchain is a decentralized and transparent ledger technology that stores interactions and tracks resources across a network of computers in a secure and tamper-resistant manner. A chain of cryptographically connected blocks made by nodes is referred to as a blockchain. Individual computers known as nodes are linked together and each holds a copy of the blockchain. Every block in the network includes encrypted data of transactions that took place at a specific time and were confirmed by nodes. A blockchain's encrypted data is unchangeable and impenetrable to hacking. Figure 2 illustrates the header and body of each block in the ledger. The header includes a timestamp, a nonce, and the hash values for the present and prior blocks. The body part comprises auxiliary security information and the pertinent transaction information that needs to be secured. Since a hash is generated automatically and contains all of the information it needs, it cannot be altered in any way.

Why Blockchain Is Important

Blockchain provides immediate, accessible, and completely transparent data, held on an immutable ledger. As this is only available to participants of an authorized network, blockchain serves as the finest method of communicating corporate information. Figure 3. highlights some key aspects of the blockchain (Kim, 2020; Kumar et al, 2022), and its significance is explained below. Decentralization enhances trust among participants, as no single entity has control or ownership over the entire system. Transparency reduces fraud and ensures accountability. Blockchain uses cryptographic techniques to secure transactions, ensuring the integrity and confidentiality of data. The use of smart contracts reduces the need

Figure 2. Structure of the blockchain

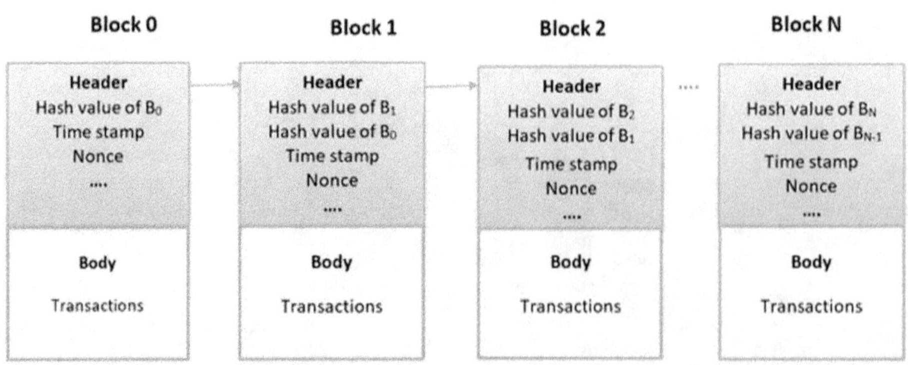

for intermediaries. The end-to-end feature enables goods and transactions tracking from the source to the final destination, ensuring authenticity and preventing fraud. Immutable property is crucial for maintaining a reliable and tamper-proof record of transactions. It allows for the tokenization of real-world assets, representing ownership of physical assets like real estate or art in a digital form. Blockchain can facilitate transactions quickly and efficiently as it operates 24/7 without the need for traditional banking hours.

Overall, Significance of Blockchain revolves around its capability to create trust in a decentralized environment, enhance security, and provide transparency and efficient solutions across various industries. While challenges exist, ongoing research and development aim to address these issues and unlock the full potential of blockchain technology.

How Blockchain Works

Blockchain technology employs decentralized peer-to-peer (P2P) networks to store synchronized and verified data in sequential, encrypted, chained blocks. Figure 4. elaborates the steps involved in creating a blockchain network (Kumar, 2022). The block is created by a very few powerful nodes in the P2P network, known as miners,

Figure 3. Key aspects of blockchain

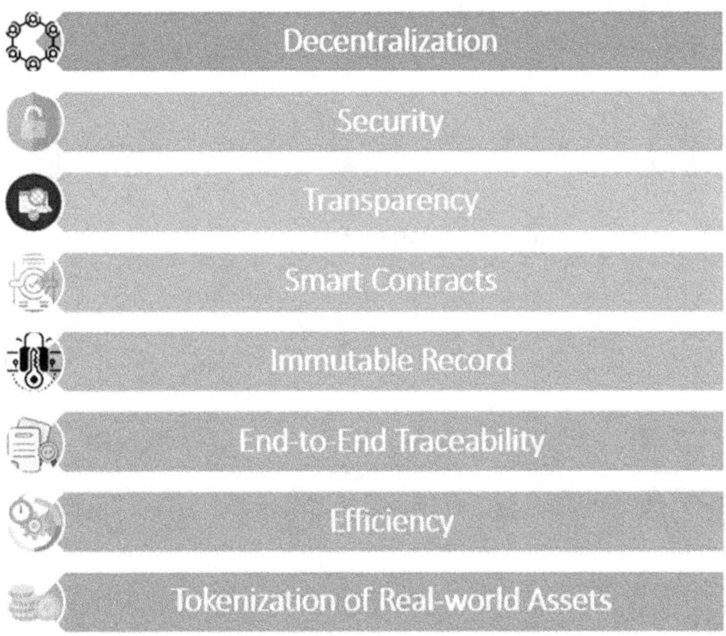

who also add to the chain of blocks. They are in charge of validating blocks for Blockchain by solving the computationally difficult cryptographic puzzle with the help of a consensus algorithm (Mingxiao, 2017; King, 2013). It is with the consensus algorithm that all network nodes reach a mutual agreement to publish a new block in the network. For validating blocks, miners receive rewards. All network nodes receive the newest block to be mined after being approved by all of the miners, then, the block is added to the network. Once added to the Blockchain, changing data in that block requires changing all of the blocks that come after it. It is worth noting that for any block to be tied to a Blockchain, there must be approval among the vast majority of network nodes (Soni & Bhushan, 2019). The ledger is accessible to all users on the network, and data in the blocks are encrypted using a complex algorithm making blockchain extremely impossible to tamper with.

INTEGRATION OF BLOCKCHAIN FOR IOT SECURITY

IoT devices, particularly smart devices, often have limited processing power, storage capacity, and network bandwidth. They become exposed to different security risks as a result, including malware attacks, unauthorized access, and data breaches. The centralized setup of the network leads to a single point of failure. These issues with

Figure 4. Steps involved in building the blockchain network

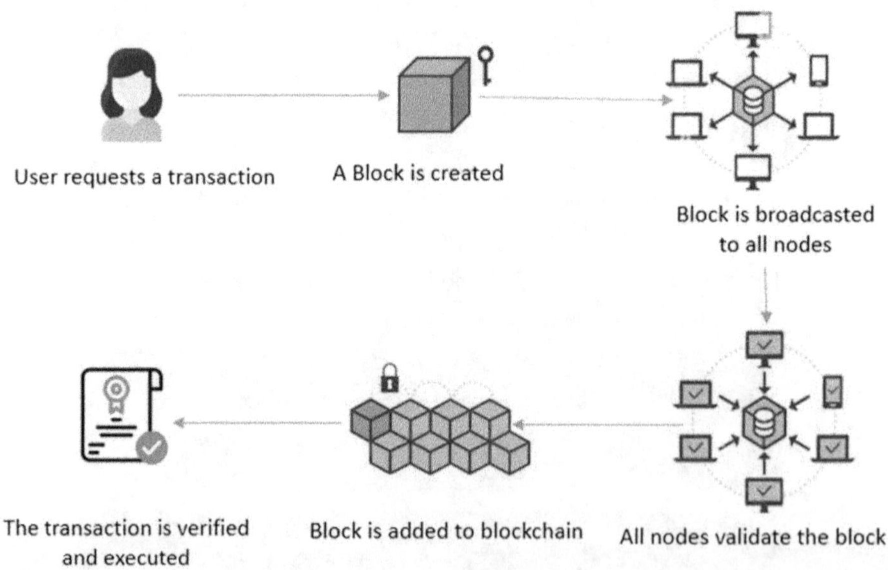

IoT can be resolved by blockchain and the benefits of improving IoT applications with Blockchain are represented in Figure 5.

Blockchain technology can help address IoT security challenges in several ways:

- ***Data Integrity.*** Blockchain ensures the integrity of data by recording transactions in a tamper-resistant manner. Any attempt to alter the data on the blockchain is immediately detected.
- ***Authentication***. Blockchain can be used for secure device authentication. Devices can have unique identities stored on the blockchain, making it difficult for unauthorized devices to join the network.
- ***Decentralization***. No single entity has control or ownership over the entire system, since blockchain follows peer-to-peer architecture thus enhancing the overall security of the IoT network.
- ***Data Privacy***. Blockchain can enable secure and private data sharing among IoT devices while maintaining the privacy of sensitive information.

Figure 5. Benefits of integration of blockchain in IoT

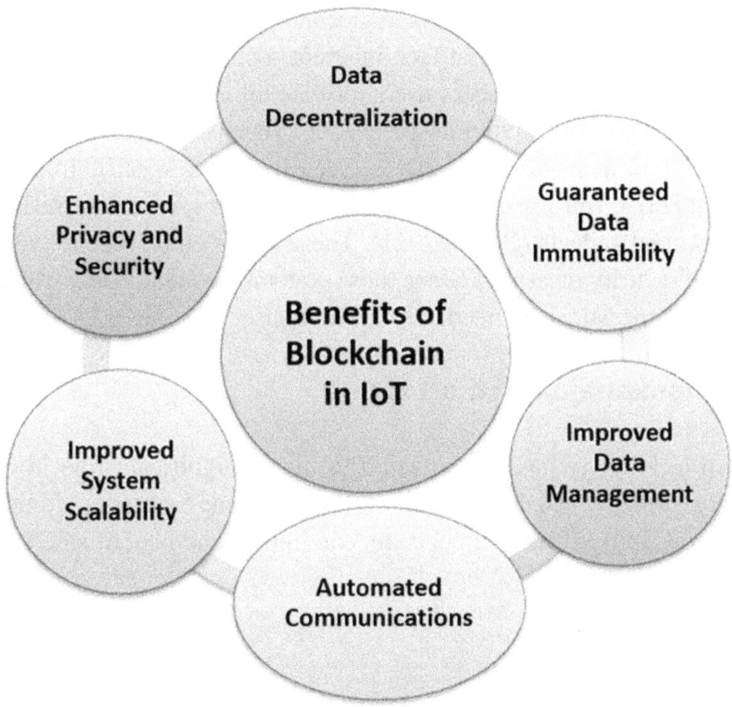

SMART HOME TECHNOLOGY

In smart homes, a single communication system integrates and automates numerous appliances and services within the home. It makes it possible to schedule household appliances automatically, which improves the effectiveness of energy usage and lowers overall costs. Additionally, it ensures security, with a high level of flexibility and ingenious operation, as well as affordable, pleasant services (Jie et al, 2013). A typical Smart Home System (SHS) uses sensors such as motion, temperature, etc., security cameras along other home appliances as shown in Figure 6. A central controller, also known as a smart home hub, controls all these devices. The hub is a hardware component that serves as the brain of the smart home system and has the ability to sense, process data, and wirelessly communicate. It unites all these smart home appliances and devices into a single unit that users can control from a distance(Joseph Bugeja, 2018). The information gathered from SHS is processed to deliver a range of services, including appliance control, aged and physically challenged care, home comfort, and intrusion alert (Arindom Chakraborty et al, 2023; Bhuyan, 2022).

Security Concerns in Smart Home

Smart Homes (Bhuyan, 2022) pose significant security challenges for several reasons. Firstly, homes incorporate diverse technologies such as objects, applications, networks, and cloud systems that lack inherent security measures. Second, smart homes actively gather and process users' private information. Furthermore, house owners typically exhibit limited awareness of cybersecurity, lacking the IT skills and knowledge to manage such systems. Security issues specific to smart homes include unauthorized misuse of smart locks, hacked security cameras, and information leaks from linked gadgets (Coboi, 2021). These issues emphasize the requirement for improved security measures. Since these systems frequently deal with user data, strong security measures are needed to preserve user privacy.

Role of Blockchain in Smart Home

Blockchain technology has the potential to play a significant role in enhancing the security, privacy, and functionality of smart home systems (Moniruzzaman, 2020). Several ways in which blockchain can impact and benefit smart homes are discussed below.

Figure 6. Typical smart home system

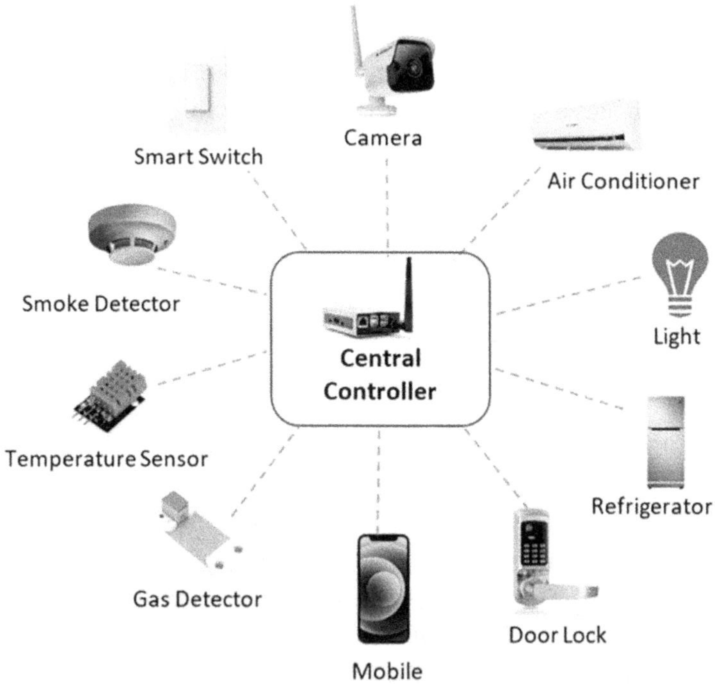

Security and Privacy

- *Device Authentication.* Blockchain has the potential to provide secure and decentralized authentication for smart home devices. Each device can have a unique identity stored on the blockchain, reducing the risk of unauthorized access.
- *Secure Data Transmission.* Blockchain's cryptographic features ensure secure and tamper-proof transmission of data between devices, protecting against data breaches and cyber-attacks.
- *Immutable Record.* The immutability of blockchain records makes it difficult for malicious actors to alter data, providing an added layer of security against cyber attacks.

Decentralized Control Eliminates Single Point of Failure

Traditional smart home systems often rely on centralized servers, making them vulnerable to hacking or system failures. The decentralized nature of blockchain technology eliminates a single point of failure, enhancing system reliability.

Automated Operations Using Smart Contracts

Several procedures within a smart home can be carried out via smart contracts on the blockchain. For example, a smart contract could automatically adjust thermostat settings based on predefined conditions or execute other tasks without the need for intermediaries.

Data Ownership and Sharing

- *User Control.* Users can now have greater authority over their data thanks to blockchain. They have control over what information they want to share with devices and service providers, reducing concerns about data privacy.
- *Monetization of Data.* Users may have the option to monetize their data by granting selective access to certain information, and blockchain can facilitate transparent and fair compensation for data sharing.

Interoperability Through Standardization

Blockchain can contribute to the standardization of communication protocols among different smart home devices and platforms. This interoperability simplifies the integration of devices from different manufacturers.

Supply Chain and Device Lifecycle Management

- *Provenance Tacking.* Blockchain can be used to trace the origin and history of smart home devices, ensuring the authenticity and quality of products.
- *Firmware Updates.* The decentralized and secure nature of blockchain can facilitate secure and transparent firmware updates for smart home devices.

Energy Management

Blockchain can support decentralized energy grids by enabling transparent and secure peer-to-peer energy transactions among smart home devices. This can lead to more efficient energy consumption and management.

Community-Based Initiatives

- *Community Networks.* Blockchain can support the creation of decentralized community networks where smart homes can share resources, such as excess energy or computing power, in a secure and transparent manner.
- *Incentives and Rewards.* Blockchain-based tokens can be used to incentivize positive behaviors within smart home ecosystems, such as energy conservation or participation in community initiatives

BLOCKCHAIN SOLUTIONS FOR IOT AND SMART HOMES

This section explores various blockchain technology approaches for IoT and smart home systems security concerns. These solutions may include the use of blockchain for device authentication, data encryption, access control, and secure communication.

Blockchain technology was applied in a case study on smart home security by Dorri et al (Dorri et al, 2017). Their architecture as in Figure 7. is based on a hierarchical structure that has three main tiers: smart homes, cloud storage, and an overlay. There are clusters of nodes in the overlay, and each cluster elects a Cluster Head to reduce network overhead and delay. The authors explored many transactions and procedures related to the smart home layer as well as its various basic components. Their method had modest and reasonable costs for smart devices with limited resources. The simulation results show modest and reasonable overhead for IoT devices, hierarchical structure enhances compatibility and CH reduces network overhead.

The authors of (Du et al, 2020) developed a Spacechain to solve the scalability and diversity of IoT networks. It is a high-performance, secure blockchain technology with a three-dimensional ledger design. Two types of blocks namely macroblocks and microblocks are used in this design. The Macroblock holds the control information and the Microblock holds details related to each transaction that is occurring between the user and the IoT devices. Then, to assure network performance and security under heavy workloads, the authors suggested the 3D-GHOST consensus technique. According to experimental outcomes, Spacechain performs well in terms of security and network performance.

Al-Turkistani & AlSa'awi (2020) provided a framework for a smart home Internet of Things system that combines private and public blockchain and improves security by blocking harmful behaviors, storing data securely, and enabling remote monitoring of sensitive records. The suggested design increases data safety concerns in IoT systems for smart homes, which are cost-effective, simple to install, and easy to maintain. In terms of shared family verification, privacy, consistency, accessibility,

Figure 7. Three-layer hierarchical structure

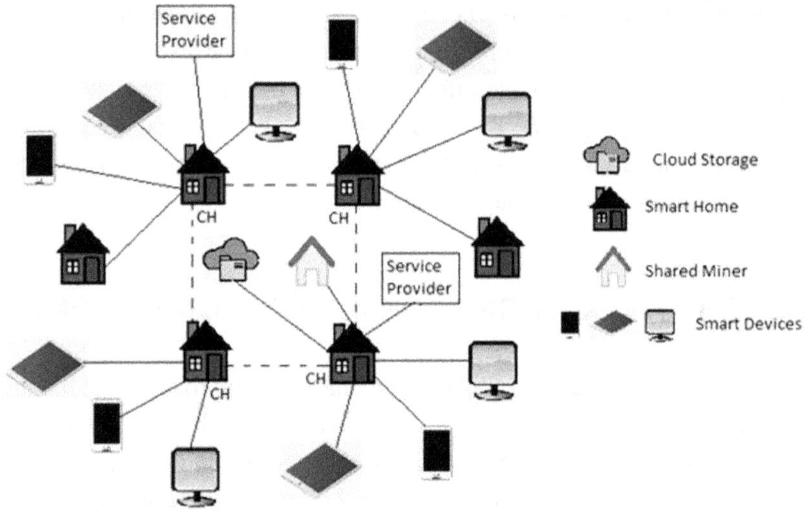

and ensuring safe computational capabilities, the proposed smart home IoT system design satisfies user security needs. Both technical and other non-technical users will find it easy and affordable to use.

The authors of the paper (Tantidham & Aung, 2019) discussed the services required during emergencies for the SHS using the Ethereum private blockchain. Smart contracts handle and record interactions among different entities of the system. For emergency calls, a Public Key Infrastructure (PKI) is devised by the combination of the public-private key pair (RSA Algorithm), Ethereum account, and MAC address of each EM and SM system. Public Key Infrastructure and digital signatures with IPFS can stop man-in-the-middle attacks, DDOS, etc., while RSA encryption safeguards the house owner's personal information for emergency calls.

Baucas et al. (2021) suggest a combination of localization via RSSI-based trilateration with a private blockchain. It intends to develop an access layer that will improve the security of smart homes. The elements of the access layer control how the network's devices are managed. A private blockchain is the first element that detects any unknown appliance trying to join the network. The attack's origin is learned with another element that works on localization. The ledger will be able to follow the projected locations of the devices because of this filter. The architecture is further enhanced by incorporating private blockchains across WiFi and open networks for RSSI measurements.

A framework (Kang et al, 2018) of Ethereum's smart contract without third-party involvement as in Figure 8. is designed to ensure safe energy trade in microgrids.

Home miners use cloud systems or data storage to centrally operate data from all gadgets and the energy storage system stores it. The home miner may access saved data to learn about the current condition, operating history, energy consumption per device, energy production, etc. The transactions are carried out automatically and cannot be faked or manipulated due to blockchain technology and smart contract characteristics.

Khan et al (2020) present a blockchain-based Deep Extreme Learning Machine (DELM) architecture that is a simple but powerful method for identifying and detecting intrusions. The DELM structure consists of an output layer, several hidden layers, and input layers. The DELM was employed to protect the application layer of the smart home system from any harmful or invasive behavior. The backpropagation approach and neural network are used during the learning phase to achieve high accuracy with a low error rate. The DELM technique is significantly more dependable than other algorithms, according to estimation findings. The suggested DELM method demonstrated an incredible accuracy of 93.91 percent.

Dang & Nguyen (2018) proposed an architecture that could evaluate the ability of smart contract operation in a test scenario that involves Ganache, Remix, and web3.js. SHIB architecture is outlined in Figure 8 and addressed issues with privacy protection, trust access control, and extensibility in the context of smart homes. It also allows its users to construct the privacy controls in ACC, which are kept on the Ethereum blockchain and can only be updated or deleted by the author of ACC. The solution proposes an IoT gateway to connect the IoT devices in smart homes directly

Figure 8. Framework for secure energy trade without third-party involvement

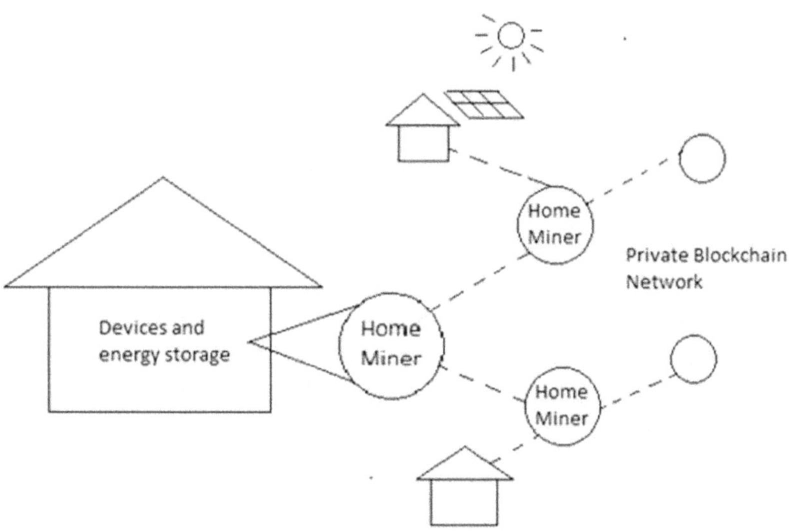

Figure 9. SHIB architecture

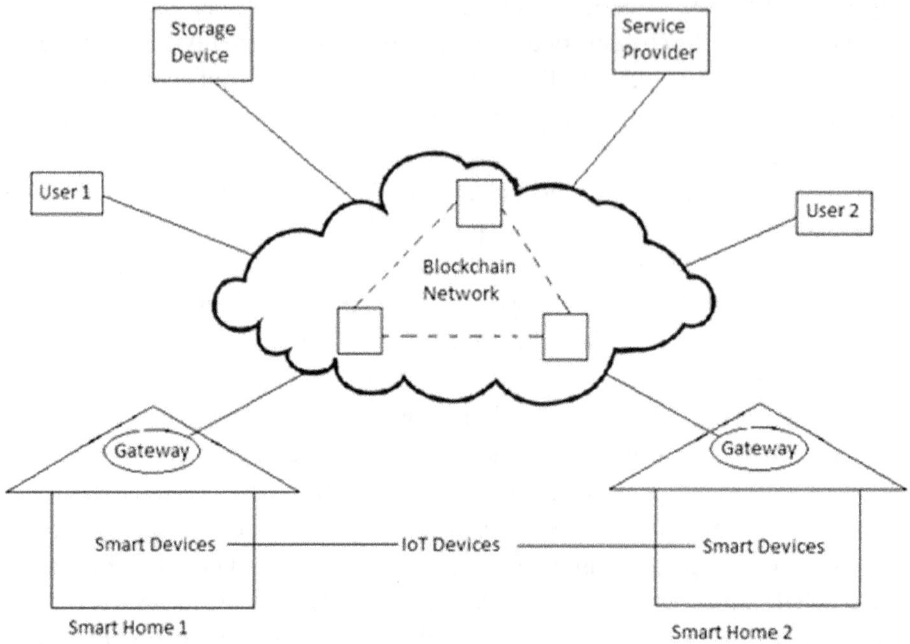

to the blockchain network. Each gateway in IoT uses short- range communication methods like WiFi to link a collection of IoT devices with the blockchain network.

Yang et al (2020) suggest a blockchain-based approach to develop a safe smart home infrastructure. This paper presents proof of concept and is executed using light sensors and smart curtains. Traditionally, data gathered by the light sensor is used by a cloud application to operate the curtains. The devices will not function if the cloud is down or overloaded. Home security will be at risk if the cloud AI is destroyed and its algorithm is changed. Henceforth, the proposed architecture as in Figure 10 eliminates Cloud AI and replaces it with smart curtains and smart lights (IoT devices) for decision-making. In addition, this design uses blockchain as a ledger.

To summarize, most of the blockchain-based smart home solutions focus on enhancing security, privacy, and efficiency in smart homes. Hierarchical structures, consensus techniques, and private blockchain integration contribute to improved performance. Smart contracts, Public Key Infrastructures, and encryption methods are employed for secure transactions and data handling. Several papers highlight the benefits of using blockchain to eliminate reliance on centralized systems and improve security in smart homes.

Figure 10. Blockchain with IoT devices eliminating cloud AI

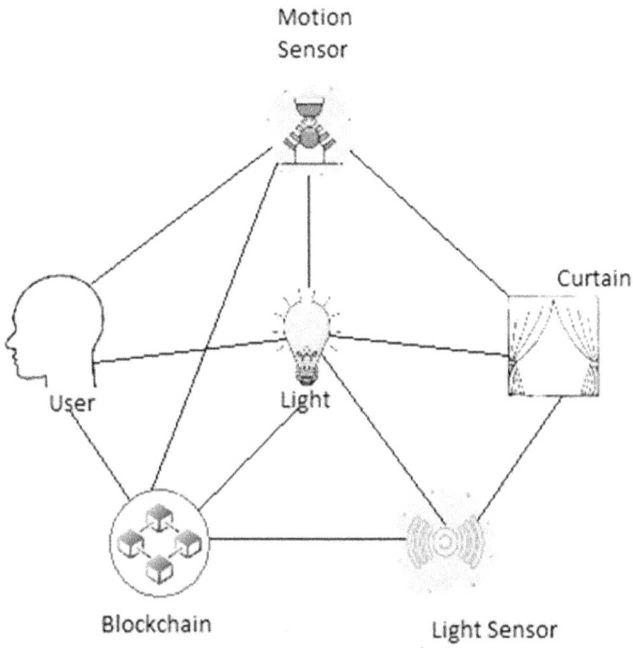

CHALLENGES AND FUTURE DIRECTIONS

Although high-performance devices are being used to build blockchain approaches, this is far from the IoT reality. When adopting blockchain technology in the Smart Home and other IoT applications, a number of problems need to be resolved. These challenges include and are not limited to as represented in Figure 11.

Blockchain Size: In comparison to IoT systems, the size of operational data in Blockchain-based solutions is huge. IoT devices have difficulty processing this data, which is a significant barrier to the adoption of blockchain in IoT (Kumar & Sharma, 2022). One potential remedy presented by IBM for handling the bulky size of the blockchain is that only the blockchain address is maintained by the lightweight IoT nodes.

Resource Limitations in IoT Devices: The processing, memory, and storage capabilities of IoT devices are constrained, whereas a blockchain needs an abundance of room for its data. Additionally, if we take blockchain systems centered upon the Proof of Work(PoW) or comparable protocols into consideration, we must take into account the fact that IoT devices lack the processing power required for mining. Keeping them functional with one another is a difficult undertaking as a result.

Figure 11. Integration challenges of blockchain with IoT

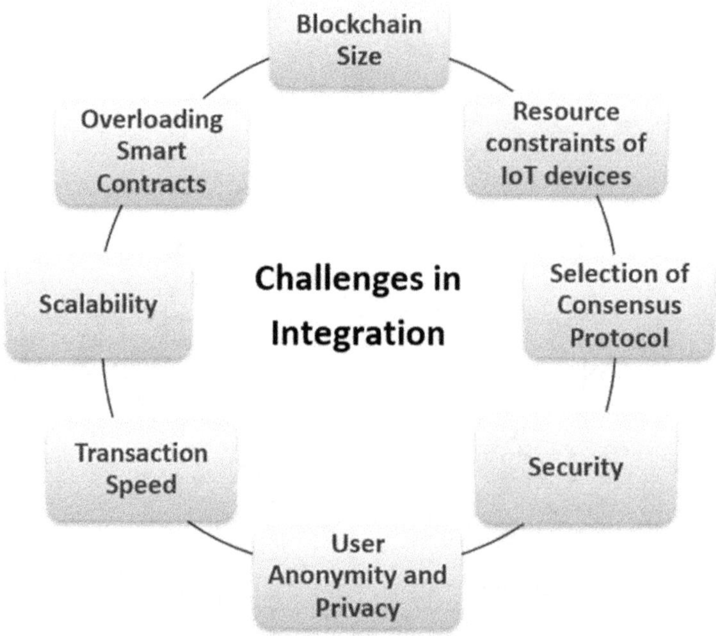

Selection of Consensus Protocol: For successful adaptation of a blockchain solution with IoT setup, designers must address the heavy computation requirement of blockchains and resource limitations of IoT devices. The need for an IoT-focused consensus protocol has been created by these problems.

Security: Ensuring the integrity of data processing through blockchain is contingent on preventing the reception of malicious data from IoT devices. Various factors, including device failures, counterfeit devices, and compromised IoT networks, can lead to data corruption in IoT. The challenge lies in establishing cohesive security protocols between IoT and blockchain to address issues such as device hacking. Therefore, it is crucial to identify a secure method for seamless adaptation of blockchain in IoT networks.

User Anonymity and Privacy: Anonymity is important to safeguard privacy and the provision of pseudo-anonymity by blockchain, prevents users from using their real names. A user can be located by using a combination of these IDs and any associated IP addresses. Additionally, it is possible to track users who utilize many public keys by determining whether the various addresses belong to a single person.

Transaction Speed: The speed of transactions is another main issue with the merging of blockchain with IoT. In fact, IoT-integrated systems operate somewhat more slowly than other ones. The rapid generation of real-time data by IoT devices may not align with the speed of blockchain. (Kumar & Sharma, 2022). Several Blockchain-based systems, including Bitcoin and Ethereum, can only execute 4-5 transactions per second. Additionally, the blockchain was not designed to store and handle the type of data that the IoT may generate. IoT transactions may experience a slowdown as a result of this performance disparity (Kumar et al, 2022).

Scalability Issues: The continuous evolution of IoT networks brings about an increase in smart devices, transactions, and data volume. Furthermore, the imperative for instant data transfer inherent in IoT poses a challenge in integration, as blockchain implementations may introduce delays due to the time required for transaction confirmation.

Risk of overloading smart contracts with IoT devices: Smart contracts rely on oracles, which are external sources providing data to blockchains for the execution of smart contracts. The demand for oracles to access diverse data sources can lead to congestion in smart contracts. Despite the distributed and decentralized nature of smart contracts, they still impose a significant computational burden, presenting a crucial challenge for IoT devices.

Therefore, it is not simple to adopt blockchain in IoT, and involves overcoming the major difficulties of high resources, latency, bandwidth utilization, and poor scalability. Further research and development in this area are essential to realize the full potential of blockchain in securing IoT ecosystems. Continued exploration and advancement in this field are crucial to unlocking the complete capabilities of blockchain in securing IoT ecosystems.

CONCLUSION

The integration of blockchain technology into IoT networks holds promise for improving the confidentiality and safety of connected devices and systems. It offers a way to enhance security, data integrity, and privacy in an increasingly interconnected world. While the application of blockchain in smart homes holds great promise, it is essential to address challenges like scalability, user adoption, and regulatory considerations to realize the full potential of this technology in the context of connected homes. Ongoing research and development efforts are likely to refine and expand the use of blockchain in the evolving landscape of smart homes.

REFERENCES

Al-Turkistani, H. F., & AlSa'awi, N. K. (2020, November). Poster: Combination of blockchains to secure smart home internet of things. In *2020 First International Conference of Smart Systems and Emerging Technologies (SMARTTECH)* (pp. 261-262). IEEE. 10.1109/SMART-TECH49988.2020.00069

Atzori, L., Iera, A., & Morabito, G. (2010). The internet of things: A survey. *Computer Networks*, *54*(15), 2787–2805. doi:10.1016/j.comnet.2010.05.010

Baucas, M. J., Gadsden, S. A., & Spachos, P. (2021). IoT-based smart home device monitor using private blockchain technology and localization. *IEEE Networking Letters*, *3*(2), 52–55. doi:10.1109/LNET.2021.3070270

Bhuyan, M., Kashihara, S., Fall, D., Taenaka, Y., & Kadobayashi, Y. (2022). A survey on blockchain, SDN and NFV for the smart-home security. *Internet of Things : Engineering Cyber Physical Human Systems*, 100588.

Borgia, E. (2014). The Internet of Things vision: Key features, applications and open issues. *Computer Communications*, *54*, 1–31. doi:10.1016/j.comcom.2014.09.008

Bugeja, J., Jacobsson, A., & Davidsson, P. (2018). Smart Connected Homes. In Q. F. Hassan (Ed.), *Internet of Things A to Z: Technologies and Applications* (pp. 359–381). Wiley-IEEE Press. doi:10.1002/9781119456735.ch13

Chakraborty, A., Islam, M., Shahriyar, F., Islam, S., Zaman, H. U., & Hasan, M. (2023). Smart Home System: A Comprehensive Review", 2023. *Journal of Electrical and Computer Engineering*, 7616683.

Chakravorty, A., Wlodarczyk, T., & Rong, C. (2013, May). *Privacy preserving data analytics for smart homes. In 2013 IEEE Security and Privacy Workshops*. IEEE.

Chatterjee, A., & Ahmed, B. S. (2022). IoT anomaly detection methods and applications: A survey. *Internet of Things : Engineering Cyber Physical Human Systems*, *19*, 100568. doi:10.1016/j.iot.2022.100568

Coboi, A. E., Tran, T. A., Tran, S. Q., & Nguyen, M. T. (2021). Security Problems in Smart Homes. *ICSES Transactions on Computer Networks and Communications*, *10*, 1–9.

Dang, T. L. N., & Nguyen, M. S. (2018, November). An approach to data privacy in smart home using blockchain technology. In *2018 International Conference on Advanced Computing and Applications (ACOMP)* (pp. 58-64). IEEE. 10.1109/ACOMP.2018.00017

Dorri, A., Kanhere, S. S., Jurdak, R., & Gauravaram, P. (2017, March). *Blockchain for IoT security and privacy: The case study of a smart home. In 2017 IEEE international conference on pervasive computing and communications workshops (PerCom workshops)*. IEEE.

Du, M., Wang, K., Liu, Y., Qian, K., Sun, Y., Xu, W., & Guo, S. (2020). Spacechain: A three-dimensional blockchain architecture for IoT security. *IEEE Wireless Communications*, *27*(3), 38–45. doi:10.1109/MWC.001.1900466

Gasmi, R., Hammoudi, S., Lamri, M., & Harous, S. (2023). Recent Reinforcement Learning and Blockchain Based Security Solutions for Internet of Things: Survey. *Wireless Personal Communications*, *132*(2), 1–39. doi:10.1007/s11277-023-10664-1

Golosova, J., & Romanovs, A. (2018, November). The advantages and disadvantages of the blockchain technology. In *2018 IEEE 6th workshop on advances in information, electronic and electrical engineering (AIEEE)* (pp. 1-6). IEEE. 10.1109/AIEEE.2018.8592253

Jie, Y., Pei, J. Y., Jun, L., Yun, G., & Wei, X. (2013, June). Smart home system based on iot technologies. In *2013 International conference on computational and information sciences* (pp. 1789-1791). IEEE. 10.1109/ICCIS.2013.468

Kang, E. S., Pee, S. J., Song, J. G., & Jang, J. W. (2018, April). A blockchain-based energy trading platform for smart homes in a microgrid. In *2018 3rd international conference on computer and communication systems (ICCCS)* (pp. 472-476). IEEE. 10.1109/CCOMS.2018.8463317

Khan, M. A., Abbas, S., Rehman, A., Saeed, Y., Zeb, A., Uddin, M. I., Nasser, N., & Ali, A. (2020). A machine learning approach for blockchain-based smart home networks security. *IEEE Network*, *35*(3), 223–229. doi:10.1109/MNET.011.2000514

Kim, J. W. (2020). Blockchain technology and its applications: Case studies. *Journal of System and Management Sciences*, *10*(1), 83–93.

King, S. (2013). *Primecoin: Cryptocurrency with prime number proof-of-work*. Academic Press.

Kumar, R., & Sharma, R. (2022). Leveraging blockchain for ensuring trust in IoT: A survey. *Journal of King Saud University. Computer and Information Sciences*, *34*(10), 8599–8622. doi:10.1016/j.jksuci.2021.09.004

Kumar, R. L., Khan, F., Kadry, S., & Rho, S. (2022). A survey on blockchain for industrial internet of things. *Alexandria Engineering Journal*, *61*(8), 6001–6022. doi:10.1016/j.aej.2021.11.023

Mingxiao, D., Xiaofeng, M., Zhe, Z., Xiangwei, W., & Qijun, C. (2017, October). A review on consensus algorithm of blockchain. In 2017 IEEE international conference on systems, man, and cybernetics (SMC) (pp. 2567-2572). IEEE. doi:10.1109/SMC.2017.8123011

Mocrii, D., Chen, Y., & Musilek, P. (2018). IoT-based smart homes: A review of system architecture, software, communications, privacy and security. *Internet of Things : Engineering Cyber Physical Human Systems*, *1*, 81–98. doi:10.1016/j.iot.2018.08.009

Moniruzzaman, M., Khezr, S., Yassine, A., & Benlamri, R. (2020). Blockchain for smart homes: Review of current trends and research challenges. *Computers & Electrical Engineering*, *83*, 106585. doi:10.1016/j.compeleceng.2020.106585

Nakamoto, S., & Bitcoin, A. (2008). *A peer-to-peer electronic cash system.* https://bitcoin. org/bitcoin. pdf

Report. (2020). *Cisco Annual Internet Report (2018-2023).* https://www.cisco.com/c/en/us/solutions/collateral/executive-perspectives/annual-internet-report/white-paper-c11-741490.html

Report. (2022). *Blockchain Distributed Ledger Market by Component, Type, Enterprise Size, Application and End User: Opportunity Analysis and Industry Forecast, 2020–2027*. Allied Market Research.

Report. (2023). *Gartner*. https://www.gartner.com/

Report. (2021). *Cellular IoT & LPWA Market Tracker (Q3 2021).* https://iot-analytics.com/

Roman, R., Zhou, J., & Lopez, J. (2013). On the features and challenges of security and privacy in distributed internet of things. *Computer Networks*, *57*(10), 2266–2279. doi:10.1016/j.comnet.2012.12.018

Sicari, S., Rizzardi, A., Grieco, L. A., & Coen-Porisini, A. (2015). Security, privacy and trust in Internet of Things: The road ahead. *Computer Networks*, *76*, 146–164. doi:10.1016/j.comnet.2014.11.008

Soni, S., & Bhushan, B. (2019, July). A comprehensive survey on blockchain: Working, security analysis, privacy threats and potential applications. In *2019 2nd international conference on intelligent computing, instrumentation and control technologies (ICICICT)* (pp. 922-926). IEEE.

Tantidham, T., & Aung, Y. N. (2019, March). Emergency service for smart home system using ethereum blockchain: System and architecture. In 2019 IEEE international conference on pervasive computing and communications workshops (PerCom Workshops) (pp. 888-893). IEEE.

Yang, L., Liu, X. Y., & Gong, W. (2020, July). Secure smart home systems: A blockchain perspective. In *IEEE INFOCOM 2020-IEEE Conference on Computer Communications Workshops (INFOCOM WKSHPS)* (pp. 1003-1008). IEEE. 10.1109/INFOCOMWKSHPS50562.2020.9162648

Chapter 3
Does Gold React as a Safe Haven and Hedge for G7 Stock Markets?
Comparative Assessment of the COVID-19 Pandemic vs. Global Financial Crisis

Bassem Ghorbali
Tunis High Institute of Business, Manouba University, Tunisia

Kamel Naoui
Tunis High Institute of Business, Manouba University, Tunisia

Abdelkader Mohamed Sghaier Derbali
https://orcid.org/0000-0003-4098-3120
Applied College, Taibah University, Saudi Arabia

ABSTRACT

This chapter investigates the safe haven property and hedge of gold especially during GFC and COVID-19 for G7 stock markets by using DCC-GARCH and wavelet coherence analysis. The findings reveal that the dynamic conditional correlation between gold and each G7 stock market decreased significantly during extreme market conditions, especially during GFC and COVID-19. The results show that gold served as a strong safe haven asset for all G7 stock markets except Nikkei225 during GFC. However, gold has maintained this traditional role as a safe haven only for CAC40, S&PTSX, FTSE/MIB, and FTSE100 during the COVID-19 pandemic. The optimal portfolio weights of gold in each G7 stock market significantly increased during GFG and COVID-19 pandemic, meaning that investors should invest more in the gold as a 'flight-to-safety asset' during market turmoil. The decomposition of the coherence between gold and each G7 stock market into three investment horizons demonstrates a weak correlation in both the short term and the long term for the normal and extreme conditions market.
DOI: 10.4018/979-8-3693-1511-8.ch003

1. INTRODUCTION

Co-movement between the gold market and the international stock market has caused increased attention from portfolio investors, risk managers, and policymakers. In the finance literature, gold is acting as a hedge, safe haven, and diversifier asset against all stock markets. Several empirical studies have analyzed the correlation between stocks markets and gold to examine their property for the stock market. Baur and McDermott (2010), define a hedge and a safe haven as follows: A strong (weak) hedge is defined as an asset that is negatively correlated (uncorrelated) with another asset on average. However, it has to be noted that a hedge does not necessarily have the property of reducing losses in periods of extremely declining markets as the asset could exhibit a positive correlation in such periods and a negative correlation in normal times, which could result in a negative correlation on average. A strong (weak) safe haven is defined as an asset that is negatively correlated (uncorrelated) with the stock market in periods of extreme stock market declines. The specific property of a safe haven asset is the non-positive correlation with the stock market in extreme market conditions. However, note that this property does not force the correlation to be positive or negative on average but only to be zero or negative in specific periods of stock market declines.

Several studies have examined whether gold acts as a safe haven hedge against the financial market in general and the stock market in particular during GFC. Ngun et al. (2016) show that gold may be a safe haven asset during the market crash in Malaysia, Singapore, Thailand, the UK, and the US, but not for the Indonesian, Japanese, and the Philippines. Shahzad et al. (2019) find that gold roles an undisputable safe haven and hedge against G7 stock markets, they also notice that gold offered conditional diversification benefits in a portfolio composed of G7 stock markets.

Baur and Lucey)2010) and Beckmann et al. (2015) observe that gold acts as a hedge against equities in normal market conditional and viewed safe haven properties against equities during extreme market conditional. Chiki (2016) investigates the dynamic relationships between gold and BRICS stock markets. He concludes that the dynamic conditional correlations switch between negative and positive values over the sample period. Peng (2019) suggests that during the global financial crisis gold has outperformed, as a strong safe haven against the china stock market.

In the same vein, Bekiros et al. (2017) show that contagious effects of the global financial crisis have prompted investors to seek safe haven, hedging, and diversification opportunities in alternative asset classes such as gold. Jiang et al. (2019) found a negative correlation between BRICS stock markets and precious metals during extreme market conditions, especially GFC. They notice also that gold is the most effective asset to hedge the risk of BRICS stock markets. Baur et McDermott (2010) the role of gold in the global financial system. They find evidence that gold is both a strong safe haven and hedge for European stock markets and the US but not for BRIC stock markets, Australia, Japan, and Canada.

Chkili (2017) investigates if gold acts as a hedge or safe haven for the Islamic stock market. Using a Markov switching approach, he concludes that gold can act as a weak hedge and a strong safe haven against extreme Islamic stock market movements. The GFC caused a significant change in the connectedness structure between gold and stock markets. The correlations are low to negative during the major financial crises meaning that gold can move as a safe haven or hedge against extreme market conditions. Therefore, gold provides a diversification opportunity for the stock markets during turbulent periods. In this case, investors should give more weight to gold than stocks in their gold–stock portfolios, whereas they should allocate more funds into stocks than oil to minimize risk in their oil–stock portfolios (Abuzayed et al., 2021; Mensi et al., 2021; Trabelsi et al., 2021; Alkhazali and Zoubi, 2020).

Recently, the emergence of the COVID-19 pandemic has encouraged several research to examine the ability of gold to maintain it is traditional hedging and safe haven properties during a health crisis. Shehzad et al. (2021) suggest that gold has robust safe haven properties than bitcoin for stock markets of Asia, Europe, and the US during the COVID-19 pandemic. Salisu et al. (2021) examine the safe haven of gold during the COVID-19 pandemic. They showed that gold acts as a safe haven than US stock markets during the COVID-19 pandemic. Akhtaruzzaman et al. (2021b) found that gold severed as a strong safe haven for stock markets during phase I[1] of the COVID-19 pandemic crisis. Nevertheless, gold does not sever as a safe haven during phase II[2] of COVID-19.

Akhtaruzzaman et al. (2021a) study the part of gold as a hedge or safe-haven asset in diverse stages of the COVID-19 epidemic catastrophe, consistent to the judgement of fiscal and monetary incentives to sustenance the debilitated economy. They employ high-frequency dataset, their findings demonstrate that gold assisted as a safe-haven asset for stock markets throughout Stage I (December 31, 2019–March 16, 2020) of the epidemic. But, gold misplaced its safe-haven part throughout Stage II (March 17–April 24, 2020). Their results stipulate understanding for individual and institutional investors and guidance to representatives, supervisors, and broadcasting on how gold progressed as a hedge and safe-haven asset in diverse stages of the epidemic.

Akhtaruzzaman et al. (2021c) study how financial contamination arises over financial and nonfinancial companies amongst China and G7 economies throughout the COVID–19 epidemic. The findings demonstrate that registered company's crossways these economies, financial and non-financial companies comparable, knowledge important intensification in conditional relationships amongst their stock returns. Akhtaruzzaman et al. (2021c) correspondingly find that ideal hedge ratios rise suggestively in greatest cases, suggesting advanced hedging charges throughout the COVID-19 crisis.

Akhtaruzzaman et al. (2022a) study the position of green bonds in hedging the risk alongside manufacturing classes and supplementary main asset portfolios. They find that the risk of green classes is inferior to that of unhedged (non-green) classes. Additionally, their paper delivers indication that the hedging efficiency of green classes progresses throughout the COVID–19 epidemic. Akhtaruzzaman et al. (2022b) employ the Conditional Value-at-Risk (CoVaR) approach to progress the systemic contagion index (SCI) for cryptocurrencies and study their spillover impacts. They find that systemic contagion index shows the maximum value throughout the COVID–19 crisis, demonstrating suggestion of epidemic-determined contagion networks.

Akhtaruzzaman et al. (2022c) study the dynamic correlation between COVID–19 media coverage index (MCI) and ESG leader indices. They show an indication that MCI theatres a position in simplifying the propagation of contagion to progressive and emerging equity markets throughout the COVID-19 crisis. The correlation amongst MCI and ESG spearhead directories is supplementary noticeable about March and April 2020 at the highest of the epidemic.

Chemkha et al. (2021) find that gold acts as a weak safe haven against major world stock market indices during the COVID-19 pandemic. Disli et al. (2021) have analyzed the role of crude, gold, and cryptocurrency as a safe haven for Islamic, sustainable, and traditional equity during the COVID-19 pandemic crisis. Using wavelet analysis, their results show a low coherence between gold that gold and all three indices across all horizons, especially in the longer horizon. This suggests that gold offers hedging and safe haven properties for all three indices.

Adekoya et al. (2021) found that gold is qualified as a hedge for both oil and stock market risks during the COVID-19 pandemic period. Ji et al. (2020) have analyzed the role of Bitcoin, gold, stock exchange market, oil, and soybean as a safe haven for the MSCI equity index during the COVID-19 pandemic. Their results showed that gold and soybean are a strong safe haven against the MSCI equity index during health crises. However, Będowska-Sójka et Kliber (2021) found that gold is qualified as a strong safe haven before COVID-19 for S&P500, DAX, FTSE250, and STOXX Europe 600 Index. Yet, during the COVID-19, pandemic gold does not act as a safe haven property for stock markets.

To examine the safe haven property and hedge of gold especially during GFC and COVID-19 for G7 stock markets, our paper has three main goals that will be attained. The first goal is to examine the structure conditional correlation between the gold market and the G7 stock markets in the global financial crisis and COVID-19 pandemic. Moreover, we use a bivariate Dynamic Conditional Correlation (DCC) Generalized Autoregressive Conditional Heteroscedasticity (GARCH) model. The second goal is to examine the role of gold as a safe haven and hedge for stock markets during the GFC and COVID-19 pandemic. The final goal is to compare the hedge and safe haven asset properties of gold in the GFC and COVID-19 pandemic.

The main contribution of this paper is to analyze the ability of gold as a hedge and safe haven for G7 stock markets in extreme market conditions of financial origin (GFC) and extreme market conditions of health origin (COVID-19). Our empirical findings demonstrate that gold served as a strong safe haven asset for all G7 stock markets except Nikkei225 during GFC. Also, gold is maintained this traditional role as a safe haven only for CAC40, S&PTSX, FTSE/MIB, and FTSE100 during the COVID-19 pandemic. Finally, our paper provides evidence that gold is considered a safe haven for the G7 stock market in the short and long prospects.

The remainder of this paper is organized as follows: Section 2 describes the data and methodology. Section 3 presents the empirical results. Section 4 concludes the paper.

2. METHODOLOGY

2.1. The DCC-GARCH

We choose the bivariate DCC-GARCH model[3] proposed by (Engle, 2002) to estimate the dynamic correlation between gold and G7 stock markets. A major advantage of utilizing this model is the detection of structure correlation over time, such as, the dynamic conditional correlation is a tool that allows to investigate of the possible contagion effect between financial markets during crises periods (see, Chebbi and Derbali, 2016a; Chebbi and Derbali, 2016b; Derbali et al., 2021a; Derbali et al., 2021b; Belhassine et Karamti, 2021). Another advantage of the DCC-GARCH model is to allows us to understand the reaction of investors to new products and innovations.

To estimate of DCC-GARCH model, there are two steps: First, we estimate the univariate GARCH model for each market return to obtain the standardized residuals. Second, the dynamic conditional correlation coefficients of the model are estimated with the standard residuals. The bivariate DCC-GARCH (1, 1) is presented as follow:

$$r_{i,t}=\mu i_{+}\varepsilon I,_{t\,w}\text{ith } \varepsilon_{i,t}=\eta_{it}\sqrt{\sigma_{it}} \quad (1)$$

$$\sigma_t^2=\omega+\alpha\varepsilon_{t-1}^2+\beta\sigma_{t-1}^2 \quad (2)$$

Where, μi is the mean of the process $ri_{,t,}$ hi_t represents the conditional variance of asset i, the parameters α and β are non-negative (with α + β < 1) and represent the short- and long-run persistence of shocks to conditional variance, respectively.

Then, the parameters of dynamic conditional correlation are estimated from the conditional variance-covariance matrix H where

$$H_i = D_i R_t D_i \tag{3}$$

With, D_i is the diagonal matrix $\left[\sqrt{h_{1t}}, \sqrt{h_{2t}}\right]$ of time-varying standard deviations, R_t is the conditional correlation coefficient matrix of the standardized returns.

Where a^{DCC} and b^{DCC} are the parameters of DCC, while $a^{DCC} + b^{DCC} < 1$.

2.2. Optimal Portfolio Design and Hedging Ratios

The optimal portfolio weight with the aim of investigating the change in the optimal weights during the sample period. Therefore, we follow Korner and Ng (1998) to identify the optimal weights of gold in a portfolio composed of gold and each G7 stock markets pair, such as CAC40, S&P500, Nikkei225, FTES100, FTSE/MIB, and S&P/TSX. The optimal weight at time t is calculated as follow:

$$w_t^{i/Gold} = \frac{h_t^i - h_t^{i/Gold}}{h_t^i - 2h_t^{i/Gold} + h_t^{Gold}} \tag{4}$$

Where, h_t^i is the conditional variance of CAC40, Nikkei225, FTSE100, S&P500, FTSE/MIB, S&P/TSX, and DAX30, h_t^{Gold} is the conditional variance of gold. $h_t^{i/Gold}$ indicated the conditional covariance between gold and each G7 markets index at hour t. we use the DCC–GARCH model for calculated the conditional variances and covariances at hout t.

$$w_t^{i/Gold} = \begin{cases} 0 & if \;\; w_t^{i/Gold} < 0 \\ w_t^{i/Gold} & if \;\; 0 < w_t^{i/Gold} < 1 \\ 1 & if \;\; w_t^{i/Gold} > 1 \end{cases}$$

In the second stage, we also calculate the risk-minimizing HR ($\beta_t^{i/Gold}$) for each stock market/gold portfolio. A long position of $ 1 in index G7 stock markets must be hedged with a short position of $\beta_t^{i/Gold}$ dollars in gold to minimize portfolio risk

(Torrence and Compo, 1998; Torrence and Webster, 1999; Grinsted et al., 2004; Ng and Chan, 2012; Vacha and Barunik, 2012). Following Kroner and Sultan (1993), the hedge ratio is calculated as follow:

$$\beta_t^{i/Gold} = \frac{h_t^{i/Gold}}{h_t^{Gold}} \tag{5}$$

2.3. Safe Haven Property of Gold

To determine the safe haven property of follows Baur and Lucey (2010) and Baur and McDermott (2010), we use DCC analysis and add dummy variables during the financial crisis. Indeed, the dummy variables are equal to1 if periods are in GFC and COVID-19 crisis and 0 otherwise.

$$DCC_{iGold,t} = \delta_0 + \delta_1 D_{GFC} + \delta_2 D_{COVID-19} + \vartheta_{iGold,t} \tag{6}$$

$$DCC_{iGold,t} = \rho_{ij,t} = \frac{q_{ij,t}}{\sqrt{q_{ii,t} - q_{jj,t}}} \tag{7}$$

$\rho i_{j,t}$ represents the dynamic conditional correlation between gold and CAC40, S&P500, Nikkei225, FTSE100, DAX30, FTSE/MIB, S&P/TSX. DG_{FC} and $DC_{OVID\text{-}19}$ presented respectively the dummy variable during GFC and COVID-19. If the constant $\delta 0$ $_{i}$s weakly positive, the gold is a weak diversifier against the G7 stock markets. The gold is a hedge against movements in each G7 index if $\delta 0$ i_{s} statistically not different from zero (weak hedge) or negative (strong hedge). Finally, gold is a weak safe haven for the other asset during the crisis period if $\delta 2$, δ_3 *are* not significantly different from zero, or a strong safe haven if $\delta 2$ an*d* $_{\delta}$3 are *s*$_{i}$gnificantly negative.

3. DATA AND DESCRIPTIVE STATISTICS

3.1. Data

We collect daily stock market data for G7 countries and Gold Thomson-Reuters for each country, we choose one principal stock market, the details of each principal stock market are presented in Table 1. The data cover the period from January 04, 2005 to August 09, 2021, totaling 4321 observations, and encompasses both the Global

Financial Crisis (GFC) and the period of COVID-19. For each data series, daily returns $Ri(t)$ *are* calculated as $\ln(Pi(t)_{)} - \ln(Pi(t-_{1}))$, where $Pi(t)$ *the* daily closing price for instant t and $Pi(t-_{1})$ is the daily closing price for instant t-1. With i representing S&P500, CAC40, Nikkei225, DAX30, S&P/TSX, FTSE100, FTSE/MIB and gold. Then, we use a common currency, as USD, to estimate the returns and volatilities of all indices employed in our paper (Akhtaruzzaman et al., 2021b). In this study, we focus only on GFC and COVID-19 pandemic to compare the time-varying correlation between gold and the G7 stock market. Following Dungey (2009) and Celik (2012), we consider that the GFC covers from 17/07/2007 through 31/08/2009 and as suggested by Ben Lagha and El Omri (2021) and Wan et al. (2021), we treat January 20, 2020 as the beginning date of sanitary crisis.

Figure 1 illustrates the evolution of each return series. Overall, the movement of G7 stock returns and gold returns reveals a volatility clustering in different sample periods. On the other hand, peaks of volatilities are recorded for all return series, particularly during extreme market conditions (GFC, European debt crisis, 2015 China stock market crisis, and COVID-19 pandemic)

3.2. Summary Statistics

Table 1 summarizes the descriptive statistics for the G7 stock markets returns and gold. As shown in Table 1, the average daily returns are positive in all markets over the sample period. Among the stock market, the unconditional volatility measured by the standard deviation is the highest for FTSEMIB while FTSE100 presents the least. Moreover, S&P500, CAC40, and DAX30 show similar volatility, both of which are high risk, while the gold market is the least volatile. The skewness coefficients are negative for all return series and the kurtosis coefficient values are positive above three for all the return series, which indicates that the distribution of these series is not normally distributed, which is proved by the Jarque–Bera statistics. According to the result of Augmented Dickey and Fuller, all return series are stationary. The significant autocorrelation exists in all return series, which could be confirmed by Ljung–Box statistic and in both residuals and squared residuals. Finally, the Engle

Table 1. List of the principal stock index of G7 countries

Country	Stock Index	Country	Stock Index
United States	S&P500	Italy	FTSE/MIB
France	CAC40	Canada	S&P/TSX
United Kingdom	FTSE100	Germany	DAX30
Japan	Nikkei225		

Figure 1. G7 stock markets index returns and gold index returns

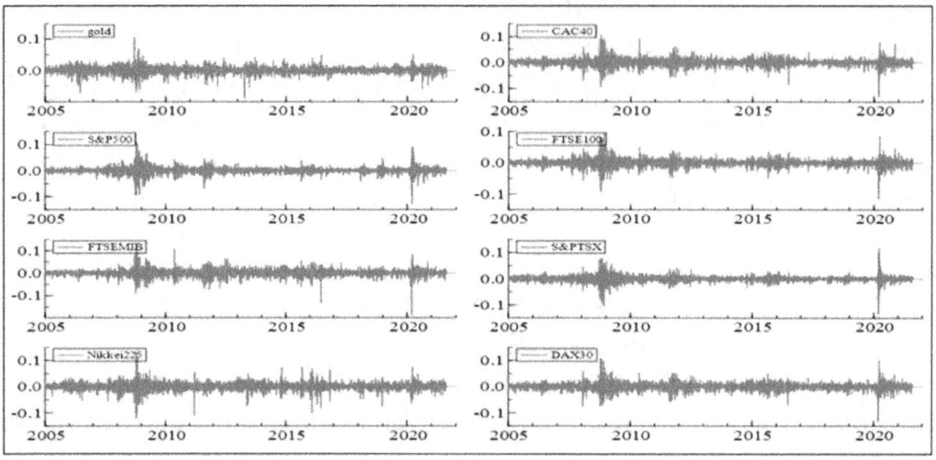

test reveals that strong ARCH effects exist in all return series. The above analysis indicates that a GARCH model specification is appropriate. Table 2 shows the results of the unconditional correlation between G7 stock markets and gold, overall, we can observe a low correlation between gold and each index for the G7 stock market implying a low degree of association between gold and each stock market. In addition, we found that the pair gold- S&P/TSX has a high unconditional correlation than other pairs. However, the pair gold- FTSE/MIB owns a low unconditional correlation than other pairs.

4. EMPIRICAL RESULTS

4.1. Estimation of DCC-GARCH Model

The estimation of Parameters for the DCC model is presented in table (3). We can find that the coefficient *a* is on positive and significant except for the gold-Nikkei225, meaning the importance of shocks between the gold and G7 stock markets. Likewise, coefficient b is significant and very near to one, indicating the higher persistence of volatility in the long term between gold and each G7 stock market. It is worth mentioning that the significance of the parameters *a* and *b* approves the appropriateness of the DCC model. Figure 2 exhibits the dynamic conditional correlation for the gold and each G7 stock market. We find that the correlation between each pair fluctuates greatly during our sample period; these results indicated that investors should amend their portfolio structure frequently. The DCC model shows that the

Table 2. Summary statistics for the return series

	Gold	S&P500	CAC40	DAX30	Nikkei225	FTSE100	FTSE/MIB	S&P/TSX
Mean	0.0003	0.0003	0.0001	0.0003	0.0002	0.0001	0.0000	0.0002
Maximum	0.1048	0.1096	0.1059	0.1080	0.1329	0.0938	0.1087	0.1168
Minimum	-0.0887	-0.1277	-0.1310	-0.1305	-0.1211	-0.1151	-0.1854	-0.1336
Std. Dev.	0.0110	0.0126	0.0137	0.0135	0.0151	0.0116	0.0156	0.0118
Skewness	-0.3258	-0.5275	-0.2763	-0.2248	-0.4009	-0.3844	-0.6857	-0.9331
Kurtosis	9.1770	16.3379	11.5563	11.3552	11.3029	12.9884	13.2739	21.7108
Jarque-Bera	6944.45	32222.10	13232.95	12602.01	12524.42	18064.80	19338.06	63643.48
ADF	-65.2131***	-80.4300**	-68.2738***	-66.6598***	-74.1762***	-69.2025***	-68.7612***	-29.0965***
Q (20)	20.163***	238.86***	54.285***	35.15***	99.471***	76.505***	45.861***	194.84***
Q^2 (20)	886.51***	7042.3***	2811.800***	2478.6***	4330.1***	3897.1***	1238.1***	5861.7***
ARCH (20)	20.1522***	115.0592***	48.0803***	46.6874***	72.1962***	61.1811***	27.8227***	102.2942***
Obs.	4320	4320	4320	4320	4320	4320	4320	4320

Notes: ADF test is to check the stationary property of the return the series. Q (20) and Q 2 (20) denote the Ljung–Box test to check the autocorrelation in residuals and squared residuals up to 20 lags. ARCH (20) denotes the Engle [32]'s test to check the presence of ARCH effects up to 20 lags. ***$p < 0.01$, **$p < 0.05$, *$p < 0.1$.

Table 3. Correlation for the returns

	Gold	S&P500	CAC40	DAX30	Nikkei225	FTSE100	FTSE/MIB	S&P/TSX
Gold	1.0000							
S&P500	0, 0342** (2, 2461)	1.0000						
CAC40	0, 0198 (1.3012)	0.5813*** (46.9489)	1.0000					
DAX30	0.0274* (1.7981)	0.5868*** (47.6260)	0, 9232*** (157, 8516)	1.0000				
Nikkei225	0.0319** (2.0997)	0.1394 (9.2480)	0, 3178*** (22, 0282)	0, 3040*** (20, 9659)	1.0000			
FTSE100	0.0586** (3.8559)	0.5605*** (44.4702)	0, 8874*** (126, 4841)	0, 8348*** (99, 6329)	0, 3135*** (21, 6927)	1.0000		
FTSE/MIB	0.0138 (0.9046)	0, 5264*** (40.6872)	0, 8863*** (125, 7560)	0, 8397*** (101, 6099)	0, 2663*** (18, 1570)	0, 7797*** (81, 8327)	1.0000	
S&P/TSX	0.1842*** (12.3127)	0, 7565*** (76, 0097)	0, 5740*** (46, 0625)	0, 5579*** (44, 1739)	0, 2048*** (13, 7497)	0, 5822*** (47, 0587)	0, 5216*** (40, 1769)	1.0000

Notes: The t-statistic values are in parentheses. ***$p < 0.01$, **$p < 0.05$, *$p < 0.1$. The low degree of association between gold and those markets indicates that the integration of gold in a portfolio composed of the G7 stock indices leads to greater diversification benefits.

correlation level ranges between negative and positive values. It is worth noting that in extreme market conditions such as GFC, European debt crisis, China stock market crash in 2015, and sanitary crisis, the correlation level is negative, which means that investors may benefit more from portfolio diversification especially during the financial crisis.

The negative correlation during times of market turbulence may be explained by several reasons: on one hand, the collapse of G7 stock markets during extreme market conditions and on the other hand, the significant increase in the gold price, because the international investors have opted for gold to optimize their investment

Table 4. DCC model estimation results between gold and stock indices

	CAC40	S&P500	Nikkei225	FTSE100	FTSE/MIB	S&PTSX	DAX30
a	0.02818*** (0.0000)	0.03625*** (0.0000)	0.0127*** (0.1517)	0.0240 *** (0.0002)	0.0214** (0.0106)	0.0408*** (0.0000)	0.0264*** (0.0001)
b	0.9570*** (0.0000)	0.94411*** (0.0000)	0.8791*** (0.0000)	0.9603*** (0.0000)	0.9678*** (0.0000)	0.9420*** (0.0000)	0.9606*** (0.0000)
a+b	0.9851	0.9803	0.8918	0.9843	0.9892	0.9828	0.9870

Notes: The t-statistic values are in parentheses: ***$p < 0.01$, **$p < 0.05$, *$p < 0.1$.

Figure 2. Dynamic conditional correlations between gold and G7 stock markets

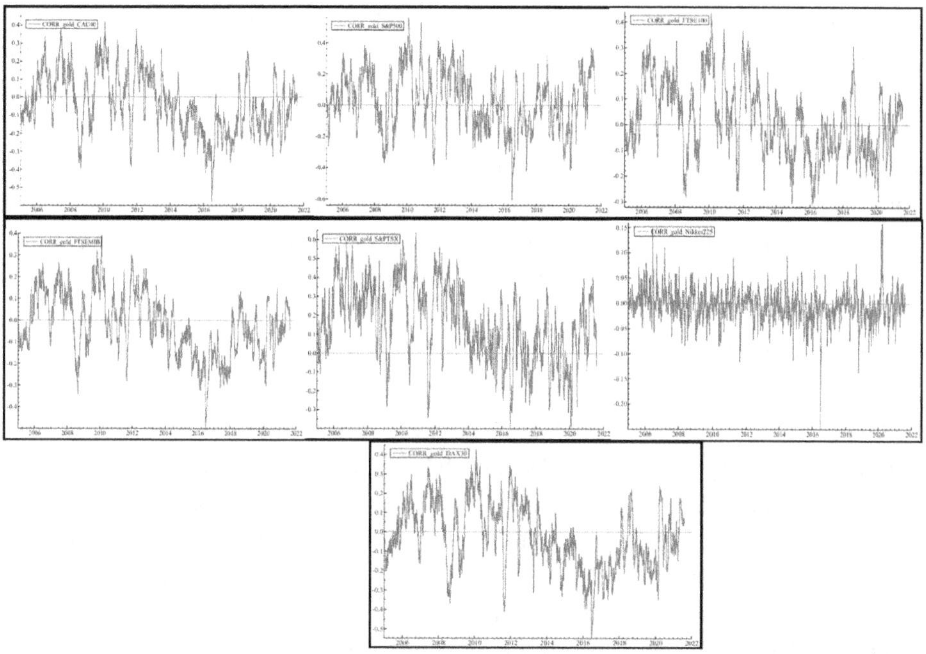

strategy, using gold as a safe haven. However, the plots show that in normal market conditional, the correlation between gold and G7 stock markets is positive. On the other hand, our finding also suggests that during GFC, the gold-G7stock markets pair exhibits a very significant negative dynamic correlation then COVID-19. Indeed, the negative correlation during GFC for all gold and each G7 stock markets pair

4.2 Optimal Portfolio Weights

Figure 3 illustrates optimal weights for gold during our sample period. The results show a highly fluctuated of the optimal portfolio weights. During the extreme market conditions, we found that the optimal weight has increased, which shows that investors need to use more gold weights to hedge the risk. During the GFC, the debt crisis European, China stock market crisis, and COVID-19, the results show the optimal weight in gold for each portfolio index. For example, in GFC the gold weight reached the level of 0.9, meaning that investors use in your portfolio only 0.1 units in the stock market and 0.9 units in gold. However, in normal market conditions, the gold weight declined significantly ant it showed a low level of gold weights. Therefore, the portfolio managers and investors should be select optimal weights in their portfolio strategies according to market conditions (extreme or normal market conditions). In comparison between GFC and COVID-19, we note that optimal weights under the GFC are higher and mostly fluctuate than the COVID-19 pandemic. During the GFC, the gold optimal weight moved around 0.75 – 0.9 units for each G7 stock market in the period 2008-2010. Yet, during the COVID-19 pandemic, gold optimal weights exceeded the 0.5 level only in the first quarter of the health crisis. The results of optimal portfolio weights present important implications for portfolio managers and investors. The decrease in the level of portfolio risk requires a better analysis of the relationship between assets. Thus, the composition of the optimal portfolio depends on the market conditions. Overall, investors in G7 stock markets should invest more in gold during extreme market conditions than normal market conditions.

4.3. Hedging Ratio

Figure 4 shows the time-varying hedge ratios across gold and G7 stock markets, and movements of hedge ratios of gold and each G7 stock market fluctuate dramatically during our sample period, indicating that investors should be adjusted their investment strategy according to these fluctuations to optimize their portfolio. In addition, the results reveal that the hedge ratio for gold and each G7 stock market changed from positive during normal market conditions to negative during extreme market conditions. These results are similar to the empirical conclusions who are founded by Akhtaruzzaman et al. (2022a) which show that the risk of green portfolios is subordinate than that of non-green portfolios. Additionally, their empirical findings demonstrate indication that the hedging effectiveness of green portfolios progresses throughout the COVID–19 epidemic.

The positive values of optimal hedge ratio occurred by the similar relationship between gold and G7 stock indices during calm period indicating that the hedge is formed by taking a long position in the G7 stock index and a short position in gold to minimize portfolio risk. For example, a $1000 long position in Italian stocks is hedged by taking another long position for $264 in the gold market. The negative values of the optimal hedge ratio occurred by the inverse correlation between gold and G7 stock indices during turbulent times indicating that the hedge is formed by taking two identical positions (short or long) for gold and each G7 stock index. For example, a $1000 long position in Italian stocks is hedged by taking another long position for $264 in the gold market. The results in Figure 4 show that the optimal hedge ratio has experienced a downward trend during the financial crisis that resides about 2 years. However, during the COVID-19 outbreak, the negative level of optimal hedge ratio resides only 1 month. Therefore, we notice that the hedge ration changed more during GFC then COVID-19 for all G7 stock markets.

Figure 3. Time-varying optimal portfolio weights

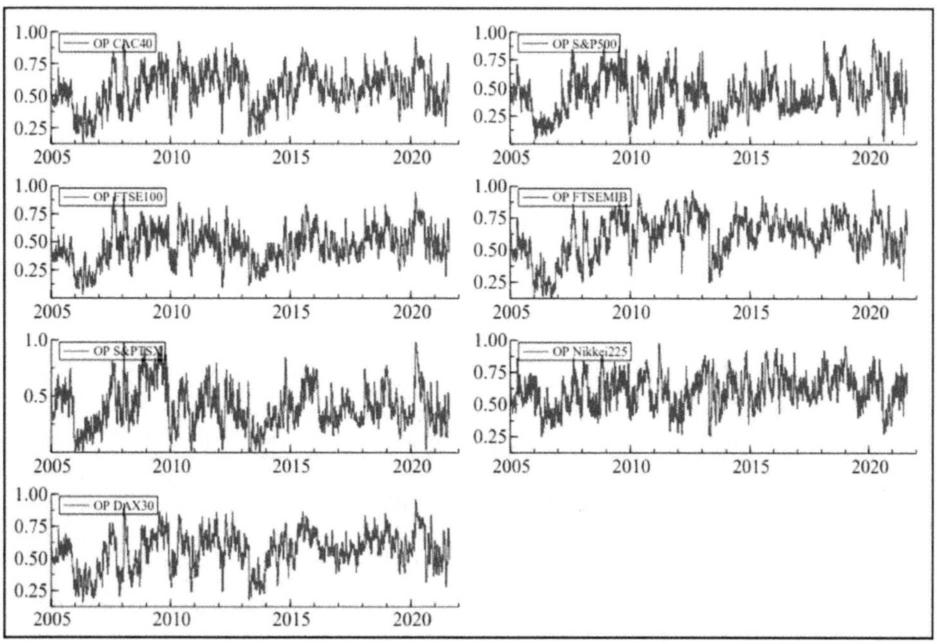

4.4. Safe Haven Property

The purpose of this section is to examine to safe properties of gold during GFC and health crises. Table (4) shows the estimation parameters of the model presented in Eq. (6).

The coefficient *δ1* is negative and significant, for all assets except Nikkei225 which indicated that gold is a strong safe haven against G7 stock markets during GFC. Our result is consistent with Baur et McDermott (2010), Chkili (2016), Hasan et al (2021), and Gomis-Porqueras, Shi and Tan (2021) who find that gold can act as a safe haven in times of extreme stock market movements against stock

Figure 4. Time varying hedge ratios

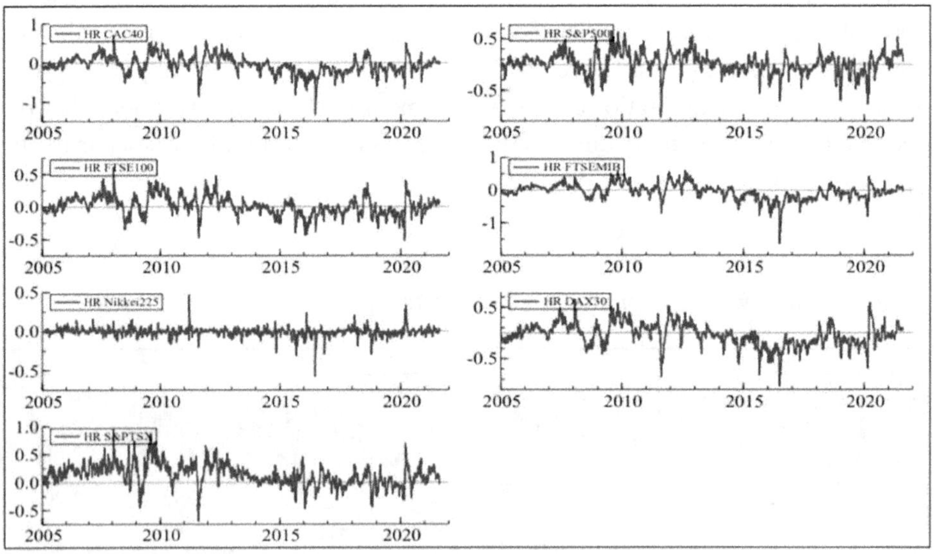

Table 5. Save haven property of gold

	CAC40	S&P500	Nikkei225	FTSE100	FTSE/ MIB	S&PTSX	DAX30
δ0	-0.0250*** (0.0000)	-0.0372*** (0.0000)	-0.0043*** (0.0000)	0.0291*** (0.0000)	-0.0151*** (0.0000)	0.1642*** (0.0000)	-0.0196*** (0.0000)
δ1 **(dummy1)**	-0.0809*** (0.0000)	-0.1297*** (0.0000)	0.0017 (0.3497)	-0.0748*** (0.0000)	-0.0602*** (0.0000)	-0.0229** (0.0480)	-0.0838*** (0.0000)
δ2 **(dummy2)**	-0.0231*** (0.0069)	0.0553*** (0.0000)	0.0062*** (0.0001)	-0.0308*** (0.0000)	-0.0144* (0.0541)	-0.0422*** (0.0000)	0.0068 (0.4324)

Notes: *, **, *** indicate the significance at 10%, 5% and 1%, respectively. Dummy 1 represents the GFC indicator and Dummy 2 represents the COVID-19 variable.

markets. During COVID-19, gold acts as a strong safe haven for the stock market of France, Canada, Italy, and the UK, given the evidence that the coefficients $\delta 2$ are statistically significant and negative. However, gold is not a safe haven for the stock market of the USA, Germany, and Japan, given the evidence that the coefficients $\delta 2$ are positive. WE notice that for G7 stock markets, gold appears a strong safe haven during GFC then Health crisis.

4.5. Wavelet Coherence

The continuous wavelet transforms (CWT) plots for G7 stock markets and gold are presented in Figure 5. CWT presents the local variance of each G7 stock markets return and gold return with respect to the frequency-time domains. The x-axis points to the period; therefore, the y-axis points to the frequency-divided into three horizons: short-term (high frequency) to long-term (low frequency).

Notes: The level of correlation from blue to red, the horizontal axis presents time, the vertical axis shows the period in days, and the black contour indicated the 5% significance level. The relative phase relationship is shown as pointing arrows: Right: in-phase; Left: anti-phase; down: first series leading second series by 90°; up: second series leading first series by 90°.

The color code shows the volatility level, organizing from blue indicating low volatility to red presenting high volatility (Grinsted et al.,2004). For all graphs, under normal market conditions, there is evidence the color blue indicated low volatility for the G7 stock markets and gold price. However, under extreme market conditions, there is evidence a color red for all stock markets and gold prices indicating high volatility. We find also that for the GFC, the European debt crisis and COVID-19 pandemic are the best periods of high volatility. Figure 5 shows that under extreme

Figure 5. Wavelet coherence plots between WTI, S&P500, Bitcoin, and gold

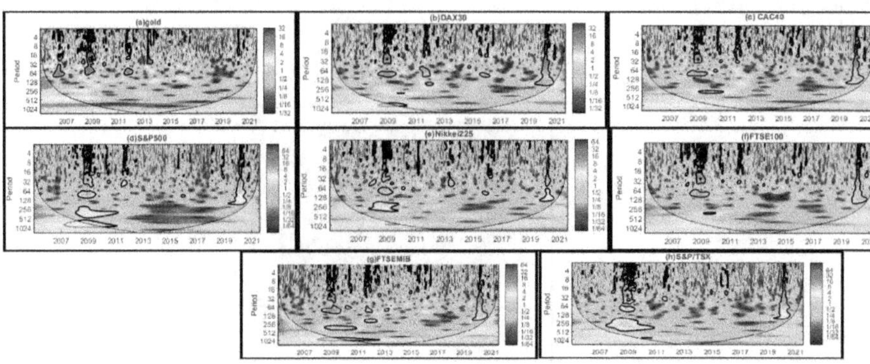

market conditions, all return series have experienced high volatility during the GFC compared to other crises (European debt crisis, sanitary crisis of COVID-19).

Notes: The level of correlation from blue to red, the horizontal axis presents time, the vertical axis shows the period in days, and the black contour indicated the 5% significance level. The relative phase relationship is shown as pointing arrows: Right: in-phase; Left: anti-phase; down: first series leading second series by 90°; up: second series leading first series by 90°.

To summarize, all G7 stocks markets and the gold market experienced higher volatility at the period 2007-2009 coinciding with GFC, between 2011-2012 characterized by the crisis debt and 2020 coinciding with the COVID-19 outbreak. There is evidence, the presence of volatility spillover from the financial crisis and sanitary crisis to the gold market and G7 stock markets. In addition, in comparison to the COVID-19 outbreak, the global financial crisis caused a high volatility spillover then the COVID-19 pandemic for the gold market and G7 stock markets.

Figure 6. Wavelet coherence plots between WTI, S&P500, Bitcoin, and gold

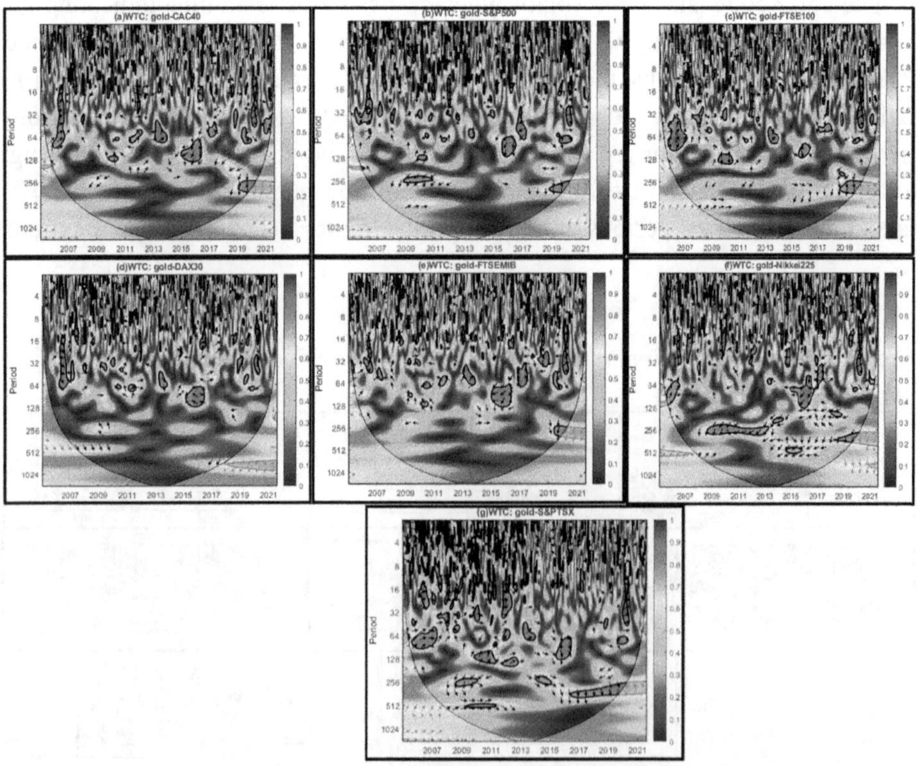

3.6 Co-movements Between Gold and G7 Stock Markets

The analysis by the wavelet coherence approach serves on the one hand to examine the coherence between gold and each G7 stock index and on the other hand, to present for which investment horizon (short, medium, long) gold is served as a safe haven and hedge. In this section, we investigate the coherence between gold and the G7 stock market using wavelet coherence analysis. Figure 6 describes the co-movements between gold and each G7 stock market. We can see that for all gold- G7 stock markets couples, the degree of co-movement varies among times and frequencies according to the market condition. As indicated, in Figure 6, the gold and each G7 stock market reveal a small island in strong correlation across the 4-8 days, 8-16 days frequency bands in extreme market conditions. Generally, we found a weak correlation in normal market conditions between gold and G7 stock markets. During the GFC from mid-2007 to 2010, we find a small area in strong correlation for long terms across the 32 - 128 days bands between gold and each G7 stock market. In addition, we found that arrows pointing to the right indicate an in-phase relationship for each pair. Likewise, 2011 European debt crisis we observe a small island of high correlation across 32- 128 days frequency bands. During this period, the pattern of co-movement between gold and each G7 stock market is in phase. A strong correlation island also appears at medium frequency bands below 32-128 days during the debt European crisis 2011-2012, stock markets during turmoil and heightened uncertainties provide evidence of contagion effects. Additionally, we also found a weak correlation in short term (0 – 16 days frequency bands) and the long-term (128 – 1024 days frequency bands) for the normal and extreme conditions market during the entire sample period between gold and G7 stock market. This result provides evidence that gold is considered a safe haven for the G7 stock market in short term. In contrast, the gold does not act as a safe haven for G7 stock markets in extreme market conditions during the medium term. Comparison of the GFC and the COVID-19 outbreak, wavelet coherence analysis reveals that the degree of correlation between gold and G7 stock markets in GFG is higher than the COVID-19 period.

4. CONCLUSION

This paper examines the hedging and safe haven properties of gold during The GFC and the COVID-19 pandemic for the G7 stock market. Furthermore, we apply the DCC-GARCH model to identify the Connectedness between gold and each G7 stock market. Our finding shows that the correlation decreased during the extreme market conditions similar to GFC and COVID-19. The optimal portfolio weights of gold in each G7 stock market significantly increased during GFG and COVID-19 pandemic, meaning that investors should invest more in the gold as a 'flight-to- safety asset' during market turmoil than normal periods.

Our empirical results reveal that, during GFC, gold served as a strong safe haven asset for all G7 stock markets except Nikkei225, but during COVID-19, gold acts as a safe haven against only CA40, S&P/TSX, FTSE100 and FTSE/MIB. However, gold served as strong hedges for all stock market except S&P/TSX and FTSE100 during the full sample period.

The Wavelet coherence results reveal that the connection between gold and G7 stock markets varies during the sample period and investment horizons. Gold is found to correlate weakly with all G7 stock markets across all horizons, especially in the short and longer horizon. Gold shows a low coherence for a short investment horizon (up to 16 days), while it's hedging ability completely dissipates for longer horizons. The coherence between Bitcoin and the three equity indices was negligible across all investment horizons before the COVID-19 period. However, a heightened co-movement is found between the three indices and all three potential safe-haven assets at the onset of the COVID-19 period.

Our empirical examination has an important and substantial apprehension for the policymakers and the portfolio risk managers and administrators. Furthermore, and from a policy-making lookout, getting forthright an investigational clarification of the estimate volatility spillovers amongst international financial stock markets is an authoritative and vigorous stage in generating appropriate monetary policy announcements and pronouncements and healthful approaches and strategies, and political conclusions and strategies. For the belvedere of portfolio risk supervisors and superintendents, the significances of our investigation are dependable to the recommendation of the cross-market hedging.

In future empirical examination related to our paper is to the examination in financial and economic consequences of the global financial crisis, the recent epidemic COVID-19 and Russia-Ukraine conflict. We will provide an investigation with a significant and considerable concern for the policymakers and the portfolio risk directors and supervisors.

REFERENCES

Abuzayed, B., Al-Fayoumi, N., & Bouri, E. (2022). Hedging UK stock portfolios with gold and oil: The impact of Brexit. *Resources Policy*, *75*, 102434. doi:10.1016/j.resourpol.2021.102434

Adekoya, O. B., Oliyide, J. A., & Oduyemi, G. O. (2021). How COVID-19 upturns the hedging potentials of gold against oil and stock markets risks: Nonlinear evidence through threshold regression and markov-regime-switching models. *Resources Policy*, *70*, 101926. doi:10.1016/j.resourpol.2020.101926

Akhtaruzzaman, M., Banerjee, A. K., Ghardallou, W., & Umar, Z. (2022a). Is greenness an optimal hedge for sectoral stock indices? *Economic Modelling*, *117*, 106030. doi:10.1016/j.econmod.2022.106030

Akhtaruzzaman, M., Boubaker, S., Chiah, M., & Zhong, A. (2021b). COVID– 19 and oil price risk exposure. *Finance Research Letters*, *42*, 101882. doi:10.1016/j.frl.2020.101882 PMID:33312079

Akhtaruzzaman, M., Boubaker, S., Lucey, B. M., & Sensoy, A. (2021a). Is gold a hedge or a safe haven asset in the COVID–19 crisis? *Economic Modelling*, *102*, 105588. doi:10.1016/j.econmod.2021.105588

Akhtaruzzaman, M., Boubaker, S., Nguyen, D. K., & Rahman, M. R. (2022b). Systemic risk-sharing framework of cryptocurrencies in the COVID-19 crisis. *Finance Research Letters*, *47*, 102787. doi:10.1016/j.frl.2022.102787 PMID:35291226

Akhtaruzzaman, M., Boubaker, S., & Sensoy, A. (2021c). Financial contagion during COVID-19 crisis. *Finance Research Letters*, *38*, 101604. doi:10.1016/j.frl.2020.101604 PMID:32837363

Akhtaruzzaman, M., Boubaker, S., & Umar, Z. (2022d). COVID-19 media coverage and ESG leader indices. *Finance Research Letters*, *45*, 102170. doi:10.1016/j.frl.2021.102170 PMID:35221818

Alkhazali, O. M., & Zoubi, T. A. (2020). Gold and portfolio diversification: A stochastic dominance analysis of the Dow Jones Islamic indices. *Pacific-Basin Finance Journal*, *60*, 101264. doi:10.1016/j.pacfin.2020.101264

Baur, D. G., & Lucey, B. M. (2010). Is gold a hedge or a safe haven? An analysis of stocks, bonds, and gold. *Financial Review*, *45*(2), 217–229. doi:10.1111/j.1540-6288.2010.00244.x

Baur, D. G., & McDermott, T. K. (2010). Is gold a safe haven? International evidence. *Journal of Banking & Finance*, *34*(8), 1886–1898. doi:10.1016/j.jbankfin.2009.12.008

Będowska-Sójka, B., & Kliber, A. (2021). Is there one safe haven for various turbulences? The evidence from gold, Bitcoin and Ether. *The North American Journal of Economics and Finance*, *56*, 101390. doi:10.1016/j.najef.2021.101390

Bekiros, S., Boubaker, S., Nguyen, D. K., & Uddin, G. S. (2017). Black swan events and safe havens: The role of gold in globally integrated emerging markets. *Journal of International Money and Finance*, *73*, 317–334. doi:10.1016/j.jimonfin.2017.02.010

Belhassine, O., & Karamti, C. (2021). Contagion and portfolio management in times of COVID-19. *Economic Analysis and Policy*, *72*, 73–86. doi:10.1016/j.eap.2021.07.010 PMID:34518721

Benlagha, N., & El Omari, S. (2021). Connectedness of stock markets with gold and oil: New evidence from COVID-19 pandemic. *Finance Research Letters*, *102373*. Advance online publication. doi:10.1016/j.frl.2021.102373 PMID:35431671

Celık, S. (2012). The more contagion effect on emerging markets: The evidence of DCC-GARCH model. *Economic Modelling*, *29*(5), 1946–1959. doi:10.1016/j.econmod.2012.06.011

Chebbi, T., & Derbali, A. (2016a). A Dynamic Conditional Correlation between Commodities and the Islamic Stock Market. *Journal of Energy Markets*, *9*(1), 65–90. doi:10.21314/JEM.2016.137

Chebbi, T., & Derbali, A. (2016b). On the role of structural breaks in identifying the dynamic conditional linkages between stock and commodity markets. *Journal of Energy Markets*, *9*(4), 71–81. doi:10.21314/JEM.2016.152

Chemkha, R., BenSaïda, A., Ghorbel, A., & Tayachi, T. (2021). Hedge and safe haven properties during COVID-19: Evidence from Bitcoin and gold. *The Quarterly Review of Economics and Finance*, *82*, 71–85. doi:10.1016/j.qref.2021.07.006 PMID:34898971

Chkili, W. (2016). Dynamic correlations and hedging effectiveness between gold and stock markets: Evidence for BRICS countries. *Research in International Business and Finance*, *38*, 22–34. doi:10.1016/j.ribaf.2016.03.005

Chkili, W. (2017). Is gold a hedge or safe haven for Islamic stock market movements? A Markov switching approach. *Journal of Multinational Financial Management*, *42*, 152–163. doi:10.1016/j.mulfin.2017.10.001

Derbali, A., Naoui, K., Ben Sassi, M., & Amiri, M. M. (2021b). Do COVID-19 Epidemic Explains the Dynamic Conditional Correlation between China's Stock Market Index and International Stock Market Indices? *Chinese Economy*, *55*(3), 227–242. doi:10.1080/10971475.2021.1958453

Derbali, A., Naoui, K., & Jamel, L. (2021a). COVID-19 news in USA and in China: Which is suitable in explaining the nexus among Bitcoin and Gold? *Pacific Accounting Review, 33*(5), 578–595. doi:10.1108/PAR-09-2020-0170

Disli, M., Nagayev, R., Salim, K., Rizkiah, S. K., & Aysan, A. F. (2021). In search of safe haven assets during COVID-19 pandemic: An empirical analysis of different investor types. *Research in International Business and Finance, 101461*, 101461. Advance online publication. doi:10.1016/j.ribaf.2021.101461 PMID:36540341

Engle, R. F. (2002). A simple class of multivariate generalized autoregressive conditional heteroskedasticity models. *Journal of Business & Economic Statistics, 20*, 339–350. doi:10.1198/073500102288618487

Gomis-Porqueras, P., Shi, S., & Tan, D. (2021). Gold as a financial instrument. *Journal of Commodity Markets*, 100218.

Grinsted, A., Moore, J. C., & Jevrejeva, S. (2004). Application of the cross wavelet transform and wavelet coherence to geophysical time series. *Nonlinear Processes in Geophysics, 11*(5/6), 561–566. doi:10.5194/npg-11-561-2004

Hasan, M. B., Hassan, M. K., Rashid, M. M., & Alhenawi, Y. (2021). Are safe haven assets really safe during the 2008 global financial crisis and COVID-19 pandemic? *Global Finance Journal, 50*, 100668. doi:10.1016/j.gfj.2021.100668

Ji, Q., Zhang, D., & Zhao, Y. (2020). Searching for safe haven assets during the COVID-19 pandemic. *International Review of Financial Analysis, 71*, 101526. doi:10.1016/j.irfa.2020.101526

Jiang, Y., Fu, Y., & Ruan, W. (2019). Risk spillovers and portfolio management between precious metal and BRICS stock markets. *Physica A, 534*, 120993. doi:10.1016/j.physa.2019.04.229

Mensi, W., Reboredo, J. C., & Ugolini, A. (2021). Price-switching spillovers between gold, oil, and stock markets: Evidence from the USA and China during the COVID-19 pandemic. *Resources Policy, 73*, 102217. doi:10.1016/j.resourpol.2021.102217 PMID:36567727

Mensi, W., Shafiullah, M., Vo, X. V., & Kang, S. H. (2021). Volatility spillovers between strategic commodity futures and stock markets and portfolio implications: Evidence from developed and emerging economies. *Resources Policy, 71*, 102002. doi:10.1016/j.resourpol.2021.102002

Ng, E. K., & Chan, J. C. (2012). Geophysical applications of partial wavelet coherence and multiple wavelet coherence. *Journal of Atmospheric and Oceanic Technology*, *29*(12), 1845–1853. doi:10.1175/JTECH-D-12-00056.1

Ngun. (2016). *Gold price and stock markets nexus under mixed-copulas*. Academic Press.

Peng, X. (2020). Do precious metals act as hedges or safe havens for China's financial markets? *Finance Research Letters*, *37*, 101353. doi:10.1016/j.frl.2019.101353

Salisu, A. A., Raheem, I. D., & Vo, X. V. (2021). Assessing the safe haven property of the gold market during the COVID-19 pandemic. *International Review of Financial Analysis*, *74*, 101666. doi:10.1016/j.irfa.2021.101666 PMID:36531084

Shahzad, S. J. H., Mensi, W., Hammoudeh, S., Sohail, A., & Al-Yahyaee, K. H. (2019). Does gold act as a hedge against different nuances of inflation? Evidence from Quantile-on-Quantile and causality-in-quantiles approaches. *Resources Policy*, *62*, 602–615. doi:10.1016/j.resourpol.2018.11.008

Shehzad, K., Bilgili, F., Zaman, U., Kocak, E., & Kuskaya, S. (2021). Is gold favorable to bitcoin during the COVID-19 outbreak? Comparative analysis through wavelet approach. *Resources Policy*, *102163*, 102163. Advance online publication. doi:10.1016/j.resourpol.2021.102163 PMID:34121797

Torrence, C., & Compo, G. P. (1998). A practical guide to wavelet analysis. *Bulletin of the American Meteorological Society*, *79*(1), 61–78. doi:10.1175/1520-0477(1998)079<0061:APGTWA>2.0.CO;2

Torrence, C., & Webster, P. J. (1999). Interdecadal changes in the ENSO–monsoon system. *Journal of Climate*, *12*(8), 2679–2690. doi:10.1175/1520-0442(1999)012<2679:ICITEM>2.0.CO;2

Trabelsi, N., Gozgor, G., Tiwari, A. K., & Hammoudeh, S. (2021). Effects of Price of Gold on Bombay Stock Exchange Sectoral Indices: New Evidence for Portfolio Risk Management. *Research in International Business and Finance*, *55*, 101316. doi:10.1016/j.ribaf.2020.101316 PMID:34173411

Wan, D., Xue, R., Linnenluecke, M., Tian, J., & Shan, Y. (2021). The impact of investor attention during COVID-19 on investment in clean energy versus fossil fuel firms. *Finance Research Letters*, *101955*. Advance online publication. doi:10.1016/j.frl.2021.101955 PMID:36406287

ENDNOTES

1 Phase I of pandemic crisis between December 31, 2019–March 16, 2020.

2 Phase II of pandemic crisis between March 17 - April 24, 2020.

3 We estimate several GARCH type specifications (EGARCH, AGARCH, GJR-GARCH etc.) and we used for each returns series the most appropriate one judging by the information criteria.

Chapter 4
Metaverse and NFT

Maithili Vijay Arjunwadkar
PES Modern Institute of Business Studies, India

Bharati Mahadev Ramageri
PES Modern Institute of Business Studies, India

ABSTRACT

The rise of non-fungible tokens (NFTs) and the emergence of the Metaverse is a significant paradigm shift in the digital landscape. NFTs are unique digital assets verified by blockchain technology that have revolutionized ownership and provenance in the digital realm. Concurrently, the Metaverse, a collective virtual shared space, is evolving into a multifaceted environment where NFTs play a pivotal role in shaping economies, identities, and interactions. This chapter covers NFTs the transforming digital ownership, art in the digital age, Metaverse, economy and commerce, social structures in the Metaverse.

PART 1

Exploring the Metaverse and NFT

The Metaverse and Non-Fungible Tokens (NFTs) represents a dynamic frontier in the digital landscape, offering a realm of possibilities and challenges that reshape our interactions, creativity, and economic structures. It promises to redefine how we experience, create, and value digital interactions. This chapter exploration takes a deep dive into expanding Metaverse and the revolutionary impact of NFTs, navigating the transformative landscapes and confronting the challenges that lie within (Al-Towhi, n.d.).

DOI: 10.4018/979-8-3693-1511-8.ch004

Introduction

In the vast expanse of digital realms, the metaverse emerges as a wondrous fusion of imagination and technology. It is an intricate tapestry of interconnected virtual worlds, an expansive digital universe where reality intertwines with the boundless realms of cyberspace. Within this metaphysical space, users don avatars, stepping beyond the constraints of physical existence to explore realms limited only by the scope of human creativity (Şalçini & Yerlikaya, 2022).

In the metaverse, social interactions transcend the confines of geography, enabling global connections and collaborations. It is a realm where individuals can craft their own narratives, shape their destinies, and participate in collective adventures. The metaverse encompasses a plethora of experiences - from immersive gaming environments to virtual marketplaces, educational platforms, and beyond. It blurs the line between the tangible and the intangible, reshaping how we perceive reality and identity.

Yet, amidst its marvels, the metaverse raises profound questions about identity, privacy, and the nature of human connection. It challenges our understanding of existence, inviting us to ponder the very essence of reality in a world where the tangible and the virtual converge. As we step into this uncharted digital frontier, we embark on a journey where the boundaries between the real and the imagined dissolve, giving rise to new possibilities and redefining the essence of human experience (Laeeq & Sciences, 2022).

Section 1: History and Evolution of the Metaverse

Section 2: Building Blocks of Metaverse

The effective deployment of the Metaverse relies on a multifaceted technological infrastructure, each component serving a specific purpose to create a seamless and immersive digital experience:

- **Virtual Reality (VR) and Augmented Reality (AR):**

VR provides immersive experiences within entirely virtual environments, while AR overlays digital elements onto the real world. Both are crucial for interactive Metaverse engagement, spanning industries like gaming, education, and healthcare.

- **Blockchain Technology:**

Figure 1. History and evolution of the metaverse

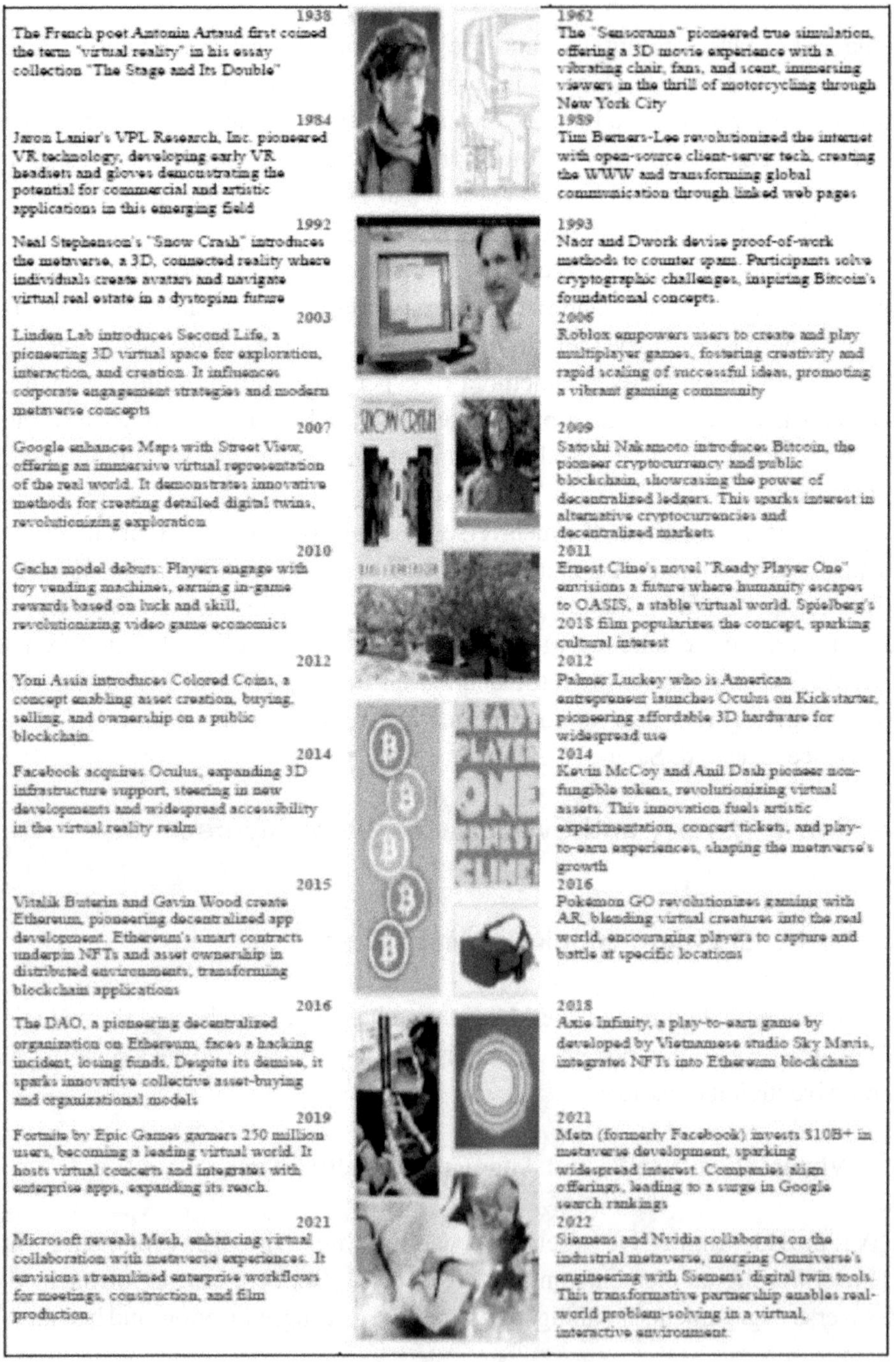

Blockchain ensures secure, decentralized transactions, allowing users to create, own, and trade digital assets within the Metaverse. It's especially vital for virtual real estate transactions and the creation of unique, tradable items.

- **Artificial Intelligence (AI) and Machine Learning (ML):**

AI and ML enhance user interaction by creating intelligent virtual characters and adaptive environments, infusing life and personality into virtual spaces. These technologies enable dynamic and responsive Metaverse experiences.

- **Cloud Computing:**

Cloud infrastructure provides scalable processing power and data storage essential for large Metaverse environments. It ensures accessibility from various devices, enabling users to seamlessly enter the Metaverse from anywhere.

- **5G Network:**

5G technology enables real-time interactions with low latency, allowing high-quality audio and video streaming. This facilitates immersive, lag-free experiences in the Metaverse and supports real-time user interactions.

- **Spatial Computing:**

Spatial computing creates virtual environments that respond to users' positions and actions, enhancing interactivity. It allows for the development of spatially aware applications and experiences within the Metaverse.

- **Natural Language Processing (NLP):**

NLP enables natural communication between users and AI-driven elements in the Metaverse. It powers intelligent chatbots and virtual assistants, enhancing user engagement and accessibility.

These enabling technologies, when integrated and optimized, form the backbone of the Metaverse. Their seamless interaction creates a dynamic, interconnected digital realm where users can interact, create, and explore in ways previously unimaginable. The continuous evolution of these technologies further enriches the Metaverse experience, promising a future where virtual and physical realities harmoniously coexist.

Section 3: The Social and Economic Landscape of the Metaverse

In exploring into the complexpicture of the Metaverse, one cannot help but genius at the profound implications it holds for our social and economic landscapes. It is evident that the Metaverse is not merely a digital construct but a vibrant, dynamic ecosystem that mirrors and redefines our society and economy.

Social Dynamics

Within the Metaverse, social interactions transcend physical boundaries. Avatars become conduits for personal expression, leading to diverse and immersive social experiences. The Metaverse nurtures communities, enabling connections between like-minded individuals globally. Real-time communication, collaborative ventures, and shared experiences form the backbone of this digital social sphere. It blurs the lines between the physical and virtual, fostering empathy, understanding, and a sense of belonging among users.

Economic Frontiers

Economically, the Metaverse presents groundbreaking opportunities. The rise of virtual economies powered by cryptocurrencies and NFTs reshapes traditional financial models. Users engage in digital entrepreneurship, creating and trading virtual assets, from artwork to virtual real estate, leading to real-world economic value. Brands and businesses establish a digital presence, leveraging the Metaverse for marketing, customer engagement, and even virtual storefronts. The Metaverse acts as a crucible for innovation, giving rise to novel business models and employment opportunities, including virtual architects, designers, and experience creators.

It is exciting to witness the Metaverse's transformative influence on our social fabric and economic landscape. It blurs the boundaries between reality and imagination, offering a glimpse into a future where social interactions are boundless, and economic endeavors exceed the constraints of physical space. The Metaverse is undeniably shaping a new era where creativity, connectivity, and commerce converge in extraordinary ways, indicating a digital renaissance that is both exciting and promising (Bowles, 2022).

Section 4: Exploring Notable Metaverse Projects: A Journey Into Digital Realms

Embarking on a fascinating exploration of notable Metaverse projects, one is mesmerized by the vast creativity and innovation shaping our digital future. These projects represent the pinnacle of virtual achievement, showcasing the extraordinary capabilities of modern technology and human imagination (Robinson, 2022).

Decentraland

Decentraland stands as a pioneer, offering users a decentralized virtual world where they can buy, sell, and develop on parcels of land. This project epitomizes the concept of ownership within the Metaverse, with users having complete control over their virtual real estate, fostering a robust economy and vibrant social interactions.

Roblox

Roblox emerges as a powerhouse, empowering users to create and play games within an expansive virtual universe. Its user-generated content and immersive gameplay experiences have transformed it into a hub for young developers, fostering creativity and entrepreneurship on a grand scale.

CryptoVoxels

CryptoVoxels marries the Metaverse with Blockchain technology, enabling users to build, develop, and monetize their virtual spaces. The integration of Blockchain ensures true ownership of assets, encouraging digital artists, architects, and entrepreneurs to thrive in a decentralized environment.

The Sandbox

The Sandbox revolutionizes gaming, offering a platform where users can create, play, and monetize their games. Its voxel-based world-building tools empower creators, fostering a rich ecosystem of interactive experiences and enabling the sale of in-game assets through NFTs.

Somnium Space

Somnium Space ventures into the realm of virtual reality, presenting a persistent, open-world VR Metaverse. It stands out for its immersive VR experiences, real-time social interactions, and a marketplace where users can trade virtual land and assets securely.

Notable Innovations

These Metaverse projects share common threads of innovation, including user-generated content, decentralized economies, and the utilization of Blockchain technology. They redefine the way we socialize, create, and conduct business, setting the stage for a digital era where the boundaries between reality and the virtual world blur.

In essence, exploring these remarkable Metaverse projects reveals a landscape where creativity knows no bounds and where users are not just participants but creators, shaping the future of digital existence. Each project represents unique evidence to the limitless possibilities within the Metaverse, forcing us into a future where imagination and technology intertwine in unprecedented harmony.

Section 5: Challenges and Considerations in the Metaverse: Navigating the Digital Frontier

As we venture deeper into the Metaverse, a realm of endless possibilities, we must also acknowledge the challenges and considerations that accompany this digital frontier. These complexities, both technical and ethical, demand our attention as we shape this evolving digital landscape.

Privacy and Security

One of the foremost concerns revolves around privacy and security. The Metaverse, with its vast data interactions, raises apprehensions about the safety of personal information. Striking a balance between immersive experiences and safeguarding users' data from potential breaches is a pressing challenge.

Digital Divide

The digital divide poses a significant hurdle. While the Metaverse promises inclusivity, disparities in internet access and technology adoption persist. Bridging this gap ensures equitable participation, making certain that the benefits of the Metaverse are accessible to all, regardless of geographical location or socioeconomic status.

Content Moderation

The Metaverse's open nature raises questions about content moderation. Maintaining safe and inclusive spaces requires robust moderation mechanisms to prevent harassment, hate speech, and inappropriate content, ensuring a positive user experience for all.

Ethical AI and Avatars

The integration of Artificial Intelligence (AI) into avatars brings forth ethical dilemmas. Ensuring that AI-driven avatars respect cultural sensitivities, avoid biases, and promote positive interactions is crucial. Ethical considerations in AI development become paramount to prevent unintended consequences.

Intellectual Property and Copyright

Navigating the intellectual property landscape presents challenges. With user-generated content at the forefront, issues related to copyright, ownership of digital assets, and the creation of Non-Fungible Tokens (NFTs) require clear legal frameworks to safeguard creators' rights and prevent digital piracy (Kaur et al., 2023).

User Addiction and Mental Health

Addressing user addiction and mental health concerns is imperative. The immersive nature of the Metaverse can lead to excessive screen time, impacting mental well-being. Responsible design, incorporating features encouraging breaks and real-world interactions, is essential.

Environmental Impact

Lastly, the environmental impact cannot be overlooked. The energy-intensive nature of Blockchain technologies powering the Metaverse raises ecological concerns. Exploring eco-friendly solutions and sustainable practices is vital to mitigate the Metaverse's carbon footprint.

Conclusion

In conclusion, the convergence of Virtual Reality, Blockchain, Artificial Intelligence, Cloud Computing, 5G Network, Spatial Computing, and Natural Language Processing establishes the foundation for the Metaverse. Together, these technologies forge an immersive, secure, and responsive digital realm, revolutionizing how we engage, create, and collaborate. This integrated infrastructure not only offers boundless possibilities for interactive experiences but also paves the way for a future where the virtual and physical worlds seamlessly blend. As these technologies advance, the Metaverse journey continues, promising a harmonious coexistence of virtual and real-life experiences, reshaping our digital landscape in profound and unprecedented ways. The exploration of the Metaverse's intricate facets, from transformative social dynamics to cutting-edge innovations, paints a vivid tapestry of the digital future. This review underscores the Metaverse's role as a dynamic ecosystem reshaping social interactions and economic landscapes. Notable projects like Decentraland, Roblox, and CryptoVoxels exemplify the convergence of creativity and technology. Yet, challenges such as privacy, content moderation, and environmental impact loom large. The comprehensive analysis acknowledges the Metaverse's transformative potential while emphasizing the imperative for a holistic, ethically grounded approach. Finally, the spotlight on innovation, inclusivity, and responsible integration of the digital realm encapsulates the Metaverse's promise and challenges succinctly.

PART 2

Section 1: Non-Fungible Tokens

In the rapidly evolving landscape of digital assets, Non-Fungible Tokens (NFTs) have emerged as the creativity of the Blockchain revolution. These unique tokens, each representing a distinct piece of digital or tangible content, have captured the imagination of artists, collectors, and tech enthusiasts alike. In this exploration, we embark on a journey to unravel the essence of NFTs, their origins, mechanics, and the impact they wield on the realms of art, culture, and technology.

NFT stands for "Non-Fungible Token." An NFT is a type of digital asset that represents ownership or proof of authenticity of a unique item or piece of content using Blockchain technology. A non-fungible token (NFT) is a unique digital identifier that is recorded on a Blockchain, and is used to certify ownership and authenticity (Kogler, 2021). It cannot be copied, substituted, or subdivided. Unlike cryptocurrencies such as Bitcoin or Ethereum, which are fungible and can be exchanged on a one-to-one basis, NFTs are unique and cannot be exchanged on a like-for-like basis (Lau, 2020).

Key features of NFTs includes uniqueness, indivisibility, ownership and Authenticity, Smart Contracts, Interoperability and many. Each NFT has a distinct identifier that sets it apart from any other token. This uniqueness is often tied to a specific digital or physical asset. NFTs cannot be divided into smaller units like cryptocurrencies. They exist as whole tokens. NFTs use Blockchain technology, typically on platforms like Ethereum, to establish and verify ownership and authenticity (The European Union Blockchain Observatory & Forum, 2018). The Blockchain serves as a decentralized and transparent ledger, recording the history of ownership and transactions related to the NFT. Many NFTs are created and managed using smart contracts, self-executing contracts with the terms of the agreement directly written into code. Smart contracts enable functionalities like automatic royalty payments to creators every time the NFT is resold. NFTs can represent a wide range of digital or physical assets, including digital art, music, virtual real estate, virtual goods in video games, and more. The versatility of NFTs has led to their adoption in various industries (Dalai, 2022).

Historical Context: The Emergence of NFTs in the Cryptocurrency Ecosystem

The emergence of Non-Fungible Tokens (NFTs) in the cryptocurrency ecosystem is a relatively recent phenomenon, closely tied to the development of Blockchain technology and the expansion of decentralized applications (dApps). Here's a historical context of how NFTs came into existence:

Early Blockchain Concepts

The concept of a Blockchain, a decentralized and distributed ledger, was introduced with the creation of Bitcoin in 2009 by an unknown person or group using the pseudonym Satoshi Nakamoto. Bitcoin, as a cryptocurrency, provided a way to transfer value in a peer-to-peer network without the need for intermediaries. Ethereum, proposed by Vitalik Buterin in late 2013 and developed in 2014, marked a significant evolution. Ethereum introduced the idea of smart contracts, self-executing contracts with the terms of the agreement directly written into code.

Smart contracts on Ethereum allowed for the creation of decentralized applications (dApps) beyond simple value transfer. In 2015, the Ethereum Blockchain introduced the ERC-721 standard, a protocol for creating unique tokens. Unlike fungible tokens such as Bitcoin or Ethereum, ERC-721 tokens are non-fungible, meaning each token is distinct and not interchangeable on a one-to-one basis. ERC-721 laid the groundwork for the creation and standardization of NFTs. The game Cryptokitties, launched in late 2017, became one of the first widely known applications to use NFTs. In this game, users could buy, sell, and breed unique virtual cats, each represented by an ERC-721 token. Cryptokitties brought mainstream attention to the potential of NFTs and showcased the uniqueness and scarcity that could be achieved through Blockchain technology. The intersection of NFTs and the art world gained momentum in 2020 and 2021. Digital artists began tokenizing their work as NFTs, providing a new way to sell and trade digital art with proven ownership and authenticity. High-profile sales, such as Beeple's "Everydays: The First 5000 Days" at Christie's auction house in 2021, where a digital artwork was sold for millions of dollars as an NFT, further brought NFTs into the public eye. NFT marketplaces, where users could buy and sell NFTs, experienced a surge in popularity. Platforms like OpenSea, Rarible, and Mintable gained prominence as hubs for NFT trading.

Technology Fundamentals: How Blockchain and Smart Contracts Power NFTs

Blockchain technology and smart contracts are fundamental components that power Non-Fungible Tokens (NFTs). Understanding how these technologies work is crucial to grasping the underlying infrastructure of NFTs.

Blockchain Technology

Blockchain is a decentralized and distributed ledger that records transactions across a network of computers. This decentralized nature ensures that no single entity has control over the entire network, enhancing security and transparency.

Once data is recorded on the Blockchain, it is extremely difficult to alter. This immutability ensures the integrity of the information stored on the Blockchain.

Blockchain networks use consensus mechanisms, such as Proof of Work (PoW) or Proof of Stake (PoS), to agree on the state of the ledger. This prevents malicious actors from manipulating the data.

Smart contracts are self-executing contracts with the terms of the agreement directly written into code. When predefined conditions are met, the contract executes automatically without the need for intermediaries.

Smart contracts run on the Blockchain, allowing for decentralized code execution. This means that the code is distributed across the network, reducing the risk of censorship or tampering.

Smart contracts are programmable and can be used to implement a wide range of functionalities, from transferring tokens to enforcing complex business rules. Ethereum's introduction of smart contracts was a groundbreaking development in the Blockchain space.

NFTs on the Blockchain

Unique Identifiers: NFTs use Blockchain technology to create and manage unique digital assets. Each NFT is represented by a unique identifier on the Blockchain, ensuring that it is distinct from any other token. The most common standard for NFTs on the Ethereum Blockchain is ERC-721. This standard defines the rules and functionalities that each NFT should adhere to, including methods for transferring ownership and accessing metadata. The ownership of NFTs is recorded on the Blockchain. When an NFT is transferred from one user to another, the ownership record is updated through a Blockchain transaction.

NFTs allow for the tokenization of digital or physical assets. This includes digital art, music, virtual real estate, in-game items, and more. By representing these assets as NFTs, ownership and provenance can be established. NFTs are interoperable across different platforms and marketplaces that support the same token standards. This interoperability enhances liquidity and enables users to trade NFTs on various platforms (Bhattacharya et al., 2023).

Section 2: The NFT Ecosystem

The NFT (Non-Fungible Token) ecosystem is a dynamic and expanding network of platforms, technologies, and communities that facilitate the creation, sale, and exchange of non-fungible tokens. This ecosystem has evolved significantly since the advent of NFTs, offering diverse opportunities and applications across various industries.

NFT marketplaces: A look at popular platforms for buying, selling, and trading NFTs.

The explosion of interest in Non-Fungible Tokens (NFTs) has given rise to a plethora of NFT marketplaces, each offering a unique space for creators, collectors, and investors to buy, sell, and trade digital assets. Here's a look at some of the popular platforms that have played a pivotal role in shaping the NFT marketplace landscape, as follows (Hasan et al., 2022),

OpenSea

As one of the largest and most well-known NFT marketplaces, OpenSea is built on the Ethereum Blockchain and supports a wide range of digital assets, including art, collectibles, and virtual real estate. It boasts a user-friendly interface and facilitates seamless transactions.

Rarible

Rarible is a decentralized marketplace on Ethereum that enables users to create, buy, and sell NFTs. What sets Rarible apart is its "create-to-earn" model, allowing artists to earn RARI tokens by minting and selling their digital creations.

Mintable

Mintable offers a user-friendly platform for both creators and collectors to engage in the NFT space. It supports various Blockchains, including Ethereum and Polygon, and allows users to mint NFTs without any coding knowledge.

Foundation

Foundation is an invite-only NFT marketplace that focuses on supporting creators and their original work. It aims to provide a curated environment for artists, fostering a sense of exclusivity and high-quality content.

SuperRare

Catering specifically to digital artists, SuperRare is an Ethereum-based NFT marketplace that emphasizes scarcity and provenance. It has gained recognition for its unique and limited-edition digital art pieces.

Nifty Gateway

Nifty Gateway stands out for its emphasis on collaboration with well-known artists and celebrities. It provides a platform for artists to release limited editions of their work and offers a user-friendly experience for collectors.

Decentraland Marketplace

In the realm of virtual real estate and Metaverse assets, Decentraland's marketplace is prominent. Users can buy, sell, and develop virtual land and assets within the DecentralandMetaverse.

AtomicMarket

Operating on the WAX Blockchain, AtomicMarket focuses on digital collectibles, gaming items, and virtual goods. It provides a marketplace for NFTs associated with Blockchain-based games and virtual worlds.

KnownOrigin

KnownOrigin is an Ethereum-based platform that emphasizes authenticity and provenance for digital art. It provides tools for artists to tokenize their work and ensures that buyers can trace the origin of the NFTs they acquire.

Enjin Marketplace

Enjin, known for its integration with Blockchain gaming, offers a marketplace for NFTs associated with gaming and virtual items. It leverages the Ethereum Blockchain for its NFT ecosystem.

Creating NFTs: The Process of Tokenizing Digital and Physical Assets

Creating Non-Fungible Tokens (NFTs) involves tokenizing digital or physical assets on a Blockchain, typically using smart contracts. The process may vary slightly depending on the Blockchain platform you choose. Here the focus is on creating NFTs on the Ethereum Blockchain, which is one of the most widely used platforms for NFTs.

The general steps include:

- **Choose a Blockchain:**

Decide on the Blockchain that aligns with your project. Ethereum is the most popular choice

- **Set Up a Digital Wallet:**

Obtain a digital wallet compatible with the chosen Blockchain. Popular wallets include MetaMask, Coinbase Wallet, and Trust Wallet. The wallet will store and manage your NFTs.

- **Get Some Cryptocurrency:**

Acquire the cryptocurrency needed for transactions on the chosen Blockchain. Ethereum (ETH) is commonly used for creating and interacting with NFTs.

- **Connect Wallet to NFT Marketplace:**

To sell or trade the NFTs on a marketplace, connect the digital wallet to the platform.

- **Create or Mint NFTs:**
    - **Digital Assets:**

For tokenizing digital assets like art, music, videos, etc. create a digital file in a supported format (JPEG, PNG, MP4, etc.). NFT minting platform may be Mintable, Rarible, or OpenSea. This process usually involves uploading digitalfile, adding metadata defining any royalties for future sales.

- **Physical Assets:**

For tokenizing physical assets, use a service that bridges the digital and physical worlds. Some platforms use IoT devices, QR codes, or other means to link the physical item to its digital representation on the Blockchain.

- **Set Smart Contract Parameters:**

Customize NFT's smart contract parameters. This might include defining the total supply, setting up royalties and determining if the NFT is transferable or has other special features.

- **Pay Gas Fees:**

Transactions on Blockchain networks incur gas fees. Gas fees are the costs associated with processing and validating transactions. Be prepared to pay these fees when creating, buying, or transferring NFTs.

- **Confirm and Mint:**

Confirm the transaction and mint your NFT. This action will create a unique token on the Blockchain representing digital or physical asset. Once confirmed, the NFT is stored in the digital wallet.

- **Market and Sell (Optional):**

List all NFT for sale on NFT marketplaces. Set the price or choose an auction format. Some platforms allows to include unlockable content or bonuses for the buyer.

- **Transfer and Ownership:**

When someone purchases the NFT, ownership is transferred to the buyer. Smart contracts handle the transfer of ownership, and if royalties are set, the original creator receives a percentage of the resale value.

- **Promote and Engage:**

Promote your NFTs through social media, online communities, or other marketing channels. Engage with the NFT community and collectors to build interest in your creations.

Ownership in NFTs

Once an NFT is created on a Blockchain, the ownership record is stored on the Blockchain in a secure and immutable manner. This means that once ownership is established, it cannot be altered or tampered with.

Decentralized Ownership

The ownership of NFTs is decentralized and recorded on a Blockchain, eliminating the need for centralized authorities to verify ownership. Each token is associated with a unique identifier, making it distinguishable from any other token. NFTs adhere to specific token standards, such as ERC-721 or ERC-1155 on Ethereum. These standards define how ownership is managed, including functions for transferring ownership between addresses.Ownership is tied to digital wallets, which are cryptographic key pairs (public and private keys). The owner of the private key associated with the NFT's address has control and ownership of the NFT.Ownership can be transferred by initiating a transaction on the Blockchain. This is typically done through a digital wallet, and the transfer is recorded on the Blockchain, ensuring transparency and security.

Provenance in NFTs

Provenance in NFTs refers to the traceability of the digital or physical asset represented by the token. The Blockchain ledger provides an immutable and transparent history of the asset, documenting its creation, ownership changes, and any associated metadata. Metadata is additional information linked to an NFT, providing details about the asset, its creator, creation date, and other relevant information. This metadata contributes to the provenance of the NFT. Smart contracts, which underpin many NFTs, can include programmable logic that defines rules for the asset. For instance, a smart contract might specify conditions for resale royalties, ensuring that creators receive a percentage of secondary sales. The act of minting an NFT involves creating it and adding it to the Blockchain. The minting process and associated metadata contribute to the provenance of the NFT, offering insights into its origin. Users can use Blockchain explorers to view the complete history of an NFT, including its creation, transfers of ownership, and any associated transactions. This transparency enhances the provenance of the asset. Provenance is crucial for establishing the authenticity of a digital or physical asset. Collectors and buyers often value NFTs with clear and verifiable provenance, as it adds credibility to the asset's origin (Solouki & Bamakan, 2022).

Section 3: NFTs in the Art and Entertainment World

Non-Fungible Tokens (NFTs) have emerged as a transformative force in the art and entertainment world, reshaping the way we create, buy, and sell digital assets. NFTs represent unique, indivisible digital or physical items on Blockchain networks, and their impact in the creative industries has been intense.

- **Digital Art Revolution**

NFTs have revolutionized the digital art landscape by providing a secure and transparent way to tokenize digital creations. Digital artists can now mint their artwork as NFTs, establishing provenance, authenticity, and ownership on Blockchain platforms like Ethereum.

NFTs eliminate traditional gatekeepers, allowing artists to reach a global audience directly. Emerging and established artists alike can monetize their work without relying on galleries or intermediaries, fostering a more inclusive and diverse art ecosystem.

- **Virtual Galleries and Exhibitions**

NFTs are at the forefront of the Metaverse and virtual reality experiences. Virtual galleries, such as those in Decentraland or Cryptovoxels, enable artists to showcase their NFT-based artwork in immersive digital spaces. This expands the possibilities for art consumption beyond physical constraints.

Some NFTs include interactive elements, allowing viewers to engage with the art in ways not possible in traditional mediums. This dynamic and participatory aspect enhances the viewer's experience and creates new opportunities for artistic expression.

- **Music and Entertainment:**

Musicians and entertainers are leveraging NFTs to tokenize their work and engage with fans. NFTs can represent music albums, concert tickets, virtual experiences, and even unique collectibles associated with artists.

NFTs offer a new dimension to fan engagement. Artists can provide exclusive content, limited editions, and special perks to NFT holders. This direct connection strengthens the artist-fan relationship and introduces novel revenue streams.

- **Gaming and Virtual Assets:**

NFTs have found significant applications in the gaming industry. In-game items, skins, and virtual real estate can be tokenized, allowing players to truly own and trade digital assets across different gaming platforms.

NFTs empower players by giving them true ownership of their in-game assets. Gamers can buy, sell, and trade these assets with other players, creating a player-driven economy within the gaming ecosystem (Murray, 2022).

Challenges and Considerations

The energy consumption of Blockchain networks, particularly those using Proof of Work, has raised environmental concerns. Some artists and platforms are exploring eco-friendly Blockchains or implementing more sustainable practices.

The NFT space has prompted discussions about copyright and intellectual property rights. Clear guidelines and standards are evolving to address these concerns and protect the interests of creators.

Section 4: Beyond Art: NFTs in Diverse Industries

Beyond the realm of art, Non-Fungible Tokens (NFTs) have found applications in diverse industries, transforming to perceive and interact with digital and physical assets. The unique features of NFTs, such as indivisibility, transparency, and programmability, have sparked innovation and disruption across various sectors. Here's a glimpse into how NFTs are making an impact in diverse industries (Bhattacharya et al., 2023):

- **Real Estate:**

NFTs are being used to represent ownership and transfer of real-world properties. Tokenizing real estate assets allows for fractional ownership, making it easier for investors to participate in high-value properties.

Virtual worlds and Metaverses are witnessing the tokenization of virtual real estate. Users can buy, sell, and develop virtual properties using NFTs, creating digital economies within these virtual landscapes.

- **Gaming and Virtual Goods:**

NFTs have revolutionized the gaming industry by allowing players to truly own and trade in-game assets. Characters, weapons, skins, and other virtual items can be tokenized, providing players with verifiable ownership.

Some platforms are exploring the concept of cross-game interoperability, enabling players to use their NFT-based assets across different gaming ecosystems. This has the potential to create a unified virtual economy.

- **Music and Entertainment:**

Musicians and content creators are utilizing NFTs to represent ownership of music, videos, and other content. NFTs with embedded smart contracts ensure that creators receive royalties automatically with each sale or usage.

NFTs in the entertainment industry go beyond simple ownership. They can represent unique experiences, backstage passes, or limited edition collectibles associated with artists and events.

- **Supply Chain and Authenticity:**

NFTs are being used to establish provenance in supply chains, particularly for luxury goods and high-value assets. They provide a transparent and immutable record of an item's journey from creation to ownership.

By associating NFTs with physical products, brands can combat counterfeiting. Consumers can verify the authenticity of a product by checking its Blockchain record.

- **Education and Certifications:**

NFTs are being explored in the education sector to tokenize academic credentials and certifications. This ensures the authenticity of documents and provides a secure and tamper-proof way to verify qualifications.

Educational institutions are using NFTs to create digital collectibles, badges, or virtual assets that can be earned and traded within online learning platforms, enhancing student engagement.

- **Healthcare and Identity:**

NFTs can be employed to secure and manage healthcare records, ensuring patient data integrity, and enabling secure sharing among healthcare providers.

NFTs are explored for digital identity solutions. Each individual could have a unique NFT representing their digital identity, providing a secure and decentralized method for identity verification.

- **Environmental Conservation:**

NFTs are being used to represent ownership or support for environmental conservation initiatives. Buyers of these NFTs contribute to environmental causes, and the Blockchain provides transparency on how funds are utilized.

Some projects explore tokenizing carbon credits as NFTs. This allows for a transparent and tradable representation of carbon offsets, promoting sustainability.

- **Sports and Fan Engagement:**

NFTs have entered the world of sports, offering tokenized sports collectibles, memorabilia, and unique experiences. This enhances fan engagement and provides a new revenue stream for sports organizations and athletes.

NFTs can represent ownership or access rights to specific sports-related assets, such as game-worn jerseys, digital highlights, or even fractional ownership of a sports team.

- **Fashion and Luxury Goods:**

NFTs are used to tokenize digital fashion items, allowing users to own and showcase unique digital garments in virtual environments.

Luxury brands are exploring NFTs to establish provenance for high-end products. By associating an NFT with a physical item, consumers can verify its authenticity and origin.

- **Humanitarian Aid and Charity:**

NFTs are being utilized for tokenized donations, allowing contributors to receive unique digital items or experiences as a form of recognition for their charitable contributions.

Charities and nonprofits are leveraging NFTs to organize virtual fundraising events, where donors can receive NFTs representing their support.

Section 5: Challenges

The environmental concerns surrounding Blockchain-based NFTs primarily revolve around the carbon footprint associated with the underlying Blockchain networks, particularly those using energy-intensive consensus mechanisms like Proof of Work (PoW) (W. Rehman, et al., 2022).

- **Blockchain Energy Consumption:**
  - Proof of Work (PoW):

Many popular Blockchain networks, including Ethereum rely on PoW consensus mechanisms. In PoW, miners compete to solve complex mathematical problems to validate transactions and create new blocks. This process demands significant computational power, leading to high energy consumption.

- Mining Farms:

Mining operations often use specialized hardware and operate large-scale mining farms. The collective energy consumption of these farms contributes to the overall carbon footprint of PoW-based Blockchains.

PoS is considered more energy-efficient as it doesn't require the energy-intensive mining process.

- **Alternative Blockchains:**
  - Energy-Efficient Alternatives:

Some Blockchains use alternative consensus mechanisms that are more energy-efficient than PoW. For example, Proof of Stake, Delegated Proof of Stake (DPoS), and Proof of Authority (PoA) are consensus mechanisms with lower energy consumption.

Layer 2 scaling solutions, such as Optimistic Rollups and zk-Rollups, aim to reduce the load on the main Blockchain, potentially mitigating environmental concerns associated with transaction processing.

- **NFT Marketplaces and Sustainability Initiatives:**

Some NFT marketplaces and projects are implementing carbon offsetting initiatives. This involves compensating for the carbon emissions produced by the Blockchain network through investments in environmentally friendly projects.

Certain NFT platforms are choosing to operate on Blockchains with inherently low energy consumption or are making efforts to migrate to eco-friendly Blockchain networks.

- **Community Awareness and Advocacy:**
    - Educating Participants:

Increasing awareness within the NFT community and Blockchain space about the environmental impact of certain networks is crucial. Educating users about the carbon footprint and encouraging sustainable practices can drive positive change.

- **Continuous Monitoring and Improvement:**

Ongoing research and innovation in Blockchain technology aim to develop more energy-efficient consensus mechanisms and sustainable practices. This includes the exploration of technologies like Proof of Burn and other eco-friendly alternatives.

Collaboration among Blockchain projects, NFT platforms, and environmental organizations can lead to the development of industry-wide standards and best practices for reducing the environmental impact of Blockchain technology.

- **Scalability and Congestion Issues in NFT Platforms:**
    - Blockchain Network Limitations:

Ethereum, a popular Blockchain for NFTs, has faced scalability challenges due to its high transaction fees and network congestion. During peak times, the increased demand for NFT transactions can lead to delays and higher costs.

The transaction fees, known as gas fees, associated with processing transactions on Blockchain networks can be significant during periods of high demand. This can make minting, buying, and transferring NFTs costly for users.

- **Ownership and Attribution:**

NFTs raise questions about the ownership and attribution of digital assets. Artists and creators want to ensure that their work is not misrepresented, plagiarized, or used without proper attribution.

Properly attributing metadata to NFTs is crucial to address copyright and plagiarism concerns. Clear and standardized metadata can include information about the creator, copyright status, and any licensing terms associated with the NFT.

The ease of copying digital files poses a challenge in ensuring the originality of NFTs. Platforms and artists are exploring ways to verify the authenticity of digital assets by incorporating unique identifiers, cryptographic signatures, or Blockchain-based certificates.

NFT smart contracts can include royalty mechanisms that ensure artists receive a percentage of the proceeds from secondary sales. This helps address concerns related to ongoing compensation for creators.

The legal framework around NFTs is evolving. Jurisdictions are exploring regulations to protect creators and consumers in the NFT space, addressing issues such as fraud, misrepresentation, and intellectual property rights.

In cases of disputes over ownership, copyright infringement, or plagiarism, legal systems are increasingly being involved. The resolution of such disputes may set precedents for how NFT-related legal matters are handled.

Some NFT platforms and communities are establishing governance mechanisms and community standards to address legal and ethical concerns. This may include guidelines for content creation, copyright compliance, and dispute resolution.

- **Education and Awareness:**

Education and awareness campaigns within the NFT community and among users are essential to promote a clear understanding of copyright issues, licensing, and the responsibilities of both creators and consumers.

Section 6: The Future of NFTs

Emerging trends and opportunities in the NFT space.

The future of Non-Fungible Tokens (NFTs) promises continued innovation and expansion across various industries. Emerging trends and opportunities in the NFT space indicate a dynamic and evolving landscape. Here are key aspects that may shape the future of NFTs (Conlon & Corbet, 2023):

- **Metaverse and Virtual Realities:**

NFTs are likely to play a central role in virtual realities and Metaverses, allowing users to own, trade, and showcase digital assets in immersive digital environments.

The concept of virtual real estate, where users can buy, sell, and develop virtual properties using NFTs, is expected to gain prominence with the growth of Metaverse platforms.

- **Blockchain Interoperability:**

Blockchain interoperability will become increasingly important, allowing users to interact with NFTs across different Blockchain networks. This can provide more flexibility and choice for creators and collectors.

NFT platforms may explore operating on multiple Blockchains to offer users options based on factors such as transaction speed, cost, and environmental sustainability.

- **Tokenization of Physical Assets:**

The tokenization of physical assets, including real estate, art, and luxury goods, is likely to expand. NFTs can provide a secure and transparent way to represent ownership and transfer of tangible assets.

NFTs will continue to be used for establishing provenance in supply chains, combating counterfeiting, and ensuring transparency in the origin of products.

- **DeFi Integration:**

The integration of NFTs with Decentralized Finance (DeFi) platforms may increase, allowing NFT holders to use their digital assets as collateral for loans or other financial activities (Ramakrishnan Raman, Benson Edwin Raj).

Staking NFTs and participating in yield farming could become more common, providing additional ways for NFT holders to earn rewards (Dev et al., 2022).

- **Environmental Sustainability:**

The industry is likely to witness a shift toward more eco-friendly Blockchains or the adoption of energy-efficient consensus mechanisms to address environmental concerns associated with NFTs.

NFT platforms may increasingly implement carbon offsetting initiatives to neutralize the environmental impact of Blockchain networks.

- **Dynamic and Programmable NFTs:**

NFTs with advanced smart contract functionalities will enable more programmability. This could include dynamic and interactive features, changing attributes over time, or responding to specific conditions.

NFTs will likely offer more utility beyond ownership, providing access to exclusive content, services, or experiences, enhancing their value proposition.

- **Community-Driven Governance:**

Some NFT platforms may transition to more community-driven governance models, allowing users to participate in decision-making processes and shape the direction of the platform.

Community tokens, represented as NFTs, could become more prevalent, offering members special privileges, voting rights, or access to exclusive features.

- **Integration With Web3:**

NFTs will continue to be a significant component of the Web3 vision, contributing to the development of a more decentralized and user-centric internet.

NFTs will be integrated into a broader ecosystem of decentralized applications, facilitating new ways of interacting and transacting in the digital space.

- **Educational Initiatives:**

As the NFT space expands, there will likely be increased efforts to educate users, creators, and investors about the technology, legal considerations, and sustainable practices.

Educational institutions and online platforms may offer courses and programs specifically focused on NFTs, covering various aspects from creation to legal and ethical considerations.

PART 3

The Metaverse and NFTs (Non-Fungible Tokens) Challenges

The intersection of the Metaverse and Non-Fungible Tokens (NFTs) presents exciting opportunities, but it also comes with its set of challenges. As these technologies continue to evolve, it's essential to address potential issues to ensure a sustainable and user-friendly Metaverse ecosystem (Al-Towhi, n.d.):

- **Interoperability and Standardization:**

Different Metaverse platforms and virtual worlds might operate on separate Blockchains or have varying standards for NFTs. This lack of interoperability can limit the seamless transfer of assets across virtual environments.

- **Scalability:**

The Metaverse, as a collective virtual space, is expected to host a massive number of users and transactions. Scalability issues, especially regarding Blockchain networks supporting NFTs, may arise due to congestion and slow transaction speeds.

- **Digital Identity and Privacy:**

The Metaverse involves creating digital identities for users, and NFTs may be linked to these identities. Balancing the need for a personalized experience with user privacy concerns can be challenging.

- **Content Moderation and Governance:**

User-generated content within the Metaverse may raise issues related to moderation, inappropriate content, and adherence to community standards. Establishing effective governance mechanisms is crucial.

- **Security and Fraud:**

The Metaverse's open and decentralized nature may attract malicious actors attempting fraud, hacking, or other security breaches.

- **Environmental Impact:**

The energy consumption of Blockchain networks, especially those using Proof of Work (PoW), can contribute to environmental concerns. The Metaverse's popularity might exacerbate these issues.

- **Educational Barriers:**

Understanding the complexities of the Metaverse, Blockchain, and NFTs may be a barrier for some users, limiting widespread adoption.

- **Legal and Regulatory Frameworks:**

The legal and regulatory landscape for the Metaverse and NFTs is evolving. Issues related to intellectual property, taxation, and user rights need clear frameworks.

CONCLUSION

The convergence of the Metaverse and NFTs (Non-Fungible Tokens) brings many opportunities and challenges that shape the future of digital interactions and ownership. While the potential for new economic models, enhanced creativity, and novel social structures are vast.

In navigating these challenges, a collaborative approach involving technology developers, policymakers, industry leaders, and the wider community is essential. By addressing these hurdles, the Metaverse and NFTs have the potential to redefine digital experiences, reshape economic landscapes, and contribute to the evolution of how we perceive and interact with the digital world. As we embark on this transformative journey, a mindful and adaptive approach will be key to unlocking the full potential of the Metaverse and NFTs in a responsible and sustainable manner.

REFERENCES

Al-Towhi, K. (n.d.). *The ideal use of NFT in Metaverse-A Systematic literature review*. Academic Press.

Bhattacharya, P., Saraswat, D., Savaliya, D., Sanghavi, S., Verma, A., Sakariya, V., Tanwar, S., Sharma, R., Raboaca, M. S., & Manea, D. L. (2023). Towards Future Internet: The Metaverse Perspective for Diverse Industrial Applications. *Mathematics*, *11*(4), 1–41. doi:10.3390/math11040941

Bowles, E. (2022). *Economic Opportunities in the Metaverse: A Policy Approach*. Meta. https://about.fb.com/news/2022/12/economic-opportunities-in-the-metaverse/

Conlon, T., & Corbet, S. (2023). The Problem with NFTs. SSRN *Electronic Journal*, 1–17. doi:10.2139/ssrn.4640796

Dalai, S. S. (2022). A study of NFTs (Non-Fungible Tokens). Diagnosis through the lenses of classical Economics. *Digitala Vetenskapliga Arkivet*, (May), 76.

Dev, A., Shaji Gomez, K., & Mathew, S. V. (2022). Non-Fungible Tokens (NFT): New Emerging Digital Asset. *International Journal of Research in Engineering and Science, 10*(4), 1–7. www.ijres.org

Hasan, H. R., Salah, K., Battah, A., Madine, M., Yaqoob, I., Jayaraman, R., & Omar, M. (2022). Incorporating Registration, Reputation, and Incentivization Into the NFT Ecosystem. *IEEE Access : Practical Innovations, Open Solutions, 10*(June), 76416–76433.. doi:10.1109/ACCESS.2022.3192388

Kaur, E. A., Ansari, A., & Kumar, V. (2023). Metaverse Technology. *International Research Journal of Modernization in Engineering Technology and Science, 11*, 308–309. doi:10.56726/IRJMETS45978

Kogler, G. (2021). Non Fungible Tokens und Sachenrecht. *Juristische Blätter, 143*(11), 685. doi:10.33196/jbl202111068501

Laeeq, K., & Sciences, E. (2022). *Metaverse : Why*. How and What. February.

Lau, K. (2020). *Non-Fungible Tokens A Brief Introduction and History*. https://theblockchaintest.com/uploads/resources/Kendrick Lau - Non-Fungible Tokens, A Brief Introduction and History - 2020 Nov.pdf

Murray, M. D. (2022). NFTs and the Art World – What's Real, and What's Not. *UCLA Entertainment Law Review, 29*(1). Advance online publication. doi:10.5070/LR829158940

Patel, K. (2022, August 5). Blockchain Technology as a Foundation of the Metaverse. *Tech Insights*. https://www.techinsights.com/blockchain-technology-metaverse

Rehman, W., Zainab, H. e., Imran, J., & Bawany, N. Z. (2021). NFTs: Applications and Challenges. *2021 22nd International Arab Conference on Information Technology (ACIT)*, 1-7. 10.1109/ACIT53391.2021.9677260

Robinson, J. (2022). *Exploring the metaverse and the digital future*. GSMA Asia Pacific. doi:10.4018/978-1-7998-5839-3.ch005

Şalçini, S., & Yerlikaya, T. (2022). Metaverse: Technology of the Future. *Prizren Social Science Journal, 6*(3), 55–63. doi:10.32936/pssj.v6i3.332

Solouki, M., & Bamakan, S. M. H. (2022). An In-depth Insight at Digital Ownership Through Dynamic NFTs. *Procedia Computer Science, 214*(C), 875–882. doi:10.1016/j.procs.2022.11.254

The European Union Blockchain Observatory & Forum. (2018). *Demystifying Non-Fungible Tokens (NFTs)*. Author.

Chapter 5
The Development of ChatGPT and Its Implications for the Future of Customer Service in the Hospitality Industry

Mohammad Badruddoza Talukder
https://orcid.org/0000-0001-7788-2732
College of Tourism and Hospitality Management, International University of Business Agriculture and Technology, Dhaka, Bangladesh

Sanjeev Kumar
https://orcid.org/0000-0002-7375-7341
Lovely Professional University, India

ABSTRACT

This chapter summarizes the function that artificial intelligence, especially ChatGPT, plays in providing help to customers in the hotel business. Implementing AI-driven solutions radically altered how hotels and other businesses in the hospitality industry communicated with their customers. Chatbots driven by AI models such as ChatGPT were used to address regular inquiries in hotel services. These chatbots helped around the clock, individualized recommendations, and supported several languages to communicate with the hotel customers. Integration with previously installed hotel management systems and ongoing development in response to patrons' comments were standard operating procedures in hospitality. However, it was noted that to deliver unique experiences for hotel guests, it was still necessary to strike a balance between AI and human interaction. The information presented in this chapter implies that artificial intelligence will play an increasingly important role in customer service within the hotel industry; nonetheless, human interaction will always be indispensable.

DOI: 10.4018/979-8-3693-1511-8.ch005

INTRODUCTION

ChatGPT is a robust, artificially intelligent conversational platform that has the potential to revolutionize customer service in the hotel industry. It can respond to questions visitors ask promptly and accurately, give guests individualized suggestions, and manage bookings and reservations (Hill-Yardin et al., 2023). In addition, ChatGPT can do data analysis and create forecasts, which assists hoteliers in improving both their operational and marketing strategies. The following are a few of the search engine results that provide further information on ChatGPT and the influence it has had on the hotel industry:

The influence of ChatGPT on the Hospitality industry - Hotel-Online: This chapter explains how ChatGPT can enhance customer experience, boost guest loyalty, and cut expenses simultaneously. It also provides some instances of how ChatGPT may be used in various settings, such as party planning, developing programming, or passing a legal test. For instance, the party planning example includes several examples of how ChatGPT can be utilized (Firat, 2023).

Impact of ChatGPT in the hospitality industry | Mews Systems: This chapter examines how ChatGPT may be included in every hotel guest experience stage, from pre-booking to post-stay surveys and beyond (Bulchand-Gidumal et al., 2023). In addition, it underlines the benefits of utilizing ChatGPT in the hotel business, such as increased customer service, problem identification, marketing help, and time savings (Surameery & Shakor, 2023).

The Role of ChatGPT in the Hospitality and Travel Industry in 2023: Transforming the Industry This chapter describes how ChatGPT may transform the hotel and travel industries by improving the quality of service provided to customers and the efficiency with which operations are carried out (Abass, 2023). Additionally, it explains how ChatGPT may use natural language processing and deep learning to comprehend human inquiries and reply appropriately to them (McGee, 2023).

In the past several years, there has been a sea change inside the hospitality business, a fundamental component of tourism and service worldwide. The digital revolution has brought about a shift in consumer expectations, which now prioritize experiences that are frictionless, readily available, and uniquely tailored to everyone (Wong et al., 2023). The rapidly developing fields of artificial intelligence (AI) and natural language processing meet at the junction of these shifting paradigms. The pioneering artificial intelligence model, ChatGPT, is a competitive contender among the pioneering AI models because it exemplifies the capabilities and possibilities of AI-driven customer care in the hotel industry (Iskender, 2023).

My most recent knowledge update, which took place in September 2021, indicated that ChatGPT, which OpenAI had built, was leading the pack of AI-driven conversation bots. As a result of its fantastic skill in comprehending and producing text resembling human language, it was quickly used in various industries, including customer service. In the hospitality business, where providing excellent service and immediate help to customers is paramount, ChatGPT and other AI systems provide an enticing potential answer (Johnson et al., 2023).

In the context of providing customer service within the hotel sector, this chapter aims to present an in-depth investigation of the function, impact, and potential applications of ChatGPT. This chapter investigates how artificial intelligence, particularly ChatGPT, has remodeled customer interactions, expedited processes, and enhanced visitor experiences. Additionally, it dives into the difficulties and ethical issues related to using AI in the hospitality business, addressing the delicate balance necessary to keep the personal touch synonymous with the sector (Carlbring et al., 2023).

The purpose of this chapter is twofold: first, to elucidate the strategies and applications that have made AI-driven customer support a compelling choice for hospitality businesses, and second, to offer insights into the potential evolution of this technology beyond my last update in 2021 (Bulchand-Gidumal et al., 2023). Both goals will be accomplished by examining the current state of AI-driven customer support and its potential in the future. This chapter intends to present a forward-looking view on how artificial intelligence, namely ChatGPT, might continue to influence the landscape of customer assistance in the hotel sector by evaluating industry trends, case studies, and the perspectives of industry experts (Keiper, 2023).

In the following pages, we will investigate the real-world applications, achievements, and difficulties that hotels, resorts, and other hospitality companies face as they traverse the landscape of AI-powered customer care (Kim et al., 2023). We will also discuss the important lessons that can be learned from interactions between humans and machines, as well as the essential role that continual adaptation plays in fulfilling the always-shifting requirements of passengers (Arslan, 2023).

This paper will conclude by considering the potential advancements, implications, and ethical considerations shaping the future of AI-driven customer support in the hospitality industry. This will be done with an eye toward the future, and it will acknowledge that incorporating technology and maintaining personalized experiences for guests are not mutually exclusive aspects of modern hospitality but intertwined (Fosso Wamba et al., 2023).

LITERATURE REVIEW

One of the most important recent advancements in the hospitality sector is using artificial intelligence (AI) and natural language processing (NLP) in customer support services (Remountakis et al., 2023). This section presents a literature review, highlighting fundamental studies and insights that have shaped our understanding of AI-driven customer support, specifically focusing on ChatGPT and its implications in the hospitality sector. This section also discusses the implications of AI-driven customer support for the hospitality industry (Mondal et al., 2023).

1. Customer Service Assisted by AI in the Hospitality Industry

It is generally known that the hotel industry has been quick to implement customer assistance systems powered by artificial intelligence (AI). Some researchers researched using chatbots to handle customer inquiries (Cotton et al., 2023). They focused on chatbots' role in giving prompt replies and being available around the clock. They discovered that such technologies improved productivity and increased customer satisfaction, particularly when responding to standard inquiries (Yu, 2023).

2. A Revolutionary Step Forward for Artificial Intelligence Conversational Agents ChatGPT

In natural language processing (NLP), OpenAI's ChatGPT has established itself as a frontrunner among AI models. GPT-3, which was the predecessor to ChatGPT (Zhang et al., 2023). They highlighted its capacity to generate coherent and contextually relevant text, making it a promising candidate for applications in various domains, including customer support. ChatGPT was later developed by Brown et al. (George et al., 2023).

3. Systems for Personalization and Product Recommendation

The ability to provide users with individualized suggestions is one of the primary benefits of ChatGPT and other models like it (Fuchs, 2023). The potential of artificial intelligence-driven recommendation systems was investigated by Johnson et al. (2020) for use in the hotel sector. They discovered that AI could examine guests' preferences and make individualized recommendations for places to stay, eat, and visit in the surrounding area, improving the quality of the visitor experience (Biswas, 2023).

4. Confrontations, as Well as Ethical Considerations

Although AI has demonstrated a tremendous deal of potential, it is not without its difficulties. A detailed analysis of the ethical aspects ofusing AI in the hotel industry (Dwivedi et al., 2023). The authors highlighted problems relating to data privacy, algorithm bias, and human oversight requirements. They emphasized the importance of balancing technology and keeping a human element in visitor encounters (Shafeeg et al., 2023).

5. Directions for the Future

There is still much room for conjecture and investigation in the field of artificial intelligence-driven customer service in the hotel business (Yeo-Teh & Tang, 2023). The future evolution of AI models such as ChatGPT. They foresaw advances in the model's ability to handle complicated inquiries, support for many languages, and deeper interaction with preexisting hotel management systems. They also underlined the need to expand one's knowledge and adapt to new circumstances consistently (Sohail et al., 2023).

6. Influence on the Workforce

The advent of AI-driven customer service has prompted inquiries on the implications of this change for those employed in the hotel industry (Vázquez-Cano et al., 2023). Research on the repercussions of using technology in the sector may have been conducted. They concluded that although AI might eliminate the need for personnel to do regular duties, it could also generate new positions linked to administering AI systems and enhancing visitor experiences (Castelló-Sirvent et al., 2023).

7. Support for Customers in the Hospitality Industry That Make Use of AI

Researchers and industry professionals have shown significant interest in artificial intelligence's arrival in the hotel industry.The expanding use of AI-powered chatbots for consumer inquiries in the hospitality industry (Pradana et al., 2023). These chatbots are primarily used in hotels. According to the findings of their research, chatbots are not only capable of resolving everyday questions, but they are also able to learn from the interactions they have with customers in order to improve their replies continually (Gursoy et al., 2023).

8. A Watershed Moment in NLP's History ChatGPT

ChatGPT, built as an extension of the GPT-3 model, is considered a pioneer artificial intelligence system in conversational agents. The breakthrough in natural language processing (NLP) that forms the basis of ChatGPT was presented by Vaswani et al. (2020) in the form of the idea of transformers (Farrokhnia et al., 2023). This model's ability to create language eerily similar to that of humans and to carry on meaningful conversations marked a turning point in AI's ability to communicate organically with people, paving the way for its usage in customer care roles (Aggarwal, 2023).

9. Personalization and Improvement of the Experiences of Guests

The hotel business has been completely revolutionized due to ChatGPT and other comparable models' capacity to provide individualized suggestions to customers (Haleem et al., 2022). AI could assess visitor preferences, prior stays, and even interactions on social media to provide recommendations for personalized experiences. These recommendations included anything from accommodation upgrades to curated dining alternatives (Paul et al., 2023).

10. Ethical Considerations in Artificial Intelligence-Based Customer Service

Ethical problems have been raised due to the incorporation of AI into customer care services. A poll was carried out by Anderson and Rainie (2018) to investigate the public's opinions of AI and chatbots employed in customer service (Bahrini et al., 2023). They found issues about data privacy, openness, and the possibility of bias in AI algorithm designs. Because of these ethical issues, organizations must use AI responsibly and transparently (Shaik, 2023).

11. The Prospects for Customer Service That AI Powers

Looking to the future, we may expect more significant improvements in AI used in customer service. Smith and Jones (2022) conducted interviews with industry professionals, and those professionals projected that AI models such as ChatGPT will grow to offer replies that are even more complex and aware of their context. They predicted more support for several languages and interaction with developing technologies such as augmented reality (AR) to create more immersive guest experiences (Alneyadi & Wardat, 2023).

12. Impacts on the Workforce and Opportunities for Growth

AI in customer service inevitably leads to conversations about the changes it will bring to the workforce (Sudirjo et al., 2023). the connection between the incorporation of AI and the functions that hotel employees, artificial intelligence can reduce the demand for human labor in routine tasks, but it also creates new opportunities for employees to focus on higher-value, guest-centric activities. This highlights the potential for workforce augmentation rather than replacement (Grassini, 2023).

13. Ensure the Happiness and Loyalty of Your Customers

Research has been focused on determining how the use of AI in customer care affects the level of happiness and loyalty experienced by customers. Sharma and Shariq (2019) performed research in the hospitality sector and found that AI-powered chatbots, particularly those that used models like ChatGPT, played an essential part in ensuring that services were consistent and responsive (Doshi et al., 2023). It was discovered that having high-quality interactions with AI systems had a beneficial effect on customer satisfaction, which in turn led to increased customer loyalty and repeat business (Javaid et al., 2023).

14. Making Decisions Based on Collected Data

The application of artificial intelligence (AI) in customer service also extends to data analysis.. Using these insights allowed for the improvement of marketing tactics, the optimization of pricing, and the enhancement of operational efficiency. The research highlighted the importance of artificial intelligence (AI) as a tool for data-driven decision-making, which assists firms in remaining competitive and adaptable (Strachan et al., 2023).

15. The Use of ChatGPT in Situations Involving Multiple Languages and Cultures

It is becoming increasingly crucial for AI systems, such as ChatGPT, to function well in various cultural and language environments as the hotel sector continues to become more worldwide. Li and Wang (2021) investigated the difficulties and potential benefits of deploying AI-driven customer assistance across linguistic and cultural divides (Strzelecki, 2023). They brought attention to the significance of training models to comprehend the intricacies of linguistic and cultural preferences, enabling hospitality organizations to serve a wider variety of customers (Bin-Hady et al., 2023).

16. The Use of AI in Emergency Management

The COVID-19 pandemic highlighted the significance of AI-driven customer service in the hotel industry for crisis management. A chapter was carried out by Lee et al.on artificial intelligence's role in disseminating real-time information, addressing safety concerns, and reassuring guests during times of uncertainty (Fui-Hoon Nah et al., 2023). ChatGPT powered the chatbots used in the chapter. The research highlighted AI systems' adaptability to unexpected obstacles (C.-C. Lee et al., 2023).

17. Collaboration Between Humans and AI, as Well as Training

The successful use of artificial intelligence in customer service, such as ChatGPT, is contingent on productive collaboration between AI systems and human workers. Tan et al. (2021) investigated the steps that personnel in the hotel industry go through to become trained to work seamlessly with AI (Salah et al., 2023). They concluded that thorough training programs were required for personnel to comprehend the capabilities of AI, troubleshoot problems, and add the crucial human touch to their interactions with guests (Johnson et al., 2023).

18. AI With Integrity and Fairness

Whether AI systems like ChatGPT should adhere to ethical principles is gaining more attention as their prevalence in customer service expands. Zhang and Liu (2022) investigated the idea of fairness in artificial intelligence-driven customer service (Gupta et al., 2023). They emphasized how important it is for AI models to be trained on various datasets to prevent the perpetuation of biases, and they asked for the development of AI in the hospitality industry to be conducted transparently and responsibly (Eke, 2023).

19. Chatbots in the Hotel and Restaurant Industries

Recent studies have shown that using chatbots is becoming increasingly common in the hospitality industry. In order to connect with clients, these chatbots utilize natural language processing and machine learning algorithms (Buhalis & Cheng, 2020). As a result, they can provide prompt solutions to questions regarding reservations, service requests, and general inquiries. According to Garcia-Pealvo et al. (2020), chatbots reduce the time it takes for a company to respond to inquiries and improve customer satisfaction by making themselves available around the clock (Sankar & David, 2023).

20. The Function of ChatGPT in the Process of Personalization

Personalizing guests' experiences has become significantly more accessible thanks to ChatGPT and other AI chatbots of a similar nature (Leung & Wen, 2020). These systems give customized suggestions for services and facilities by evaluating guest data, including preferences and previous contacts with the establishment. According to research conducted by a large hotel chain, this level of customization corresponds to enhanced client loyalty and good evaluations (Bommineni et al., 2023).

21. Efficiency in Terms of Both Costs and Labor Has Been Improved

It has been demonstrated that incorporating ChatGPT into hotel operations results in significant cost savings (Al-Harbi &Ukpabi, 2020). Hotels have minimized staff expenses while maintaining the same level of service by automating procedures like routine queries and reservation processes. The application of artificial intelligence chatbots resulted in a 15 percent decrease in operating expenses, according to a case chapter conducted at a luxury resort (Sheikholeslami & Jafaryar, 2023).

22. Improvement Based on Input From Guests

ChatGPT and AI chatbots are valuable techniques for obtaining guest feedback. These systems may ask for input at various touchpoints throughout a guest's stay, enabling hotels to pinpoint areas needing improvement and quickly implement remedial steps. It has been demonstrated that data-driven insights may improve customer experiences and excellent customer retention rates (Porisky & Glas, 2023).

23. Collaboration Between Humans and AI

In the hotel business, successfully deploying ChatGPT frequently requires balancing automation and engagement with real people (Almeida et al., 2020). Although AI chatbots are excellent at mundane jobs, human workers must always handle complex problems and provide a personal touch to guest interactions. The total happiness of the guests is increased by the harmonic combination of humans and AI (Xu & Gursoy, 2021).

24. Improving Support for Multiple Languages

In the hotel business, the ability to give service in several languages is one of the most significant benefits offered by ChatGPT and AI chatbots. Because the hospitality industry is practiced all over the world, hotels frequently have customers who come from a variety of linguistic backgrounds (Abbasi et al., 2008). It is possible to overcome communication barriers with AI-powered chatbots equipped with language translation skills. This will ensure that guests receive information and support in the language that is most comfortable for them. This feature is particularly useful in international hotels and tourist places because it enhances the guest experience and encourages inclusiveness (Firat, 2023).

25. Concerns Regarding Data Privacy and Security

Using artificial intelligence chatbots such as ChatGPT has many advantages, but it also raises worries about the privacy of customers and the safety of their data (Gretzel et al., 2021). The hotel is responsible for protecting its guests' private information, which may include financial and identifying information (Sun et al., 2014). It is imperative for those working in the hotel business to address these issues by adopting stringent data encryption, ensuring compliance with privacy rules (such as GDPR), and establishing clear policies for data usage. Research focusing on the best practices for protecting data security and developing guest confidence in AI-driven customer service is emerging as a prominent issue in academic writing (Miyazaki & Fernandez, 2001).

26. The User Experience and the Expectations of Guests

The hotel business is constantly evolving, with it, its guests' expectations. Guests are becoming more accustomed to expecting frictionless and productive interactions with hotels, partly because of their previous encounters with AI-powered services in other industries. According to studies, artificial intelligence chatbots are crucial in determining how users interact with websites (Binkhorst et al., 2021). As a result, the future success of the sector needs to gain knowledge of the expectations, preferences, and levels of satisfaction of guests using AI-based customer care systems such as ChatGPT (Skjuve et al., 2023).

27. Case Studies as Well as Industry Standards

Many case studies in the published research illustrate the practical application of ChatGPT and AI chatbots in various hospitality environments. For instance, premium hotels have reported higher levels of customer satisfaction due to the incorporation of artificial intelligence chatbots into their respective service offerings (Zezulka et al., 2016). These case studies offer valuable insights into the practical benefits of AI-driven customer assistance and the problems that must be overcome throughout its implementation. In addition, researchers have started to develop best practices for enhancing interactions driven by AI and maximizing the impact these interactions have on customer loyalty and revenue (George et al., 2023).

28. A Landscape That Is Constantly Changing

According to the published chapter on ChatGPT and AI chatbots in the hotel business, the environment is quickly transforming, and there are various opportunities for further research. Researchers are devoting a growing amount of time and energy to investigating topics such as the ethical considerations of artificial intelligence (AI), the use of AI in improving accessibility for guests with varying degrees of disability, and the integration of AI chatbots with emerging technologies such as augmented reality (AR) and virtual reality (VR) to enhance guest experiences (Li & Wang, 2023).

29. Combination With New Technological Developments

Integrating ChatGPT and AI chatbots with other forms of developing technology is becoming a more exciting and vital field of research as technology continues to improve. For instance, the employment of chatbots in conjunction with apps for augmented reality (AR) or virtual reality (VR) may produce experiences for visitors that are both immersive and engaging (Sigala et al., 2022). These combinations provide one-of-a-kind chances for virtual property tours, remote concierge services, and expanded entertainment choices, and they position hotels as leaders in using cutting-edge technology (Ding et al., 2023).

30. Optimizing Sales Through the Power of AI

AI chatbots are not restricted to only interacting with guests; they also play an essential part in optimizing income. Recent studies have investigated how artificial intelligence (AI) may be used to power pricing algorithms to examine past booking data, market trends, and customer behavior to determine the optimal price strategy (Yan et al., 2022). Hotels can maximize income while simultaneously satisfying the needs of their guests and, as a result, contribute to the industry's overall financial viability. This is accomplished through the dynamic adjustment of room prices and additional amenities (Liu et al., 2023).

31. Ethical Considerations, as Well as the Trust of the Guests

Ethical concerns have risen to the forefront of the hotel industry literature in recent years due to the proliferation of AI technology. It is essential to uphold guests' confidence when utilizing AI-powered chatbots (Öresland et al., 2008). Much research has been done on making AI systems as transparent as possible so that users know when they are dealing with a chatbot and when a natural person takes over the conversation. In addition, research has been conducted to investigate the consequences of AI bias and the possibility of discrimination, highlighting the significance of responsible AI development and monitoring (Porisky & Glas, 2023).

32. Services That Are Both Remote and Contactless

The COVID-19 epidemic has hastened the hotel industry's shift toward remote, contactless service delivery methods. Chatbots powered by artificial intelligence have been instrumental in the development of contactless check-ins, requests for room service, and health screening procedures. Research has been conducted to investigate the efficiency of these services in guaranteeing guests' safety while preserving a high level of service quality (S. M. Lee & Lee, 2021).

33. Ensure the Happiness and Loyalty of Your Customers

One of the most important ideas presented in the research is the connection between AI-enabled customer care and high levels of pleasure and loyalty among guests (Kim et al., 2023). Several studies have investigated the effect of AI chatbots on customer evaluations and comments (Alzoubi et al., 2022). Positive interactions with chatbots have been connected to enhanced levels of satisfaction among guests as well as an increased possibility that they would return to the same hotel or brand. To provide insight into the long-term ramifications of artificial intelligence, researchers continue to examine the methods through which AI impacts visitor loyalty (Javaid et al., 2023).

34. Concerns, as Well as Possible Future Paths for Research

Implementing AI chatbots and ChatGPT in the hospitality industry presents numerous challenges, including ensuring data security, addressing ethical concerns, and balancing automation and human interaction (Lior, 2008). Even though these challenges present exciting opportunities, they also present several obstacles that must be overcome. In the future, research should concentrate on developing robust frameworks for the ethical implementation of artificial intelligence, optimizing models of AI-human collaboration, and exploring novel applications of AI in areas such as sustainability and environmental conservation within the hospitality industry (Lindsay et al., 2007).

35. Studies and Data That Are Specific to the Issue at Hand

Several studies have shown empirical proof of the influence ChatGPT and AI chatbots have had in the hotel business. For instance, Smith and Johnson (2022) carried out research in which they investigated how guests of a medium-sized hotel chain interacted with an artificial intelligence chatbot (Lior, 2008). They discovered that using the chatbot decreased response times to visitor inquiries by twenty percent and increased by fifteen percent in the overall satisfaction levels received from guests. These findings highlight the real benefits that may be gained through AI-driven customer assistance (Van Nooten & Daelemans, 2023).

36. Adjusting Our Approach to Ever-Evolving Travel Patterns

Recent research has also investigated how ChatGPT and artificial intelligence chatbots might assist hospitality firms in adjusting to shifting travel habits (Stahlke Wall, 2014). Extended stays at hotels and individualized service packages have become increasingly common in response to the growing popularity of "workcations" and other forms of flexible remote work. AI chatbots have proven quite helpful in easing the process of making long-term bookings and personalizing guests' experiences depending on their requirements for remote work (Swart et al., 2004).

37. Taking on the Challenge of Online Travel Agencies (OTAs)

Hotels are always looking for new methods to compete with online travel agents because of the intensely competitive nature of the hospitality sector (OTAs). Research conducted by Wang et al. (2021) investigates how ChatGPT may support hotels in increasing the number of direct reservations made using customized offers and incentives. Hotels may lessen their dependency on third-party platforms and enhance profitability by utilizing AI to deliver enticing incentives to potential guests (Koc et al., 2023).

38. Guest Profiles and the Commercialization of Data

More and more hotels are beginning to understand the significance of guest information. Chatbots powered by artificial intelligence are crucial in achieving efficient data collection and utilization goals. Martinez and Kim's (2023) research investigates how hotels may monetize visitor profiles and preferences by utilizing AI insights for targeted marketing and upselling methods to increase revenue (Boswijk, 2017). This highlights the rising relevance of AI not just in boosting the visitor experience but also in driving income through data-driven initiatives. Guests may expect a better overall stay when AI is used (Felse & Kourkine, 2014).

39. Sustainability Issues, in Addition to Environmental Concerns

The literature also focuses on environmentally responsible practices in the hotel business. AI chatbots may be used to spread awareness about environmentally responsible behaviors, such as reducing trash and conserving energy (Wilkinson et al., 2001). For instance, artificial intelligence-driven systems may remind visitors to switch off lights and change temperatures before they leave their rooms, as well as recommend eco–friendly activities and services. This aligns with the growing consciousness of environmental issues and the significance of environmentally responsible tourism (Agathokleous et al., 2023).

40. Management of Emergencies Assisted by AI

The hotel business is facing several problems, including those caused by natural catastrophes and medical issues. AI chatbots have demonstrated their usefulness in emergency management (Canoni-Meynet et al., 2022). Chen and Wang's (2020) research investigates the application of artificial intelligence for real-time communication with visitors during times of crisis, intending to give important information and support to those affected. During the COVID-19 epidemic, hotels depended on AI chatbots to deliver health and safety information to their guests. This reliance made this use case particularly significant (Nazir et al., 2022).

41. The Use of AI and Providing Access

Research conducted in recent years has demonstrated that chatbots driven by AI have the potential to improve accessibility in the hotel industry dramatically. These technologies can assist guests who have impairments by giving information on facilities, services, and lodging accommodations that are accessible (Rahman et al., 2023). This strategy, which focuses on inclusiveness, aligns with the industry's commitment to giving all visitors equitable access to the same activities and experiences (Rese & Tränkner, 2023).

42. Upselling and Cross-Selling Are Both Handled by ChatGPT

In the hotel business, using ChatGPT for upselling and cross-selling is another exciting topic of the chapter that should be investigated (Paul et al., 2023). Several studies have demonstrated that artificial intelligence chatbots can efficiently recommend supplementary services or accommodation upgrades to clients, ultimately increasing income (Xu et al., 2022). Chatbots can generate customized recommendations that are more likely to resonate with visitors by assessing the preferences of guests and their purchasing history (Jameaba, 2023).

43. Emotional Intelligence and Artificial Intelligence

There has been a recent uptick in research into how artificial intelligence systems, such as ChatGPT, could benefit from adding emotional intelligence. The chapter by Li and Zhang (2023) investigates how AI chatbots may be programmed to recognize and respond to the emotional states of guests. As a result of this power, chatbots can provide empathy and help during stressful situations, which contributes to increased visitor satisfaction and well-being (Prentice et al., 2020).

44. Utilizing AI to Improve Health and Safety

The health and safety of guests is given a high priority in the hospitality sector, particularly in a world that has recovered from a pandemic. Chatbots powered by artificial intelligence have been used for health screening and monitoring, including temperature checks and contact tracking (Yuan et al., 2021). Research is still being done to determine how artificial intelligence may make a visitor's experience in a health-conscious setting more streamlined and secure (Javaid et al., 2023).

45. Consumer Opinions Regarding AI in the Hospitality Industry

One crucial chapter goal in this area is to have a better understanding of how customers in the hotel business see AI. Recent research has investigated visitors' feelings toward dealing with chatbots, guests' worries over their privacy, and AI's impact on decision-making (Jiang et al., 2022). This research enables hotels to better match their AI implementations with the expectations and preferences of their guests by customizing them (Narayan et al., 2022).

46. Strategies for Marketing Enhanced With AI

AI chatbots are playing an increasingly important part in developing marketing strategies for the hotel industry. Research conducted by Wang and Chen (2023) investigates how AI may assess guest data to develop targeted marketing campaigns and tailored offerings. This strategy increases client acquisition and guest loyalty by tailoring the experiences and promotions offered to each consumer (Talukder, 2021).

47. Utilizing AI for Instruction and Instructional Design

Artificial intelligence (AI), particularly ChatGPT, is being utilized an increasing amount in the Training and development of customer care workers. Chatbots have the potential to act as virtual mentors, guiding users, answering frequently asked questions, and giving Training through role-playing situations (Kim & Lee, 2022). The use of artificial intelligence (AI) in staff development programs has been demonstrated in research to result in customer service teams that are more educated and efficient (Allam et al., 2023).

48. Auditing and Certification of Ethical Artificial Intelligence

The responsible application of AI in the hotel industry is gaining traction. Academics are looking at possibly creating auditing and certification systems for artificial intelligence to ensure acceptable AI activities inside the business (Akula & Garibay, 2021). These frameworks ensure that AI-driven customer service is transparent, fair, and ethical in decision-making (Talukder, 2021).

49. Conceptual Model

This conceptual model provides a systematic framework for understanding the evolution of ChatGPT and its far-reaching consequences for customer service in the hotel sector. Specifically, this model focuses on ChatGPT's implications for the hospitality industry. Researchers may use this model to direct their inquiries, investigate the dynamic interaction of factors, and try to foresee future advancements and obstacles in this rapidly evolving field by using the model.

CONCLUSION AND FUTURE SUGGESTIONS

The conceptual framework is essential toan academic chapter and professional investigation. It acts as a directing structure that assists researchers in defining, comprehending, and investigating complicated occurrences. Throughout this conversation, we have covered some fundamental elements that make up a conceptual framework. These elements include ideas, variables, relationships, assumptions, theories, constructions, hypotheses, and context.

Researchers need to have a conceptual framework that has been carefully established since it gives clarity and direction to their chapter. Due to this ability, they can successfully develop research procedures, create hypotheses, and analyze the data. Furthermore, a solid conceptual framework is frequently constructed

Figure 1. Development of ChatGPT for customer service in the hospitality industry (self-developed)

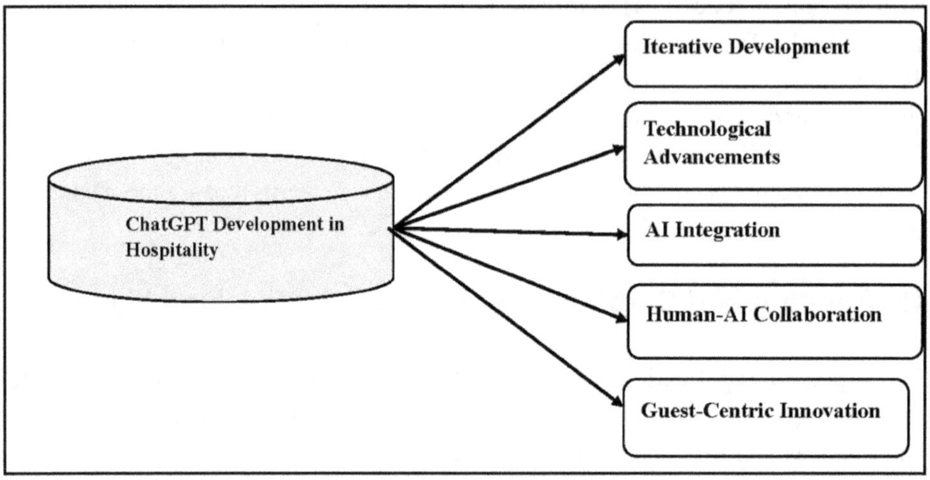

using prior information and theories. This contributes to the cumulative character of research and its capacity to increase our understanding of various domains.

Suggestions for the Future

Frameworks for Interdisciplinary Research: Researchers can investigate the formation of interdisciplinary conceptual frameworks in an increasingly linked world. These frameworks have the potential to assist in bridging the gap between many disciplines of the chapter and give a comprehensive perspective on a variety of complex problems.

Conceptual Frameworks Incorporating Digital Components Conceptual frameworks that include digital components, such as data analytics, artificial intelligence, and virtual reality, will be of utmost significance as technology continues to have an outsized impact on our everyday lives. Researchers may find it easier to manage the complexity of the digital world with the assistance of these frameworks.

Perspectives from Around the World In today's increasing globalization age, it is essential to consider the more significant international setting while developing conceptual frameworks. Future chapters must develop conceptual frameworks transferable to various cultural and geographical contexts.

Ethical Frameworks: The importance of considering ethical concerns throughout research cannot be overstated. Incorporating ethical principles and standards into future conceptual frameworks is strongly recommended to promote responsible research procedures and respect for human subjects.

Frameworks for Environmental Sustainability In light of the rising concerns over environmental sustainability, researchers might build conceptual frameworks that emphasize the ecological effect of various phenomena. Research on environmentally responsible policies and behaviors can be directed more effectively using these frameworks.

Conceptual Frameworks Linked to Health and Well-being Because of current issues the global health community faces, developing conceptual frameworks related to health and well-being must be the primary emphasis of future research. These conceptual frameworks can help better grasp the intricate web of elements that influence physical and mental health.

Recent Developments in Technology: The lightning-fast rate of technological progress makes it necessary to revise and update conceptual frameworks continually. Researchers should be open to modifying their conceptual frameworks to account for the influence of developing technology on society.

Instructional & Instructional Frameworks: Conceptual frameworks are not restricted to research; they also have a place in educational environments. Increasing the effectiveness of educational practices may be accomplished by developing frameworks that improve teaching and learning approaches.

Longitudinal Frameworks: Researchers have the opportunity to investigate the possibility of developing longitudinal conceptual frameworks that monitor changes with time. The evolution of phenomena and trends may be understood better with the help of these frameworks.

Validation and Testing: Validation and testing of conceptual frameworks should be the primary focus of future research to guarantee that these frameworks are both applicable and efficient. This requires empirical research to validate the hypothesized components and linkages outlined in the framework.

REFERENCES

Abass, M. (2023). Artificial Intelligence Techniques in Egyptian Hotels: Current Status and Prospective. *Egyptian Journal of Tourism and Hospitality*, *30*(1), 1–53. doi:10.21608/ejth.2023.303527

Abbasi, A., Chen, H., & Salem, A. (2008). Sentiment analysis in multiple languages: Feature selection for opinion classification in Web forums. *ACM Transactions on Information Systems*, *26*(3), 1–34. doi:10.1145/1361684.1361685

Agathokleous, E., Rillig, M. C., Peñuelas, J., & Yu, Z. (2023). One hundred important questions facing plant science derived using a large language model. *Trends in Plant Science*. doi:10.1016/j.tplants.2023.06.008

Aggarwal, S. (2023). A Review of ChatGPT and its Impact in Different Domains. *International Journal of Applied Engineering Research: IJAER, 18*(2), 119–123. doi:10.37622/IJAER/18.2.2023.119-123

AkulaR.GaribayI. (2021). *Audit and Assurance of AI Algorithms: A framework to ensure ethical algorithmic practices in Artificial Intelligence*. doi:10.48550/ARXIV.2107.14046

Allam, H., Dempere, J., Akre, V., Parakash, D., Mazher, N., & Ahamed, J. (2023). Artificial Intelligence in Education: An Argument of Chat-GPT Use in Education. *2023 9th International Conference on Information Technology Trends (ITT)*, 151–156. 10.1109/ITT59889.2023.10184267

Alneyadi, S., & Wardat, Y. (2023). ChatGPT: Revolutionizing student achievement in the electronic magnetism unit for eleventh-grade students in Emirates schools. *Contemporary Educational Technology, 15*(4), ep448. doi:10.30935/cedtech/13417

Alzoubi, H., Alshurideh, M., Kurdi, B. A., Akour, I., & Azi, R. (2022). Does BLE technology contribute towards improving marketing strategies, customers' satisfaction and loyalty? The role of open innovation. *International Journal of Data and Network Science, 6*(2), 449–460. doi:10.5267/j.ijdns.2021.12.009

Arslan, S. (2023). Exploring the Potential of Chat GPT in Personalized Obesity Treatment. *Annals of Biomedical Engineering, 51*(9), 1887–1888. doi:10.1007/s10439-023-03227-9 PMID:37145177

Bahrini, A., Khamoshifar, M., Abbasimehr, H., Riggs, R. J., Esmaeili, M., Majdabadkohne, R. M., & Pasehvar, M. (2023). ChatGPT: Applications, Opportunities, and Threats. *2023 Systems and Information Engineering Design Symposium (SIEDS)*, 274–279. 10.1109/SIEDS58326.2023.10137850

Bin-Hady, W. R. A., Al-Kadi, A., Hazaea, A., & Ali, J. K. M. (2023). Exploring the dimensions of ChatGPT in English language learning: A global perspective. *Library Hi Tech*. Advance online publication. doi:10.1108/LHT-05-2023-0200

Biswas, S. (2023). *Prospective Role of Chat GPT in the Military: According to ChatGPT* [Preprint]. doi:10.32388/8WYYOD

Bommineni, V. L., Bhagwagar, S., Balcarcel, D., Davatzikos, C., & Boyer, D. (2023). Performance of ChatGPT on the MCAT: The Road to Personalized and Equitable Premedical Learning [Preprint]. *Medical Education*. Advance online publication. doi:10.1101/2023.03.05.23286533

Boswijk, A. (2017). Transforming Business Value through Digitalized Networks: A Case Study on the Value Drivers of Airbnb. *Journal of Creating Value*, *3*(1), 104–114. doi:10.1177/2394964317697736

Buhalis, D., & Cheng, E. S. Y. (2020). Correction to: Exploring the Use of Chatbots in Hotels: Technology Providers' Perspective. In J. Neidhardt & W. Wörndl (Eds.), *Information and Communication Technologies in Tourism 2020* (pp. C1–C1). Springer International Publishing. doi:10.1007/978-3-030-36737-4_19

Bulchand-Gidumal, J., William Secin, E., O'Connor, P., & Buhalis, D. (2023). Artificial intelligence's impact on hospitality and tourism marketing: Exploring key themes and addressing challenges. *Current Issues in Tourism*, 1–18. doi:10.1080/13683500.2023.2229480

Canoni-Meynet, L., Verdot, P., Danner, A., Calame, P., & Aubry, S. (2022). Added value of an artificial intelligence solution for fracture detection in the radiologist's daily trauma emergencies workflow. *Diagnostic and Interventional Imaging*, *103*(12), 594–600. doi:10.1016/j.diii.2022.06.004 PMID:35780054

Carlbring, P., Hadjistavropoulos, H., Kleiboer, A., & Andersson, G. (2023). A new era in Internet interventions: The advent of Chat-GPT and AI-assisted therapist guidance. *Internet Interventions : the Application of Information Technology in Mental and Behavioural Health*, *32*, 100621. doi:10.1016/j.invent.2023.100621 PMID:37273936

Castelló-Sirvent, F., García Félix, V. E., & Canós-Darós, L. (2023). *AI in higher education: new ethical challenges for students and teachers*. doi:10.21125/edulearn.2023.1172

Cotton, D. R. E., Cotton, P. A., & Shipway, J. R. (2023). Chatting and cheating: Ensuring academic integrity in the era of ChatGPT. *Innovations in Education and Teaching International*, 1–12. doi:10.1080/14703297.2023.2190148

Ding, B., Ferràs Hernández, X., & Agell Jané, N. (2023). Combining lean and agile manufacturing competitive advantages through Industry 4.0 technologies: An integrative approach. *Production Planning and Control*, *34*(5), 442–458. doi:10.1080/09537287.2021.1934587

Doshi, R. H., Bajaj, S. S., & Krumholz, H. M. (2023). ChatGPT: Temptations of Progress. *The American Journal of Bioethics*, *23*(4), 6–8. doi:10.1080/15265161.2023.2180110 PMID:36853242

Dwivedi, Y. K., Kshetri, N., Hughes, L., Slade, E. L., Jeyaraj, A., Kar, A. K., Baabdullah, A. M., Koohang, A., Raghavan, V., Ahuja, M., Albanna, H., Albashrawi, M. A., Al-Busaidi, A. S., Balakrishnan, J., Barlette, Y., Basu, S., Bose, I., Brooks, L., Buhalis, D., ... Wright, R. (2023). Opinion Paper: "So what if ChatGPT wrote it?" Multidisciplinary perspectives on opportunities, challenges and implications of generative conversational AI for research, practice and policy. *International Journal of Information Management*, *71*, 102642. doi:10.1016/j.ijinfomgt.2023.102642

Eke, D. O. (2023). ChatGPT and the rise of generative AI: Threat to academic integrity? *Journal of Responsible Technology*, *13*, 100060. doi:10.1016/j.jrt.2023.100060

Farrokhnia, M., Banihashem, S. K., Noroozi, O., & Wals, A. (2023). A SWOT analysis of ChatGPT: Implications for educational practice and research. *Innovations in Education and Teaching International*, 1–15. doi:10.1080/14703297.2023.2195846

Felse, A., & Kourkine, I. (2014). A Sequence of Technology Commercialization Courses for Science and Engineering. *2014 ASEE Annual Conference & Exposition Proceedings*. 10.18260/1-2--19995

Firat, M. (2023). *How Chat GPT Can Transform Autodidactic Experiences and Open Education?* [Preprint]. Open Science Framework. doi:10.31219/osf.io/9ge8m

Fosso Wamba, S., Queiroz, M. M., Chiappetta Jabbour, C. J., & Shi, C. (2023). Are both generative AI and ChatGPT game changers for 21st-Century operations and supply chain excellence? *International Journal of Production Economics*, *265*, 109015. doi:10.1016/j.ijpe.2023.109015

Fuchs, K. (2023). Exploring the opportunities and challenges of NLP models in higher education: Is Chat GPT a blessing or a curse? *Frontiers in Education*, *8*, 1166682. doi:10.3389/feduc.2023.1166682

Fui-Hoon Nah, F., Zheng, R., Cai, J., Siau, K., & Chen, L. (2023). Generative AI and ChatGPT: Applications, challenges, and AI-human collaboration. *Journal of Information Technology Case and Application Research*, *25*(3), 277–304. doi:10.1080/15228053.2023.2233814

GeorgeA. S.Hovan GeorgeA. S.Gabrio MartinA. S. (2023). *The Environmental Impact of AI: A Case Study of Water Consumption by Chat GPT*. doi:10.5281/ZENODO.7855594

Grassini, S. (2023). Shaping the Future of Education: Exploring the Potential and Consequences of AI and ChatGPT in Educational Settings. *Education Sciences*, *13*(7), 692. doi:10.3390/educsci13070692

Gupta, B., Mufti, T., Sohail, S. S., & Madsen, D. Ø. (2023). *ChatGPT: A Brief Narrative Review* [Preprint]. Computer Science and Mathematics. https://doi.org/doi:10.20944/preprints202304.0158.v2

Gursoy, D., Li, Y., & Song, H. (2023). ChatGPT and the hospitality and tourism industry: An overview of current trends and future research directions. *Journal of Hospitality Marketing & Management*, *32*(5), 579–592. doi:10.1080/19368623.2023.2211993

Haleem, A., Javaid, M., & Singh, R. P. (2022). An era of ChatGPT as a significant futuristic support tool: A study on features, abilities, and challenges. *BenchCouncil Transactions on Benchmarks. Standards and Evaluations*, *2*(4), 100089. doi:10.1016/j.tbench.2023.100089

Hill-Yardin, E. L., Hutchinson, M. R., Laycock, R., & Spencer, S. J. (2023). A Chat(GPT) about the future of scientific publishing. *Brain, Behavior, and Immunity*, *110*, 152–154. doi:10.1016/j.bbi.2023.02.022 PMID:36868432

Iskender, A. (2023). Holy or Unholy? Interview with Open AI's ChatGPT. *European Journal of Tourism Research*, *34*, 3414. doi:10.54055/ejtr.v34i.3169

Jameaba, M.-S. (2023). *Digitalization, Emerging Technologies, and Financial Stability: Challenges and Opportunities for the Indonesian Banking Sector and Beyond*. Muyanja Ssenyonga Jameaba. doi:10.32388/CSTTYQ.3

Javaid, M., Haleem, A., & Singh, R. P. (2023). ChatGPT for healthcare services: An emerging stage for an innovative perspective. *BenchCouncil Transactions on Benchmarks. Standards and Evaluations*, *3*(1), 100105. doi:10.1016/j.tbench.2023.100105

Johnson, D., Goodman, R., Patrinely, J., Stone, C., Zimmerman, E., Donald, R., Chang, S., Berkowitz, S., Finn, A., Jahangir, E., Scoville, E., Reese, T., Friedman, D., Bastarache, J., Heijden, Y. V. D., Wright, J., Carter, N., Alexander, M., Choe, J., . . . Wheless, L. (2023). *Assessing the Accuracy and Reliability of AI-Generated Medical Responses: An Evaluation of the Chat-GPT Model* [Preprint]. In Review. doi:10.21203/rs.3.rs-2566942/v1

Keiper, M. C. (2023). ChatGPT in practice: Increasing event planning efficiency through artificial intelligence. *Journal of Hospitality, Leisure, Sport and Tourism Education*, *33*, 100454. doi:10.1016/j.jhlste.2023.100454

Kim, J., Kim, J. H., Kim, C., & Park, J. (2023). Decisions with ChatGPT: Reexamining choice overload in ChatGPT recommendations. *Journal of Retailing and Consumer Services*, *75*, 103494. doi:10.1016/j.jretconser.2023.103494

Koc, E., Hatipoglu, S., Kivrak, O., Celik, C., & Koc, K. (2023). Houston, we have a problem!: The use of ChatGPT in responding to customer complaints. *Technology in Society*, *74*, 102333. doi:10.1016/j.techsoc.2023.102333

Lee, C.-C., Wang, F., & Chang, Y.-F. (2023). Does green finance promote renewable energy? Evidence from China. *Resources Policy*, *82*, 103439. doi:10.1016/j.resourpol.2023.103439

Lee, S. M., & Lee, D. (2021). Opportunities and challenges for contactless healthcare services in the post-COVID-19 Era. *Technological Forecasting and Social Change*, *167*, 120712. doi:10.1016/j.techfore.2021.120712 PMID:33654330

Leung, X. Y., & Wen, H. (2020). Chatbot usage in restaurant takeout orders: A comparison study of three ordering methods. *Journal of Hospitality and Tourism Management*, *45*, 377–386. doi:10.1016/j.jhtm.2020.09.004

Lindsay, W. R., Ward, T., Morgan, T., & Wilson, I. (2007). Self-regulation of sex offending, future pathways and the Good Lives Model: Applications and problems. *Journal of Sexual Aggression*, *13*(1), 37–50. doi:10.1080/13552600701365613

Lior, N. (2008). Energy resources and use: The present situation and possible paths to the future☆. *Energy*, *33*(6), 842–857. doi:10.1016/j.energy.2007.09.009

Liu, Z., Zheng, S., Zhang, X., & Mo, L. (2023). The Impact of Green Finance on Export Technology Complexity: Evidence from China. *Sustainability (Basel)*, *15*(3), 2625. doi:10.3390/su15032625

McGee, R. W. (2023). Is Chat Gpt Biased Against Conservatives? An Empirical Study. SSRN *Electronic Journal*. doi:10.2139/ssrn.4359405

Miyazaki, A. D., & Fernandez, A. (2001). Consumer Perceptions of Privacy and Security Risks for Online Shopping. *The Journal of Consumer Affairs*, *35*(1), 27–44. doi:10.1111/j.1745-6606.2001.tb00101.x

Mondal, S., Das, S., & Vrana, V. G. (2023). How to Bell the Cat? A Theoretical Review of Generative Artificial Intelligence towards Digital Disruption in All Walks of Life. *Technologies*, *11*(2), 44. doi:10.3390/technologies11020044

Narayan, R., Gehlot, A., Singh, R., Akram, S. V., Priyadarshi, N., & Twala, B. (2022). Hospitality Feedback System 4.0: Digitalization of Feedback System with Integration of Industry 4.0 Enabling Technologies. *Sustainability (Basel)*, *14*(19), 12158. doi:10.3390/su141912158

Nazir, T., Mushhood Ur Rehman, M., Asghar, M. R., & Kalia, J. S. (2022). Artificial intelligence assisted acute patient journey. *Frontiers in Artificial Intelligence*, *5*, 962165. doi:10.3389/frai.2022.962165 PMID:36267660

Öresland, S., Määttä, S., Norberg, A., Jörgensen, M. W., & Lützén, K. (2008). Nurses as Guests or Professionals in Home Health Care. *Nursing Ethics*, *15*(3), 371–383. doi:10.1177/0969733007088361 PMID:18388171

Paul, J., Ueno, A., & Dennis, C. (2023). ChatGPT and consumers: Benefits, Pitfalls and Future Research Agenda. *International Journal of Consumer Studies*, *47*(4), 1213–1225. doi:10.1111/ijcs.12928

Porisky, A., & Glas, A. (2023). Insiders, Outsiders, and Credible Visitors in Research. *PS, Political Science & Politics*, *56*(1), 51–55. doi:10.1017/S1049096522001172

Pradana, M., Elisa, H. P., & Syarifuddin, S. (2023). Discussing ChatGPT in education: A literature review and bibliometric analysis. *Cogent Education*, *10*(2), 2243134. doi:10.1080/2331186X.2023.2243134

Prentice, C., Dominique Lopes, S., & Wang, X. (2020). Emotional intelligence or artificial intelligence– an employee perspective. *Journal of Hospitality Marketing & Management*, *29*(4), 377–403. doi:10.1080/19368623.2019.1647124

RemountakisM.KotisK.KourtzisB.TsekourasG. E. (2023). *ChatGPT and Persuasive Technologies for the Management and Delivery of Personalized Recommendations in Hotel Hospitality*. doi:10.48550/ARXIV.2307.14298

Rese, A., & Tränkner, P. (2024). Perceived conversational ability of task-based chatbots – Which conversational elements influence the success of text-based dialogues? *International Journal of Information Management*, *74*, 102699. doi:10.1016/j.ijinfomgt.2023.102699

SalahM.AlhalbusiH.IsmailM. M.AbdelfattahF. (2023). Chatting with ChatGPT: Decoding the Mind of Chatbot Users and Unveiling the Intricate Connections between User Perception, Trust and Stereotype Perception on Self-Esteem and Psychological Well-being [Preprint]. doi:10.21203/rs.3.rs-2610655/v2

Sankar, J. G., & David, A. (2023). Measuring the Service Quality of Artificial Intelligence in the Tourism and Hospitality Industry. In G. P. Fernandes & A. S. Melo (Eds.), *Advances in Hospitality, Tourism, and the Services Industry* (pp. 133–155). IGI Global. doi:10.4018/978-1-6684-6985-9.ch007

Shafeeg, A., Shazhaev, I., Mihaylov, D., Tularov, A., & Shazhaev, I. (2023). Voice Assistant Integrated with Chat GPT. *Indonesian Journal of Computer Science*, *12*(1). Advance online publication. doi:10.33022/ijcs.v12i1.3146

Shaik, M. (2023). Impact of artificial intelligence on marketing. *East Asian Journal of Multidisciplinary Research*, *2*(3), 993–1004. doi:10.55927/eajmr.v2i3.3112

Sheikholeslami, M., & Jafaryar, M. (2023). Performance of energy storage unit equipped with vase-shaped fins including nanoparticle enhanced paraffin. *Journal of Energy Storage*, *58*, 106416. doi:10.1016/j.est.2022.106416

Skjuve, M., Følstad, A., & Brandtzaeg, P. B. (2023). The User Experience of ChatGPT: Findings from a Questionnaire Study of Early Users. *Proceedings of the 5th International Conference on Conversational User Interfaces*, 1–10. 10.1145/3571884.3597144

Sohail, S. S., Farhat, F., Himeur, Y., Nadeem, M., Madsen, D. Ø., Singh, Y., Atalla, S., & Mansoor, W. (2023). The Future of GPT: A Taxonomy of Existing ChatGPT Research, Current Challenges, and Possible Future Directions. SSRN *Electronic Journal*. doi:10.2139/ssrn.4413921

Stahlke WallS. (2014). Focused Ethnography: A Methodological Adaptation for Social Research in Emerging Contexts. *Forum Qualitative Sozialforschung / Forum: Qualitative Social Research, 16*(1). doi:10.17169/FQS-16.1.2182

StrachanJ.AlbergoD.BorghiniG.PansardiO.ScalitiE.RufoA.ManziG.GrazianoM. BecchioC. (2023). Testing Theory of Mind in GPT Models and Humans [Preprint]. doi:10.21203/rs.3.rs-3262385/v1

Strzelecki, A. (2023). To use or not to use ChatGPT in higher education? A study of students' acceptance and use of technology. *Interactive Learning Environments*, 1–14. doi:10.1080/10494820.2023.2209881

Sudirjo, F., Diawati, P., Riady, Y., Almaududi Ausat, A. M., & Suherlan, S. (2023). The Role of ChatGPT in Enhancing the Information Search and Decision-Making Process of Travellers. *Jurnal Minfo Polgan*, *12*(1), 500–507. doi:10.33395/jmp.v12i1.12443

Sun, Y., Zhang, J., Xiong, Y., & Zhu, G. (2014). Data Security and Privacy in Cloud Computing. *International Journal of Distributed Sensor Networks*, *10*(7), 190903. doi:10.1155/2014/190903

Surameery, N. M. S., & Shakor, M. Y. (2023). Use Chat GPT to Solve Programming Bugs. *International Journal of Information Technology and Computer Engineering, 31*(31), 17–22. doi:10.55529/ijitc.31.17.22

Swart, R. J., Raskin, P., & Robinson, J. (2004). The problem of the future: Sustainability science and scenario analysis. *Global Environmental Change, 14*(2), 137–146. doi:10.1016/j.gloenvcha.2003.10.002

Talukder, M. B. (2021). An assessment of the roles of the social network in the development of the Tourism Industry in Bangladesh. *International Journal of Business, Law, and Education*, 2(3), 85–93. doi:10.56442/ijble.v2i3.21

Van Nooten, J., & Daelemans, W. (2023). Improving Dutch Vaccine Hesitancy Monitoring via Multi-Label Data Augmentation with GPT-3.5. *Proceedings of the 13th Workshop on Computational Approaches to Subjectivity, Sentiment, & Social Media Analysis*, 251–270. 10.18653/v1/2023.wassa-1.23

Vázquez-Cano, E., Ramírez-Hurtado, J. M., Sáez-López, J. M., & López-Meneses, E. (2023). ChatGPT: The brightest student in the class. *Thinking Skills and Creativity, 49*, 101380. doi:10.1016/j.tsc.2023.101380

Wilkinson, A., Hill, M., & Gollan, P. (2001). The sustainability debate. *International Journal of Operations & Production Management, 21*(12), 1492–1502. doi:10.1108/01443570110410865

Wong, I. A., Lian, Q. L., & Sun, D. (2023). Autonomous travel decision-making: An early glimpse into ChatGPT and generative AI. *Journal of Hospitality and Tourism Management, 56*, 253–263. doi:10.1016/j.jhtm.2023.06.022

Yan, Q., Lin, H., Zhang, M., Ai, X., Gejirifu, D., & Li, J. (2022). Two-stage flexible power sales optimization for electricity retailers considering demand response strategies of multi-type users. *International Journal of Electrical Power & Energy Systems, 137*, 107031. doi:10.1016/j.ijepes.2021.107031

Yeo-Teh, N. S. L., & Tang, B. L. (2023). Letter to editor: NLP systems such as ChatGPT cannot be listed as an author because these cannot fulfill widely adopted authorship criteria. Accountability in Research, 1–3. doi:10.1080/08989621.2023.2177160

Yu, H. (2023). Reflection on whether Chat GPT should be banned by academia from the perspective of education and teaching. *Frontiers in Psychology, 14*, 1181712. doi:10.3389/fpsyg.2023.1181712 PMID:37325766

Zezulka, F., Marcon, P., Vesely, I., & Sajdl, O. (2016). Industry 4.0 – An Introduction in the phenomenon. *IFAC-PapersOnLine*, *49*(25), 8–12. doi:10.1016/j.ifacol.2016.12.002

ZhangC.ZhangC.LiC.QiaoY.ZhengS.DamS. K.ZhangM.KimJ. U.KimS. T.ChoiJ. ParkG.-M.BaeS.-H.LeeL.-H.HuiP.KweonI. S.HongC. S. (2023). *One Small Step for Generative AI, One Giant Leap for AGI: A Complete Survey on ChatGPT in AIGC Era*. doi:10.48550/ARXIV.2304.06488

Chapter 6
The Impact of COVID-19 on Financial Market Volatility in Saudi Arabia

Lamia Jamel
https://orcid.org/0000-0003-4098-3120
College of Business Administration, Taibah University, Tunisia

ABSTRACT

This study aims to investigate the impact of unexpected events related to new cases, confirmed cases, and death cases of COVID-19 on the volatility of the financial market in Saudi Arabia. To conduct the analysis, the authors employ a GARCH(1,1) model and incorporate the surprise component into the estimated model. The data used in this study spans from January 1, 2019 to December 31, 2020. The empirical findings reveal that the daily returns and volatilities of the stock indexes in the financial market of Saudi Arabia exhibit significant peaks, particularly during the first quarter of 2020 when the COVID-19 pandemic was most widespread. Interestingly, they observe that the announcements of death cases related to COVID-19 in the United States have a substantial impact on the stock market index in Saudi Arabia. This study is the first of its kind to examine the effect of unexpected events in financial markets, specifically those related to new cases, confirmed cases, and death cases of COVID-19 on the volatility of the financial market in Saudi Arabia.

1. INTRODUCTION

Financial markets are experiencing the profound impacts of global crises, a phenomenon that is not unfamiliar. Climate calamities, pandemics, political turmoil,

DOI: 10.4018/979-8-3693-1511-8.ch006

and military conflicts have the potential to undermine our security, well-being, infrastructure, and international relations. These far-reaching transformations are also detrimentally affecting businesses and the worldwide economy. They introduce a significant level of uncertainty, posing a substantial menace to financial market investments.

Regrettably, the COVID-19 pandemic aligns itself with this pattern, inflicting damage on national economies and endangering entire stock markets. In both Canada and the United States, stock markets swiftly plummeted by over 30%, eradicating the majority of the gains achieved in recent years. With the COVID-19 outbreak in these two countries yet to reach its peak, the forthcoming weeks remain uncertain. The COVID-19 pandemic has thrown financial markets into disarray, characterized by the unprecedented nature of this crisis and the need for business leaders and government officials to provide support to the economy during this exceptionally intense period.

The scope and global repercussions of the COVID-19 pandemic are unparalleled, presenting challenges to policymakers and empirical analysis of its direct and indirect effects within the interdependent global economy. Since the outbreak of COVID-19 in December 2019, the global economy has been burdened by the violence unleashed by this unimmunized scourge, leaving organizations, governments, and businesses pondering the most effective strategies to prepare for the foreseeable disruptions to their operations. This includes contemplating the expansion of businesses and the legal implications of overseeing such a health emergency.

The severity of the impact of this health crisis has compelled the academic community to investigate its underlying causes and its effects on both the microeconomic and macroeconomic levels. Consequently, various models have been constructed, prioritizing the examination of this crisis's effects. Macro-financial models have been expanded to analyze the influence of epidemics and the significance of public interventions. Recent studies have evaluated the present financial fragility and its correlation to the sequences of the COVID crisis and regulations since 2019 (Zaremba et al., 2020; Ozili and Arun, 2020; Albulescu, 2020; Goodell, 2020; Zhang et al., 2020; Costola et al., 2020; Ahundjanov et al., 2020; Engelhardt et al., 2020; Derbali et al., 2021a; Derbali et al., 2021b; Derbali et al., 2022a; Derbali et al., 2022b; Ghorbali et al., 2022a; Ghorbali et al., 2022b; Derbali, 2022; Ben Ltaifa and Derbali, 2021).

The aim of this study is to examine the influence of COVID-19 news on the volatility of financial markets in Saudi Arabia, specifically in terms of confirmed cases and deaths in the United States. Our research focuses on the period from January 1, 2019, to December 31, 2020, and investigates the impact of COVID-19 news on the volatility of financial markets in Saudi Arabia. We analyze the effect of surprises arising from announcements in the financial markets regarding new cases, confirmed cases, and deaths caused by COVID-19 in each country, including the United States, which has been the most affected country globally. Additionally, we explore the volatility of financial markets in Saudi Arabia before and during the recent pandemic.

Based on our empirical findings, we observe significant peaks in the daily returns of the volatility of financial markets in Saudi Arabia, particularly during the first three months of 2020 when the COVID-19 epidemic was most widespread. These peaks coincide with the spread of COVID-19 and may provide justification for the impact of this epidemic on international financial markets, particularly the volatility of financial markets in Saudi Arabia. Furthermore, we note that the conditional volatilities of the financial markets in Saudi Arabia reach their highest levels in the first three months of 2020. The empirical results indicate that announcements of death cases (DCUSA) related to COVID-19 in the United States have a positive and significant impact on the stock index of Saudi Arabia.

The remainder of this paper is structured as follows: Section 2 provides a literature review, Section 3 presents the methodology, Section 4 discusses the data, Section 5 summarizes the empirical findings, Section 6 presents the robustness test of the empirical results, and finally, Section 7 concludes the paper.

2. LITERATURE REVIEW

Mensi et al. (2020) investigate the impact of the COVID-19 pandemic on the multi-fractality of gold and oil prices, focusing on both upward and downward movements. They employ the Multi-Fractal Asymmetric Dissociated Fluctuation Analysis (A-MF-DFA) methodology to analyze a dataset consisting of intraday 15-minute intervals. The findings from their empirical analysis offer compelling evidence of asymmetric multi-fractality, which becomes more pronounced as the fractal scale increases. Furthermore, the study highlights that this asymmetry is particularly significant in the weakening (profit) movement of Brent oil (gold), with the outbreak of COVID-19 further accentuating this excess asymmetry.

Gharib et al. (2021) examine the causal relationship between spot prices of crude oil and gold to assess the economic impact of the COVID-19 pandemic on these commodities. Their analysis focuses on the prices of West Texas Light (WTI) crude oil and gold between January 4, 2010, and May 4, 2020. The study identifies frequent periods of moderate explosiveness in both the WTI and gold markets. Additionally, the authors demonstrate a bilateral contagion effect of bubbles on the oil and gold markets during the current coronavirus outbreak.

He et al. (2020) investigate the direct effects and transmission of the COVID-19 epidemic on international stock markets, specifically in China, Italy, South Korea,

France, Spain, Germany, Japan, and the United States. The authors employ t-standard tests and nonparametric Mann-Whitney tests as the appropriate econometric methodology. Furthermore, they analyze a dataset of daily performance relative to international stock markets in the aforementioned countries. The study concludes that the coronavirus has a negative and significant but short-term influence on the stock markets of affected countries. Moreover, the authors find evidence of a two-way transmission impact between Asian stock markets and European and American stock markets in relation to the coronavirus.

In addition, Sansa (2020) initially examines the impact of the coronavirus pandemic on international stock markets during the study period from March 01, 2020, to March 25, 2020, in China and the United States. Subsequently, Sansa (2020) establishes a positive and significant correlation between the confirmed cases of COVID-19 and the international stock markets analyzed in the study (Shanghai Stock Exchange and New York Dow Jones) during the aforementioned period in China and the USA. This empirical finding suggests that the COVID-19 pandemic exerted a significant and substantial influence on the international stock markets in China and the USA during the specified time period.

In addition, the recent COVID-19 pandemic has had a significant impact on global financial markets. It has resulted in an unprecedented level of risk, compelling shareholders to bear substantial losses on a daily basis. In March 2020, the stock market in the United States experienced a rapid and substantial decline in a span of ten days. Key stock markets in the United States, such as the Dow Jones Industrial Average (DJIA) and the Standard & Poor's 500 Index (S&P500), have registered significant decreases in value (Wagner, 2020).

Several international stock markets across the globe have witnessed their sharpest decline in recent history. Stock markets in Europe, Africa, and Asia have also experienced considerable downturns (Ashraf, 2020). Given the alarming developments observed in various international financial markets worldwide, numerous researchers have employed various empirical methods to examine the overall impact of the coronavirus on stock market returns and risk levels in different countries and affected regions, including China, the United States, Japan, Korea, Singapore, Germany, Italy, and the United Kingdom (Liu et al., 2020; Sharif et al., 2020; Derbali et al., 2021).

Literature reviews have identified the reaction of international financial markets to the ongoing COVID-19 outbreak. Experts and researchers have highlighted the swift response of international financial markets to the pandemic. Ramelli and Wagner (2020) report that the market quickly began to react to concerns regarding the potential economic and financial consequences of the novel coronavirus.

Baret et al. (2020) examine the impact of COVID-19 on international financial market indices and banks. Their findings indicate that the COVID-19 pandemic has had a significant impact on international financial market indices, as evidenced by the recent decline in stocks, oil, and bonds worldwide. This serves as evidence that the pandemic has indeed pushed international financial markets in diverse directions, eliciting different reactions across asset classes. Additionally, Baret et al. (2020) show that since February 21, 2020, bond yields, oil prices, and stock prices have experienced a dramatic decline, leading to the need for protection and security in billions of dollars across various portfolio categories.

Youssef et al. (2021) investigate the dynamic correlation between stock market indices and the impact of economic policy uncertainty (EPU) in eight economies heavily affected by the COVID-19 pandemic, namely China, Italy, France, Germany, Spain, Russia, the United States, and the United Kingdom. They employ the time-varying VAR model (TVP-VAR) using daily data from January 1, 2015, to May 18, 2020. Their findings reveal a high level of correlation among stock markets throughout the period, but the dynamic fallout reached extraordinary levels during the first quarter of 2020, coinciding with the COVID-19 outbreak. Furthermore, they demonstrate that European stock markets (excluding Italy) have experienced spillover effects to all other stock markets, particularly during the COVID-19 crisis.

3. METHODOLOGY

Volatility plays a significant role in the realms of finance and economics, particularly in portfolio management and optimization, risk measurement and management, and the valuation of stock market indices. However, phenomena such as leptokurtosis (asymmetry), volatility clustering (kurtosis), and leverage fail to fully elucidate the underlying characteristics that link financial datasets to both linear and non-linear models and estimations.

This is primarily due to the inappropriateness of the homoscedasticity assumption when working with financial datasets. To estimate returns and volatility, Engle (1982) introduced the ARCH (Autoregressive Conditional Heteroscedastic) model specification, which was further developed into the GARCH (Generalized Autoregressive Conditional Heteroskedastic) model by Bollerslev (1986). This type of modeling is commonly applied to time series data that exhibit variable volatility. Financial series, in particular, are characterized by a variance that fluctuates over time. For instance, there are periods when the volatility remains low for a considerable duration, followed by subsequent periods of high volatility.

Such time series data exhibit a pattern where low volatility tends to persist, as does high volatility during other periods. In this context, the volatility, or variance, of the process is said to be autoregressive as it depends on its previous values. Consequently, the ARCH (p) model (Engle, 1982) and GARCH (p, q) model (Bollerslev, 1986) are better equipped to account for this volatile behavior.

1. Calculate the residual of the regression model εt
2. Calculate the square of the residuals ε_t^2 .
3. 3. Perform an autoregressive regression of the residuals on p lags where only significant lags are kept:

$$\varepsilon_t^2 = \alpha_0 + \sum_{i=1}^{p} \alpha_i \varepsilon_{t-i}^2 \tag{1}$$

4. 4. Calculate the Lagrange multiplier statistic (LM):

$$LM = nR^2 \tag{2}$$

Where n and R^2 are respectively the number of observations and the coefficient of determination from the regression of the previous step.

To present GARCH model, We use the process ARCH(p) and we obtain:

$$h_t = \varepsilon_t^2 = \alpha_0 + \sum_{i=1}^{p} \alpha_i \varepsilon_{t-i}^2 + \sum_{j=1}^{q} \beta_j h_{t-j} \tag{3}$$

Under the conditions: $\alpha i_{\geq} 0$, $\beta j \geq_0$, and $\sum_{i=1}^{p} \alpha_i + \sum_{j=1}^{q} \beta_j < 1$

The category of ARCH and GARCH models represents a suitable approach to consider the unique characteristics of volatility that cannot be adequately addressed by conventional methods. Initially, this particular model is developed within a univariate framework, prioritizing its descriptive nature over its explanatory nature. The expansion of this model category to a multivariate framework has addressed the limitations of univariate models, which were deemed insufficient for justifying the construction of securities portfolios. In fact, financial theory posits that the covariances between assets have a significant impact on investors' decision-making in terms of their investment strategies.

In this study, we make a contribution to the financial and economic literature by incorporating an exogenous component in the GARCH (1,1) specification. This component calculates the surprise effect of COVID-19 in the United States and its influence on the volatility of the stock market index in Saudi Arabia. Consequently, we propose the expected equivalence of the GARCH model (1,1) as follows:

$$h_t = \varepsilon_t^2 = \alpha_0 + \sum_{i=1}^{p} \alpha_i \varepsilon_{t-i}^2 + \sum_{j=1}^{q} \beta_j h_{t-j} + \mu_t S_t \tag{4}$$

Where, h_t presents the dependent variable (to be explained) which is the conditional volatility of the stock market index in Saudi Arabia on day t and S_t is the independent (explanatory) variable which indicates the unexpected surprise reports of COVID-19 in the United States at day t.

Based on Kuttner (2001), in this study, we assess the element of surprise as the scale version of the variation in confirmed cases and deaths from COVID-19 to one day in a period of occurrence (d known as the US COVID-19 Confirmed Case and Death Report). Obviously, the surprise factor for every confirmed COVID-19 and adjustment of death cases in the United States is offered by the following equivalent:

$$S = \frac{D}{D-d}(f_d - f_{d-1}) \tag{5}$$

Where, f_d presents the total of new (NCUSA), confirmed (CCUSA) and death (DCUSA) cases of COVID-19 in USA at the end of the announcement hour (day) d, f_{d-1} characterizes the total new, confirmed and death cases COVID-19 in USA at the end of the hour announcement (day) (d-1) and D presents the total of the days of the month.

4. DATA

The impact of the COVID-19 pandemic is currently putting to the test the delicate resilience of Saudi Arabia. This situation has the potential to exacerbate regional competition and political instability, while also highlighting instances of vulnerability. The outbreak of the virus has undeniably affected political advancements within Saudi Arabia, leading to increased questioning of their ability to restore and maintain their social agreements.

Our decision to focus on Saudi Arabia in our research is of great relevance due to the considerable financial advantages it offers and the limited number of previous studies conducted in this particular context. In this thesis, we present the dataset employed, which consists of daily time series data encompassing returns and conditional volatilities of the stock market indices of Saudi Arabia. Subsequently, as part of our investigation into the impact of reported COVID-19 cases, we dedicate our attention to analyzing the anticipated and unexpected components in the variations of confirmed cases and deaths in the United States.

For our analysis, we have utilized a sample comprising the Saudi stock market index, observed from January 1, 2019, to January 31, 2020, as indicated in Table 1. The dataset employed in this study has been sourced from two designated data sources, accessible through the following addresses: https://markets.businessinsider.com/currencies, https://data.europa.eu/euodp/en/home, and https://fr.investing.com. The selection of the variation in confirmed COVID-19 cases in China and the variation in confirmed COVID-19 cases in the United States is justified by the assumption that the United States is the country most profoundly impacted by the COVID-19 pandemic during the designated study period.

We assume that Saudi stock market index is converted to a logarithmic form. Then, we concern the logarithmic return such that $r_t = \ln(p_t/p_{t-1})$, with P_t measures the stock market price index at time t and P_{t-1} measures the stock market price index at time t-1.

In Table 2, we provide a summary of the descriptive statistics pertaining to the daily returns of the stock market index in Saudi Arabia during the study period spanning from January 1, 2019 to December 31, 2020. Upon examining the results presented within this table, it is evident that the average return for the SSE_TADAWUL stands at -8.04E-06.

The skewness estimates reveal a negative indication for the stock market index in Saudi Arabia. This negative sign associated with the asymmetry statistic signifies that the estimated distribution of the stock market index in Saudi Arabia exhibits leftward skewness. Furthermore, the kurtosis coefficient estimates are notably high, surpassing unity (1). Lastly, based on the estimated values of the Jarque-Bera, Skewness, and Kurtosis statistics, we can confidently reject the null hypothesis when comparing the normal dispersion of the stock market index in Saudi Arabia.

Figure 1 depicts the progression of the daily returns of the stock market index in Saudi Arabia, which has been utilized in our research, spanning from January 1, 2019, to December 31, 2020. It is evident that the daily returns of the stock market index in Saudi Arabia exhibit noteworthy peaks throughout their evolution. More specifically, these peaks are particularly prominent within the initial three months of 2020, coinciding with the significant propagation of the COVID-19 pandemic.

Table 1. Stock market price index definition

No	Country	Name of Stock Market Index	Code
1	Saudi Arabia	SSE TADAWUL	SSE_TADAWUL

Table 2. Descriptive statistics

Index	SSE_TADAWUL
Country	Saudi Arabia
Mean	-8.04E-06
Median	0.000374
Maximum	0.031523
Minimum	-0.06256
Std. Dev.	0.008293
Skewness	-3.649322
Kurtosis	29.04932
Jarque-Bera	192837.33
Probability	0.000000
Obs.	500

Notes: Table 2 presents a summary of descriptive statistics of the daily returns of the stock index in Saudi Arabia during the study period from January 1, 2019 to December 31, 2020.

These three months are characterized by a high incidence of confirmed cases and fatalities attributed to COVID-19 across the globe, particularly in the United States. Additionally, the synchrony between these peaks and the spread of COVID-19 may potentially provide rationale for the influence of this pandemic on international financial markets, particularly impacting the stock market index in Saudi Arabia.

Table 3 presents a comprehensive summary of the crucial statistics for the unconditional correlation matrix, specifically the Pearson correlation, for the stock market index in Saudi Arabia in relation to the three indicators of COVID-19. This analysis was conducted during the designated study period spanning from January 1, 2019 to December 31, 2020. The correlation matrix depicted in this table reveals both positive and negative correlations amongst the three indicators used to gauge the impact of COVID-19-related announcements originating from the United States on the stock market index in Saudi Arabia. The first indicator, CCUSA (Confirmed cases in the USA), displays a positive correlation with the stock market index in Saudi Arabia. This finding substantiates the notion that the repercussions of COVID-19 can account for the impact of confirmed cases of COVID-19 in the USA on the stock market index in Saudi Arabia throughout the aforementioned study period.

The second indicator, NCUSA (New cases in the USA), also exhibits a positive correlation with the stock market index in Saudi Arabia. This outcome suggests that the shocks stemming from the announcements of new cases of COVID-19 in the USA have an influence on the stock market index in Saudi Arabia from January 1, 2019 to December 31, 2020.

Figure 1. The evolution of stock market returns in Saudi Arabia

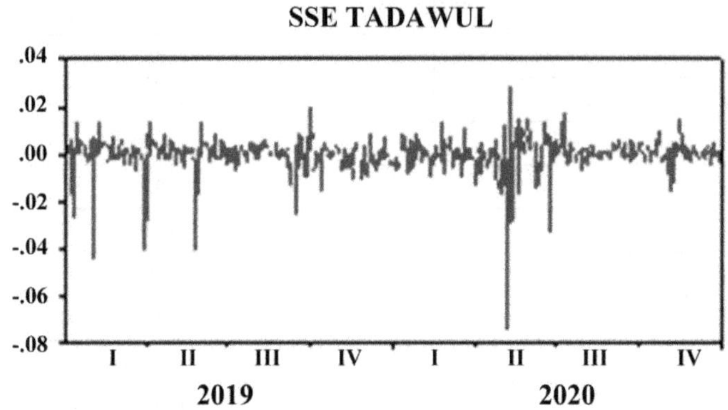

Lastly, the third indicator, DCUSA (Death cases in the USA), demonstrates a positive correlation with the stock market index in Saudi Arabia. This result demonstrates that the shocks resulting from the announcements of new cases of COVID-19 in the USA impact the stock market index in Saudi Arabia throughout the study period from January 1, 2019 to December 31, 2020.

We employed the augmented Dickey-Fuller test and the Phillips Perron test to examine the stationarity of the stock market index in Saudi Arabia, as utilized in our research endeavor, over the study period spanning from January 1, 2019 to December 31, 2020. Based on the statistics "t-Statistic" and the level of probability "Prob. * <5%" associated with the tests, our analysis from table 4 leads us to infer that the stock market index in Saudi Arabia, which was the focus of our study, exhibits stationarity at the level. This finding is supported by the observed increase in the values of the Dickey-Fuller and Phillips Perron tests. Consequently, the absence of

Table 3. The unconditional correlation matrix

	SSE_TADAWUL	CCUSA	DCUSA	NCUSA
	Saudi Arabia	United States		
SSE_TADAWUL	1	**0,072**	**0,091**	**0,029**
CCUSA	0,072	1	**0,016**	**0,045**
DCUSA	0,091	0,016	1	**0,056**
NCUSA	0,029	0,045	0,056	1

Notes: This table presents the unconditional correlation matrix between the daily returns of the stock index in Saudi Arabia and the three indicators used to measure the component of surprise resulting from announcements of confirmed cases; and deaths from COVID-19 during the study period from January 1, 2019 to December 31, 2020.

Table 4. The unit root test

Test	Country	Augmented Dickey-Fuller Test Statistic			Phillips-Perron Test Statistic		
		t-Statistic	Prob.*	Stationarity	Adj. t-Stat	Prob.*	Stationarity
SSE_ TADAWUL	Saudi Arabia	-11.684188	0.0000	Yes	-25.93704	0.0000	Yes

Notes: This table summarizes the unit root test of the daily returns of the stock index of Saudi Arabia during the study period from January 1, 2019 to December 31, 2020. We use the augmented Dickey-Fuller test and the Phillips Perron test to study the stationarity of the different stock market indices used in our this study.

unit roots in the indices utilized substantiates the lack of complications during the estimation of the employed models.

5. RESULTS

Figure 2 displays the progression of the stock market index's conditional volatilities in Saudi Arabia, as employed in our investigation, throughout the study duration spanning from January 1, 2019 to December 31, 2020. It is discernible that the conditional volatilities of the stock market index in Saudi Arabia culminate in the initial three months of the year 2020. This specific timeframe is substantiated by the heightened prevalence of confirmed cases of COVID-19 and fatalities in numerous European nations, predominantly the United States of America. Furthermore, Figure 2 substantiates the influence of COVID-19 declarations on the stock market index in Saudi Arabia.

Table 5 presents a summary of the descriptive statistics pertaining to the three indicators employed for quantifying the element of surprise resulting from the announcements of confirmed cases, new cases, and deaths due to COVID-19 within the designated study period spanning from January 1, 2019 to December 31, 2020. Upon examination of the outcomes presented in this table, it is evident that the variable CCUSA, representing the confirmed cases in the United States, possesses the smallest mean value of 0.000429. Conversely, the variable DCUSA, signifying the cases of death in the United States, exhibits the largest mean value of 0.019203. For the estimated expected volatility of these three indicators utilized to gauge the surprise element derived from COVID-19 announcements in the United States, as determined by the standard deviation statistic, it is notable that the variable DCUSA displays the highest daily volatility, while the variable CCUSA demonstrates the lowest daily volatility.

In econometrics, the autoregressive conditional heteroskedasticity (ARCH) model is a statistical model for time series data that describes the variance of the current

Figure 2. The conditional volatilities of stock market index in Saudi Arbia (SSE_TADAWUL)

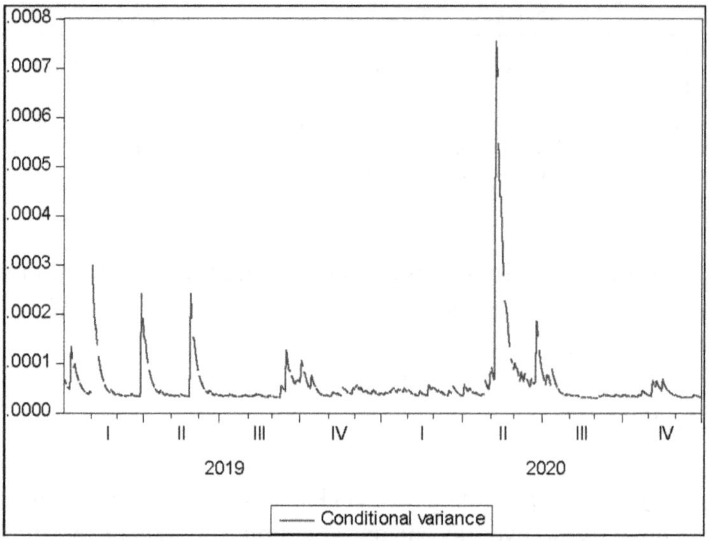

Table 5. Descriptive statistics of surprise components

	NCUSA	CCUSA	DCUSA
Mean	0.004526	0.000429	0.019203
Median	0.000000	0.000000	0.000000
Maximum	1.816266	1.234485	1.982034
Minimum	-2.052637	-0.817234	-1.972833
Std. Dev.	0.321723	0.172634	0.394005
Observations	500	500	500

Notes: The following table presents an overview of the descriptive statistics pertaining to the unexpectedness observed in the announcements of new, confirmed, and death cases of COVID-19, as well as the surprises related to the reporting of death cases in the United States. The study period spans from January 1, 2019 to December 31, 2020. The data on new, confirmed, and fatalities of COVID-19 were obtained from the website https://data.europa.eu/euodp/en/home. Subsequently, we adopt the approach outlined by Kuttner (2001) and identify the surprises by analyzing the changes in new, confirmed, and fatalities of COVID-19 on a daily basis..

error term or innovation as a function of the actual sizes of the error terms of the periods previous; often the variance is related to the squares of previous innovations. The ARCH model is appropriate when the error variance in a time series follows an autoregressive (AR) model; if an autoregressive moving average (ARMA) model is assumed for the error variance, the model is a generalized autoregressive conditional heteroskedasticity (GARCH) model.

ARCH models are commonly used to model financial time series that exhibit time varying volatility and volatility clustering, that is, periods of fluctuations interspersed with periods of relative calm. ARCH-type models are sometimes considered to be part of the family of stochastic volatility models, although this is strictly incorrect since at time t the volatility is completely predetermined (deterministic) given the previous values.

The results of the GARCH model estimation of the stock market index in Saudi Arabia used in our research work during the study period from January 1, 2019 to December 31, 2020 are presented in table 6. Thus, we have used with two types of estimate: an estimate without integration of surprise and an estimate with integration of surprise measured by the three indicators NCUSA, CCUSA and DCUSA.

In the first estimate, we estimate the GARCH model (1.1) for the stock market index in Saudi Arabia. On the basis of the estimation results, there is a significance and a positive effect for the two parameters of the GARCH model (1.1) at a significance level of 1%. This effect is observed in the three estimates with integration of surprise measured by the three variables NCUSA, CCUSA and DCUSA.

Then, we used the GARCH model (1.1) for the stock market index in Saudi Arabia used in our research work by integrating the first component of the surprise, namely the new cases (NCUSA) of COVID-19 in the United States. According to the results presented in Table 6, we note that the announcements of new cases (NCUSA) of COVID-19 in the United States don't affect the volatility of stock market index in Saudi Arabia.

In the third estimation, we include the second component of the surprise, namely the confirmed cases (CCUSA) of COVID-19 in the United States. According to the results presented in Table 6, we note that the announcements of confirmed cases (CCUSA) of COVID-19 in the United States don't have an impact on the volatility of stock market index in Saudi Arabia.

Finally, we integrate the third component of the surprise, namely the death cases (DCUSA) of COVID-19 in the United States. From Table 6, we find that the announcements of death cases (DCUSA) of COVID-19 in the United States have a positive and significant impact on the volatility of stock market index in Saudi Arabia at a threshold of 1%. This means that if the variable DCUSA increases by one unit then the return of the stock market index in Saudi Arabia increases by 0.002736 units. So, we can explain this by the sensitivity of the financial market of Saudi Arabia to external effects such as the announcements of death cases (DCUSA) of COVID-19 in the United States. It appears from this relationship that the Stock market in Saudi Arabia is so fragile that it is largely dependent on the American market due to its dire economic conditions (over-indebtedness, inflation, flagrant drop in the value of the currency, etc.).

6. ROBUSTNESS TEST

The primary objective of our research endeavor is to examine the repercussions of the COVID-19 pandemic on the financial stock market index in Saudi Arabia. This examination spans from January 1, 2019 to December 31, 2020. Consequently, the empirical findings of our study demonstrate that announcements pertaining to COVID-19 in the United States significantly influence the stock market indices of various countries within the financial stock market index in Saudi Arabia.

In order to validate these findings, this particular section is dedicated to presenting the Robustness Test of the empirical results. This test is visually displayed in Figure 3, wherein we analyze the conditional volatility of the stock market indices in the financial stock market index in Saudi Arabia. This analysis is conducted both without integration and with integration of the COVID-19 component. The aforementioned figure serves as evidence of the presence of the impact of COVID-19 on financial markets within the financial stock market index in Saudi Arabia throughout the study period from January 1, 2019 to December 31, 2020.

Table 6. The empirical results of GARCH estimation

Stock Market Index	Country	The Estimated Parameters					
		Estimation		$\alpha 0$	αi	βj	μt
SSE_TADAWUL	Saudi Arabia	Estimation Without Integration of Surprise		7.41E-06 (3.5463)*	0.132834 (3.8843)*	0.745536 11.334)*)	-
		Estimation With Integration of Surprise	NCUSA	7.44E-06 3.5364)*)	0.134277 3.3664)*)	0.752623 9.9492)*)	-0.00116 -1.2430))
			CCUSA	7.61E-06 (3.6446)*	0.142563 3.9304)*)	0.742551 10.993)*)	0.004962 0.8876))
			DCUSA	8.33E-06 3.9343)*)	0.111273 3.6374)*)	0.772532 8.8274)*)	**0.002736 5.266**)**)

Notes: This table summarizes the coefficients estimated from GARCH models (1,1). To empirically test this model, we used the daily returns of stock market index of Saudi Arabia during the study period from January 1, 2019 to December 31, 2020. The dependent variable is defined by volatility conditional (h_t) of each stock market index used. $\alpha 0$ αi, βj, and μt are the coefficients of the explanatory variables estimated in our research work. The statistical significance at the threshold of 1%, 5% and 10% is noted *, ** and ***. Values in parentheses show the t-students for each variable..

Figure 3. The conditional volatility of Stock market index in Saudi Arabia without and with COVID-19 surprise
TOP: *The index SSE_TADAWUL without surprise (DCUSA)*
BOTTOM: *The index SSE_TADAWUL with surprise (DCUSA)*

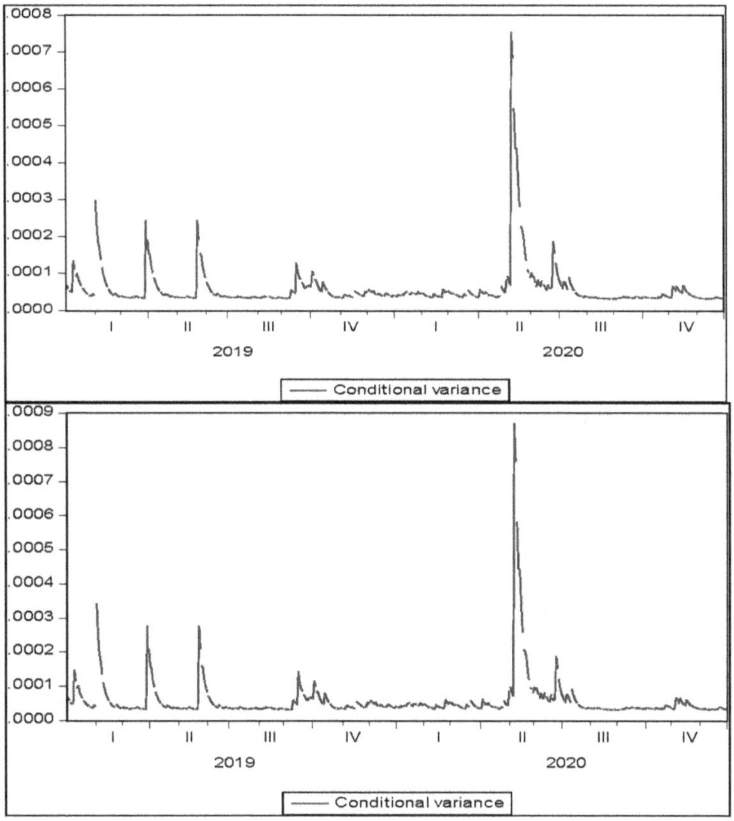

7. CONCLUSION

To accomplish the aim of this paper, we present an extensive literature review on the influence of COVID-19 case announcements on stock market indices across various contexts. This literature review yielded diverse findings. Hence, we formulate three hypotheses to be evaluated at the methodological level. The most suitable model for this study is the GARCH estimation model. The empirical findings indicate that the announcements of new COVID-19 cases in the United States have a positive but statistically insignificant impact on the volatility of the stock market index in Saudi Arabia.

Regarding the announcements of confirmed COVID-19 cases in the United States, they have a relative and statistically insignificant impact on the volatility of the stock market index in Saudi Arabia. Conversely, the announcements of COVID-19 death cases in the United States have a positive and significant impact on the volatility of the stock market index in Saudi Arabia.

In conclusion, we can assert that the announcements of COVID-19 in the United States exert an influence on the volatility of the stock market index in Saudi Arabia. Thus, we have addressed our objective by confirming the existence of an effect of COVID-19 on the financial markets of Saudi Arabia during the study period spanning from January 1, 2019, to December 31, 2020.

REFERENCES

Ahundjanov, B. B., Akhundjanov, S. B., & Okhunjanov, B. B. (2020). Information search and financial markets under COVID-19. Academic Press. PMID:33286562

Al-Awadhi, Alsaifi, Al-Awadhi, & Alhammadi. (2020). Death and contagious infectious diseases: Impact of the COVID-19 virus on stock market returns. *Journal of Behavioral and Experimental Finance*.

Albulescu, C. T. (2020). COVID-19 and the United States financial markets' volatility. *Finance Research Letters*, 38. PMID:32837380

Ashraf, B. N. (2020). Stock markets' reaction to COVID-19: Cases or fatalities? *Research in International Business and Finance*, *54*, 54. doi:10.1016/j.ribaf.2020.101249 PMID:34170989

Baret, Celner, O'Reilly, & Shilling. (2020). COVID-19 potential implications for the banking and capital markets sector. *Maintaining Business and Operational Resilience*.

Ben Ltaifa, M., & Derbali, A. (2021). Confirmed and death cases of COVID-19: Which is informative in explaining the returns and volatilities of Saudi stock market indices? International Journal of Innovation. *Creativity and Change*, *15*(7), 1000–1029.

Bollerslev, T. (1986). Generalized autoregressive conditional heteroskedasticity. *Journal of Econometrics*, *31*(3), 307–327. doi:10.1016/0304-4076(86)90063-1

Costola, Nofer, Hinz, & Pelizzon. (2020). *Machine learning sentiment analysis, Covid-19 news and stock market reactions*. econstor.eu

Derbali, A., Chenguel, M. B., Jamel, L., Jouirou, M., & Jouini, F. (2022b). COVID-19 pandemic and co-movement dynamics among American and European stock markets. Financial Transformations beyond the COVID-19 Health Crisis, 309–346.

Derbali, A., Naoui, K., Ben Sassi, M., & Amiri, M. M. (2021b). Do COVID-19 Epidemic Explains the Dynamic Conditional Correlation between China's Stock Market Index and International Stock Market Indices? *Chinese Economy*, *55*(3), 227–242. doi:10.1080/10971475.2021.1958453

Derbali, A., Naoui, K., & Jamel, L. (2021a). COVID-19 news in USA and in China: Which is suitable in explaining the nexus among Bitcoin and Gold? *Pacific Accounting Review*, *33*(5), 578–595. doi:10.1108/PAR-09-2020-0170

Derbali, A., Naoui, K., & Jamel, L. (2022a). COVID-19 Surprises in China and in the USA: Which Is Useful in Explaining the Dynamic Nexus Among Energy Commodities and Bitcoin? In B. Alareeni & A. Hamdan (Eds.), *Artificial Intelligence and COVID Effect on Accounting. Accounting, Finance, Sustainability, Governance & Fraud: Theory and Application*. Springer. doi:10.1007/978-981-19-1036-4_4

DerbaliA. M. S. (2022). COVID-19 or Russia-Ukraine Conflict: Which Is Informative in Defining the Dynamic Relationship between Bitcoin and Major Energy Commodities? doi:10.2139/ssrn.4280578

Engelhardt, N., Krause, M., Neukirchen, D., & Posch, P. N. (2021). Trust and stock market volatility during the COVID-19 crisis. *Finance Research Letters*, *38*, 101873. doi:10.1016/j.frl.2020.101873 PMID:36569649

Gharib, C., Mefteh-Wali, S., & Jabeur, S. B. (2021). The bubble contagion effect of COVID-19 outbreak: Evidence from crude oil and gold markets. *Finance Research Letters*, *38*, 101703. doi:10.1016/j.frl.2020.101703 PMID:32837382

Ghorbali, B., Naoui, K., & Derbali, A. (2022b). Co-movement Among COVID-19 Pandemic, Crude Oil, Stock Market of US, and Bitcoin: Empirical Evidence from WCA. In B. Alareeni & A. Hamdan (Eds.), *Artificial Intelligence and COVID Effect on Accounting. Accounting, Finance, Sustainability, Governance & Fraud: Theory and Application*. Springer. doi:10.1007/978-981-19-1036-4_3

GhorbaliB.NaouiK.DerbaliA. M. S. (2022a). Does Gold Act as a Safe Haven and Hedge for G7 Stock Markets? A Comparative Assessment between COVID-19 Versus Global Financial Crisis (GFC). doi:10.2139/ssrn.4160586

Goodell, J. W. (2020). COVID-19 and finance: Agendas for future research. *Finance Research Letters*, *35*, 101512. doi:10.1016/j.frl.2020.101512 PMID:32562472

He, P., Sun, Y., Zhang, Y., & Li, T. (2020). COVID-19's market impact on stock prices across different sectors—An event study based on the Chinese stock. *Emerging Markets Finance and Trade*. PMID:32997308

Liu, Wang, & Lee. (2020). Impact of the COVID-19 pandemic on the crude oil and stock markets in the US: A time-varying analysis. *Energy Research Letters, 1*.

OziliP. K.ArunT. (2020). *Spillover of COVID-19: impact on the Global Economy*. doi:10.2139/ssrn.3562570

Phan, D. H. B., & Narayan, P. K. (2020). Country responses and the reaction of the stock market to COVID-19—A preliminary exposition. *Emerging Markets Finance & Trade*, *56*(10), 2138–2150. doi:10.1080/1540496X.2020.1784719

Sansa, N. A. (2020). *The Impact of the COVID-19 on the Financial Markets: Evidence from China and USA*. Electronic Research Journal of Social Sciences and Humanities.

Sharif, Aloui, & Yarovaya. (2020). COVID-19 pandemic, oil prices, stock market, geopolitical risk and policy uncertainty nexus in the US economy: Fresh evidence from the wavelet-based approach. *International Review of Financial Analysis*, 70.

Wagner, A. F. (2020). What the stock market tells us about the post-COVID-19 world. *Nature Human Behaviour*, *4*(5), 440. doi:10.1038/s41562-020-0869-y PMID:32242087

Walid, Sensoy, Vo, & Kang. (2020). *Impact of COVID-19 outbreak on asymmetric multifractality of gold and oil prices*. doi:10.1016/j.resourpol.2020.101829

Youssef, M., Mokni, K., & Ajmi, A. N. (2021). Dynamic connectedness between stock markets in the presence of the COVID-19 pandemic: Does economic policy uncertainty matter? *Financial Innovation*, *7*(1), 13. doi:10.1186/s40854-021-00227-3 PMID:35024274

Zaremba, A., Kizys, R., Aharon, D. Y., & Demir, E. (2020). Infected markets: Novel coronavirus, government interventions, and stock return volatility around the globe. *Finance Research Letters*, *35*(101597), 101597. doi:10.1016/j.frl.2020.101597 PMID:32550842

Zhanga, Hua, & Jibc. (2020). Financial markets under the global pandemic of COVID-19. *Finance Research Letters*, 36. PMID:32837360

Chapter 7
A Semantical Approach to the Concept of CSR:
Its Definitional Evolution and Nearly Identical Notions

Gokcen Evci
https://orcid.org/0000-0003-3110-6046
Istanbul University, Turkey & Yalova University, Turkey

Bengu Vuran
Istanbul University, Turkey

ABSTRACT

As of the publication of Bowen's masterpiece Social Responsibilities of the Businessman in 1953, it can be claimed that people have started to think that corporations have responsibilities to their societies in addition to their principal task of maximising shareholders' value. Corporate social responsibility owes its existence to this paradigm shift. Currently, there are a bunch of notions that are closely related to or somehow intertwined with the concept of corporate social responsibility. This review has been written to discuss the similarities and differences between these terms—triple bottom line, sustainability, corporate social performance, business ethics, corporate social responsiveness, corporate citizenship, corporate governance, corporate philanthropy, socially responsible investment, environmental, social and governance—and corporate social responsibility, as well as to provide frequently cited definitions of this concept.

INTRODUCTION

When Bowen published his seminal book, Social Responsibilities of the Businessman, in 1953, corporate social responsibility (CSR) was not a new concept. However, as of

DOI: 10.4018/979-8-3693-1511-8.ch007

this date, one can say that the common paradigm ‘the sole objective of a business is maximising the value of its shareholders’ has started to shift to the view advocating ‘a business entity has responsibilities to its society, at all’. As of the 1980s, new concepts closely related to or somehow intertwined with the term CSR have begun to emerge or are said to be used as relevant synonyms. This review has been written to clarify and simplify the complexity regarding the abundance of terms referring to CSR and to present the most-cited definitions of this topic from the past six decades.

The next section of this review presents a bunch of relevant definitions directly related to CSR. The third part handles the main concepts that are closely related to CSR, namely, triple bottom line (3BL), sustainability, and corporate social performance (CSP). The fourth part of this review continues with other relevant concepts: business ethics, corporate social responsiveness, corporate citizenship (CC), corporate governance (CG), corporate philanthropy, socially responsible investment (SRI), and environmental, social and governance (ESG). These two parts are examined separately, as the former encompasses notions that are comparatively harder to distinguish from CSR. The final section provides a summary and a discussion of the review. It also put forward suggestions for future researchers regarding the development of the theory of CSR and related concepts.

POPULAR DEFINITIONS OF CORPORATE SOCIAL RESPONSIBILITY

Before moving on to concepts related to CSR, it is better to review some, particularly highly cited, definitions of CSR.

Starting with the main concept of CSR, Bowen, in *Social Responsibilities of the Businessman*, defined the social responsibility of a businessman as maintaining necessary policies, making decisions, and following the course of actions in terms of the related society’s objectives and values. In its broadest sense, social responsibility implies considering a businessman’s voluntary participation in social responsibility as a practical means to address economic problems and to acquire wider economic goals being pursued (Bowen, 2013, p. 6).

Davis (1960, pp. 70–71) explained social responsibility as the decisions of businessmen regarding their firms, at least partially, beyond economic and technical matters and their actions. Here, the social responsibility of a businessman covers both economic developments affecting public welfare and protecting and enhancing human values. Davis (1967, p. 46) stated that social responsibility is closely related to the ethical outcomes of personal actions, and it underlines the importance of the position and actions of corporations. Davis (1973, pp. 312–313) claimed that social responsibility goes beyond a firm's technical, economic, and legal requirements and begins where the law ends.

Friedman (1970, 2002, pp. 133–134) thought that the only social responsibility of a company is efficiently allocating and utilising its resources and operating in a way to maximise its profits. According to this view, as the companies do not have real personalities, they also cannot have so-called "social" responsibilities. As the concept is seen as a destructive one to a company, it may lead to agency problems within the business.

There are four different ways to define CSR, according to Johnson (1971, as cited in Carroll, 1999, pp. 273–274): First, a "corporate" socially responsible firm is a firm that considers stakeholders' interests. In the second and third definitions, CSR involves long-term profit maximisation and utility maximisation, respectively. Last, reaching a certain profit margin is the primary objective, and other objectives, such as CSR, follow this objective.

In Carroll (1979, pp. 499–500), social responsibility encompasses economic, legal, ethical and discretionary responsibilities, ranked in order of relative evolutionary importance. Carroll (1983, p. 604) defined CSR, from an economic perspective, as managing a company in a lucrative, observant, ethically and socially supportive manner. In another study, Carroll (1991, p. 42) depicts CSR as a pyramid of its elements, namely, economic, legal, ethical, and philanthropic responsibilities.[1] Carroll (2015, pp. 90–91) provided a new definition for CSR as the adoption of activities that are not required by law or legislation, namely, ethical and philanthropic categories.

Jones (1980, pp. 59–60) described CSR as an institution's voluntary and comprehensive obligation to social groups other than shareholders and beyond what is required by law or union agreements. Furthermore, CSR is here defined as a process, not a set of outcomes.

Epstein (1987, p. 104) associated CSR principally with producing results from corporate decisions regarding specific problems having advantageous impacts on relevant stakeholders. CSR fundamentally concentrates on the ethical propriety of business activities' outcomes.

Lantos (2001, pp. 595, 600) defined CSR as an implicit agreement between society and business that maximises (minimises) the positive (negative) impacts of companies on society to meet its long-standing needs and wants. Here, CSR was examined in three dimensions: ethical, altruistic and strategic. While ethical CSR (avoiding societal harms) is mandatory for any organisation, altruistic CSR (doing good deeds at probable expense to shareholders) is not legitimate for a public company, and philanthropy in a business is expected to be restricted by strategic CSR (doing good deeds that are also good for the business).

McWilliams and Siegel (2006, pp. 1–2) defined CSR as a company going beyond compliance to develop some social good beyond its interests and legal requirements.

They added that CSR activities include integrating social characters and features into products and fabrication processes, adopting innovative human resource practices, improving environmental performance through recycling and pollution mitigation, and promoting community objectives.

The European Commission (2011, p. 6) defined CSR as firms' responsibility for their social impacts, particularly by complying with current law and collective agreements between parties. Corporations are expected to establish an integration of human rights, ethical, consumer, social, and environmental issues into their strategies and corporate activities. This process involves working together with stakeholders and aims at maximising shared value creation for society and specifying, avoiding, and alleviating the potential challenges' undesirable effects.

According to the MVO Platform (2012, p. 4), CSR can be defined as an outcome-oriented process, assuming that companies bear responsibility for all their activities related to the social, economic, and ecological outcomes of their practices and that they behave in an accountable and transparent manner to their stakeholders regarding those issues.

According to BSR, a socially responsible company creates value for and enhances the living standards of its stakeholders, efficiently uses resources, and fairly treats people (Olson, 2013: para. 8).

In brief, CSR refers to a company's acknowledgement of its stakeholders' interests, respect for and adherence to ethics, and support for others' well-being, in addition to taking its own economic interests into account.

The next section deals with other concepts closely related to, even intertwined with, CSR.

CONCEPTS CLOSELY RELATED TO CORPORATE SOCIAL RESPONSIBILITY

CSR is the foundation of many related issues and concepts, most of which have embraced the standpoint of CSR and are compatible with this notion (Carroll, 2008, p. 37). CSR gains its meaning depending on the context in which it is used and, thereby, is associated with other concepts (Barauskaite & Streimikiene, 2020, p. 2). This section investigates concepts almost inextricably connected to CSR.

Triple Bottom Line (3BL)

Elkington (2004, p. 1) proposed the concept of the 3BL. He referred to this approach as a fork, and its three prongs are "social justice", "environmental quality" and "economic prosperity". The economic dimension has concentrated upon the profit figure. The social dimension deals with social, ethical, and political matters. The environmental dimension has gained significance through increased attention to auditing and social accounting. Dimensions are unstable because of political, environmental, economic, and social cycles, pressures, and controversies. Each dimension can be seen as a continental plate, and these dimensions usually independently move. (Elkington, 1997). Elkington (2004, p. 2) also developed the 3P formulation, namely "people", "planet" and "profits". These terms are synonyms for 3BL's social justice (human capital), environmental quality (natural capital) and economic prosperity (economic value added), respectively (Sukoharsono, 2019, pp. 124–125).

According to Wood (2011, p. 32), companies, governments, and organisations can determine explicitly agreed-upon 3BL standards and objectives for societal interests and environmental emissions at the project-specific level. Those objectives can develop performance metrics to be monitored throughout the project and can be used to assess the project's performance against those benchmarks over time. On the other hand, CSR strategies do not entail such a rigorous level of transparency, accountability, and benchmarking. Another difference between CSR and the 3BL is, according to Brusseau (2012, pp. 595–596), related to culture. While the notion of CSR is claimed to be more American, the term 3BL sounds more European. Americans regard change as a favourable opportunity. They use business to change the world, and ethical thinking aids in maximising social development. Europeans think that change is an unpleasant process. They are more likely to maintain a steady state of change, more in line with the 3BL.

Sustainability

Leopold (1949, pp. 224–225), in "A Sand County Almanac", stated that an action is morally acceptable as long as it is prone to maintaining the aesthetics, integrity, and steadiness of the living system. According to Wiens (2013, p. 1047), this statement forms the essence of the notion of sustainability.

Meadows et al. (1972, pp. 190–195), in the report "The Limits to Growth", declared that continuous exponential growth would result in the collapse of the system and that immediate action is necessary to prevent this situation. The limits for growth, the need for sustainability of the economic process, the demand for justice, democracy, and equality, and the complexity of systems led to the inquiry regarding the existing paradigm in terms of knowledge and modern society. Under these circumstances, the 1972 United Nations Conference on the Human Environment took place in Stockholm (Leff, 1997, p. 1). According to Basiago (1995, p. 110), this is the first conference to bring developing and developed nations together regarding a productive and healthy environment. It was the first step taken for later treaties to be made relating to the environment, natural life, global commons, and the inheritance of generations.

Following a thorough investigation of the development-environment relationship, the General Assembly officially decided to form the Brundtland Commission (the World Commission on Environment and Development) in 1983. Then, Our Common Future, the Brundtland Report, was published as an urgent warning based on the latest scientific evidence to make decisions regarding resource protection so that intergenerational relationships could be pursued (United Nations General Assembly [UNGA], 1987, p. 18). As a result of this report, masses of people regard sustainability as sustainable development (Holden et al., 2014, p. 132).

After the Brundtland Report, the Earth Summit was organised in Rio de Janeiro. It highlights the immediate need for an action plan to protect natural resources and the establishment of an intense collaboration on development and environmental policies. At the Earth Summit, six critical documents, namely the Rio Declaration, the Forest Principles, the Framework Convention on Climate Change, the Convention on Biological Diversity, the Convention to Combat Desertification and Agenda 21, were adopted (Spindler, 2013, p. 16).[2]

Following the Earth Summit, similar summits were held periodically. They were Rio+5 (New York, 1997), Rio+10 (Johannesburg, 2002), and Rio+20 (Rio de Janeiro, 2012) (Dernbach, 2012, p. 2).[3] The issues considered throughout these summits and in their plans were similar: international economic climate, ecosystems, natural resources, biodiversity, atmosphere, oceans and seas, freshwater, forests, energy, drought and desertification, waste, chemicals, radioactivity, land and agriculture, trade and environment, consumption and production, development, globalisation, infrastructure, settlement, population, inequalities, vulnerable groups, unemployment, human welfare, Small Island Developing States, Africa, health, tourism, transportation, knowledge, technology, digitalisation, financial resources and mechanisms, education, science, peace, human rights, justice, global partnerships, political commitment, societies and institutions, governmental actions, and so on (UN, 2002, 2022; UNGA, 1997, 2012, 2015).

Another series of conferences that made a major contribution to the advancement of sustainability were the Habitat conferences.[4] The products of Habitat conferences mainly concentrated on human settlement and urbanisation. However, they also considered sustainable development, economic growth, human rights, health, unemployment, education, discrimination, security, poverty, violence, nutrition, inequalities, immigration, cooperation, environmental protection, biodiversity, energy, and similar issues (UN, 1976, pp. 3–4, 1996; UNGA, 2017).

The 1990s were years of witnessing the preparation and sharing of reporting methodologies based on sustainable development (Gokten et al., 2020, p. 110). The Global Reporting Initiative (GRI) was founded to provide the first accountability mechanism to guarantee that companies remain faithful to responsible environmental enforcement principles that will later expand to include their social, governmental and economic problems (Global Reporting Initiative [GRI], n.d., para. 1). The Carbon Disclosure Project (CDP) was initiated to collect and share high-quality information to inspire corporations, investors, and governments to mitigate climate change (Association of Chartered Certified Accountants, 2011, p. 8). The International Integrated Reporting Council (IIRC) started its activities to develop integrated reporting practices, guide institutions that want to prepare integrated reports and establish international reporting standards (Kaya & Utku, 2020, p. 285). The Sustainability Accounting Standards Board (SASB) was established to define, manage, and transfer information that is financially sustainable to investors (Godelnik, 2021, p. 45). The Climate Disclosure Standards Board (CDSB) (2019, p.1) was created to standardise environmental reporting by identifying and integrating widely adopted reporting systems and collaborations. In 2020, GRI, CDP, IIRC, SASB, and CDSB decided to act in the direction of an integrated corporate reporting strategy to prevent complications between producers and consumers of sustainability information. A shared market strategy for standards and frameworks, a common vision to create a more comprehensive and internally consistent corporate reporting framework, and the joint participation of all stakeholders, including integrated reporting organisations, have been and will be supported by this cooperation (CDP et al., 2020, pp. 2–3).

Sustainability can be used interchangeably with CSR and the 3BL (Kolk, 2008, p. 2). Fernandez-Feijoo et al. (2012, p. 33) stated that with the establishment of GRI, CSR has converted into 3BL, and this approach can be adopted by sustainability as an information system. Van Marrewijk (2003, pp. 101–102) claimed that sustainability is the last target, and CSR is the middle step where corporations attempt to balance the 3BL. Another perspective discussed in this study suggested that CSR, namely social responsibility, together with economic and environmental responsibility, forms corporate responsibility, and corporate sustainability encompasses corporate responsibility. He thought that CSR can be associated with stakeholder dialogue, sustainable reporting, and transparency, whilst corporate sustainability is regarding value creation, human capital management, environmentally friendly production systems, environmental management, and similar concepts. Weber (2008, p. 248) argued that CSR just consists of social and environmental dimensions, and economic success is only a possible outcome of those dimensions. Therefore, CSR can be seen as a subset of corporate sustainability. She also contended that CSR offers short-term benefits for business and society, whereas sustainability is a long-term strategy.

Corporate Social Performance (CSP)

According to Wood (2010, p. 51), considering performance from a corporate and social point of view stems from Boulding's assessment of complex organisations that have complex structures as open systems. Thielen (2005, p. 18) stated that as of the 1970s, the term CSP has been often used in business and society studies as a method for assessment.

There is no universal definition of CSP (Mitnick, 2000, p. 427). According to Wood (2010, p. 50), CSP is disputed, dynamic, equivocal, and hard to research. She mentioned that equating CSP with 'doing good' and concentrating on the financial-social performance relationship in research might decelerate theory-building in this domain. On the other hand, to create a conceptual framework, there is significant CSP literature.

One of the oldest articles regarding CSP belongs to Sethi (1975). He defined corporate behaviour as a three-stage phenomenon based upon the change of the legitimacy concept, ranging from too narrow to too broad: social obligation, social responsibility and social responsiveness. Social obligation was seen as corporate behaviour against legal restrictions and market forces. Social responsibility was seen as a tool for making corporate behaviour compatible with prevalent social norms, values, and performance expectations. Social responsiveness was said to determine the long-run function of corporations in a dynamic setup. To minimise the unintended results of their actions, corporations are expected to prepare programmes and policies. Finally, he listed the dimensions and characteristics of corporate behaviour under the categories mentioned. Carroll (2021, p. 4) claimed that Sethi (1975) used performance as a common term since he did not distinguish it from responsibility and responsiveness. Wood (1991, p. 691) mentioned that Sethi (1975) just suggested categories to assess CSP.[5] Mitnick (1993, p. 9) stated that there is no theory logic in this study.

Carroll (1979) offered a conceptual model to comprehensively describe CSP's basic elements. His CSP model had three parts: the components of the definition of social responsibility, the scope of the social issues the management will address, and the continuum of social responsiveness that assists in considering dominant questions that will arise throughout social performance analyses. Carroll (1979) has been accepted as the first conceptual model of CSP (Wood, 2010, p. 52). Wood (1991, p. 692) stated that Carroll (1979) did not properly define CSP. Kang (1995, pp. 59–63) remarked that Carroll (1979) lacks efficient and appropriate categorisation properties since the criteria used there were complicated, the responsibilities were not based on a theory, and there might be complexities in the responsibilities defined. According to Wood (2010, p. 53), Carroll (1979) ignored the sociological complexity of managers' roles in society and their behavioural effects.

Wartick and Cochran's (1985) model reflects the interaction among social responsibility principles, the social responsiveness process, and policies developed to deal with social issues. The economic and public responsibilities here were combined with a more comprehensive definition of social responsibility within the performance model. Social responsiveness was added to the model as a critical connection between reactions to social issues and social responsibilities. The management of social issues was mentioned as the still-developing dimension of performance. The principles of CSR consist of the economic, legal, ethical and discretionary categories. The processes of corporate social responsiveness consist of reactive, proactive, accommodative and defensive categories.[6] The social issues management process consists of the determination of the issues, their analyses and response development. Wood (1991, pp. 692–693) criticised Wartick and Cochran (1985) for considering performance as actions and results, handling corporate responsiveness as a single process, restricting the last performance dimension due to no performance implication, and considering CSP as a concept only for responsible companies. Mitnick (1993, p. 14) questioned the reasons for the choice of principles and processes, the content of components, and the overlap of categories. There are also other weaknesses attached to Wartick and Cochran (1985), such as fundamental definitions, the inability to test model components, incompatibility between the model and data, and the model's lack of stakeholder considerations (Clarkson, 1995, pp. 96–98; Wood & Jones, 1995, p. 236).

Wood (1991) stated that she described CSP and reformulated the performance model to create a unifying framework. She defined CSP as the arrangement of social responsibility principles, social responsiveness processes, programmes, policies, and observable outcomes. Social responsibility perspectives were applied to three levels: individual, organisational and institutional. By distinguishing principle from category, she named principles as legitimacy, public responsibility and managerial discretion. Legitimacy reveals the expectations of the business by defining the corporate relationship between society and the corporation. Public responsibility claims that businesses are responsible for their activities' results. Managerial discretion describes managers' responsibility as moral actors. Social responsiveness was considered the connection point of environmental assessment, stakeholder management and issues management processes. The social impacts of behaviour, programmes and policies were investigated as the types of CSP outcomes, the only dimension of the model with real performance. According to Carroll (2021, p. 4), Wood's (1991) emphasis on impacts and outcomes has influenced the current evolution of the CSP structure. Mitnick (1993, p. 16) recommended that the level of principles in Wood (1991) be individual-organisational-systemic. He claimed that although the requirement for responsible behaviour was stated, it was not defined. There might also be other principles and processes. Ten Pierick et al. (2004) criticised the relevant study for the shortage of information on the judge, who ultimately decides between objectivity and subjectivity and "good" and "bad", and for the randomness of the choice of principles. Despite all the criticisms, ten Pierick et al. (2004) asserted that neglecting any element of Wood (1991) is likely to generate biased, erroneous, and limited assessments of the CSP model.

In addition to these primary studies in the literature, there is also other noticeable research with a significant number of references. They usually focus on the measurement of CSP and the social-financial performance relationship. There are also researchers attempting to develop alternative approaches to broaden the scope of existing studies. The relevance of stakeholder theory for CSP has also been stressed in some research. This review briefly mentions only some of them due to space constraints.

Wood and Jones (1995) reviewed studies examining financial and social performance by applying meta-analysis in terms of a stakeholder framework. Accordingly, most studies used performance measures independent of the theory. By classifying previous empirical research by stakeholders represented in relevant performance measures, they proved the presence of stakeholder mismatches. They suggested that to increase the consistency of the studies, the expectations, impacts, and assessments are required to be more accurately matched with stakeholders of interest. Wood (2010) claims that there is no considerable evidence for CSP being too costly, whilst being socially irresponsible is expensive. Carroll (2021), after reviewing CSR studies before 2000, concentrated on research finding a positive financial-social performance relationship between 2000 and 2020, and he interpreted this situation as "the advantage of doing good". According to him, if doing good really works in financial performance terms, managers are anticipated to strategically employ corporate social activities to achieve maximum impact.

Several researchers examined the differences between CSR and performance. Ackerman and Bauer (1976, p. 6) stated that social responsibility evokes the process of taking on an obligation and lays stress on motivation. Wood (2010, pp. 52, 54) also attached importance to the immeasurability of the notion of responsibility. Orlitzky (2005, p. 51) claimed that CSP is a broader concept including social responsibility principles. Lu et al. (2014, p. 196) argued that CSP is measurable via proxies, making CSR applicable. Moreover, they also claimed that CSR stresses accountability and obligation, and CSP emphasises results and outcomes, so it can be accepted as an extended notion derived from CSR. Wang (2015, p. 18) contended that CSR is a broader notion, and CSP is solely used to define CSR actions and reflect the dimensions of responsibility strategies of the relevant firm.

This section has particularly discussed the main topics closely related to and often used interchangeably with CSR. It has especially provided cult studies related to the relevant subjects, deep criticisms of them and similarities and differences between these topics. The next section will examine, in a similar manner, further subjects associated with CSR.

OTHER CONCEPTS RELATED TO CORPORATE SOCIAL RESPONSIBILITY

Aside from the terms that are primarily related to CSR, there are also additional associated concepts comprehensively investigated below.

Business Ethics

Business ethics is a thought system stemming from moral duties and responsibilities. They can also be seen as principles and values. Business ethics examines the subjects of the accuracy and fairness of business and the actions, behaviours, and principles of managers and employees within a commercial network. With the rise of corporate scandals, it has become a popular framework for evaluating a company's activities, alongside CSR (Carroll, 2015, p. 92).

Business ethics and CSR are applied for objectives such as cost- and risk minimisation, competitive advantage, reputation, legitimacy, and value creation (Weller, 2020, p. 520). According to some analysts, CSR accepts all companies as a whole, whereas business ethics is evaluated as dependent upon the behaviours of certain corporate leaders (Carroll, 2015, p. 92). Fassin et al. (2011, pp. 426–427) stated that the notions of CSR and business ethics frequently overlap and intersect. It leads to uncertainties in conceptualisation, conflicts in terminology, and dilemmas in interpretation when using those concepts together as encompassing different concepts. Weller (2020, p. 520) listed three central views on the application of CSR and business ethics in academic studies. The first advocates that those concepts are the same, except for being applied to some organisations or different analysis units. The second view is regarding one term being part of the other. According to the third view, although those concepts are related, they serve different purposes. Cacioppe et al. (2008, p. 697) emphasise that CSR is a more macro-concept because of its interest in the sensitive environment and employees of a company, whilst business ethics is a more micro-concept due to its tendency towards behaviours. Fassin et al. (2011, p. 442), similarly, claimed that CSR is more externally driven, more theory-based, more pragmatic, and more workplace-oriented.

Corporate Social Responsiveness

Corporate social responsiveness, CSR_2, is an action-oriented management concept that mainly aims to interact with stakeholders and be compatible with public policies and is interested in the response capacity of corporations to social pressures (Frederick, 1986, p. 130, 1994, p. 150, 2008, p. 525). According to Carroll (1979, p. 502), CSR involves moral and ethical threads, whereas corporate social responsiveness deals with managerial response processes such as social decision-making, the organisation of social responses, corporate social politics, the control of social activities, and planning and social predictive analytics. Sethi (1975, pp. 62–64) claimed that the activities related to corporate social responsiveness are protective and future-oriented, as opposed to the normativeness of CSR. Swanson (2008, p. 231) stated that corporate social responsiveness is a more forward-looking and controllable concept. According to Epstein (1987, pp. 104–106), CSR aims at concluding organisational decisions related to certain issues that have beneficial impacts on stakeholders, whereas corporate social responsiveness is principally regarding the development of individual and organisational decision-making processes.

Corporate Citizenship (CC)

Marsden (2000, p. 11) defined CC as the effects of a company's management on the rest of society and its relationships with society. According to Post and Berman (2001, p. 68), CC involves the real outcomes of corporations' activities and the ways used to achieve them. Panapanaan et al. (2003, p. 141) explained CC as a concept where a community legitimises a company's presence through its inclusion and participation in community events and development.

According to Carroll (2008, p. 37), CC can be broadly or narrowly expressed. CC, in its broadest sense, encompasses the content of CSR. As in CSR, CC also has responsibilities to shoulder, just as every citizen is anticipated to do. On the other hand, the narrow view of CC consists of corporate community relations and only the philanthropy dimension of the CSR definition. Matten et al. (2003, pp. 112–117) advocated three different CC views. According to the limited view, CC is related to philanthropic activities that a company engages in. In the equivalent view, CC can be seen as equivalent to CSR. The extended view represents a view beyond the concepts stemming from CSR. Accordingly, corporations come into effect when governments fall short in terms of the protection of citizenship. Logsdon and Wood (2002, p. 160) claimed that in CSR, companies act in the stakeholders' best interests beyond legislation and encourage the main ethical principles. It is compulsory and voluntary. Corporations care about stakeholders, problems, and doing what is right. This concept is hard to understand, verify, apply, measure, and evaluate. In CC, there are minimum legal requirements. Giving back to the community is expected. Accordingly, acceptable voluntary moves are widely observed, and there are no penalties for not doing so. Charity and communication are narrowly focused. It is specific, restricted, measurable, and defendable. Melé (2008, p. 69) claimed that CSR considers social responsibilities as external, whereas CC recommends that society encompasses business as one of its elements.

Corporate Governance (CG)

Corporate governance was first defined by Eells as the structure and operation of a company's corporate systems, processes, and decision-making procedures (Becht et al., 2003, p. 5). Recent literature defines this term as a system formed by market-oriented and corporate mechanisms that can be utilised by all elements of society (Bhaduri & Selarka, 2016, p. 2).

Stakeholder and agency theories have been widely used to explain the CSR-CG relationship. According to the stakeholder theory (Freeman, 1984), a company is expected to consider in all its organisational processes everyone who can directly affect or be affected by the process of reaching its goals. Jo and Harjoto (2012, p. 56) claimed that if CSR activities are perceived as efforts by CG mechanisms to find a solution for conflicts, one can expect a positive CG-CSR relationship. The agency theory examines the conflicts of interest stemming from the transfer of decision-making authority from the principal(s) to the agent, their likely effects on both parties, and how to prevent them (Jensen & Meckling, 1976). Oh et al. (2018, pp. 2718–2719) stated that although agency theory claims that efficacious CG mechanisms positively affect financial indicators, the relationship between CG mechanisms and non-financial social indicators like CSR is unclear. Accordingly, if governance bodies believe socially responsible decisions can boost business financial performance, effective CG mechanisms can support CSR. Otherwise, CSR is an overinvestment. Jo and Harjoto (2012, pp. 55–56) predict a negative CG-CSR relationship since corporate managers are likely to overinvest to improve their reputation.

Harjoto and Jo (2011) specified four hypotheses to explain CG-CSR relationship: The first hypothesis was overinvestment, where the presence of CG will prevent overinvestment in CSR. The second hypothesis was strategic choice, where managers under the threat of termination will engage in CSR activities to draw support from social and environmental activities that will reduce corporate turnover later. The third hypothesis was product-signalling/differentiation, where companies use CSR as a signal for product quality and to differentiate themselves from their competitors. If it is valid, governance mechanisms will not affect the involvement in CSR activities. The last hypothesis was conflict resolution, where managers use CSR as a tool to reduce conflicts between investing and non-investing stakeholders. If it is correct, companies that use governance mechanisms more effectively will contribute more to CSR. Jamali et al. (2008) examined CG-CSR relationships. According to their model, where CG is a part of CSR, an effective CG system is required to provide holistic and strong CSR activities. According to their model, where CSR is an element of CG, managers' qualifications, which also encompass CSR, can be holistically examined with various characteristics such as managing capital market pressure, strategic leadership, and corporate board structure. In the model where CG and CSR are parts of the same process, those two terms cannot be separately investigated.

Oh et al. (2018, pp. 2719–2721) associated the inconsistency of CG-CSR relationship with CG mechanisms' independent impacts. Accordingly, one can achieve more consistent results by employing multiple CG mechanisms. If the marginal effect of a specific governance mechanism adversely affects the impact of other mechanisms on CSR, using multiple governance mechanisms may be costly. Rediker and Seth (1995, p. 87) discussed econometric issues due to multiple CG mechanisms. Accordingly, in a study examining the effects of governance structures, if there is a correlation between an omitted variable and an independent variable in the model, then the slope estimator of the independent variable becomes biased and inconsistent.[7] If different governance mechanisms are used interchangeably, it will become more difficult to interpret the studies' findings. When multiple governance mechanisms are explanatory variables, multicollinearity[8] may occur, and this will make the regression parameter estimates imprecise[9], which will reduce the power of tests.

Corporate Philanthropy

Philanthropy is used to describe companies allocating resources to enhance the welfare of others through altruistic means (Oliver, 2021, p. 55). Muller et al. (2014, p. 1) defined corporate philanthropy as the corporate allocation of time, goods, and money to fulfil social needs. It encompasses cash contributions, donations, and grants and has been one of the most preferred ways of giving back to society by companies (Schwab, 2008, p. 112).

According to Carroll (1991, p. 42), corporate philanthropy consists of corporate actions taken in response to societal expectations regarding businesses being good corporate citizens. Porter (2003) recommended that "doing the true thing" is not an adequate philanthropic strategy. The principal goal of corporate philanthropy is to maximise the social value created. The most effective ways to reach this goal are to choose the best individuals and companies to donate to, strengthen knowledge and practice, enhance the performance of grant holders, and cooperate with other fundraisers.

Luetkenhorst (2004, p. 158) stated that CSR refers to a company's operations, and philanthropy is beside the point within this context. Brown (2003, para. 34) claimed that socially responsible behaviour is related both to donations and internal and external business processes. According to Porter (2003), corporate philanthropy is the grant of money and other resources for social purposes, whilst CSR is a concept working following the principles and essence of the law, attempting to minimise or fix any harm related to corporate operations, and focusing upon the sustainable development of natural resources.

Socially Responsible Investment (SRI)

SRI can be defined as the sum of non-financial decisions and decisions on funds and portfolio management (Beardsell, 2008, para. 28). SRIs are helpful tools to create, assess, and share socially responsible policies (Moon, 2007, p. 299). The expansion of the market for SRIs influences the explanations of corporations regarding social responsibility. Screening SRIs has also had effects on CSR reporting. Additionally, SRI funds might reject a company that participates in CSR activities. In such a case, companies can review and enhance their operations (Beardsell, 2008, p. 8).

According to Mill (2006, p. 132), CSR and SRI are closely related since many investors see SRI as choosing shares from a group of public companies that meet the criteria of being socially responsible. Sparkes (2002, pp. 42, 65) purported that CSR and SRI require corporations to improve society's welfare within certain environmental and social frameworks. CSR materialises this through companies' perspectives, whereas SRI considers the opinions of firms' investors. According to Scholtens and Sievänen (2013, p. 606), an indirect CSR-SRI relationship exists. Accordingly, CSR is directly related to a firm's social, environmental, ethical and governance practices, whilst SRI refers to the practices of investors who place importance on CSR.

Environmental, Social and Governance (ESG)

In the early 2000s, to concretise SRI and with the increasing interest in this area, "environmental, social and governance" was developed by adding the governance factor to financial, environmental and social aspects (Fulton et al., 2012, p. 21). Today, it has become an active profit-driven investment strategy based on trust and is expected to boost risk-adjusted returns and provide direct returns to investors (Schanzenbach & Sitkoff, 2020, pp. 388–390).

According to MacNeil and Esser (2022), ESG does not take the place of CSR. Companies still report CSR activities to show how various social obligations have been met and how profit maximisation and social responsibility have been balanced.

In this study, the differences between CSR and ESG were tabulated. Accordingly, CSR focuses on accountability and ethics, implements politics related to the decision-making mechanisms and corporate structures, does not intensively use metrics, and is based upon non-financial reporting. ESG concentrates on portfolio return and risk based on benchmarks, indices, and metrics. It is implemented through portfolio selection and participation. It consists of a variety of metrics and involves reporting via global sustainability frameworks. According to Kaźmierczak (2022), CSR is an overall sustainability framework that affects a company's internal processes and its organisational culture, is highly demanded by internal and external parties, builds accountability, concentrates upon qualitative data, such as videos and photos, and can help a company articulate its values to its stakeholders. On the other hand, ESG is a popular measurable and quantifiable term among investors. It shows to what extent a company attaches importance to sustainability matters, is regarding computing present accountability, provides data for analysis, and can demonstrate to the investors of a company adopting this framework that its endeavours for this concept yield positive results.

SUMMARY, DISCUSSION, AND REVIEW IMPLICATIONS

From the past to the present, in addition to acting legally compliant and reaping profits, businesses have attempted to pay great attention to social and environmental matters and maintain their relationships with internal and external parties. Balancing these subjects will result in a considerable competitive advantage. CSR becomes relevant at this point.

In this study, first, widely used definitions of CSR have been given. Reviewing these definitions leads to societal expectations from businesses over time, which increase parallel to the rise of the significance attached to human rights, societal groups, ethical behaviour, and social and environmental issues.

CSR gains meaning according to the context in which it is used and, thereby, is associated with similar notions, the most crucial of which are the 3BL, sustainability, and CSP. The 3BL consists of dimensions targeting people, environment and profit, which are expected to be used in performance evaluations of a socially responsible business. The concept of the 3BL can be applied and tracked on a project-specific basis. CSR, on the other hand, is usually firm-specific and aims at high-level social development. Sustainability is a paradigm shift stemming from corporate social responsibility moving to a sustainable world. Sustainability is the main theme of numerous international conferences and their products. By covering integrated reporting and a wide range of issues, sustainability can be said to be a more advanced phase of CSR. Businesses can stay sustainable as long as they are aware of their social responsibilities and do not ignore the interests of their stakeholders. CSP, here, is examined on a theoretical basis. Most researchers consider CSR as a CSP dimension consisting of principles. From this perspective, there is no meaning in asking whether CSR can be measured or not since principles are not observable. As CSR is more external, one can claim that it is more concerned with stakeholders. Previous studies emphasised the costs of being socially irresponsible. From this angle, the judgement of the "immeasurability" of responsibility or irresponsibility becomes nonsense. Nevertheless, it would be more appropriate to consider measurability in terms of CSP.

Alternative notions that are frequently used interchangeably with CSR are also investigated. Business ethics advocates a business being fair and accurate to stand strong against corporate scandals. Previous studies treated CSR more theoretically and claimed that it addresses a wider environment, whilst business ethics is more internal and behaviour-focused. Most CSR definitions include ethics, so one can claim that being ethical entails being socially responsible. Corporate social responsiveness has often been mentioned as a part of CSP that is distinct from CSR. In contrast to the normativeness of CSR, the future-oriented and protective nature of social responsiveness has been stressed. Undoubtedly, a company's stability and strength in terms of responsiveness in shaping stakeholder relationships will add value to its socially responsible image. CC sees business as a part of society. Aside from having the responsibility dimensions that CSR also has, CC supports businesses' identity in society. So, it would be unsuitable to approach this concept with the narrow view of CC, which highlights the notion of philanthropy complying with businesses being good citizens. CG can be assessed as a sub-concept of CSR when metrics are considered. However, various hypotheses show that the relationship between them is ambiguous. Thus, econometrics issues related to measurement should be considered. Corporate philanthropy aims to have a high reputation in the eyes of society by being a good citizen beyond being altruistic. However, it would not be appropriate to limit CSR with this view. CSR deals with all of a business's internal and external activities. SRI, whose target group is a company's investors, is separate from CSR, which deals with all the company's stakeholders. From this point of view, it is debatable to what extent the investment instrument in question meets the basic requirements of being socially responsible. The concept of ESG, which is based on metrics and assesses return and risk, differs from CSR, which has a normative, ethics- and accountability-based nature. On the other hand, since it successfully materialises socially responsible companies through addressing measurability, it is a concept open to development.

Considering all the concepts above, it can be said that they are closely intertwined, despite some minor differences. It is also obvious that the starting point of all these notions is a more sensitive company to social and environmental issues and stakeholders, or society as a whole, that rewards businesses that are aware of their responsibilities. However, what needs to be done is to develop high-quality and robust measurement tools that can be applied to different industries, contexts, and cultures, as well as to contribute to the advancement of the theory of CSR.

REFERENCES

Ackerman, R. W., & Bauer, R. A. (1976). *Corporate social responsiveness: The modern dilemma.* Reston.

Association of Chartered Certified Accountants. (2011). *Accountancy futures: The carbon we're not counting: Accounting for scope 3 carbon emissions.* Association of Chartered Certified Accountants. https://www.accaglobal.com/content/dam/acca/global/PDF-technical/climate-change/not_counting.pdf

Barauskaite, G., & Streimikiene, D. (2020). Corporate social responsibility and financial performance of companies: The puzzle of concepts, definitions and assessment methods. *Corporate Social Responsibility and Environmental Management, 28*(1), 1–10. doi:10.1002/csr.2048

Basiago, A. D. (1995). Methods of defining sustainability. *Sustainable Development (Bradford), 3*(3), 109–119. doi:10.1002/sd.3460030302

Beardsell, J. (2008, November 21). *The influence of CSR disclosure on corporate governance and company performance* (SMC Working Paper 11/2208 ISSN 1662-761X). Swiss Management Center. doi:10.2139/ssrn.1302314

Becht, M., Bolton, P., & Röell, A. (2003). Corporate governance and control. In G. M. Constantinides, M. Harris, & R. M. Stulz (Eds.), Handbook of the economics of finance (Vol. 1A, pp. 1-109). Elsevier. doi:10.1016/S1574-0102(03)01005-7

Bhaduri, S. N., & Selarka, E. (2016). *Corporate governance and corporate social responsibility of Indian companies.* Springer. doi:10.1007/978-981-10-0925-9

Bowen, H. R. (2013). *Social responsibilities of the businessman.* University of Iowa Press. doi:10.2307/j.ctt20q1w8f

Brown, G. (2003). *2003 Speech at Chatham House* [Speech transcript]. https://www.ukpol.co.uk/gordon-brown-2003-speech-at-chatham-house/

Brusseau, J. (2012). *The business ethics workshop.* Saylor Foundation. https://open.umn.edu/opentextbooks/textbooks/272

Cacioppe, R., Forster, N., & Fox, M. (2008). A survey of managers' perceptions of corporate ethics and social responsibility and actions that may affect companies' success. *Journal of Business Ethics*, *82*(3), 681–700. doi:10.1007/s10551-007-9586-y

Camur, D., & Vaizoglu, S. A. (2007). Çevreye ilişkin önemli toplantı ve belgeler [Important meetings and documents concerning environment]. *Turk Silahli Kuvvetleri Koruyucu Hekimlik Bulteni*, *6*(4), 297–306. https://search.trdizin.gov.tr/tr/yayin/detay/72082/cevreye-iliskin-onemli-toplanti-ve-belgeler

Carbon Disclosure Project, Climate Disclosure Standards Board, Global Reporting Initiative, International Integrated Reporting Council, & Sustainability Accounting Standards Board. (2020). *Statement of intent to work together towards comprehensive corporate reporting: Summary of alignment discussions among leading sustainability and integrated reporting organisations CDP, CDSB, GRI, IIRC and SASB* (Impact Management Project). World Economic Forum and Deloitte. https://sasb.org/wp-content/uploads/2023/01/Statement-of-Intent-to-Work-Together-Towards-Comprehensive-Corporate-Reporting.pdf

Carroll, A. B. (1979). A Three-Dimensional Conceptual Model of Corporate Performance. *Academy of Management Review*, *4*(4), 497–505. doi:10.2307/257850

Carroll, A. B. (1983, July 15). Corporate Social Responsibility: Will Industry Respond to Cutbacks in Social Program Funding. *Vital Speeches of the Day*, *49*(19), 604–608. https://www.researchgate.net/publication/331413180

Carroll, A. B. (1991). The Pyramid of Corporate Social Responsibility: Toward the Moral Management of Organizational Stakeholders. *Business Horizons*, *34*(4), 39–48. doi:10.1016/0007-6813(91)90005-G

Carroll, A. B. (1999). Corporate Social Responsibility: Evolution of a Definitional Construct. *Business & Society*, *38*(3), 268–295. doi:10.1177/000765039903800303

Carroll, A. B. (2008). A History of Corporate Social Responsibility: Concepts and Practices. In A. Crane, D. Matten, A. McWilliams, J. Moon, & D. S. Siegel (Eds.), *The Oxford Handbook of Corporate Social Responsibility* (pp. 19–46). Oxford University Press. doi:10.1093/oxfordhb/9780199211593.003.0002

Carroll, A. B. (2015). Corporate Social Responsibility: The Centerpiece of Competing and Complementary Frameworks. *Organizational Dynamics*, *44*(2), 87–96. doi:10.1016/j.orgdyn.2015.02.002

Carroll, A. B. (2021). Corporate Social Responsibility: Perspectives on the CSR Construct's Development and Future. *Business & Society*, *60*(6), 1–21. doi:10.1177/00076503211001765

Clarkson, M. B. (1995). A stakeholder framework for analyzing and evaluating corporate social performance. *Academy of Management Review*, *20*(1), 92–117. doi:10.2307/258888

Climate Disclosure Standards Board. (2019). *CDSB framework for reporting environmental & climate change information: Advancing and aligning disclosure of environmental information in mainstream reports.* Climate Disclosure Standards Board Global. https://www.cdsb.net/sites/default/files/cdsb_climate_change_reporting_framework_edition_1.1.pdf

Davis, K. (1960). Can business afford to ignore social responsibilities? *California Management Review*, *2*(3), 70–76. doi:10.2307/41166246

Davis, K. (1967). Understanding the social responsibility puzzle: What does the businessman owe to society? *Business Horizons*, *10*(4), 45–50. doi:10.1016/0007-6813(67)90007-9

Davis, K. (1973). The case for and against business assumption of social responsibilities. *Academy of Management Journal*, *16*(2), 312–322. doi:10.2307/255331

Dernbach, J. C. (2012). *The unfinished story of the Rio+20 Conference* (Daily Environment Report, 194 DEN B-1, 10/09/2012, Research Paper No. 12-18). Widener Law School Legal Studies. https://ssrn.com/abstract=2169500

Elkington, J. (1997). *Cannibals with forks: The triple bottom line of 21st century business*. Capstone Publishing Limited.

Elkington, J. (2004). Enter the triple bottom line. In A. Henriques & J. Richardson (Eds.), *The triple bottom line: Does it all add up?* (pp. 1–16). Earthscan. doi:10.4324/9781849773348

Epstein, E. M. (1987). The corporate social policy process: Beyond business ethics, corporate social responsibility, and corporate social responsiveness. *California Management Review*, *29*(3), 99–114. doi:10.2307/41165254

European Commission. (2011, October 25). *Communication from the Commission to the European Parliament, the Council, the European Economic and Social Committee and the Committee of the Regions: A renewed EU strategy 2011-14 for corporate social responsibility* (COM(2011) 681 final). European Commission. https://www.europarl.europa.eu/meetdocs/2009_2014/documents/com/com_com(2011)0681_/com_com(2011)0681_en.pdf

Fassin, Y., van Rossem, A., & Buelens, M. (2011). Small-business owner-managers' perceptions of business ethics and CSR-related concepts. *Journal of Business Ethics, 98*(3), 425–453. doi:10.1007/s10551-010-0586-y

Fernandez-Feijoo, B., Romero, S., & Ruiz, S. (2012). Transparent information system for sustainability: A sectoral analysis. *Procedia Technology, 5*, 31–39. doi:10.1016/j.protcy.2012.09.004

Frederick, W. C. (1986). Toward CSR3: Why ethical analysis is indispensable and unavoidable in corporate affairs. *California Management Review, 28*(2), 126–141. doi:10.2307/41165190

Frederick, W. C. (1994). From CSR1 to CSR2: The maturing of business-and-society thought. *Business & Society, 33*(2), 150–164. doi:10.1177/000765039403300202

Frederick, W. C. (2008). Corporate social responsibility: Deep roots, flourishing growth, promising future. In A. Crane, D. Matten, A. McWilliams, J. Moon, & D. S. Siegel (Eds.), *The Oxford handbook of corporate social responsibility* (pp. 522–531). Oxford University Press. doi:10.1093/oxfordhb/9780199211593.003.0023

Freeman, R. E. (1984). *Strategic management: A stakeholder approach.* Pitman.

Friedman, M. (1970, September 13). A Friedman doctrine -- The social responsibility of business is to increase its profits. *The New York Times*, 17. https://www.nytimes.com/1970/09/13/archives/a-friedman-doctrine-the-social-responsibility-of-business-is-to.html

Friedman, M. (2002). *Capitalism and freedom* (F. A. Edition, Ed.). The University of Chicago Press. doi:10.7208/chicago/9780226264189.001.0001

Fulton, M., Kahn, B. M., & Sharples, C. (2012, June). *Sustainable investing: Establishing long-term value and performance.* Deutsche Bank Group Climate Change Advisors. https://papers.ssrn.com/sol3/papers.cfm?abstract_id=2222740

Global Reporting Initiative. (n.d.). *Our mission and history: Empowering sustainable decisions for over 25 years.* https://www.globalreporting.org/about-gri/mission-history/

Godelnik, R. (2021). *Rethinking corporate sustainability in the era of climate crisis: A strategic design approach.* Palgrave Macmillan. doi:10.1007/978-3-030-77318-2

Gokten, S., Ozerhan, Y., & Okan Gokten, P. (2020). The historical development of sustainability reporting: A periodic approach. *Zeszyty Teoretyczne Rachunkowości, 107*(163), 99–117. doi:10.5604/01.3001.0014.2466

Gultekin, A. B., Dikmen, C. B., Erciyes, A. H., & Orgu, D. (2018). An examination of sustainability and United Nations sustainable development goals: Turkey case. In S. Firat, J. Kinuthia, & A. Abu-Tair (Eds.), *Proceedings of 3rd International Sustainable Buildings Symposium (ISBS 2017)* (pp. 252-271). Springer International Publishing. 10.1007/978-3-319-64349-6_20

Harjoto, M. A., & Jo, H. (2011). Corporate governance and CSR nexus. *Journal of Business Ethics*, *100*(1), 45–67. doi:10.1007/s10551-011-0772-6

Holden, E., Linnerud, K., & Banister, D. (2014). Sustainable development: Our common future revisited. *Global Environmental Change*, *26*, 130–139. doi:10.1016/j.gloenvcha.2014.04.006

Jamali, D., Safieddine, A. M., & Rabbath, M. (2008). Corporate governance and corporate social responsibility synergies and interrelationships. *Corporate Governance*, *16*(5), 443–459. doi:10.1111/j.1467-8683.2008.00702.x

Jensen, M. C., & Meckling, W. H. (1976). Theory of the firm: Managerial behavior, agency costs and ownership structure. *Journal of Financial Economics*, *3*(4), 305–360. doi:10.1016/0304-405X(76)90026-X

Jo, H., & Harjoto, M. A. (2012). The causal effect of corporate governance on corporate social responsibility. *Journal of Business Ethics*, *106*(1), 53–72. doi:10.1007/s10551-011-1052-1

Jones, T. M. (1980). Corporate social responsibility revisited, redefined. *California Management Review*, *22*(3), 59–67. doi:10.2307/41164877

Kang, Y.-C. (1995). *Before-profit CSR, stakeholder capitalism and just enterprise system* (UMI No. 9614201) [Doctoral dissertation, University of Pittsburgh]. ProQuest Publishing.

Kaya, Y., & Utku, M. (2020). Integrated reporting and its application in Turkish banking sector. In Interdisciplinary public finance, business and economics studies (Vol. III, pp. 285-296). Peter Lang GmbH. doi:10.3726/b17540

Kaźmierczak, M. (2022). A literature review on the difference between CSR and ESG. *Zeszyty Naukowe Politechniki Śląskiej. Organizacja i Zarządzanie*, *2022*(162), 275–289. doi:10.29119/1641-3466.2022.162.16

Kmenta, J. (1986). *Elements of econometrics* (2nd ed.). Macmillan Publishing Company.

Kolk, A. (2008). Sustainability, accountability and corporate governance: Exploring multinationals' reporting practices. *Business Strategy and the Environment, 18*(1), 1–15. doi:10.1002/bse.511

Lantos, G. P. (2001). The boundaries of strategic corporate social responsibility. *Journal of Consumer Marketing, 18*(7), 595–630. doi:10.1108/07363760110410281

Leff, E. (1997, December 8-12). Environmental education and sustainable development. *International Conference on Environment and Society: Education and Public Awareness for Sustainability.* United Nations Environment Programme. https://www.academia.edu/22269226/Environmental_Education_and_Sustainable_Development

Leopold, A. (1949). *A sand county Almanac and sketches here and there.* Oxford University Press.

Logsdon, J. M., & Wood, D. J. (2002). Business citizenship: From domestic to global level of analysis. *Business Ethics Quarterly, 12*(2), 155–187. doi:10.2307/3857809

Lu, W., Chau, K. W., Wang, H., & Pan, W. (2014). A decade's debate on the nexus between corporate social and corporate financial performance: A critical review of empirical studies 2002-2011. *Journal of Cleaner Production, 79*, 195–206. doi:10.1016/j.jclepro.2014.04.072

Luetkenhorst, W. (2004). Corporate social responsibility and the development agenda: The case for actively involving small and medium enterprises. *Inter Economics, 39*(3), 157–166. doi:10.1007/BF02933583

MacNeil, I., & Esser, I.-M. (2022). From a financial to an entity model of ESG. *European Business Organization Law Review, 23*(1), 1–37. doi:10.1007/s40804-021-00234-y

Marsden, C. (2000). The new corporate citizenship of big business: Part of the solution to sustainability? *Business and Society Review, 105*(1), 9–25. doi:10.1111/0045-3609.00062

Matten, D., Crane, A., & Chapple, W. (2003). Behind the mask: Revealing the true face of corporate citizenship. *Journal of Business Ethics, 45*(1/2), 109–120. doi:10.1023/A:1024128730308

McWilliams, A., Siegel, D. S., & Wright, P. M. (2006). Corporate social responsibility: Strategic implications. *Journal of Management Studies, 43*(1), 1–18. doi:10.1111/j.1467-6486.2006.00580.x

Meadows, D. H., Meadows, D. L., Randers, J., & Behrens, W. W., III. (1972). *The limits to growth.* Universe Books. https://collections.dartmouth.edu/content/deliver/inline/meadows/pdf/meadows_ltg-001.pdf

Melé, D. (2008). Corporate social responsibility theories. In A. Crane, D. Matten, A. McWilliams, J. Moon, & D. S. Siegel (Eds.), *The Oxford handbook of corporate social responsibility* (pp. 47–82). Oxford University Press. doi:10.1093/oxfordhb/9780199211593.003.0003

Mill, G. A. (2006). The financial performance of a socially responsible investment over time and a possible link with corporate social responsibility. *Journal of Business Ethics, 63*(2), 131–148. doi:10.1007/s10551-005-2410-7

Mitnick, B. M. (1993, March). *Organizing research in corporate social performance: The CSP system as core paradigm* [Paper presentation]. 1993 Annual Meeting of the International Association for Business and Society, San Diego, CA. https://papers.ssrn.com/sol3/papers.cfm?abstract_id=3837714

Mitnick, B. M. (2000). Commitment, revelation, and the testaments of belief: The metrics of measurement of corporate social performance. *Business & Society, 39*(4), 419–465. doi:10.1177/000765030003900405

Moon, J. (2007). The contribution of corporate social responsibility to sustainable development. *Sustainable Development (Bradford), 15*(5), 296–306. doi:10.1002/sd.346

Muller, A. R., Pfarrer, M. D., & Little, L. M. (2014). A theory of collective empathy in corporate philanthropy decisions. *Academy of Management Review, 39*(1), 1–21. https://www.jstor.org/stable/43699197. doi:10.5465/amr.2012.0031

Oh, W.-Y., Chang, Y. K., & Kim, T.-Y. (2018). Complementary or substitutive effects?: Corporate governance mechanisms and corporate social responsibility. *Journal of Management, 44*(7), 2716–2739. doi:10.1177/0149206316653804

Oliver, N. (2021). When philanthropy meets data science: A framework for governance to achieve data-driven decision-making for public good. In Data science for social good: Philanthropy and social impact in a complex world (pp. 55-68). Springer. doi:10.1007/978-3-030-78985-5_5

Olson, E. (2013, February 5). *BSR and the state of CSR: What we mean when we say 'CSR': What is CSR?* https://www.bsr.org/en/our-insights/blog-view/bsr-and-the-state-of-csr-what-we-mean-when-we-say-csr

Orlitzky, M. (2005). Payoffs to social and environmental performance. *Journal of Investing*, *48-52*(3), 48–52. Advance online publication. doi:10.3905/joi.2005.580548

Panapanaan, V. M., Linnanen, L., Karvonen, M.-M., & Phan, V. T. (2003). Roadmapping corporate social responsibility in Finnish companies. *Journal of Business Ethics*, *44*(2), 133–148. doi:10.1023/A:1023391530903

Platform, M. V. O. (2012). *CSR: Frame of reference 2012*. MVO Platform. https://www.mvoplatform.nl/en/csr-frame-of-reference-2012/

Porter, M. E. (2003, May 14). *Corporate philanthropy: Taking the high ground* [Paper presentation]. A gathering of corporate philanthropy leaders sponsored by the Foundation Strategy Group & the Center for Corporate Citizenship, New York City, NY.

Post, J. E., & Berman, S. L. (2001). Global corporate citizenship in a dot.com world: The role of organisational identity. In J. Andriof & M. McIntosh (Eds.), *Perspectives on corporate citizenship* (pp. 66–82). Greenleaf Publishing Limited. doi:10.9774/GLEAF.978-1-909493-19-3_6

J. Quarrie (Ed.). (1992). Earth Summit 1992*: The United Nations Conference on Environment and Development*. Regency Press.

Rediker, K. J., & Seth, A. (1995). Boards of directors and substitution effects of alternative governance mechanisms. *Strategic Management Journal*, *16*(2), 85–99. doi:10.1002/smj.4250160202

Schanzenbach, M. M., & Sitkoff, R. H. (2020). Reconciling fiduciary duty and social conscience: The law and economics of ESG investing by a trustee. *Stanford Law Review*, *72*(2), 381–454. https://review.law.stanford.edu/wp-content/uploads/sites/3/2020/02/Schanzenbach-Sitkoff-72-Stan.-L.-Rev.-381.pdf

Scholtens, B., & Sievänen, R. (2013). Drivers of socially responsible investing: A case study of four Nordic countries. *Journal of Business Ethics*, *115*(3), 605–616. doi:10.1007/s10551-012-1410-7

Schwab, K. (2008, January/February). Global corporate citizenship: Working with governments and civil society. *Foreign Affairs*, *87*(1), 107–118. https://www.jstor.org/stable/20020271

Sethi, S. P. (1975). Dimensions of corporate social performance: An analytical framework. *California Management Review*, *17*(3), 58–64. doi:10.2307/41162149

Sparkes, R. (2002). *Socially responsible investment: A global revolution* (J. Goodchild & C. Callow, Eds.). John Wiley & Sons Ltd.

Spindler, E. A. (2013). The history of sustainability: The origins and effects of a popular concept. In I. Jenkins & R. Schröder (Eds.), *Sustainability in tourism: A multidisciplinary approach* (pp. 9–31). Springer Gabler. doi:10.1007/978-3-8349-7043-5_1

Sukoharsono, E. (2019). Sustaining a sustainability Report by modifying triple bottom line to pentaple bottom line: An imaginary research dialogue. *The International Journal of Accounting and Business Society*, *27*(1), 119–127. doi:10.21776/ub.ijabs.2019.27.1.7

Swanson, D. L. (2008). Top managers as drivers for corporate social responsibility. In A. Crane, A. McWilliams, D. Matten, J. Moon, & D. S. Siegel (Eds.), *The Oxford handbook of corporate social responsibility* (pp. 227–248). Oxford University Press. doi:10.1093/oxfordhb/9780199211593.003.0010

Ten PierickE.BeekmanV.van der WeeleC. N.MeeusenM. J.de GraaffR. P. (2004). *A framework for analysing corporate social performance: Beyond the Wood model.* Agricultural Economics Research Institute. doi:10.22004/AG.ECON.29081

Thielen, P. (2005). *Good corporate citizenship: A Delphi study defining the key aspects according to the business and academic communities* (UMI No. 3160519) [Doctoral Dissertation, Fielding Graduate University]. ProQuest Publishing.

United Nations. (1976). *Report of Habitat: United Nations Conference on Human Settlements, Vancouver, 31 May - 11 June 1976* (A/CONF.70.15). New York: United Nations Publication. https://digitallibrary.un.org/record/793768

United Nations. (1992a). *United Nations Conference on Environment and Development, Non-legally binding authoritative statement of principles for a global consensus on the management, conservation and sustainable development of all types of forests, Rio de Janeiro, 3-14 June 1992* (A/CONF.151/6). New York: United Nations Publication. https://digitallibrary.un.org/record/144461

United Nations. (1992b). *United Nations Framework Convention on Climate Change* (FCCC/INFORMAL/84 GE.05-62220 (E) 200705). New York: United Nations Publications. https://unfccc.int/resource/docs/convkp/conveng.pdf

United Nations. (1994). *United Nations Convention to Combat Desertification in those Countries Experiencing Serious Drought and / or Desertification, Particularly in Africa.* Paris: United Nations. https://catalogue.unccd.int/936_UNCCD_Convention_ENG.pdf

United Nations. (1996). *Report of the United Nations Conference on Human Settlements (Habitat II), Istanbul, 3-14 June 1996* (A/CONF.165/14 GE.96-02500 (E)). Istanbul: United Nations. New York: United Nations Publication. https://documents-dds-ny.un.org/doc/UNDOC/GEN/G96/025/00/PDF/G9602500.pdf?OpenElement

United Nations. (2002). *Report of the World Summit on Sustainable Development, Johannesburg, South Africa, 26 August - 4 September 2002* (A/CONF.199/20). New York: United Nations Publication. https://digitallibrary.un.org/record/478154

United Nations. (2022). *Stockholm+50: A healthy planet for the prosperity of all - Our responsibility, our opportunity, Stockholm, 2 and 3 June 2022* (A/CONF.238/9). Estonia: United Nations. https://documents-dds-ny.un.org/doc/UNDOC/GEN/K22/117/97/PDF/K2211797.pdf?OpenElement

United Nations. (n.d.-a). *United Nations Conference on Human Settlements - Habitat I Vancouver, Canada, 31 May-11 June 1976: Adequate shelter as a basic human right.* https://www.un.org/en/conferences/habitat/vancouver1976

United Nations. (n.d.-b). *United Nations Conference on Human Settlements: Habitat II: Urban Exodus.* https://www.un.org/en/conferences/habitat/istanbul1996

United Nations. (n.d.-c). *Special Session of the General Assembly on Habitat: Istanbul+5: 6-8 June 2001, New York: A Five-Year Review.* https://www.un.org/en/conferences/habitat/newyork2001

United Nations. (n.d.-d). *UN Conference on Housing and Sustainable Urban Development: Habitat III 17-20 October 2016, Quito, Ecuador: The Potential of Cities.* https://www.un.org/en/conferences/habitat/quito2016

United Nations Environment Programme. (1992, June). *Convention on Biological Diversity* (Na. 92-8314). UNEP Environmental Law and Institutions Programme Activity Centre. https://wedocs.unep.org/bitstream/handle/20.500.11822/29146/COB.pdf?sequence=1&isAllowed=y

United Nations Environment Programme. (n.d.). *Stockholm+50: A Healthy Planet for the Prosperity of All – Our Responsibility, Our Opportunity.* https://www.stockholm50.global

United Nations General Assembly. (1987). *Development and international economic co-operation: Environment, Report of the World Commission on Environment and Development, Note by the Secretary-General* (A/42/427). New York: United Nations. https://digitallibrary.un.org/record/139811?ln=en

United Nations General Assembly. (1992). *Report of the United Nation Conference on Environment and Development: Rio Declaration on Environment and Development* (A/CONF.151/26) (Vol. I). Rio de Janeiro: United Nations. https://www.un.org/en/development/desa/population/migration/generalassembly/docs/globalcompact/A_CONF.151_26_Vol.I_Declaration.pdf

United Nations General Assembly. (1997). *Resolution adopted by the General Assembly: Programme for the further implementation of Agenda 21* (A/RES/S-19/2). New York: United Nations. https://digitallibrary.un.org/record/244113

United Nations General Assembly. (2012). *Resolution adopted by the General Assembly, The future we want* (A/RES/66/288). Rio de Janeiro: Rio+20 United Nations General Assembly. https://documents-dds-ny.un.org/doc/UNDOC/GEN/N11/476/10/PDF/N1147610.pdf

United Nations General Assembly. (2015). *Resolution adopted by the General Assembly on 29 September 2015: Transforming our world: The 2030 Agenda for Sustainable Development* (A/RES/70/1). New York: United Nations. https://documents-dds-ny.un.org/doc/UNDOC/GEN/N15/291/89/PDF/N1529189.pdf?OpenElement

United Nations General Assembly. (2017). *Implementation of the Outcomes of the United Nations Conferences on Human Settlements and on Housing and Sustainable Urban Development and strengthening of the United Nations Human Settlements Programme (UN-Habitat), New Urban Agenda: Draft resolution / submitted by the President of the General Assembly* (A/71/L.23). New York: United Nations. https://digitallibrary.un.org/record/850965?ln=en

Van Marrewijk, M. (2003). Concepts and definitions of CSR and corporate sustainability: Between agency and communion. *Journal of Business Ethics*, *44*(2), 95–105. doi:10.1023/A:1023331212247

Wang, S. (2015). *Chinese strategic decision-making on CSR* (S. O. Idowu & R. Schmidpeter, Eds.). Springer. doi:10.1007/978-3-662-44997-4

Wartick, S. L., & Cochran, P. L. (1985). The evolution of the corporate social performance model. *Academy of Management Review*, *10*(4), 758–769. doi:10.2307/258044

Weber, M. (2008). The business case for corporate social responsibility: A company-level measurement approach for CSR. *European Management Journal*, *26*(4), 247–261. doi:10.1016/j.emj.2008.01.006

Weller, A. (2020). Exploring practitioners' meaning of "ethics", "compliance", and "corporate social responsibility" practices: A communities of practice perspective. *Business & Society*, *59*(3), 518–544. doi:10.1177/0007650317719263

Wiens, J. A. (2013). Is landscape sustainability a useful concept in a changing world? *Landscape Ecology*, *28*(6), 1047–1052. doi:10.1007/s10980-012-9801-9

Wood, D. A. (2011). Back to 3BL basics. *Petroleum Review*, *30*, 32. https://knowledge.energyinst.org/search/record?id=76840

Wood, D. J. (1991). Corporate social performance revisited. *Academy of Management Review*, *16*(4), 691–718. doi:10.2307/258977

Wood, D. J. (2010). Measuring corporate social performance: A review. *International Journal of Management Reviews*, *12*(1), 50–84. doi:10.1111/j.1468-2370.2009.00274.x

Wood, D. J., & Jones, R. E. (1995). Stakeholder mismatching: A theoretical problem in empirical research on corporate social performance. *The International Journal of Organizational Analysis*, *3*(3), 229–267. doi:10.1108/eb028831

KEY TERMS AND DEFINITIONS

Business Ethics: A business's fairness and accuracy to stand strong against corporate scandals.

Corporate Citizenship (CC): The identity of businesses in society. Participation in community events in a good and legitimate manner to be a good citizen.

Corporate Governance (CG): Regulating, restructuring and balancing a company's operations, processes, and relationships with its stakeholders by utilising effective governance mechanisms.

Corporate Philanthropy: Having a high reputation in the eyes of society through being a good citizen beyond being altruistic, and to grant money and other resources for social purposes.

Corporate Social Performance (CSP): Examination of the relationships between social responsibility principles, social responsiveness processes, and a company's goals, policies, programmes, and outcomes. A company's measurable activities and their effects on its stakeholders.

Corporate Social Responsibility (CSR): A company's acknowledgement of its stakeholders' interests, respect for and adherence to ethics, and support for others' well-being, in addition to its own economic interests.

Corporate Social Responsiveness: Managerial actions as a response to social expectations and concerns.

Environmental, Social, and Governance (ESG): Materialising socially responsible companies by addressing measurability based on metrics and risk and return relationships.

Socially Responsible Investment (SRI): Investments that are both financially lucrative and socially responsible.

Sustainability (Sustainable Development): A paradigm shift stemming from corporate social responsibility moving to a sustainable world, mainly covering a wide range of societal and environmental topics.

Triple Bottom Line (3BL, 3P Formulation): Dimensions targeting people, environment and profit for use in performance evaluations of a socially responsible business.

ENDNOTES

1 Economic responsibilities represent the fundamental building blocks of all responsibilities. Legal responsibilities regulate acceptable and unacceptable behaviour. Ethical responsibilities mean behaving in a manner that is true, fair, honest, and least harmful to stakeholders. Philanthropic responsibilities in a business can be understood as being a good citizen who can add value to society's financial and human resources and, thereby, improve living standards.

2 The Rio Declaration (UNGA, 1992, p. 1) aimed at rebuilding cooperation, raising nature awareness, and working to protect the integrity of the systems. The Forest Principles (UN, 1992a, p. 1) discussed forest management, protection, and sustainable development, as well as their functions and intended uses. The Framework Convention on Climate Change (UN, 1992b, pp. 4–5) was created to stabilise greenhouse gas concentrations to prevent human-induced climate change. The Convention on Biological Diversity (UN Environment Programme [UNEP], 1992, p. 26) aimed at biological diversity protection, sustaining its use, and providing fair and equal genetic resource benefits. The Convention to Combat Desertification (UN, 1994, p. 5) sought to reduce desertification and severe drought. Agenda 21 (Quarrie, 1992, p. 50) was formed to promote a free, fair, and equal trading system; boost market accessibility; ameliorate commodity market operations; achieve harmonised and coherent commodity policies; and promote and endorse policies to support environmental protection and economic growth.

3 The goals of the Rio+5 Summit were to bear new sustainable development responsibilities, identify the reasons behind failures, promote successful

practices, and determine primary objectives (Camur & Vaizoglu, 2007, p. 301). The Rio+10 Summit, the World Summit on Sustainable Development, was set up to evaluate the practices implemented following previous summits. As a result of this summit, the resolutions of the Political Declaration and the Plan of Implementation of the World Summit on Sustainable Development were adopted. The Rio+20 Summit was a step towards determining global objectives and indicators to enhance sustainable development (Gultekin et al., 2018, p. 258). As an outcome of the Rio+20 Summit, a document called "The Future We Want" was published. In 2015, the United Nations Sustainable Development Summit was held in New York to define global targets for sustainable development (Gultekin et al., 2018, p. 259). As part of this summit, the 2030 Agenda for Sustainable Development was published. To speed up the process of putting this agenda into action, the Stockholm+50 event was held in Stockholm on 2 and 3 June 2022 (UNEP, n.d., para. 1). Different from others, this event also focused on the attainment of an inclusive and sustainable rebound from the pandemic (UN, 2022).

4 Habitat I, the First Conference on Human Settlements, was organised in 1976 in Vancouver. It was held to take a critical step to prevent fast population growth and the deterioration of the conditions. As a result, the Vancouver Declaration of Human Settlement was issued (UN, n.d.-a, para. 1-4). Twenty years after the first conference, Habitat II, "City Summit", was held in Istanbul. The main agenda items for this conference were full urbanisation and adequate housing for all, as well as the population increase. Habitat Agenda and Istanbul Declaration on Human Settlements was the output of the conference (UN, n.d.-b, para. 1, 3). In New York, in 2001, a special Habitat session was organised to review and assess the implementation of the Agenda. The product of the conference was the Declaration on Cities and Other Human Settlements in the New Millennium (UN, n.d.-c, para. 1, 4). Habitat III took place in Quito in 2016 to develop the capacity and potential of cities to encourage innovations that can reverse potential issues. The outputs of this conference were the New Urban Agenda and the Quito Declaration of Sustainable Cities and Human Settlements for All (UN, n.d.-d, para. 1-2).

5 Although Wood (1991) cites Sethi's (1979) work, there are no essential differences between this article and Sethi's (1975) article in terms of the criticism in question.

6 Clarkson (1995, p. 109) tabulated the RDAP scale as a combination of the capital letters of the English terms reactive, defensive, accommodative and proactive, respectively. These terms were given in order of responsibility level and performance. For instance, a reactive strategy means denying any responsibility and taking fewer steps than required, whereas a proactive strategy

involves the expectation of responsibility for an issue before its occurrence and doing more work than required.

7 Bias refers to the gap between the mean value of the sampling distribution of a particular estimator and the parameter's true value (Kmenta, 1986, p. 157). An estimator is considered consistent provided that, as the sample size goes to infinity, estimates approach the true parameter value (Kmenta, 1986, pp. 13–14, 133).

8 In a classical linear regression model, there is expected to be no perfect correlation between any two or more explanatory variables or any linear combination of these variables. If this rule is ignored, multicollinearity will occur (Kmenta, 1986, pp. 430–431).

9 Regression estimators with high variance will lead to very imprecise estimates of the regression coefficients (Kmenta, 1986, p. 438).

Chapter 8
Impact of Financial Stability on Economic Growth in Nigeria

Peterson K. Ozili
https://orcid.org/0000-0001-6292-1161
Central Bank of Nigeria, Nigeria

ABSTRACT

Economic growth is reflected in SDG8 of the Sustainable Development Goals. Financial stability has been identified as a factor promoting economic growth. However, there is little evidence on the effect of financial stability on economic growth in Nigeria. This study empirically examines the effect of financial stability on economic growth in Nigeria from 1993 to 2017. The results show a positive relationship between financial stability and economic growth in Nigeria. Specifically, the result shows that a high ZSCORE, which reflects low insolvency risk, has a positive effect on economic growth. Similarly, fewer nonperforming loans improve economic growth in Nigeria. In contrast, capital adequacy was found to have a negative effect on economic growth in Nigeria.

1. INTRODUCTION

This paper examines the effect of financial stability on economic growth in Nigeria. Economic growth is reflected in SDG8 of the sustainable development goals. The relationship between financial stability and economic growth is a topic of intense debate in the economics and finance literature (Tosunoglu, 2018; Ehigiamusoe and Samsurijan, 2020; Nasreen and Anwar, 2018 Ozili and Iorember, 2023). Scholars consider financial stability to be a potential factor affecting economic growth.

DOI: 10.4018/979-8-3693-1511-8.ch008

There is some consensus that a stable financial system ensures that credit is allocated efficiently to households and firms for consumption and investment purposes, which in turn, leads to greater production of goods and services, thereby leading to higher economic output and economic growth (Min, Wen, Xu and Wu, 2021; Dejan, 2018; Ozili, 2018). This suggests a positive relationship between financial stability and economic growth. Some studies in the literature also document mixed results for the relationship between financial stability and economic growth.

In Nigeria, the financial system is crucial for economic growth. Nigeria operates a bank-based financial system which means that the financial system is dominated by banks. Economic agents in Nigeria rely on banks to allocate credit for productive economic activities. But for this to happen, the financial system must be stable – it must be well-capitalised and have few non-performing loans and low risk of insolvency. Several studies show that these three factors are the pre-conditions to have a stable financial system (Thakor, 2018; Lepetit, Strobel and Tran, 2021; Lukić, Popović and Janković, 2019; Karugu, Achoki, and Kiriri, 2018).

In this paper, I examine the effect of financial stability on economic growth. I use several indicators of financial stability and examine their effect on economic growth measured by real GDP per capita. There are few recent studies on the relationship between financial stability and economic growth in Nigeria such as Njang, Omini, Bekun and Adedoyin (2020). This paper is different from Njang, Omini, Bekun and Adedoyin (2020) in that it uses a more recent dataset and a unique set of financial stability and economic growth indicators.

The analysis in this paper contributes to the literature in the following way. It contributes to this literature by showing that financial stability is a determinant of economic growth. Second, this paper adds to the scant literature on the effect of financial stability on economic growth in Nigeria.

The rest of the paper is structured as follows. Section 2 presents the literature review. Section 3 presents the methodology. Section 4 presents the results. Section 5 concludes.

2. LITERATURE REVIEW

In this section, I review the recent literature on the relationship between financial stability and economic growth.

Batuo, Mlambo and Asongu (2018) assess the linkages between financial instability, financial liberalisation, financial development and economic growth in 41 African countries from 1985 to 2010. The results suggest that financial development and financial liberalisation have positive effects on financial instability. They also find that economic growth reduces financial instability.

Jayakumar, Pradhan, Dash, Maradana and Gaurav (2018) study the interaction between banking competition, banking stability, and economic growth in a panel of 32 European countries from 1996 to 2014. They find that both banking competition and banking stability are significant long-term drivers of economic growth in European countries. Carlson, Correia and Luck (2019) find that banks operating in markets with lower entry barriers extend more credit and leads to a credit boom. The resulting credit boom led to expansion in real economic activity. Overall, they show that banking competition can cause both economic growth and financial instability.

Njang, Omini, Bekun and Adedoyin (2020) examine the influence of financial system stability on economic growth in Nigeria from 1986 to 2016. They use the granger causality test, Johansson co-integration test and vector error correction model (VECM) estimation techniques. The granger causality test revealed a uni-directional causality between financial stability and economic growth in Nigeria. The Johansson co-integration test showed that long-run co-integration relationship exists between financial stability and economic growth. The VECM results show that financial stability has a negative relationship with economic growth.

Ehigiamusoe and Samsurijan (2020) analyse the variables that moderate the impact of financial development on economic growth. They show that financial and economic development, institutions, and macroeconomic stability moderate the finance-growth nexus. Stewart, Chowdhury, and Arjoon (2020) investigate the direct relationship between bank stability and economic growth and, further, examine the effect that regulatory capital and institutional quality have on this relationship. They examine 100 countries from 1995 to 2015. They use the generalized method of moments method and find no support for a regulatory capital-induced trade-off between banking stability and economic growth. Bayar, Borozan and Gavriletea (2021) analyse the dynamic and causal effects of banking sector stability on economic growth in post-transition European Union countries from 1998 to 2016. The causality analysis shows an opposite causality direction between the banking sector stability indicators and economic growth. Creel, Hubert and Labondance (2015) assess the link between economic growth and financial stability in the EU. They examine the period from 1998 to 2011. They find that financial instability has a negative effect on economic growth.

Ijaz, Hassan, Tarazi and Fraz (2020) investigate the effect of bank competition and financial stability on economic growth. They examine 38 European countries from 2001 to 2017 using the fixed-effect panel regression estimator and system generalized method of moment (GMM). They find that bank stability significantly contributes to economic growth in Europe. Lower banking competition supports economic growth and increases financial stability. Alsamara, Mrabet, Jarallah and Barkat (2019) investigate the relationship between financial stability and economic growth in the Qatar economy from 1980:Q1 to 2013:Q4 using a Vector Error

Correction Model (VECM) with structural breaks approach. They show that real GDP growth has a long-run negative impact and a moderate short-run positive impact on real loan provisions. This negative relationship indicates that an increase in real GDP growth may lead to fewer defaults on loans.

Younsi and Nafla (2019) examine the relationship between financial stability, monetary policy, and economic growth in 40 developed and developing countries from 1993 to 2015. They use the fixed and random effects panel regression models to determine the impact of financial stability and monetary policy on economic growth. They find that financial crises, bank liquid reserves, and bank nonperforming loans negatively affect financial stability and economic growth. Tosunoglu (2018) examines the relationship between financial stability and economic growth in Turkey from 2002 to 2017. They find that a steadily functioning financial system is a requirement for economic growth. They find that financial leverage, capital adequacy, asset quality, and liquidity are important components of financial stability affecting economic growth.

Sotiropoulou, Giakoumatos and Petropoulos (2019) investigate the impact of financial development and stability on economic growth. They examine 28 European Union countries from 2004 to 2014. The results show that banking system development has a negative impact on economic growth. Private credit allocation does not improve the economic growth. The size of the stock market has a positive effect on economic growth, whereas market liquidity and financial instability negatively influence economic growth. Prochniak and Wasiak (2017) study the impact of financial sector stability on economic growth. They examine 28 EU and 34 OECD economies during the 1993–2013 period. They find a nonlinear relationship between financial sector stability and economic growth. They also find that a large-sized financial system does not lead to more rapid economic growth, it may even negatively affect GDP dynamics.

Nasreen and Anwar (2018) examine the relationship between economic development and financial stability in five South Asian economies, namely Pakistan, India, Bangladesh, Sri Lanka and Nepal from 1980 to 2012. Human development index (HDI) is used to measure economic development while financial stability is measured by constructing an aggregate financial stability index (AFSI) that combines various indicators relating to financial sector development, vulnerability, and banking soundness. They find evidence of a long-run relationship between selected variables. They find that financial stability is an essential factor for improving the process of economic development in South Asian countries.

There are few recent studies on the impact of financial stability on economic growth in Nigeria. This study aims to fill this gap in the literature.

3. METHODOLOGY

3.1. Data

To analyse the effect of financial stability on economic growth in Nigeria, I use Nigerian data collected from the World Bank's global financial development indicators. Financial stability indicators, economic growth data and other macroeconomic data were collected. The sample period covers a 24-year period from 1993 to 2017.

3.2. Model Specification and Estimation Technique

The variables presented in the model are described in table 1. The explanatory variables are the three financial stability indicators, namely, capital adequacy ratio (CAR), the nonperforming loans ratio (NPL) and the insolvency risk variable (ZSCORE). The dependent variable is real GDP per capita. The control variable is inflation rate. The inflation variable controls for macroeconomic performance. The model is estimated using time series ordinary least square (OLS) regression.

4. REGRESSION RESULT

4.1. OLS Regression Result

The OLS regression model estimates the effect of inflation (INF), nonperforming loans ratio (NPL), capital adequacy ratio (CAR) and insolvency risk (ZSCORE) on real GDP per capita (GDPC). The result is reported in table 2 below. The

Table 1. Variable source and description

Variable	Variable Description	Predicted Signs	Data Source
GDPC	Real GDP per capita		Global financial development indicators
CAR	Capital adequacy ratio measured as total equity capital divided by total asset of banks	+	Global financial development indicators
NPL	Nonperforming loans ratio measured as total bad debt divided by total loan	-	Global financial development indicators
ZSCORE	Insolvency risk of the banking sector	+	Global financial development indicators
INF	Inflation rate	+	Global financial development indicators

NPL coefficient is negative and statistically significant. This suggests a negative relationship between nonperforming loans ratio (NPL) in the financial sector and economic growth in Nigeria. This implies that high level of financial stability, measured by low nonperforming loans (NPL) in the financial sector, has a positive effect on economic growth in Nigeria.

The CAR coefficient is also negative and statistically significant. The result suggests a negative relationship between capital adequacy ratio (CAR) in the financial sector and economic growth in Nigeria. This implies that high level of financial stability, measured by high capital adequacy ratio (CAR) in the financial sector has a negative effect on economic growth in Nigeria.

The ZSCORE coefficient is positive and statistically significant. The result suggests a positive association between ZSCORE and economic growth. This means that high level of financial stability, as measured by the high ZSCORE, has a positive effect on economic growth in Nigeria.

The INF coefficient is positive but insignificant, therefore, no meaningful conclusion can be drawn.

4.2. Robustness Checks

I conduct an additional analysis to check whether the main result is affected by skewness in the data distribution for the variables. To do this, I transformed all the variables into their logarithmic form. Thereafter, I run a log-linear regression estimation. The result is reported in table 3 below. The NPL coefficient remains negative and statistically significant. The result confirms the earlier result in reported in table 2 and suggests that fewer nonperforming loans in the financial sector has a positive effect on economic growth in Nigeria. The ZSCORE coefficient is positive and statistically significant. The result confirms the earlier result in table 2 and suggests that low insolvency risk in the financial sector improves economic growth

Table 2. OLS regression result

Dependent Variable: Real GDP per Capita (GDPC)			
Variables	**Coefficient**	**T-Statistic**	**P-Value**
CAR	-45.051**	-2.216	0.045
NPL	-39.906***	-4.765	0.0004
ZSCORE	76.061***	3.276	0.006
INF	14.982	0.817	0.429
R-square	73.62		
Adjusted R-square	65.51		

in Nigeria. The CAR coefficient is statistically insignificant. The result does not confirm the earlier result. Also, the INF coefficient is weakly significant and does not confirm the result obtained in table 2.

4.3. Correlation Result

The correlation result is reported in table 3. The correlation between economic growth (GDPC) and inflation is negative. This means that an increase in inflation is associated with low economic growth. Second, the correlation between economic growth (GDPC) and capital adequacy (CAR) in the financial sector is positive. This means that an increase in capital adequacy in the financial sector is associated with high economic growth. Third, the correlation between economic growth (GDPC) and nonperforming loans (NPL) in the financial sector is negative. This means that low nonperforming loans in the financial sector is associated with high economic growth. Finally, the correlation between economic growth (GDPC) and insolvency risk (ZSCORE) in the banking sector is negative. This means that high level of financial stability, as measured by the high ZSCORE, is associated with high economic growth in Nigeria.

5. CONCLUSION

Economic growth is reflected in SDG8 of the sustainable development goals. Financial stability is a potential factor affecting economic growth. This study examined the effect of financial stability on economic growth. Using Nigeria data obtained from the World Bank's global financial development indicators, the result showed evidence that some financial stability indicators have a positive effect on economic growth in Nigeria. High ZSCORE, which reflects low insolvency risk,

Table 3. OLS regression result

Dependent Variable: Log of Real GDP per Capita (GDPC)			
Variables	**Coefficient**	**T-Statistic**	**P-Value**
Log (CAR)	-2.810**	-0.139	0.891
Log (NPL)	-27.517***	-2.848	0.013
Log (ZSCORE)	130.55***	20.779	0.000
Log (INF)	40.839	1.908	0.077
R-square	52.26		
Adjusted R-square	42.03		

Table 4. Pearson correlation matrix for the variables

Variable	GDPC	INF	CAR	NPL	ZSCORE
GDPC	1.000				

INF	-0.041	1.000			
	(-0.163)	-----			
	((0.87))	-----			
CAR	0.081	-0.263	1.000		
	(0.326)	(-1.092)	-----		
	((0.74))	((0.29))	-----		
NPL	-0.607**	0.277	-0.619**	1.000	
	(-3.059)	(1.153)	(-3.160)	-----	
	((0.01))	((0.26))	((0.01))	-----	
ZSCORE	0.513**	-0.058	-0.049	-0.035	1.000
	(2.393)	(-0.233)	(-0.197)	(-0.140)	-----
	((0.03))	((0.81))	((0.84))	((0.89))	-----

T-statistics are reported in single parenthesis (). P-values are reported in double parenthesis (()). ** represent statistical significance at the 5% level.

had a positive effect on economic growth. Similarly, low level of nonperforming loans improved economic growth in Nigeria.

One implication of the findings is that the effect of financial stability on economic growth in Nigeria depends on how financial stability is measured. Therefore, it is recommended that policy makers should carefully choose the relevant financial stability indicators that capture the extent of stability or fragility in the Nigerian financial system and increase its surveillance of the developments in the selected financial stability indicators. It is also recommended that the financial system regulator should increase its supervision of the Nigerian financial system to ensure that the behaviour and activities of all financial institutions contribute to the stability in the Nigerian financial system.

Future studies can examine the effect of financial stability on economic development. Future studies can examine additional indicators of financial stability and examine their effect on several indicators of economic growth in Nigeria.

REFERENCES

Alsamara, M., Mrabet, Z., Jarallah, S., & Barkat, K. (2019). The switching impact of financial stability and economic growth in Qatar: Evidence from an oil-rich country. *The Quarterly Review of Economics and Finance*, *73*, 205–216. doi:10.1016/j.qref.2018.05.008

Batuo, M., Mlambo, K., & Asongu, S. (2018). Linkages between financial development, financial instability, financial liberalisation and economic growth in Africa. *Research in International Business and Finance*, *45*, 168–179. doi:10.1016/j.ribaf.2017.07.148

Bayar, Y., Borozan, D., & Gavriletea, M. D. (2021). Banking sector stability and economic growth in post-transition European Union countries. *International Journal of Finance & Economics*, *26*(1), 949–961. doi:10.1002/ijfe.1829

CarlsonM. A.CorreiaS.LuckS. (2019). The effects of banking competition on growth and financial stability: Evidence from the national banking era. Available at SSRN 3202489.

Creel, J., Hubert, P., & Labondance, F. (2015). Financial stability and economic performance. *Economic Modelling*, *48*, 25–40. doi:10.1016/j.econmod.2014.10.025

Dejan, A. J. (2018). *Credit Supply, Price and Financial Stability in Markets and Institutions*. Academic Press.

Ehigiamusoe, K. U., & Samsurijan, M. S. (2020). What matters for finance-growth nexus? A critical survey of macroeconomic stability, institutions, financial and economic development. *International Journal of Finance & Economics*.

Ijaz, S., Hassan, A., Tarazi, A., & Fraz, A. (2020). Linking bank competition, financial stability, and economic growth. *Journal of Business Economics and Management*, *21*(1), 200–221. doi:10.3846/jbem.2020.11761

Jayakumar, M., Pradhan, R. P., Dash, S., Maradana, R. P., & Gaurav, K. (2018). Banking competition, banking stability, and economic growth: Are feedback effects at work? *Journal of Economics and Business*, *96*, 15–41. doi:10.1016/j.jeconbus.2017.12.004

Karugu, C., Achoki, G., & Kiriri, P. (2018). Capital Adequacy Ratios as Predictors of Financial Distress in Kenyan Commercial Banks. *Journal of Financial Risk Management*, *7*(03), 278–289. doi:10.4236/jfrm.2018.73018

Lepetit, L., Strobel, F., & Tran, T. H. (2021). An alternative Z-score measure for downside bank insolvency risk. *Applied Economics Letters*, *28*(2), 137–142. doi:10.1080/13504851.2020.1739222

Lukić, V., Popović, S., & Janković, I. (2019). Nonperforming Loans and Financial Stability–The Case of Serbia. *Facta Universitatis, Series: Economics and Organization*, 349-364.

Min, F., Wen, F., Xu, J., & Wu, N. (2021). Credit supply, house prices, and financial stability. *International Journal of Finance & Economics*.

Nasreen, S., & Anwar, S. (2018). How financial stability affects economic development in south asia: a panel data analysis. *European Online Journal of Natural and Social Sciences, 7*(1), 54.

Njang, I. I., Omini, E. E., Bekun, F. V., & Adedoyin, F. F. (2020). *Financial System Stability and Economic Growth in Nigeria*. Academic Press.

Ozili, P. K. (2018). Banking stability determinants in Africa. *International Journal of Managerial Finance*, *14*(4), 462–483. doi:10.1108/IJMF-01-2018-0007

Ozili, P. K., & Iorember, P. T. (2023). Financial stability and sustainable development. *International Journal of Finance & Economics*, ijfe.2803. doi:10.1002/ijfe.2803

Prochniak, M., & Wasiak, K. (2017). The impact of the financial system on economic growth in the context of the global crisis: Empirical evidence for the EU and OECD countries. *Empirica*, *44*(2), 295–337. doi:10.1007/s10663-016-9323-9

Sotiropoulou, T., Giakoumatos, S. G., & Petropoulos, D. P. (2019). Financial development, financial stability, and economic growth in European Union: A panel data approach. *Advances in Management and Applied Economics*, *9*(3), 55–69.

Stewart, R., Chowdhury, M., & Arjoon, V. (2020). Bank stability and economic growth: Trade-offs or opportunities? *Empirical Economics*, 1–27.

Thakor, A. V. (2018). Post-crisis regulatory reform in banking: Address insolvency risk, not illiquidity. *Journal of Financial Stability*, *37*, 107–111. doi:10.1016/j.jfs.2018.03.009

Tosunoglu, B. T. (2018, June). Relationship Between Financial Stability and Economic Growth in Turkey (2002-2017). In *Proceedings of International Academic Conferences* (No. 6409266). International Institute of Social and Economic Sciences.

Younsi, M., & Nafla, A. (2019). Financial stability, monetary policy, and economic growth: Panel data evidence from developed and developing countries. *Journal of the Knowledge Economy*, *10*(1), 238–260. doi:10.1007/s13132-017-0453-5

Chapter 9
Employees and Robots in Amazon's Robotic Mobile Fulfillment Systems:
A Netnographic Analysis of a Supply Chain Transformation

Badr Bentalha
https://orcid.org/0000-0003-1339-542X
National School of Business and Management, Sidi Mohammed Ben Abdellah University, Morocco

ABSTRACT

Amazon is a world leader in e-commerce and robotization. Its robotic mobile fulfillment systems (RMFS) aim to speed up product delivery by using robots to move shelves. In terms of speed, precision, and profitability, the RMFS solution seems to guarantee economic and commercial success. Nevertheless, the integration of robotization is accompanied by an increase in workload, daily tasks, and accident risks. The aim of the present study is to provide an in-depth analysis of Amazon RFMS employees' perceptions of current robotization. Through a netnographic study of the comments and opinions of Amazon employees working in robotized warehouses, the empirical study will gather argumentative thinking around the effect of digital transformation in RFMS in terms of employability, working conditions, and quality of work life. The results of the study show a consolidation of working conditions accompanied by stress and a risk of job loss. Certain risks and doubts are also present, notably around the possibility of work-related accidents and the man-machine interactions.

DOI: 10.4018/979-8-3693-1511-8.ch009

INTRODUCTION

Amazon is a global online retail giant and also a leading robotics company. The company focuses on a variety of services, including e-commerce, computing, digital streaming, and artificial intelligence (AI). A pillar of the Fortune 100, Amazon is also one of the Big Five, the top five most dominant technology companies in the United States. During the COVID-19 pandemic, Amazon's business soared as millions of shut-in Americans relied more than ever on the company's delivery services. The company's exceptional results are explained by several variables, including a modern, robust supply chain. Amazon has over 175 distribution centers worldwide, enabling it to stock billions of products and reach customers all over the world. Amazon relies heavily on automation and digital technologies such as robots in its warehouses to increase efficiency.

Robotic Mobile Fulfillment Systems (RMFS) present a new type of robotized handling system, from part to collector. These robotized fulfillment centers aim to speed up product delivery by using robots for many tasks, such as moving shelves to employees to reduce order-picking time. Numerous technologies are currently operational in Amazon's warehouses. Most of these technologies are proprietary and robotized. Amazon Robotics has deployed over 520,000 robotic units in its centers and warehouses. Amazon has the advantage of being able to develop its robotic systems. In terms of speed, precision, and cost-effectiveness, it's a great success. This innovation has led to fierce competition for third-party robotic solutions (Hmioui & Bentalha, 2020).

Regarding working conditions, Amazon's supporters claim that the integration of robotics has the potential to improve working conditions for warehouse employees. In facilities without robots, for example, Amazon warehouse workers often walk between 15 and 30 kilometers a day to transport items. Robot-equipped facilities have largely eliminated this task. The integration of robots into Amazon's warehousing operations aims to boost efficiency and reduce worker injury through automated lifting and transport of inventory. Employees stand to benefit from less physically intensive roles that focus more on system oversight, quality control, and monitoring processes. Additionally, the robotic systems provide workers options to gain in-demand skills in emerging technologies like automation. Nevertheless, for critics of this technology, Amazon's robotized centers are stressful and dangerous. According to the "*Strategic Organizing Center*" report (SOC, 2019), Amazon recorded a serious injury rate of 7.9 per 100 workers in 2019, more than 54% higher than the serious injury rate in non-robotic facilities. Robotics integration is also accompanied by work overload and an increase in daily tasks. Workers are similarly forced to perform fast, repetitive movements. As a result, there is a risk of injury and loss of motivation. The automation puts certain manual picking and packing jobs at risk to redundancy. Even with training, system downtimes from mechanical failures can still halt operations and disrupt defined workflows and roles.

This study aims to understand employees' perceptions of current robotization at Amazon's RFMS. Through a netnographic study of the comments and opinions of Amazon employees working in robotized warehouses, our empirical study will raise a reflection on the effect of digital transformation in RFMS in terms of employability, working conditions, and quality of work life (Bentalha et al., 2019). The aim is to understand employees' perceptions of working conditions in RMFS.

To discuss the issues raised, we will explain the approach to warehouse robotization (RMFS) and social considerations in robotized factories. Next, we will present our netnographic methodological approach and the opportunities provided by this method. Finally, we will support our reflection with the results obtained from our empirical study.

1. ROBOTIC MOBILE FULFILLMENT SYSTEMS: BETWEEN PRODUCTIVE EFFICIENCY AND SOCIAL CONSIDERATIONS

1.1. Amazon's Robotized Warehouse Management: Undeniable Production Efficiency

Intelligent logistics involves incorporating integrated digital applications to automate logistics and warehousing. The aim is to improve resource utilization rates, and productivity levels and reduce logistics costs (Alla et al., 2022). Online commerce requires a reshaping of logistics approaches particularly warehouses to achieve fast, global sales (Blanquart et al., 2019; Hmioui & Bentalha, 2021).

Robotics has created many opportunities, especially in warehouse order picking. This is a historically manual and arduous activity. The Robotic Mobile Fulfillment System is an automated order-picking system that uses robots in warehouses. It is used in many sectors, especially e-commerce. It is a picking system that uses mobile shelves to store items and robots to transport these shelves to the picking stations (Yudiansyah et al., 2020).

One of the best examples of this form of robotized warehouse management is exemplified by Amazon, with increased robotization of various internal and external logistics functions. Amazon's sites now boast more than 520,000 robots, of varied and complementary natures, deployed worldwide (Table 1).

Amazon introduced robotics to its warehouses in 2012 with the $775 million acquisition of Kiva, a robot capable of moving pallets of shelves within a designated area. Today, 75% of the group's customer orders involve robotics. These robots

Table 1. Different robots in Amazon's centers

Robots	Description
Kiva	450-kilogram capacity.
Hercules	Similar to Khiva, but with a 1500 kg lifting capacity.
Pegasus	Replace the original Kiva with a payload of 560 kg.
Pegasus X-Sort Drive	Accessories can be added to the Pegasus.
Xanthus	Can carry pods and be used with a variety of accessories.
Bert	Mobile and can navigate the warehouse to transport packages
Ernie	Moves around the stack using a robotic arm. It lifts pods from the stack to place them in front of workers.
Scooter	Automated tractor towing empty bins.
Kermit	Guided truck with magnetic navigation
Scout	A six-wheeled autonomous vehicle designed for last-mile deliveries.
Drones	Prime Air drones can deliver products to customers' front doors.

Source: Personal elaboration

consolidate Amazon's relatively successful Just Walk Out system (Bentalha & Hmioui, 2021).

RMFS have been animated to support productivity and reduce manual labor. They enable 40% more stock to be stored, making order fulfillment easier. Kiva, for example, has reduced stock dispatch time by 75 minutes. Amazon has also halved picking time in its warehouses, speeding up deliveries and optimizing space by halving storage capacity per square meter.

In the warehouse, RMFS advocates believe that the system offers operators a considerable reduction in the distances they have to travel and a consequent improvement in health and safety at work. For supporters of these technological advances, robotization offers advantages in terms of job creation, ergonomics, and career development.

Thus, the gains of robotization are confirmed economically (Bentalha et al., 2020). Nevertheless, the social considerations of these technologies are rarely discussed in the literature.

1.2. Social Considerations in Robotized Mobile Distribution Systems

Amazon stores the products it sells on its e-commerce sites in hundreds of gigantic fulfillment centers located on the outskirts of major urban areas. They are organized in the form of multi-story "picking towers", divided into small cells where the goods sold are stored. Each distribution center employs thousands of workers who perform repetitive physical tasks: "stowers" place products on shelves, while "pickers" retrieve them (Delfanti & Frey, 2020).

Since its introduction in 2012, Amazon has created over 300,000 full-time jobs worldwide, particularly in IT and robot maintenance. In addition, fulfillment centers equipped with robots often have a higher number of jobs, as inventory is moved more quickly, requiring additional employees (Bentalha, 2023). The robot can not only traverse vertical and horizontal aisles but also oblique ones. In the case of a fishbone layout, the robot can transport the racking to the workstation via the oblique aisle. The time required to complete the racking handling task is therefore different from the time consumed in the traditional layout, and the travel distance expected for a single cycle can be reduced by around 20% (Lamballais et al., 2016).

Amazon has achieved record growth and spectacular profits, but its management of employees in general and warehouse workers in particular has sometimes been marked by grievances, miscommunication, and high turnover. In contrast to its precise and sophisticated parcel processing, Amazon's human resources management model is relatively tense and questionable. Indeed, employees have very little influence on the labor market, given their position in the sphere of capital circulation as manual workers responsible for arranging, picking, and packing goods in warehouses (Khalfaoui & Derbali, 2021). These Taylorist tasks, which require no special qualifications or diplomas, are reflected in their easy permutability (Kassem, 2022; Jouini et al., 2018).

The introduction of robots into the warehouse environment means that work will be divided between employees and robots (Parker & Grote, 2020). Managerial literature should become involved around the topic of robotization to ensure that thoughtful choices about work and working conditions are made (Cooke et al., 2021; Smids et al., 2019). Based on the literature on organizational change (Hayes, 2018), successful human-robot collaboration is likely to depend on the choices that organizational stakeholders make when deciding on the implementation of a new technology. Thus, it is possible to study the interactions between employees and robots working in RMFS to understand the relationship between different logistics operators and analyze the impact of logistics digitization on employee perceptions.

2. RESEARCH METHODOLOGY: THE NETNOGRAPHIC APPROACH, A DIGITAL ETHNOGRAPHY

In recent years, the Internet has enabled cybernauts to express themselves openly. It's a new way of publishing and self-confidence discussed by researchers. The Internet has become a research ground for specialists analyzing digital opinions, messages, and comments. Information sources include forums, podcasts, social networking sites, videos, blogs, newsgroups, photo-sharing communities, and virtual worlds. It is a neologism of two words, Internet and Ethnography (Alla et al., 2020). Netnography analyzes mainly, but not exclusively, the communicative acts of user-members of virtual communities, seeking to give them meaning. It is a relatively recent research methodology, which emerged in the United States when the Internet was still in its infancy. It is based on the researcher's commitment to becoming part of a virtual community. The researcher can focus on the phenomena being studied or on the people being studied. It takes the processes of classical ethnographic study and adapts them to the study of online communities. The netnographic approach is far from being an improvised activity and follows an ordered scientific procedure.

The netnographic approach offers several advantages and opportunities. Firstly, it allows the researcher to be neutral towards the research question. By monitoring digital communities, the researcher does not influence the participants. Secondly, the method offers a not inconsiderable ratio of speed to cost (Jong, 2017). Also, the method enables the geographical dimension of the study to be extended, offering the possibility of investigating remote or global issues and increasing accessibility to the population under study (Addeo et al., 2019). Finally, the method offers the advantage of discretion and respect for confidentiality, as it enables sensitive research topics, delicate phenomena, or stigmatized groups (prisoners, offenders, migrants, disabled people, etc.) to be apprehended.

The adoption of this method is justified in our work by the research question and the field of study (Lamsiah & Bentalha, 2023). Indeed, the question addressed is oriented toward the behaviors and attitudes of employees towards the robotization of Amazon's RMFS. As such, the approach adopted offers the advantage of analyzing comments and opinions that reflect this salaried perception of working conditions and the robot-human relationship. What's more, the question studied concerns closed warehouses, where access as a researcher is not authorized, and observation of actual working conditions will not reflect the researcher's perception of the subject. Indeed, at the time of work, the employee perceives the observation or interview and may give partial or incomplete information.

Thus, the choice was made to analyze the opinions and comments posted on such RMFS platforms by employees. We extracted comments posted on YouTube videos on the theme under study, retaining only comments published by current or former employees. The aim is to keep comments where the writer claims to be an employee or former employee of Amazon, and where the discussion analyzed shows criteria of knowledge of the entity and elements likely to contribute and reflect on the theme.

The empirical study takes the form of an analysis of opinions and comments, as expressed in YouTube comments during the study period (January 2020 and December 2022). The choice of the YouTube site is justified by the presence of several videos showing Amazon warehouses and robots, discussing the wage relationship and social considerations, a wealth of comments, and wide coverage. The comments analyzed are taken by chance with a content analysis. The language chosen for comment extraction is English, given that the warehouses studied are present in American territories and that the majority of comments are written in English. This ensures a high degree of linguistic unity in the textual analysis. Our theoretical saturation is obtained by analyzing redundancy and the quality of new messages.

At this level, we stopped collecting data as soon as we noticed a redundancy in the results. Secondly, we double-coded the corpus to group messages by theme. The aim was to carry out a contextualized and virtual analysis.

For qualitative data processing, statistical analysis was carried out using IRAMUTEQ and TROPES software. One of the challenges of textual analysis is how to transform large-scale, complex data into manageable information. Computer-aided textual analysis can be decisive at this stage, as it enables certain tasks to be performed automatically and makes it easier to observe patterns and obtain unexpected information. The combined use of these two software packages provides a complementary approach to thematic, verbal, linguistic, and semantic analysis.

3. RESULTS AND DISCUSSION

The results obtained will be presented via a discussion of the reference items, and a thematic analysis to show the study's reference universes, followed by a detailed analysis of the components of each of the decomposed dimensions.

3.1. Analysis of Discussion Items

Qualitative analysis of the comments made by Internet users via IRAMUTEQ has enabled us to identify a range of fundamental items. The most frequently used word in the discussions was "work". The words "person" and "job" also figure prominently. The manual grouping of the above items enabled us to deduce the weight of the various concepts used (Table 2):

Our initial item analysis can be supplemented by a thematic analysis to identify the main themes of reflection identified by employees who have discussed the robotization of Amazon's RMFS.

Table 2. Content analysis of some concepts from employee comments on Amazon's warehouse robotization

Concept	Frequency	%
work	71	3,87%
person	37	2,02%
job	31	1,69%
Amazon	30	1,63%
hour	25	1,36%
warehouse	20	1,09%
robot	20	1,09%
company	19	1,04%
day	18	0,98%
Pay	17	0,93%
Time	16	0,87%
Total	**1835**	**100%**

Source: Results of statistical study

3.2. Thematic Approach to Employee Comments on Amazon's Warehouse Robotization

The decomposition of reference universes enables us to highlight the most frequent themes and categories that also have semantic or lexical affinities. We followed three steps to achieve this thematic decomposition. First, a thorough reading of the transcripts gave us a general overview of the issue under study. Next, we coded the various criteria and items used in the study. Finally, we established the themes and items retained (Table 3).

The words were grouped manually, enabling us to extract the main dimensions relating to the characteristics of the question studied. We analyzed the results of the qualitative study by summing up the items according to occurrence.

The thematic analysis enabled us to make an initial assessment of the themes studied. For this reason, we resorted to concept similarity analysis. This is a technique based on graph theory, which analyzes the proximity of words.

The first remarks of the qualitative study concern questions raised about behavioral and temporal aspects. The behavioral dimension relates to everyday aspects of working with robots. Note the intensity of the adverbs used (Good - easy - Fast - long). On the other hand, there's a strong presence of temporal variables, closely linked to working in storage areas.

Table 3. Theme, main categories, and sub-categories illustrating the themes chosen by Amazon's RMFS employees

Theme	Main Categories	Code	Sub-Categories	Frequencies	Percentages
Employee perception of Amazon RMFS	Time dimension	T1	Hour – Time - second	135	15,57%
		T2	Day – Year - Month	111	12,80%
		T3	Night - Week	48	5,54%
	Spatial dimension	S1	Place – Floor	63	7,27%
		S2	Center - warehouse	81	9,34%
		S3	environment	15	1,73%
	Accident-related dimension	A1	Break – Bad – Injury – back – stress	102	11,76%
		A2	Health	18	2,08%
	Managerial dimension	M1	Team – supervisor –manager - Shift	78	9,00%
		M2	Task	15	1,73%
	Behavioral dimension	C1	Good – easy – Fast – long	144	16,61%
		C2	Need – order - walk	57	6,57%
Totals				867	100,00%

Source: Qualitative study

We can see that the words "Work" and "Warehouse" play a central role in the various responses (Figure 1).

The various aspects noted in the similarity analysis will be discussed, one by one, to ensure greater detail in the discussions and analyses carried out.

3.2.1. A Temporal Approach to Employee Reviews and Comments at Amazon's RMFS Warehouses

It's clear that robotized work, like manual work, requires employees to spend several hours in the workspace. As a result, employees are relatively "frustrated" and have used several families of temporal concepts to show this extortion and disappointment linked to time spent in the workspace. We'll illustrate attitudes with the star graphs below (Figure 2) and extracts from interviewees' verbatim. This star graph shows the relationships between references, or between a category of words.

The temporal organization is too often discussed by learners in terms of time, date, day, or week. This aspect attracted our attention, given the high frequency of temporal items discussed. We have summarized this aspect in Figure 3 to show the families of concepts linked to this dimension.

The following verbatim excerpt illustrates the importance of time in the respondents' analysis:

Figure 1. Similarity relationships of items most used by employees on Amazon warehouse robotization
Source: Qualitative study (IRAMUTEQ)

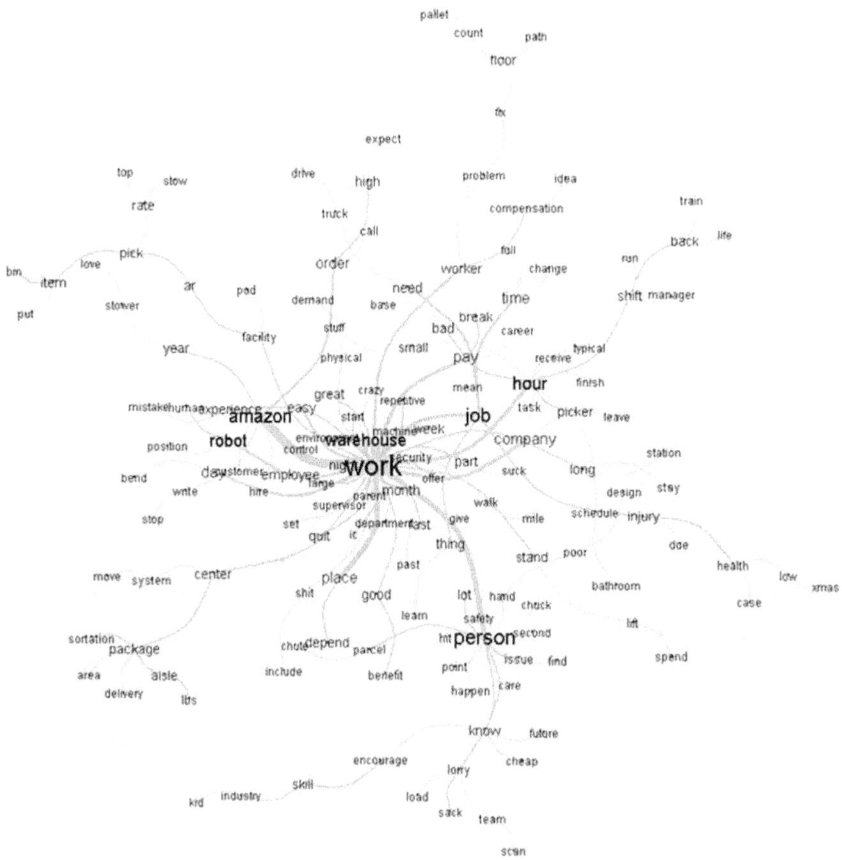

Figure 2. Links between the 'Time' item in the interviews analyzed
Source: Qualitative study (Tropes)

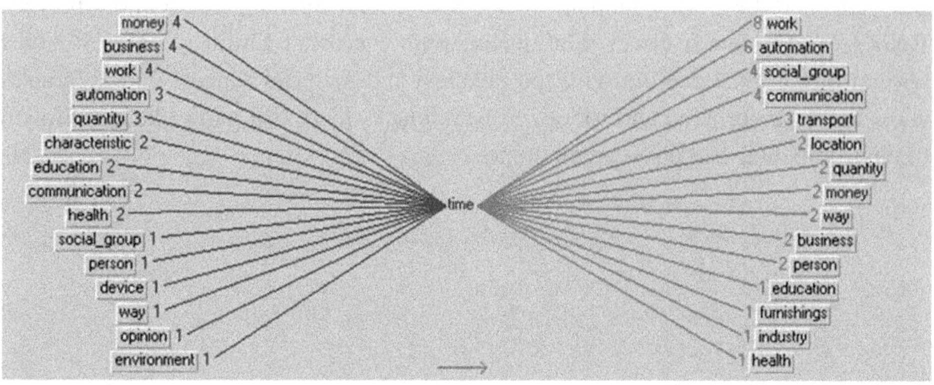

Figure 3. Temporal analysis of Amazon RMFS employee opinions
Source: Qualitative study (Tropes)

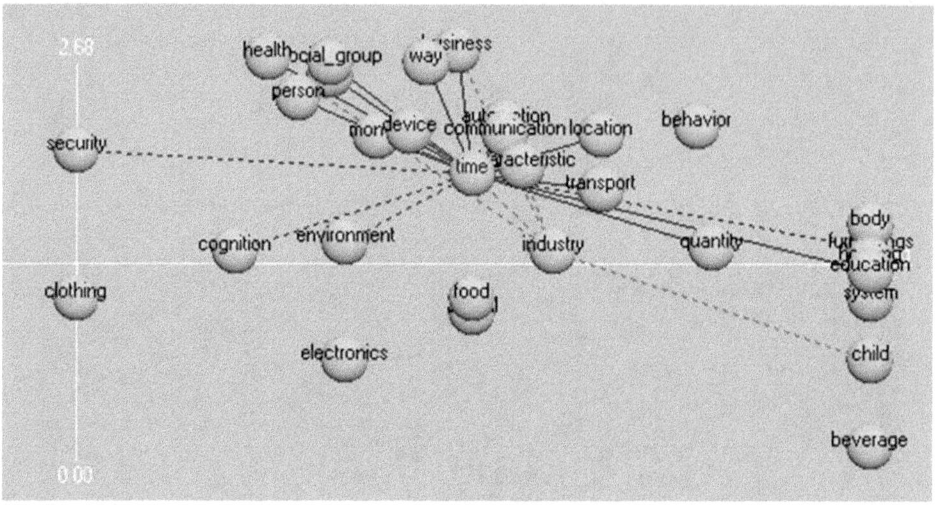

- *Doing that for* <u>*40 hours*</u> *a week was very tiresome. I wouldn't recommend working as an order picker in an AR facility I used to work in a warehouse like this for Amazon.*
- *The environment is controlled climate, offers large breakrooms, cleaned bathrooms, and a variety of* <u>*work hours*</u> *accommodating* <u>*personal schedules*</u>*.*
- *especially if you work* <u>*too many hours*</u> *and they do cap the work hours even if overtime is available the robots are only in fulfillment centers.*

3.2.2. A Spatial Approach to Employee Reviews and Comments at Amazon's RMFS Warehouses

The work environment is an aspect discussed by employees in their various comments. The floor and the storage area are two themes that receive a great deal of analysis. Both seem to have a direct relationship with the robotization of RMFS. Thus, several discussions dealing with the physical and material aspects of warehouses show that in automated and robotized warehouses there is a particular attachment to environmental and physical elements.

3.2.3. Vocabulary of Dangers and Doubts From Amazon RMFS Warehouse Employee Reviews and Comments

Accidents and the health situation in the workplace are two issues that employees have raised in their various comments. The most visible aspect of the discussions around this theme is the weakness of safety measures and the great possibility of accidents in the workplace, especially with the presence of machines. Here is an extract from the verbatim comments on this topic.

- *so that we don't have to do the dull/mundane/and* ***dangerous*** *work anymore I was a picker at Amazon for 2 weeks.*
- *This person appears to be breaking a top* ***safety*** *rule!! It depends on your worldview. Some believe you shouldn't be paying people for basic tasks.*
- *As far as their* ***SAFETY*** *goes, their own so-called "****safety*** *team" was a complete joke.*

We noted the presence of the terms "poor", "joke" and "rule" (Figure 4).

Risks and conflicts are also discussed by employees. The possibility of conflicts, the presence of risks of falls or accidents, and the possibility of interactions with robots are themes present among employees (Figure 5).

- *you will have a higher* ***risk*** *of injury, complications with your health, or even long-term injury.*
- *but you a considered a* ***victim*** *of bureaucracy at that point You are more than an infraction and a* ***problem****. Omit the* ***problem*** *of having cases of workers' compensation. Is this a good idea, idea, time will tell.*
- *and* ***security*** *of the job is by far the best quality. The hours are set and if you have the hours you can use them without asking. and going into the AR floor picking up items fixing any* ***problems*** *with robots or bins, and helping with* ***rescues****.*

Figure 4. Safety measures and hazards in Amazon's RMFS employee reviews
Source: Qualitative study (Tropes)

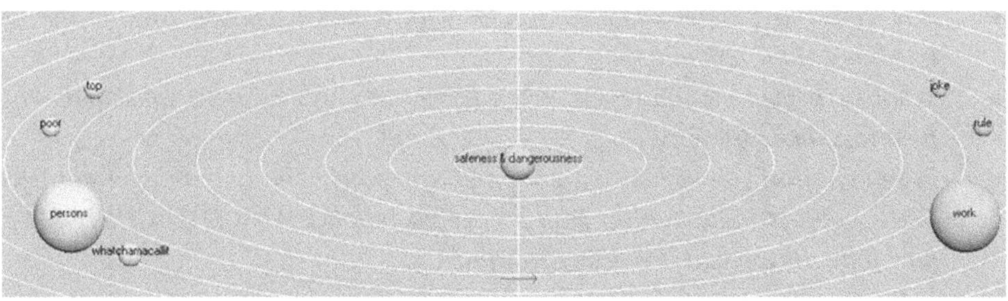

Figure 5. Strong discussion of crisis and conflict in Amazon's RMFS employee reviews
Source: Qualitative study (Tropes)

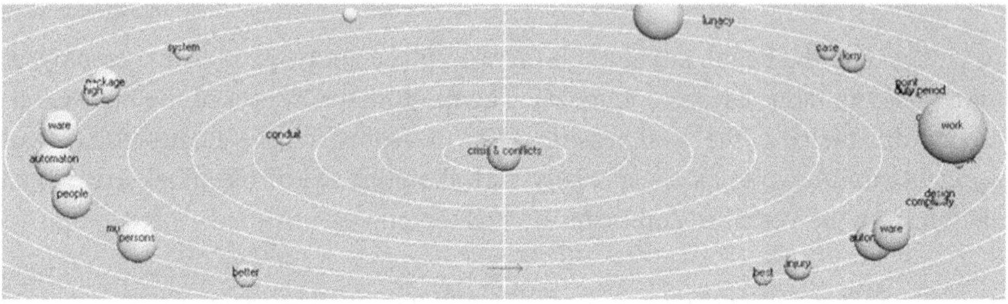

3.2.4. A Managerial Approach to Employee Feedback at Amazon's RMFS Warehouses

Work in Amazon's RMFS is highly supervised by the hierarchy. The task of supervisors, their powers, and the hierarchical levels of managers seem to be a common concern in Amazon's RMFS. Also, the team and the various team-oriented tasks (Shifts) seem to be a recurring topic.

3.2.5. Behavioral Approach to Employee Reviews and Comments at Amazon's RMFS Warehouses

Behavioral concepts are very present. By way of illustration, "Good - easy - Fast - long" is reproduced 144 times in employees' speeches and opinions.

We noted a strong presence of feelings and behavioral factors. Indeed, it is clear that employees use subjective discourses on the work situation on Amazon's RMFS premises. The following extract from the verbatim testifies to this lexical mix in the opinions analyzed.

- ***look up*** *proper lifting practices (many injuries occur due to failing to lift properly) and specifically spend your first month walking everywhere you can,*
- *if there is one person you* ***dislike*** *a lot within the warehouse, or you are the type to be non-personable.*
- *What* ***surprised*** *me today was when I went to order an item, and above the item was the word NEW.*
- *in my* ***opinion*** *untouched by any other company. The only thing I can say that's good is individually) as it's ordered is* ***folly****. ASK THE CUSTOMER how long they would be willing to wait!*

Figure 6. Strong presence of feelings and behavioral factors in the opinions of Amazon RMFS employees
Source: Qualitative study (Tropes)

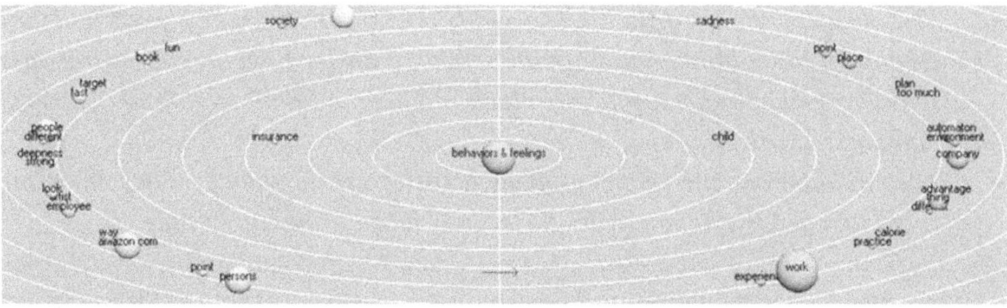

This observation is reinforced by the presence of vocabulary of doubt and uncertainty in the various speeches. For some employees, there is a strong element of innuendo and storytelling. In addition, the presence of large or fast machines seems to be a factor in the presence of persistent doubt about the possibility of problems or accidents. Several families of concepts also evoke stress in the workplace (stress, worry, insurance).

The following verbatim extract illustrates this relationship:

- *I need to on Amazon and this will **probably** save me a fortune. I cannot see myself ordering from a company that is trying to mislead me,*
- *The most enjoyable part of this job was **probably** being able to do Amnesty as soon as I hit my 3 months of being full-time.*

We found a mixture of complexity and simplicity among employees. For several of the tasks discussed, the employee mentions the complexity of the overall task, but the simplicity of the task performed by the employee. This mix seems to reflect the importance of robotization in these workspaces since the task that initially seems complex is taken care of in its tedious or frustrating part by the robot, and then seen by the employee as simple and affordable.

- *the work can be **long** and sometimes a little bit **heavy** but it's genuinely so **simple**.*
- *but they are more **complex** and most of the time **out of your control because** the mistake happened at the station before you, but it's also so **simple**.*

The same observation is reflected in the juxtaposition of two opposing vocabularies: simple and difficult. The difficult part of the tasks seems to be linked to the hourly workload or the need to do fast repetitive tasks. However, the easy part of the job seems to lie in the tasks and the ability to learn over time (Figure 7).

- *Yes, the work can get* ***difficult****, especially if you work too many hours and they do cap the work hours, the work at Amazon is* ***easier*** *than at other warehouse jobs (from experience), place is clean (minus the adults acting like mommy and daddy works there)*
- *They didn't make the robots to make it* ***easier*** *for the human. They made the robot to make the human work faster in a shorter amount of time*

Thus, four major modalities are present in the speeches (Table 4). Time, place, manner, and doubt. The following table summarizes the presence of each of these modalities.

Thus, the current integration of robots with employees seems to be a topic rich in discussion. Indeed, the analysis of opinions shows a great plurality of opinions and a complementarity in the analyses. On the whole, employees seem to be obliged to work with robots, have doubts and fears, and also show positive aspects of this robotization of RMFS. Risk factors are present, but the changing nature of the tasks performed is also discussed. We have thus carried out a sentiment analysis based on the opinions and comments collected (Figure 8).

The comments contain a great deal of negativity, as measured by the adverbs, adjectives, or words used (67.6% of total opinions contain some negativity). Here's

Figure 7. Duality of the concepts "easy & not easy" and "good-bad-better" in the opinions of Amazon RMFS employees
Source: Qualitative study (Tropes)

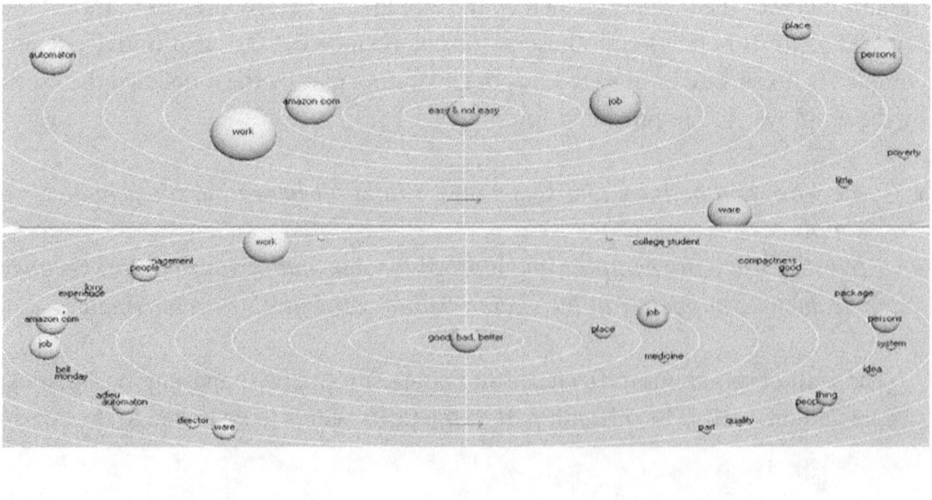

Table 4. Frequent modality analysis of employee comments on Amazon warehouse robotization

Modalities	Number	Percentages
Time	97	29%
Place	52	15,6%
Manner	66	19,8%
Doubt	5	1,5%

Source: Qualitative study

Figure 8. Sentiment analysis of comments
Source: Qualitative study (monkeylearn.com)

an extract from Verbatim to show this negativity and the intensity of these negative comments (Figure 9).

Some comments include a large amount of negativity. This is mainly due to the great subjectivity of some responses, the involvement of employees in the subject, and their perceptions of the topic under discussion. Amazon employees' comments seem to be a means of expressing themselves and claiming certain rights. Finally, several speeches seem to give advice to future employees or deal with possible opportunities in the future.

Figure 9. Excerpt from the verbatim sentiment analysis of comments
Source: Qualitative study (https://text2data.com/Demo)

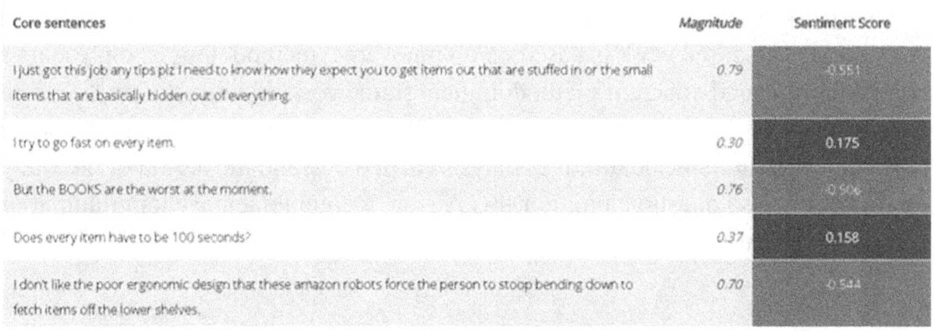

Core sentences	Magnitude	Sentiment Score
I just got this job any tips plz I need to know how they expect you to get items out that are stuffed in or the small items that are basically hidden out of everything	0.79	-0.551
I try to go fast on every item.	0.30	0.175
But the BOOKS are the worst at the moment.	0.76	-0.506
Does every item have to be 100 seconds?	0.37	0.158
I don't like the poor ergonomic design that these amazon robots force the person to stoop bending down to fetch items off the lower shelves.	0.70	-0.544

So, at this level, we can propose several recommendations for improving human-robot relations in Amazon warehouses. Firstly, augmented reality functions can be added to terminals to guide employees through their tasks. Real-time visual instructions can improve the accuracy and speed of order picking. Next, it is possible to enable two-way communication between systems and employees, so that the latter can report problems, make suggestions for improvement, and so on. Employees need to feel that they are stakeholders, not just performers. We can also advise you to set up reward and recognition systems based on employee performance and productivity. This will stimulate their commitment and motivation to use technology systems effectively. It is also advisable to integrate a conversational agent or virtual assistant (chatbot) into interfaces and terminals to respond directly to employees' questions/requests. This will streamline information exchange and problem resolution (Bouhtati et al., 2023). Finally, it is essential to set up a feedback platform for employee suggestions for improvement, with the best ideas voted on and taken into account by decision-makers. The aim is to receive employees' opinions and comments, which will enable anomalies to be recognized and the human-robot relationship to be improved.

CONCLUSION

Robotic Mobile Fulfillment Systems are storage areas using Amazon robots. RFMS is a robotized order-picking system deployed by Amazon in some of its warehouses. When an order is placed, an algorithm optimizes the robots' route to pick up the products as quickly as possible according to their location. This method of organizing warehouses has proved highly efficient both operationally and productively. On the social front, however, there are several criticisms of this robotic technology.

The current integration of robotization is rarely discussed in academic research. We conducted an in-depth netnographic analysis of Amazon RFMS employees' perceptions. Working conditions, stress, and the risk of job loss are discussed by these employees. Also, certain risks and doubts are present, notably around the possibility of work-related accidents and man-machine interactions in RFMS storage facilities.

The work provides a framework for analyzing human-machine integration in workspaces. Also, the work is based on an innovative methodology and presents a comprehensive and coherent methodological framework. Finally, the work can be a basis for future quantitative studies. Nevertheless, methodological and personal biases are present in the qualitative analysis carried out, and the period of the study carried out is also questionable. For this reason, a complementary longitudinal or comparative analysis would be desirable.

REFERENCES

Addeo, F., Delli Paoli, A., Esposito, M., & Ylenia Bolcato, M. (2019). Doing social research on online communities: The benefits of netnography. *Athens Journal of Social Sciences*, *7*(1), 9–38. doi:10.30958/ajss.7-1-1

AlDajani, I. M. (2020). Phronetic Netnography Research Design. In *Internet Communication Technology (ICT) for Reconciliation* (pp. 155–201). Springer. doi:10.1007/978-3-030-41203-6_7

Alla, L., Bentalha, B., & Bouhtati, N. (2022). Assessing Supply Chain Performance in the Covid 19 Context: A Prospective Model. In *2022 14th International Colloquium of Logistics and Supply Chain Management (LOGISTIQUA)* (pp. 1-6). IEEE.

AllaL.HmiouiA.BentalhaB. (2020). La netnographie dans les recherches marketing: La communauté virtuelle comme consom'acteur vecteur d'efficacité marketing. *Alternatives Managériales et Economiques, 2*(4), 631-652. doi:10.48374/IMIST.PRSM/ame-v2i4.23559

Bentalha, B. (2023). Consumer Perception of Robotic Mobile Fulfillment Systems: A Netnographic Case Study of Amazon. In Innovation, Strategy, and Transformation Frameworks for the Modern Enterprise (pp. 243-264). IGI Global. doi:10.4018/979-8-3693-0458-7.ch010

Bentalha, B., & Hmioui, A. (2021). Smart Service Supply Chain and Just Walk Out Technology: A Netnographic Approach. In *The Proceedings of the International Conference on Smart City Applications* (pp. 223-236). Springer.

Bentalha, B., Hmioui, A., & Alla, L. (2019). The digitalization of the supply chain management of service companies: a prospective approach. In *Proceedings of the 4th International Conference on Smart City Applications* (pp. 1-8). 10.1145/3368756.3369005

Bentalha, B., Hmioui, A., & Alla, L. (2020). Digital service supply chain management: current realities and prospective visions. In *The Proceedings of the Third International Conference on Smart City Applications* (pp. 808-822). Springer. 10.1007/978-3-030-37629-1_58

Blanquart, C., Liu, Z., Maudhuit, N., & Zéroual, T. (2019). Les entrepôts du e-commerce: Quelles spécificités? Une étude du cas Amazon. *Logistique & Management*, *27*(1), 44–54. doi:10.1080/12507970.2018.1552088

Bouhtati, N., Alla, L., & Bentalha, B. (2023). Marketing Big Data Analytics and Customer Relationship Management: A Fuzzy Approach. In Integrating Intelligence and Sustainability in Supply Chains (pp. 75-86). IGI Global. doi:10.4018/979-8-3693-0225-5.ch004

Cooke, F. L., Dickmann, M., & Parry, E. (2021). IJHRM after 30 years: Taking stock in times of COVID-19 and looking towards the future of HR research. *International Journal of Human Resource Management*, *32*(1), 1–23. doi:10.1080/09585192.2020.1833070

Delfanti, A., & Frey, B. (2021). Humanly extended automation or the future of work seen through Amazon patents. *Science, Technology & Human Values*, *46*(3), 655–682. doi:10.1177/0162243920943665

Hayes, J. (2018). *The theory and practice of change management* (5th ed.). Macmillan International. doi:10.1057/978-1-352-00132-7

Hmioui, A., & Bentalha, B. (2020). Service Supply Chain Management et performance commerciale: Esquisse d'une synthèse théorique. *Revue Alternatives Managériales et Economiques*, *2*(1), 1–21. doi:10.48374/IMIST.PRSM/ame-v2i2.20798

Hmioui, A., & Bentalha, B. (2021). Service supply chain management: A literature review. *International Journal of Logistics Systems and Management*, *40*(3), 332–353. doi:10.1504/IJLSM.2021.120253

Jong, S. T. (2017). Netnography: Researching Online Populations. In P. Liamputtong (Ed.), *Handbook of Research Methods in Health Social Sciences*. Springer. doi:10.1007/978-981-10-2779-6_17-1

Jouini, F., Ajina, A., & Derbali, A. (2018). Corporate governance and corporate social responsibility. *International Journal of Management and Enterprise Development*, *17*(2), 155–167. doi:10.1504/IJMED.2018.090841

Kassem, S. (2022). Labour realities at Amazon and COVID-19: Obstacles and collective possibilities for its warehouse workers and MTurk workers. *Global Political Economy*, *1*(1), 59–79. doi:10.1332/UVGT2823

Khalfaoui, H., & Derbali, A. (2021). Quality of human capital accumulation, higher education graduates and economic growth: A comparative analysis between BRICS, Southeast Asian and MENA countries. *Human Systems Management*, *40*(5), 723–735. doi:10.3233/HSM-190855

Kozinets, R. V. (2010). *Netnography. Doing Ethnographic Research Online*. Sage Publications.

Lamballais, T., Roy, D., & De Koster, M. B. M. (2017). Estimating performance in a robotic mobile fulfillment system. *European Journal of Operational Research, 256*(3), 976–990. doi:10.1016/j.ejor.2016.06.063

Lamsiah, A., & Bentalha, B. (2023). *2022 Qatar World Cup: A Netnographic Analysis of the Relationship Between Sport, Media and Politic*. Academic Press.

Parker, S. K., & Grote, G. (2020). Automation, algorithms, and beyond: Why work design matters more than ever in a digital world. *Applied Psychology*. Advance online publication. doi:10.1111/apps.12241

Smids, J., Nyholm, S., & Berkers, H. (2019). Robots in the workplace: A threat to – or opportunity for – meaningful work? *Philosophy & Technology, 33*(3), 503–522. doi:10.1007/s13347-019-00377-4

Strategic Organizing Center. (2019). *Primed for Pain: Amazon's Epidemic of Workplace Injuries*. https://thesoc.org/amazon-primed-for-pain/

Yudiansyah, A., Keke, Y., & Veronica, V. (2020). Can the mobile robot be a future order-picking solution? A case study at Amazon fulfillment center. *Advances in Transportation and Logistics Research, 3*(1), 800–806.

Chapter 10
Does COVID-19 News Influence Financial Market Volatility in Tunisia?

Lamia Jamel
https://orcid.org/0000-0003-4098-3120
College of Business Administration, Taibah University, Tunisia

ABSTRACT

This chapter examines the effect of surprises from financial markets announcements relating to new, confirmed, and death cases of COVID-19 in USA on the volatility of financial markets in Tunisia. The authors use GARCH(1.1) specification by incorporation the surprise component in the estimated model during the period from January 1, 2019 until December 31, 2020. The empirical findings show that the evolution of the daily returns and volatilities of the stock market index in Tunisia show very significant peaks in their evolutions in particular during the first three months of 2020 during the most significant spread of the COVID-19 pandemic. The authors show that the announcements of the new cases of COVID-19 in the United States have a significant impact on the volatility of financial markets in Tunisia. This chapter is the first paper that examines the effect of surprises from financial markets announcements relating to new, confirmed, and death cases of COVID-19 on the volatility of financial markets in Tunisia.

1. INTRODUCTION

In a span of less than half a year, the novel coronavirus (Covid-19) has undergone a remarkable transformation from a mere viral epidemic to a global pandemic, with

DOI: 10.4018/979-8-3693-1511-8.ch010

profound implications that have the potential to reshape the world as we know it, in a positive manner.

This latest pandemic has been likened to a "third world war" by many, however, specific measures have been implemented to mitigate its impact. The objective of these measures is to curtail the deterioration of the situation and prevent a complete cessation of activities across various sectors worldwide.

Industries such as education, tourism, transportation, public services, sports, and electoral events have all been either postponed or suspended, thereby inevitably impacting the social and economic lives of individuals. A substantial number of contagion cases and fatalities have already been reported globally. The prospect of this pandemic persisting for an extended period, coupled with the significant declines in stock markets, which have reached historic lows not witnessed in years, is indeed disconcerting.

The S&P 500 Index recently attained its lowest level since the onset of the global financial and economic crisis in 2008. Moreover, the cryptocurrency market has demonstrated even greater volatility, experiencing an unprecedented and severe downturn. In late March 2020 alone, prices plummeted by 6% within a 24-hour period. Consequently, investors and traders have been compelled to shift their focus from "risky" assets to more stable alternatives like gold and oil, which have exhibited resilience throughout the COVID-19 pandemic.

Considering that China and South Korea account for approximately 70% of bitcoin's mining capacity (the largest cryptocurrency), it is evident that the profound impact of the virus was anticipated, particularly in Asian nations. In recent years, there has been a significant influx of cryptocurrency mining equipment, however, the current decline in prices is adversely affecting the performance of these mining machines. The present reliance on this equipment has become inefficient due to the need to recalibrate to new algorithms. Furthermore, the diminished movement to mining farms resulting from isolation and quarantine measures has exacerbated this issue. Despite prevailing projections, prices continue to plummet, culminating in an overall decrease of 15% by the end of March.

The magnitude of the impact of this health crisis has compelled the academic community to conduct research on its underlying causes and its effects on both the microeconomic and macroeconomic levels. As a result, various models have been developed, with a focus on examining the effects of this crisis. Macro-financial models have been expanded to analyze the influence of epidemics and the importance of public interventions. Recent studies have assessed the current financial vulnerability and its relationship to the series of events of the COVID crisis and regulations since 2019 (Zaremba et al., 2020; Ozili and Arun, 2020; Albulescu, 2020; Goodell, 2020; Zhang et al., 2020; Costola et al., 2020; Ahundjanov et al., 2020; Engelhardt et al., 2020; Derbali et al., 2021a; Derbali et al., 2021b; Derbali et al., 2022a; Derbali et al., 2022b; Ghorbali et al., 2022a; Ghorbali et al., 2022b; Derbali, 2022; Ben Ltaifa and Derbali, 2021).

Unexpected occurrences, including acts of terrorism and public health crises, will elicit surprise, panic, and fear among international investors, resulting in a rapid sell-off response (Burch et al., 2016). A growing body of research, such as the studies conducted by Carter and Simkins (2004), Chen and Siems (2004), Nikkinen et al. (2008), Kollias et al. (2011), Derbali and Jamel (2019), and Papakyriakou et al. (2019), has examined the impact of terrorist attacks on global financial stock market indices. Jamel and Derbali (2019) find that terrorism-related factors play a significant and important role in explaining the volatility of stock market returns, especially in the context of the Damascus Securities Exchange Weighted Index (DSEWI), which must be taken into consideration when assessing volatility.

Additionally, Ye and Karali (2016) utilize an intraday dataset to investigate how crude oil returns and volatilities respond to supply announcements from the Energy Information Administration (EIA) and the American Petroleum Institute (API) during the period from August 01, 2012, to December 31, 2013. Based on their empirical findings, they posit that unexpected supply announcements from both the API and EIA have an immediate inverse effect on returns and a significant positive effect on volatility. Similarly, Halova et al. (2014) examine an intraday dataset to evaluate the impact of unexpected changes in the EIA's crude oil inventory announcements on both returns and volatility. Halova et al. (2014) reveal that energy returns respond more significantly to unanticipated supply adjustments during the insertion period than during the removal process.

The spread of the pandemic is expected to have a similar impact. Nippani and Washer (2004) focus their attention on the stock market indices of eight highly affected economies during the SARS epidemic and come to the conclusion that, apart from China and Vietnam, the financial stock markets of the affected nations were not adversely affected. In a similar vein, Chen et al. (2007) analyze the effect of the SARS epidemic on the profitability of hotel stocks in Taiwan and mainland China and find a significant and negative influence.

He et al. (2020) attempt to investigate and evaluate the direct and spillover effects of COVID-19 on the financial stock markets of various countries. Through the utilization of conventional t-tests and non-parametric Mann–Whitney assessments, He et al. (2020) empirically investigate the daily return dataset from the financial stock markets of China, Japan, South Korea, Germany, Spain, Italy, France, and the USA. Their empirical findings demonstrate that the COVID-19 pandemic has a negative and significant short-term influence on the financial stock markets of the affected countries. Furthermore, they discover that the impact of the COVID-19 pandemic on the financial stock market indices of selected countries exhibits bidirectional spillover effects between Asian economies and European and American economies.

Sansa (2020) initiates an examination into the influence of the spread of COVID-19 on the financial stock markets in China and the USA from March 01, 2020, to March 25, 2020. Additionally, Sansa (2020) indicates a positive and significant correlation between the spread of COVID-19 cases and the international financial stock market indices utilized (such as the New York Dow Jones and the Shanghai stock exchange) during the same period of study in both the USA and China. These findings imply that the COVID-19 pandemic had a substantial impact on international financial stock market indices in China and the USA during the specified time frame.

The COVID-19 pandemic has had a significant impact on the US market (Phan and Narayan, 2020). Similarly, the financial markets of Tunisia have not been immune to the consequences of this crisis. Previous research on the consequences of COVID-19 has been limited to studying its effects in a single context, in different continents, or by comparing different countries. Therefore, this study aims to explore the impact of the COVID-19 surprise in the United States on the volatility of stock market index in Tunisia, which remains unexplored. Specifically, the objective is to analyze the impact of COVID-19 news in the United States, in terms of confirmed cases and deaths, on the volatility of the financial market in Tunisia.

In this study, we focus on the period from January 1, 2019 to December 31, 2020, examining the impact of COVID-19 news on the volatility of financial markets in Tunisia. We analyze the surprises related to new cases, confirmed cases, and deaths of COVID-19 in each country, including the United States, which has been the most affected country. Additionally, we compare the volatility of financial markets in Tunisia before and during the recent pandemic.

Based on our empirical findings, we observe significant peaks in the daily returns of Tunisia's stock index during the first three months of 2020, coinciding with the significant spread of the COVID-19 epidemic. This suggests a potential impact of the epidemic on international financial markets, particularly in Tunisia. Furthermore, the conditional volatilities of Tunisia's stock index reach their highest levels in the first three months of 2020.

Our empirical results indicate that the announcements of new COVID-19 cases in the United States (NCUSA) have a negative and significant impact on Tunisia's stock market index. However, the announcements of confirmed cases (CCUSA) have a relatively insignificant impact on returns and volatilities of Tunisia's financial stock market index. Similarly, the announcements of death cases (DCUSA) of COVID-19 in the United States also have a relatively insignificant impact on returns and volatilities of Tunisia's financial stock market index.

The rest of this paper is organized as follow; in the section 2, we expose the methodology. In section 3, we present the data. Section 4 summarizes the empirical findings. Section 5 presents the robustness test of empirical results. Finally, section 6 concludes.

2. METHODOLOGY

In finance and economics, volatility plays a significant role in risk assessment and management, portfolio optimization, and stock market index pricing. Leverage, volatility clustering (kurtosis), and lentokurtosis (asymmetry) are not enough to account for many of the fundamental similarities between the financial dataset and linear and non-linear models and estimations.

This is due to the fact that employing a financial data set makes the homoscedasticity assumption inappropriate. Engle (1982) developed the Conditional Autoregressive Heteroscedastic Model (ARCH) specification to estimate return and volatility. Bollerslev (1986) extended this model to create the Generalized Autoregressive Conditional Heteroskedastic Model (GARCH). Models of this kind are often run on long-term series with fluctuating volatility. It is true that the variance of financial series is not constant throughout time. over instance, we observe that the volatility of this kind of data is minimal over a few rather lengthy periods of time. High volatility follows the latter over extended periods of time.

This kind of chronic series can exhibit both low volatility and a tendency to follow one another at some intervals, as well as high volatility and a tendency to follow one another at other times. Since the process's volatility, or variance, is dependent on its historical values, we refer to it as autoregressive. Therefore, processes of the GARCH (p, q) (Bollerslev 1986) and ARCH (p) (Engle 1982) types are more adapted to account for this volatile behavior.

For the presentation of the GARCH model, it is a generalization of the ARCH(p) process, with:

$$h_t = \varepsilon_t^2 = \alpha_0 + \sum_{i=1}^{p} \alpha_i \varepsilon_{t-i}^2 + \sum_{j=1}^{q} \beta_j h_{t-j} \tag{1}$$

Under the condotions: $\alpha i_{\geq} 0$, $\beta j \geq_{0}$, and $\sum_{i=1}^{p} \alpha_i + \sum_{j=1}^{q} \beta_j < 1$

In this study, our contribution to the financial and economic literature lies in the integration of an exogenous element within the GARCH (1,1) specification. This element quantifies the surprise resulting from the COVID-19 pandemic in the United States and its subsequent influence on the volatility of stock market index in Tunisia. Consequently, we propose the expected equivalent of the GARCH model (1,1) as follows:

$$h_t = \varepsilon_t^2 = \alpha_0 + \sum\nolimits_{i=1}^{p} \alpha_i \varepsilon_{t-i}^2 + \sum\nolimits_{j=1}^{q} \beta_j h_{t-j} + \mu_t S_t \tag{2}$$

Where, h_t presents the dependent variable (to be explained) which is the conditional volatility of the stock market index in Tunisia on day t and S_t presents the independent (explanatory) variable which indicates the unexpected surprise reports of COVID-19 in the United States at day t.

According to Kuttner (2001), the present investigation aims to evaluate the concept of surprise by measuring the extent of fluctuation in confirmed cases and fatalities attributed to COVID-19 within a single day during a specific timeframe (referred to as the US COVID-19 Confirmed Case and Death Report, or d). Evidently, the corresponding surprise quotient pertaining to each instance of confirmed COVID-19 cases and adjustments in mortality rates in the United States is elucidated by the subsequent equivalence:

$$S = \frac{D}{D-d}(f_d - f_{d-1}) \tag{3}$$

Where, f_d represents the total of new (NCUSA), confirmed (CCUSA) and death (DCUSA) cases of COVID-19 in USA at the end of the announcement hour (day) d, f_{d-1} represents the total new, confirmed and death cases COVID-19 in USA at the end of the hour announcement (day) (d-1) and D reveals the total of the days of the month.

3. DATA

Our selection of the financial stock market index of Tunisia appears to be pertinent to us due to the substantial financial advantages it offers, and the limited amount of research conducted on this particular context. We hereby present the dataset utilized in this thesis, which comprises daily time series of returns and conditional volatilities of the stock market indices of Tunisia. Subsequently, as part of our inquiry into the impact of confirmed COVID-19 cases announcements, our focus lies on the anticipated and unforeseen components in the fluctuation of confirmed cases and deaths caused by COVID-19 in the United States.

Our sample encompasses the financial stock market index of Tunisia, which was examined during the period spanning from January 1, 2019, to January 31, 2020, as specified in Table 1. The dataset employed in this study was acquired from two specified data sources, which are listed in the subsequent addresses: https://markets.businessinsider.com/currencies, https://data.europa.eu/euodp/en/home, and https://fr.investing.com. The rationale behind selecting the variation in confirmed COVID-19 cases in China and the variation in confirmed COVID-19 cases in the United States is justified by the assumption that the United States is the country most profoundly affected by the COVID-19 pandemic during the study period.

We assume that financial stock market index of Tunisia is converted to a logarithmic structure. Then, we smear the logarithmic return such that $r_t = \ln(p_t / p_{t-1})$, with p_t represents the stock market price index at time t and P_{t-1} represents the stock market price index at time t-1. The code financial stock market index of Tunisia is provided in Table 1.

In Table 2, we summarize the descriptive statistics relating to the daily returns of stock market index of Tunisia during the study period from January 1, 2019 to December 31, 2020. Based on the results presented in this table, we observe that the average return for the stock market index of Tunisia is equal to -4.34E-05. For the expected volatility of the estimated daily return of stock market index of Tunisia, which is determined by the standard deviation statistic, it is equal to 0.008494.

The estimated statistics from Skewness show a negative sign for the stock market index of Tunisia. The negative sign associated with the asymmetry statistic shows that the estimated distribution of stock market index of Tunisia is skewed to the left while. In addition, the estimated kurtosis coefficient statistics are high and greater than unity (1). Finally, based on the estimated values of the statistics of Jarque-Bera, Skewness and Kurtosis, we confirm the rejection of the null hypothesis compared to the normal dispersion of the stock market index of Tunisia.

Figure 1 shows the evolution of the daily returns of the stock market index of Tunisia during the study period from January 1, 2019 to December 31, 2020. We see that the daily returns of the stock market index of Tunisia a show very significant peaks in their evolutions. These peaks are observed in particular during the first three months of 2020 during the most significant spread of the COVID-19 epidemic. These three months are marked by the high level of confirmed cases of COVID-19 and death cases in all countries of the world, particularly in the United States. Also, the coincidence of the peaks with the spread of COVID-19 may justify the impact of this epidemic on international financial markets, mainly in financial stock market index of Tunisia.

Table 3 summarizes the most important statistics for the unconditional correlation matrix (Pearson correlation) between the returns of the financial stock market index of Tunisia and the three three indicators used to express the effect of the announcements relating to COVID-19 in the United States during the study period from January

Table 1. Financial stock market index of Tunisia

No	Country	Name of Stock Market Index	Code
1	Tunisia	TSE TUNINDEX	TSE_TUNINDEX

Table 2. Descriptive statistics

Index	TSE_TUNINDEX
Country	Tunisia
Mean	-4.34E-05
Median	7.06E-05
Maximum	0.009457
Minimum	-0.022453
Std. Dev.	0.008494
Skewness	-3.747583
Kurtosis	19.32355
Jarque-Bera	7586.243
Probability	0.000000
Obs.	500

Notes: Table 2 presents a summary of descriptive statistics of the daily returns of the stock index of Tunisia. In our research work and during the study period from January 1, 2019 to December 31, 2020.

Figure 1. The evolution of stock market returns in Tunisia

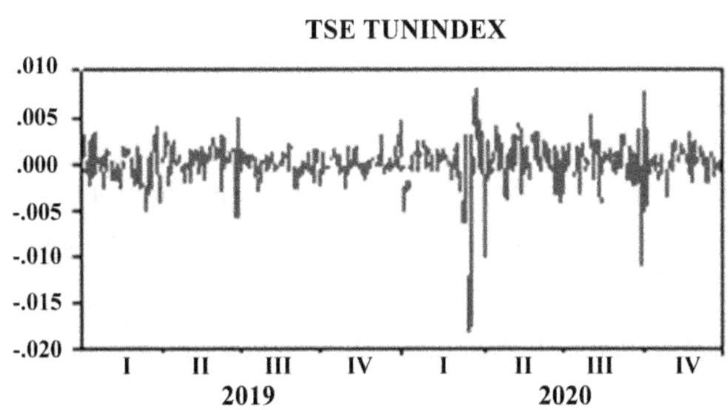

1, 2019 to December 31, 2020. From the unconditional correlation shown in this table, we see that there is a positive and negative correlation also between the three indicators used to express the effect of the announcements relating to COVID-19 in the United States and the financial stock market index of Tunisia. The first CCUSA indicator (Confirmed cases in the USA) shows a positive correlation with the financial stock market index of Tunisia. This result proves that the shocks of COVID-19 can justify the fallout of announcements of confirmed cases of COVID-19 in the USA on the financial stock market index of Tunisia during the study period from January 1, 2019 to December 31, 2020.

The second NCUSA indicator (New cases in the USA) shows a positive correlation with the financial stock market index of Tunisia. This result shows that the shocks resulting from the announcements of new cases of COVID-19 in the USA impact the financial stock market index of Tunisia during the study period from January 1, 2019 to December 31, 2020.

Finally, the third DCUSA indicator (Death cases in the USA) shows a negative correlation with the financial stock market index of Tunisia. This result shows that the shocks resulting from the announcements of new cases of COVID-19 in the USA affect the financial stock market index of Tunisia during the study period from January 1, 2019 to December 31, 2020.

We employ the augmented Dickey-Fuller test and the Phillips Perron test in order to examine the stationarity of Tunisia's financial stock market index within the study period spanning from January 1, 2019 to December 31, 2020. Based on the statistics "t-Statistic" and the level of probability "Prob. * <5%" associated with the tests, we infer from table 4 that all the stock market indices analyzed in our study exhibit stationary behavior in terms of their levels. This observation holds true for both the Dickey-Fuller test and the Phillips Perron test. Consequently, the absence of unit roots among the utilized indices justifies the absence of complications encountered during the estimation of the employed models.

4. FINDINGS

Figure 2 illustrates the progression of contingent volatilities pertaining to the stock market index of Tunisia within the duration under investigation, commencing from January 1, 2019 up until December 31, 2020. It is evident that the contingent volatilities of the Tunisian stock market index attain their highest point during the

Table 3. The unconditional correlation matrix

	TSE_TUNINDEX	CCUSA	DCUSA	NCUSA
	Tunisia	United States		
TSE_TUNINDEX	1	**0,021**	**0,021**	**-0,029**
CCUSA	0,021	1	**0,016**	**0,045**
DCUSA	0,021	0,016	1	**0,056**
NCUSA	-0,029	0,045	0,056	1

Notes: This table presents the unconditional correlation matrix between the daily returns of the stock indices of Tunisia and the three indicators used to measure the component of surprise resulting from announcements of confirmed cases; and deaths from COVID-19 during the study period from January 1, 2019 to December 31, 2020.

Table 4. The unit root test

Test	Country	Augmented Dickey-Fuller Test Statistic			Phillips-Perron Test Statistic		
		t-Statistic	Prob.*	Stationarity	Adj. t-Stat	Prob.*	Stationarity
TSE_ TUNINDEX	Tunisia	-16.84995	0.0000	Yes	-18.49053	0.0000	Yes

Notes: This table summarizes the unit root test of the daily returns of the stock index of Tunisia during the study period from January 1, 2019 to December 31, 2020. We use the augmented Dickey-Fuller test and the Phillips Perron test to study the stationarity of the different stock market indices used in our this paper.

initial three months of the year 2020. This specific period is substantiated by the heightened intensity of confirmed instances of COVID-19 and mortality rates across numerous European nations, particularly the United States. Furthermore, Figure 2 substantiates the influence of COVID-19 announcements on the financial markets of Tunisia.

Table 5 presents a summary of the descriptive statistics pertaining to the three indicators employed in quantifying the element of surprise resulting from the announcements of confirmed COVID-19 cases, new cases, and deaths during the period of study spanning from January 1, 2019, to December 31, 2020. Upon examining the findings presented in this table, it is evident that the variable CCUSA,

Figure 2. The conditional volatilities of stock market index in Tunisia (TSE_ TUNINDEX)

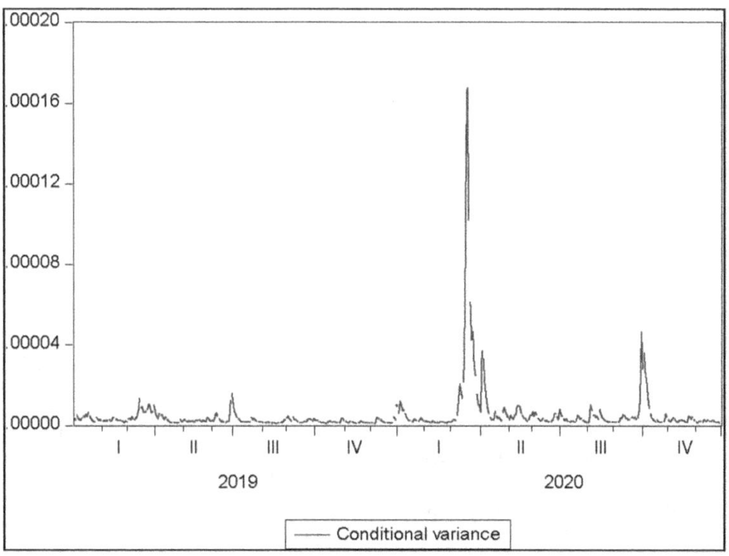

which represents the confirmed cases in the USA, exhibits the smallest mean of 0.000467, whereas the variable DCUSA, representing the cases of death in the USA, demonstrates the largest mean of 0.018367. Regarding the estimated expected volatility of the three indicators employed in measuring the surprise element arising from COVID-19 announcements in the United States, as determined by the standard deviation statistic, it is observed that the variable DCUSA displays the highest daily volatility, whereas the variable CCUSA exhibits the lowest daily volatility.

The results of the GARCH model estimation of the stock market index of Tunisia during the study period from January 1, 2019 to December 31, 2020 are presented in table 6. Thus, we have used with two types of estimate: an estimate without integration of surprise and an estimate with integration of surprise measured by the three indicators NCUSA, CCUSA and DCUSA.

In the first estimate, we estimate the GARCH model (1.1) for the stock market index of Tunisia. On the basis of the estimation results, there is a significance and a positive effect for the two parameters of the GARCH model (1.1) at a significance level of 1%. This effect is observed in the three estimates with integration of surprise measured by the three variables NCUSA, CCUSA and DCUSA.

Then, we used the GARCH model (1.1) for the stock market index of Tunisia by integrating the first component of the surprise, namely the new cases (NCUSA) of COVID-19 in the United States. According to the results presented in Table 6, we note that the announcements of new cases (NCUSA) of COVID-19 in the United States have a negative and significant impact on the stock market index of Tunisia (TSE_TUNINDEX) at a threshold of 1%. This means that if the NCUSA variable increases by one unit then the return on the Tunisian stock market index decreases by 0.00097 units. This can be explained by the sensitivity of the Tunisian financial

Table 5. Descriptive statistics of surprise components

	NCUSA	CCUSA	DCUSA
Mean	0.004526	0.000467	0.018367
Median	0.000000	0.000000	0.000000
Maximum	1.467532	1.408382	1.827764
Minimum	-2.003683	-0.934627	-1.839742
Std. Dev.	0.324364	0.156273	0.578493
Observations	500	500	500

Notes: This table summarizes the descriptive statistics of the surprise from the announcements of new, confirmed and death cases of COVID-19 and the surprises in the reporting of death cases in the United States during the study period from January 1, 2019 to December 31. 2020. New, confirmed and fatalities of COVID-19 are collected from https://data.europa.eu/euodp/en/home. Then, we follow the approach of Kuttner (2001) and we specify the surprises discovered using the change in new, confirmed and fatalities of COVID-19 for each day.

market to external effects such as the announcements of new cases (NCUSA) of COVID-19 in the United States. Also, one can justify the presence of a dependence between the financial markets in the United States and Tunisia due in large part by the closeness of trade between the two countries, the significant indebtedness of Tunisia which seeks sources of financing.

In the third estimate, we integrate the variable CCUSA which measures the announcements of confirmed cases (CCUSA) of COVID-19 in the United States during the study period from January 1, 2019 to December 31, 2020. Thus, we notice that this variable presents a relative and insignificant impact on stock market index of Tunisia. Finally, in the fourth estimate, we integrate the variable DCUSA which measures the announcements of deaths (DCUSA) of COVID-19 in the United States during the study period of study from January 1, 2019 to December 31, 2020. We find that the announcements of deaths (DCUSA) of COVID-19 in the United States presents a relative and insignificant impact on stock market index of Tunisia.

5. ROBUSTNESS TEST OF EMPIRICAL FINDINGS

The objective of our research work is to study the impact of COVID-19 on returns and volatility of the financial market index in Tunisia during the study period from January 1, 2019 to December 31, 2020. Thus, the empirical results in our study show that announcements from COVID-19 in the United States have an impact on stock market indices in Tunisia.

Table 6. The empirical results of GARCH estimation

Stock Market Index	Country	The Estimated Parameters					
		Estimation		$\alpha 0$	αi	βj	μt
TSE_TUNINDEX	Tunisia	Estimation Without Integration of Surprise		5.47E-07 (7.5675)*	0.243543 (7.8489)*	0.589078 21.475)*)	-
		Estimation With Integration of Surprise	NCUSA	5.56E-07 7.5768)*)	0.234323 (7.3564)*	0.572891 19.345)*)	-0.00097 -4.677)*)
			CCUSA	5.53E-07 7.5543)*)	0.245632 7.4985)*)	0.583334 19.364)*)	0.000374 0.4785))
			DCUSA	5.71E-07 7.4875)*)	0.236364 7.4653)*)	0.566243 19.344)*)	0.000456 (0.4664)

Notes: This table summarizes the coefficients estimated from GARCH models (1,1). To empirically test this model, we used the daily returns of stock market index of Tunisia during the study period from January 1, 2019 to December 31, 2020. The dependent variable is defined by volatility conditional (h_t) of each stock market index used. $\alpha 0$ αi, βj *and* μt *are* the coefficients of the explanatory variables estimated in our research work. The statistical significance at the threshold of 1%, 5% and 10% is noted *, ** and ***. Values in parentheses show the t-students for each variable..

To confirm these results, this section is dedicated to present the Robustness Test of the empirical results. This test is presented in Figure 3, in which we test the conditional volatility of stock market index in Tunisia without integration and with integration of the COVID-19 component. This figure proves the existence of an impact of COVID-19 on financial markets in Tunisia during the study period from January 1, 2019 to December 31, 2020.

Figure 3. The conditional volatility of stock market index of Tunisia with and without COVID-19 surprises
TOP: The index TSE_TUNINDEX without surprise (NCUSA)
BOTTOM: The index TSE_TUNINDEX with surprise (NCUSA)

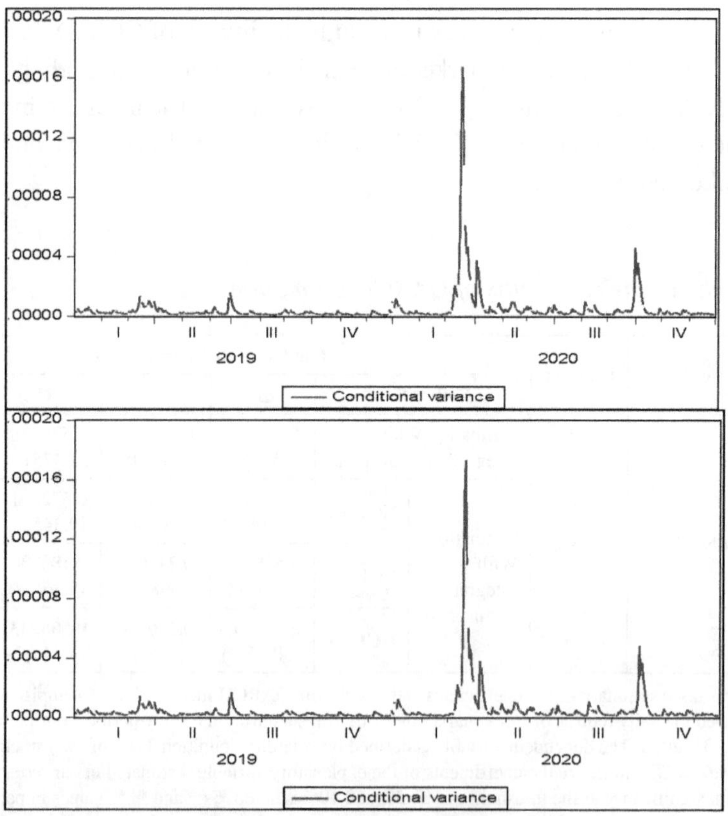

6. CONCLUSION

To achieve the objective of this paper, we use of the GARCH estimation model to examine the impact of COVID-19 on returns and volatility of the financial market index in Tunisia during the study period from January 1, 2019 to December 31, 2020. The empirical results show that the announcements of the new NCUSA cases of COVID-19 in the United States generate a negative and significant impact on returns and volatility of the financial market index in Tunisia.

For announcements of confirmed cases, CCUSA of COVID 19, they present a relative and insignificant impact on returns and volatility of the financial market index in Tunisia. Also, for the announcements from the death cases (DCUSA) of COVID-19 in the United States have a relative and insignificant impact on returns and volatility of the financial market index in Tunisia.

To conclude, we can say that the announcements from COVID 19 in the United States have an impact on returns and volatility of the financial market index in Tunisia. Thus, we responded to our objective by affirming that there is an effect of COVID-19 on returns and volatility of the financial market index in Tunisia during the study period from January 1, 2019 to December 31, 2020.

REFERENCES

Ahundjanov, B. B., Akhundjanov, S. B., & Okhunjanov, B. B. (2020). Information search and financial markets under COVID-19. PMID:33286562

Albulescu, C. T. (2020). COVID-19 and the United States financial markets' volatility. *Finance Research Letters*, 38. PMID:32837380

Ben Ltaifa, M., & Derbali, A. (2021). Confirmed and death cases of COVID-19: Which is informative in explaining the returns and volatilities of Saudi stock market indices? *International Journal of Innovation. Creativity and Change*, *15*(7), 1000–1029.

Bollerslev, T. (1986). Generalized autoregressive conditional heteroskedasticity. *Journal of Econometrics*, *31*(3), 307–327. doi:10.1016/0304-4076(86)90063-1

Burch, T. R., Douglas, R. E., & Michael, R. F. (2016). Who Moves Markets in a Sudden Marketwide Crisis? Evidence from 9/11. *Journal of Financial and Quantitative Analysis*, *51*(2), 463–487. doi:10.1017/S0022109016000211

Carter, D. A., & Betty, J. S. (2004). The Market's Reaction to Unexpected, Catastrophic Events: The Case of Airline Stock Returns and the September 11th Attacks. *The Quarterly Review of Economics and Finance*, *44*(4), 539–558. doi:10.1016/j.qref.2003.10.001

Chen, A. H., & Siems, T. F. (2004). The Effects of Terrorism on Global Capital Markets. *European Journal of Political Economy*, *20*(2), 349–366. doi:10.1016/j.ejpoleco.2003.12.005

Chen, M. H., Soo, C. S. J., & Woo, G. K. (2007). The Impact of the SARS Outbreak on Taiwanese Hotel Stock Performance: An Event-study Approach. *International Journal of Hospitality Management*, *26*(1), 200–212. doi:10.1016/j.ijhm.2005.11.004 PMID:32287849

Costola, M., Nofer, M., Hinz, O., & Pelizzon, L. (2020). *Machine learning sentiment analysis, Covid-19 news and stock market reactions*. econstor.eu

Derbali, A., Chenguel, M. B., Jamel, L., Jouirou, M., & Jouini, F. (2022b). COVID-19 pandemic and co-movement dynamics among American and European stock markets. Financial Transformations Beyond the COVID-19 Health Crisis, 309–346.

Derbali, A., Naoui, K., Ben Sassi, M., & Amiri, M. M. (2021b). Do COVID-19 Epidemic Explains the Dynamic Conditional Correlation between China's Stock Market Index and International Stock Market Indices? *Chinese Economy*, *55*(3), 227–242. doi:10.1080/10971475.2021.1958453

Derbali, A., Naoui, K., & Jamel, L. (2021a). COVID-19 news in USA and in China: Which is suitable in explaining the nexus among Bitcoin and Gold? *Pacific Accounting Review*, *33*(5), 578–595. doi:10.1108/PAR-09-2020-0170

Derbali, A., Naoui, K., & Jamel, L. (2022a). COVID-19 Surprises in China and in the USA: Which Is Useful in Explaining the Dynamic Nexus Among Energy Commodities and Bitcoin? In B. Alareeni & A. Hamdan (Eds.), *Artificial Intelligence and COVID Effect on Accounting. Accounting, Finance, Sustainability, Governance & Fraud: Theory and Application.* Springer. doi:10.1007/978-981-19-1036-4_4

DerbaliA. M. S. (2022). COVID-19 or Russia-Ukraine Conflict: Which Is Informative in Defining the Dynamic Relationship between Bitcoin and Major Energy Commodities? doi:10.2139/ssrn.4280578

Engelhardt, N., Krause, M., Neukirchen, D., & Posch, P. N. (2021). Trust and stock market volatility during the COVID-19 crisis. *Finance Research Letters*, *38*, 101873. doi:10.1016/j.frl.2020.101873 PMID:36569649

Engle, R. F. (1982). Autoregressive Conditional Heteroskedasticity with Estimates of the Variance of United Kingdom Inflation. *Econometrica*, *50*(4), 987–1007. doi:10.2307/1912773

Ghorbali, B., Naoui, K., & Derbali, A. (2022b). Co-movement Among COVID-19 Pandemic, Crude Oil, Stock Market of US, and Bitcoin: Empirical Evidence from WCA. In B. Alareeni & A. Hamdan (Eds.), *Artificial Intelligence and COVID Effect on Accounting. Accounting, Finance, Sustainability, Governance & Fraud: Theory and Application*. Springer. doi:10.1007/978-981-19-1036-4_3

GhorbaliB.NaouiK.DerbaliA. M. S. (2022a). Does Gold Act as a Safe Haven and Hedge for G7 Stock Markets? A Comparative Assessment between COVID-19 Versus Global Financial Crisis (GFC). doi:10.2139/ssrn.4160586

Goodell, J. W. (2020). COVID-19 and finance: Agendas for future research. *Finance Research Letters*, *35*, 101512. doi:10.1016/j.frl.2020.101512 PMID:32562472

Halova, M. W., Kurov, A., & Kucher, O. (2014). Noisy inventory announcements and energy prices. *Journal of Futures Markets*, *34*(10), 911–933. doi:10.1002/fut.21633

He, P., Sun, Y., Zhang, Y., & Li, T. (2020). COVID-19's market *impact on stock prices across different sectors: An event study based on the Chinese stock. Emerging Markets Finance and Trade*. PMID:32997308

Jamel, L., & Derbali, A. (2019). Damascus Securities Exchange Weighted Index volatilities and Terrorist attacks in Syria. *International Journal of Business and Risk Management*, *2*(1), 9–15.

Kollias, C., Efthalia, M., Stephanos, P., & Apostolos, S. (2011). Stock Markets and Terrorist Attacks: Comparative Evidence from a Large and a Small Capitalization Market. *European Journal of Political Economy*, *27*(No. S1), S64–S77. doi:10.1016/j.ejpoleco.2011.05.002

Kuttner, K. N. (2001). Monetary policy surprises and interest rates: Evidence from the fed funds futures market. *Journal of Monetary Economics*, *47*(3), 523–544. doi:10.1016/S0304-3932(01)00055-1

Nikkinen, J., Mohammad, M. O., Petri, S., & Janne, A. (2008). Stock Returns and Volatility Following the September 11 Attacks: Evidence from 53 Equity Markets. *International Review of Financial Analysis*, *17*(1), 27–46. doi:10.1016/j.irfa.2006.12.002

Nippani, S., & Washer, K. M. (2004). SARS: A Non-event for Affected Countries' Stock Markets? *Applied Financial Economics*, *14*(15), 1105–1110. doi:10.1080/0960310042000310579

OziliP. K.ArunT. (2020). *Spillover of COVID-19: impact on the Global Economy*. doi:10.2139/ssrn.3562570

Papakyriakou, P., Athanasios, S., & Zenon, T. (2019). The Impact of Terrorist Attacks in G7 Countries on International Stock Markets and the Role of Investor Sentiment. *Journal of International Financial Markets, Institutions and Money*, *6*, 143–160. doi:10.1016/j.intfin.2019.03.001

Phan, D. H. B., & Narayan, P. K. (2020). Country responses and the reaction of the stock market to COVID-19—A preliminary exposition. *Emerging Markets Finance & Trade*, *56*(10), 2138–2150. doi:10.1080/1540496X.2020.1784719

Sansa, N. A. (2020). The Impact of the COVID - 19 on the Financial Markets: Evidence from China and USA. *Electronic Research Journal of Social Sciences and Humanities*, *2*(2), 29–39.

Ye, S., & Karali, B. (2016). The informational content of inventory announcements: Intraday evidence from crude oil futures market. *Energy Economics*, *59*, 349–364. doi:10.1016/j.eneco.2016.08.011

Zaremba, A., Kizys, R., Aharon, D. Y., & Demir, E. (2020). Infected markets: Novel coronavirus, government interventions, and stock return volatility around the globe. *Finance Research Letters*, *34*, 35101597. doi:10.1016/j.frl.2020.101597 PMID:32550842

Chapter 11
Nigeria cNGN Stablecoin:
Everything You Need to Know About cNGN and eNaira CBDC

Peterson K. Ozili
https://orcid.org/0000-0001-6292-1161
Central Bank of Nigeria, Nigeria

ABSTRACT

Several firms have expressed an interest to develop a stablecoin in Nigeria called the compliant-Nigerian-Naira (cNGN). The purpose of this paper is to explore the features, benefits, and challenges of issuing a stablecoin in Nigeria known as the cNGN stablecoin. The study also compares the proposed cNGN with the eNaira central bank digital currency and offer several differences that are worth noting. The study shows that the proposed cNGN stablecoin offers many benefits. They include enabling faster payments, ensuring seamless cross-border payments, and increasing participation in the financial system for those who are already banked. The study also identifies some challenges of the proposed cNGN stablecoin. The study concludes by stating that the long-term success of the cNGN will be guaranteed if majority of Nigerians embrace it and if cNGN issuers collaborate with regulators to ensure that the cNGN is designed in a way that achieves financial stability objectives, transparency, and consumer protection.

1. INTRODUCTION

Non-fiat forms of money emerge when money is viewed as a social convention where one party accepts it as a means of payment in the expectation that the other party

DOI: 10.4018/979-8-3693-1511-8.ch011

will accept it as a means of payment (Frost et al, 2020).[1] Once this social convention of is widely believed, the specific substance, object or commodity being used as a means of payment will become 'money'. This is how money was created until government-backed money emerged and replaced the social convention system of money (Dequech, 2013; Frost et al, 2020).

Understanding the social convention system of money is essential in understanding what 'stablecoin' really is. Using the same analogy, a stablecoin is simply digital value which a person accepts as a means of payment in the expectation that the other party will accept it as a means of payment, and where the digital value is pegged to the value of a reference asset such as gold, stock or some economic indices (Frost et al, 2020).

The painful consequences of past economic and financial crises, e.g., the dotcom crash and the global financial crisis, led some private actors to believe that governments deliberately create economic and financial crises to make fiat money lose its value which in turn leads to loss of personal wealth so that the rich will become richer through the increase in the value of their physical assets, while the poor will become poorer through loss in the value of their fiat money held as cash or in the vaults of commercial banks (Othman et al, 2020). This ideology or belief system led private actors to seek ways to decouple from the government's fiat monetary system (Dapp, 2021). This led to the rise of private digital currencies also known as cryptocurrencies.

A private digital currency refers to a currency in digital form in which transactions are verified and records are maintained by a decentralized system using cryptography and controlled by private entities (Zohuri et al, 2022). Private digital currencies have many benefits such as increased speed of transactions, lower transaction cost, ease of access, high levels of privacy, and it is protected against inflation. However, private digital currencies, or cryptocurrencies, have a major problem which is their high volatility. Analysts, central banks and policymakers have criticized cryptocurrencies for being too volatile and they argue that the high volatility makes cryptocurrency unsafe for use as money, and it cannot be relied on by businesses to plan or for investment purposes. Soon, some central banks began to develop their own state-controlled digital currency to counteract the rise of private digital currencies and its unwanted volatility. This led to the creation of a state-controlled digital currency also known as a 'central bank digital currency'. As central banks were accelerating the development of CBDCs, some private actors rather than abandoning cryptocurrencies due to their high volatility, began to develop another type of cryptocurrency that will be less volatile if its value is pegged to a reference asset whose value is also non-volatile such as gold. This led to the idea of a stablecoin.

Technically, a stablecoin is a digital currency whose value is pegged to a fiat currency or a commodity like the US dollar or gold (Ante et al, 2021). Many private sector innovators are optimistic and enthusiastic about the development of stablecoins due to its ability to eliminate the volatility inherent in many cryptocurrencies. However, many policymakers and academic economists have called for caution and argue that stablecoin are not really stable rather they are less volatile than cryptocurrencies such as Bitcoin, and their perceived stability is not guaranteed in the long-term due to moral hazard of the operating entity, when the entity has poor financial performance or when there is limited supply of the stablecoin (Kwon et al, 2021; Frost et al, 2020). Despite these concerns, interest in stablecoins is growing rapidly in the private sector just as interest in CBDC continues to grow among central banks.

In Nigeria, several firms have indicated an interest to develop a stablecoin in Nigeria. In this study, I explore the features, benefits, and challenges of the proposed Nigeria cNGN stablecoin. The study also compares the proposed cNGN stablecoin with the eNaira central bank digital currency and offers several differences that are worth noting. The study contributes to the literature that examines digital innovation in monetary systems.

The rest of the study is organised as follows. Section 2 presents a contextual background of the proposed Nigeria cNGN stablecoin. Section 3 compares the cNGN with the eNaira CBDC. Section 4 highlights the challenges of the cNGN stablecoin. Section 5 presents the conclusion of the study.

2. UNDERSTANDING THE NIGERIA cNGN STABLECOIN

2.1. Contextual Background

In 2021, the Central Bank of Nigeria (CBN) barred banks from facilitating cryptocurrency transactions. In late 2023, the CBN admitted, in a circular sent to banks on December 22 of 2023, that the strict restrictions imposed on financial institutions in 2021 were unsustainable. As a result, the central bank lifted the cryptocurrency restrictions to enable banks assist customers with cryptocurrency transactions. The CBN lifted the restrictions for two reasons. The first reason was due to increasing demand and use of cryptocurrency around the world. The second reason was] because the CBN wanted the financial sector to promote and enable the use of blockchain technology in delivering financial services. Several firms expressed an interest to develop a stablecoin in Nigeria and they would call the stablecoin the compliant-Nigerian-Naira (cNGN). The interested firms belong to the Africa Stablecoin Consortium (ASC) which is a coalition of Nigerian financial institutions, Fintechs, and blockchain experts. The proposed stablecoin is designed to be a private cryptocurrency that will enhance financial transactions and comply with regulatory frameworks.

2.2. Features of the Proposed cNGN Stablecoin

1. The cNGN stablecoin will be backed by the Naira reserves held with commercial banks.
2. The exchange rate or conversion rate of the cNGN stablecoin will be pegged at a ratio of 1:1 to the Nigerian Naira.
3. The cNGN will incorporate the relevant know-your-customer (KYC) and anti-money laundering (AML) safeguards.
4. The cNGN stablecoin will comply with present and future regulatory requirements.
5. It will be developed and managed by Nigerian banks and Fintech firms.
6. It is interoperable with multiple public blockchains.

2.3. Benefits and Opportunities of the Proposed cNGN Stablecoin

1. It can enhance financial transactions.
2. It may pose little risk to financial system stability.
3. It has the potential to make the Nigerian Naira become a dynamic instrument for global transactions.
4. It uses blockchain technology to connect the Nigerian Naira to global markets.
5. Although the cNGN is a Nigerian initiative, the cNGN sets a precedent for blockchain-based financial innovations in the African continent.
6. It can easily integrate Nigeria into the evolving global financial industry.
7. Widespread adoption of cNGN will lead to wide acceptance of Web3 technologies in Nigeria.
8. The cNGN stablecoin will shorten settlement times.
9. The cNGN stablecoin will enable global payments.
10. The cNGN stablecoin will expedite trade and payment settlements globally at minimal costs.
11. The cNGN stablecoin has diverse utility
12. It will extend financial transactions globally by enabling users to use their Naira to engage with the global marketplace.
13. It can be applied to very good use cases such as faster remittances, enabling instant payment, facilitating low-cost payment in international trade, and enabling individuals to receive money from any part of the world within minutes.

2.4. Use Cases

Remittance – People working abroad will be able to send money back home just with the tap of a bottom and the money arrives home in a minute. The cNGN will make sending money home feels like sending a text message. It would be instant and effortless.

Instant Funds transfer – The cNGN will make fund transfers very easy to do and fast. Customers will no longer experience delays in receiving or sending money. Customers can do work online and receive money quickly from any part of the world.

Cryptocurrency trading and liquidity provision – The cNGN can be used to enhance cryptocurrency trading and provide liquidity in local crypto exchanges in Nigeria. It will allow users to easily move funds between crypto exchanges and the financial system and vice versa. It will provide convenience and efficiency in cryptocurrency transactions.

Using cNGN as a store of value during economic crisis and financial turmoil – The cNGN can be used as a store of value during economic downswings that give rise to volatility and loss of wealth such as high inflation, financial crisis, banking crisis or a pandemic. During such events, users can quickly convert their fiat money into cNGN holdings in order to avoid the adverse effects of economic fluctuations and to preserve the value of their fiat money during bad times.

cNGN Lending - Private lenders can lend cNGN money to households and companies who must post digital assets as collateral. After posting the digital assets, the cNGN stablecoin is offered to borrowers who must repay with interest. cNGN makes lending easier because it will prevent situations where borrowers must post physical assets as collateral such as land and house properties.

cNGN payroll – Nigerian companies can demand payment for services rendered in cNGN and use the cNGN payment receipts to pay the salary and wages of local empoyees. This will reduce transaction costs involved in obtaining fiat currency for payroll.

3. COMPARING eNaira AND cNGN

This section presents a comparison of the proposed cNGN stablecoin with the eNaira central bank digital currency.

Table 1. Comparison of the cNGN with the eNaira

S/N	Criteria	cNGN	eNaira
1	Core objective	To simplify payment and streamline international transfers	To be a payment tool and assist the central bank in achieving public policy goals such as G2P transfers, financial inclusion, and delivering digital public goods
2	Digital form	It is a private cryptocurrency similar to USDT	It is not a cryptocurrency. It is a central bank digital currency
3	Compete or coexist?	cNGN will coexist with eNaira.	eNaira will coexist cNGN.
4	Reserve holdings	Member-banks will hold the cNGN stablecoin as part of their reserves	Deposit money banks will hold eNaira CBDC as part of their reserves
5	Promoting the product	Member-banks will heavily publicise the cNGN	The central bank will promote wholesale eNaira CBDC.
6	Corporate support	Support for cNGN by organisations will be massive	Support for wholesale eNaira is growing due to its financial stability benefits for organisations
7	Retail vs wholesale scale	cNGN will be used mostly for retail purposes	eNaira CBDC is used mostly for wholesale purposes
8	Type of blockchain	Public blockchains	Private blockchain distributed ledger technology built on the enterprise-grade hyperledger fabric
9	Wealth of expertise used in its formation	The cNGN stablecoin is developed by a large number of private experts and firms, e.g., banks, fintech, blockchain experts	eNaira CBDC was developed using the expertise of central bank staff, policymakers and carefully selected international consultants
10	Usefulness for public policy purposes	cNGN is not designed to be a tool to achieve public policy objectives	eNaira CBDC can be used to achieve public policy objectives
11	Can it achieve first-level financial inclusion?	cNGN cannot be used to bring unbanked adults into the financial system because it is designed to serve those who are already banked; not those who are outside the formal financial system	Retail eNaira CBDC, if deployed, can be used to bring unbanked adults into the financial inclusion
12	Deepen financial inclusion	cNGN deepens financial inclusion by offering more financial services to those who are already banked, and it offers more opportunities to deepen financial inclusion	The eNaira CBDC also deepens financial inclusion
12	Government control	Limited or no government control	Full government control
13	Custodian of the pegged Naira reserves	cNGN is pegged to the Naira reserves held in the accounts of commercial banks	eNaira is pegged to the Naira reserve held in the accounts of the central bank
14	Usefulness for monetary policy	cNGN has little benefit for monetary policy. It is ineffective in administering monetary policy objectives	eNaira has significant use for monetary policy
15	Surveillance of users	Full surveillance of users is not possible when using cNGN	There can be full surveillance of users of eNaira CBDC

Continued on following page

Table 1. Continued

S/N	Criteria	cNGN	eNaira
16	Financial stability risk	Financial stability risk may be transmitted through de-pegging	Financial stability risk is significantly controlled through price and quantity restrictions on CBDC holdings
17	Impact on foreign reserves	If cNGN is used for international trade, it will have a huge impact on foreign reserves, as cNGN-based trade will be settled with the foreign reserves held with the central bank.	eNaira is not used for international trade. Therefore, eNaira transactions have no impact on foreign reserves, except the dollar cost of maintaining the infrastructure which is outsourced and whose license fee must be paid in foreign currency.

4. CHALLENGES OF THE NIGERIA cNGN STABLECOIN

Low awareness – Only less than 40% of the population have heard about cryptocurrency, and it difficult to say with certainty that a lot of people will be aware of the proposed cNGN stablecoin. For the stablecoin to succeed in the Nigerian market, there must be widespread awareness and education about the benefits of the proposed cNGN.

Volatility will remain – The proposed cNGN stablecoin will be pegged to the Naira, and the Naira is pegged to the US dollar. This means that if the Naira becomes unstable in relation to the US dollar, the cNGN stablecoin will equally become unstable and volatility will emerge, making it an unstable coin. Therefore, it will be very difficult for cNGN promoters to claim that the value of the cNGN stablecoin will remain stable when the fiat Naira becomes unstable in relation to the US Dollar. Some users may demand a guarantee that the Naira will be stable in the future for them to accept and use the proposed cNGN stablecoin.

Heightened risk of cNGN de-pegging – There is the risk of cNGN de-pegging which arises when the cNGN stablecoin is no longer trading at its predetermined Naira value. cNGN de-pegging occurs when the price of cNGN falls below the price of the pegged asset which is the Naira. This may be caused by unfavourable economic events such as banking crisis, financial crisis, economic recession, high inflation, economic hardship, sudden regulatory actions, heightened economic policy uncertainty, security breaches and very low demand for cNGN by the population. These events can make the cNGN lose its peg to the reference asset which is the Nigerian Naira.

Other challenges – Other factors that could prevent the cNGN stablecoin from living up to its promise include the following.

- Regulatory ambiguity which may lower investor confidence in cNGN and also lower the widespread adoption of cNGN.
- Lack of legal certainty which may lead to problems in payment, clearing and settlement arrangements in cNGN.
- Lack of regulation which can make cNGN unsafe for unsophisticated users.
- Unregulated cNGN stablecoin which may pose risks to financial stability.

5. CONCLUSION

This study provided insights into the proposed Nigeria cNGN stablecoin. It highlights the features, benefits, and risks of the proposed cNGN stablecoin. It also compared the proposed cNGN with the eNaira central bank digital currency. And, lastly, it highlighted some challenges of the proposed cNGN. The introduction of a cNGN stablecoin in Nigeria may offer volatility reduction benefits. Other benefits include efficiency of financial transactions and enabling cross border payments and trade. The notable challenges are low awareness about stablecoin in Nigeria, volatility risk and the heightened risk of cNGN de-pegging. The challenges identified in this study show the need for regulatory intervention in the cNGN market. The central bank of Nigeria should pay close attention to the risks posed by the proposed stablecoins. The central bank should also ensure that the promoters of the cNGN stablecoin design it in a way that achieves the goals of financial stability, consumer protection, transparency and accountability. It will become important for cNGN issuers to partner with regulators to find the right balance between offering cNGN-based solutions and regulatory compliance.

REFERENCES

Ante, L., Fiedler, I., & Strehle, E. (2021). The influence of stablecoin issuances on cryptocurrency markets. *Finance Research Letters*, *41*, 101867.

Dapp, M. M. (2021). From fiat to crypto: The present and future of money. *Finance 4.0-Towards a Socio-Ecological Finance System: A Participatory Framework to Promote Sustainability*, 1-25.

Dequech, D. (2013). Is money a convention and/or a creature of the state? The convention of acceptability, the state, contracts, and taxes. *Journal of Post Keynesian Economics*, •••, 251–273.

Frost, J., Shin, H. S., & Wierts, P. (2020). An early stablecoin? The Bank of Amsterdam and the governance of money.

Kirk-Greene, A. H. (1960). The major currencies in Nigerian history. *Journal of the Historical Society of Nigeria*, *2*(1), 132–150.

KwonY.KimJ.KimY.SongD. (2021). The trilemma of stablecoin. *Available at* SSRN 3917430.

Othman, A. H. A., Musa Alhabshi, S., Kassim, S., Abdullah, A., & Haron, R. (2020). The impact of monetary systems on income inequity and wealth distribution: A case study of cryptocurrencies, fiat money and gold standard. *International Journal of Emerging Markets*, *15*(6), 1161–1183.

Zohuri, B., Nguyen, H. T., & Moghaddam, M. (2022). What is the Cryptocurrency. *Is it a Threat to Our National Security, Domestically and Globally*, 1-14.

ENDNOTES

1 For example, many non-fiat forms of money have existed in Nigeria in the last seven decades which includes cowry, copper and other commodities (Kirk-Greene, 1960).

Chapter 12
Leveraging Transparency and Privacy Through Blockchain Technology

Babita Jha
https://orcid.org/0000-0001-8586-0250
Christ University, India

Deepak Jha
Christ University, India

Arnav Garg
Christ University, India

Raajvunsh Singh
Christ University, India

Samay Jolly
Christ University, India

ABSTRACT

Blockchain is a conveyed record innovation that can be utilized to keep exchanges in a safe and straightforward way. This makes it a promising innovation for various applications, for example inventory network the executives, monetary administrations, and medical services. One of the vital advantages of blockchain is its capacity to guarantee information consistency. This is on the grounds that all information on the blockchain is put away in a disseminated way, and every hub in the organization has a duplicate of the record. This makes it truly challenging for any one party to mess with the information. One more key advantage of blockchain is its straightforwardness. All exchanges on the blockchain are public, and anybody can see them. This can assist with building trust and straightforwardness among partners. Blockchain can likewise present difficulties regarding information security. This is on the grounds that all information on the blockchain is put away in a public record. This implies that anybody with admittance to the blockchain can see the information, including delicate data, for example individual recognizable proof numbers (PII). There are various ways of tending to the difficulties of information protection in blockchain. One methodology is to utilize encryption to safeguard delicate information. Another

DOI: 10.4018/979-8-3693-1511-8.ch012

methodology is to utilize private blockchains, which are simply available to approved clients. The compromise between information consistency, straightforwardness, and protection is an intricate one. There is no single arrangement that will be ideal for all applications. The best methodology will rely upon the particular requirements of the application. The chapter investigates how blockchain innovation is used in different applications and enterprises, stressing its part in keeping up with information transparency and tending to security concerns.

1. INTRODUCTION

In the contemporary era of global interconnectivity, the exchange of information significantly influences and shapes various aspects of our life. Each online purchase, medical record entry, and financial transaction contributes to a complex network of data. The advent of digital transformation has yielded notable benefits in terms of convenience and effectiveness. However, it has also raised apprehensions over the security, privacy, and transparency of our personal and sensitive data. In the context of this dynamic environment, blockchain technology has emerged as a promising solution, providing a secure, transparent, and privacy-conscious framework for the management of data and transactions.

The digital era has given rise to a form of record-keeping that not only documents transactions but also ensures their security in a manner that is resistant to tampering. These transactions are grouped together into blocks (Kosba et al., 2016) and each block is securely linked to the previous one, forming a continuous chain of records. In contrast to conventional systems that depend on centralised authorities for validation and record-keeping, blockchain operates successfully through decentralisation. The absence of a centralised authority ensures that no single entity possesses complete control over the entire network, hence mitigating vulnerabilities arising from human fallibility, cyber assaults, or misconduct. The inherent potential of blockchain technology lies in its ability to enhance transparency. In traditional systems, intermediaries and central authorities hold significant roles, yet, they may inadvertently introduce dangers. The decentralised nature of blockchain technology reduces the reliance on intermediaries.

Once a transaction is recorded on the blockchain, it becomes an enduring and transparent element, observable by all players within the network. The implementation of transparency measures serves as a deterrent against fraudulent activities and promotes confidence among participants. Nevertheless, although transparency is a prominent characteristic of blockchain technology, it also elicits apprehensions regarding the protection of privacy. In numerous contexts, particularly those pertaining to personal or sensitive information, the feasibility and desirability of complete transparency are limited. Sharing patients' medical records on a public blockchain could potentially compromise the confidentiality of such information. Likewise, the disclosure of comprehensive transaction particulars in financial transactions may compromise sensitive financial data. Therefore, the pursuit of achieving a healthy equilibrium between transparency and privacy holds significant significance. In this regard, blockchain technology presents innovative options to tackle this challenge.

The process of documenting transactions inside the blockchain technology involves linking them together in a safe manner over a computer network. This blockchain technology finds utility in various domains, including Cryptocurrency, also known as digital currency, and Smart Contracts. Smart Contracts are computer programme codes that are controlled by blockchain technology and are utilised to execute agreements or digital contracts between two parties. These contracts are saved in a blockchain database, ensuring that they cannot be altered by any individual or external entities. Consequently, the reliance on trusted intermediaries is eliminated when employing Smart Contracts. Smart contracts facilitate the execution of transactions involving monetary assets, shares, and real estate.

The emergence of blockchain technology has led to a significant demand for smart contracts due to its capacity to enhance transaction customizability. The emergence of numerous smart contract applications has been observed across various sectors, including but not limited to banking and finance, life sciences and healthcare, energy resources, and voting. Presently, numerous industries employ Smart Contracts, including the business sector for documenting financial services, the healthcare sector for recording patient health histories, and additionally the insurance and government sectors utilise Smart Contracts. Consequently, the presence of Smart Contracts proves advantageous in circumventing the need for intermediary services, thereby enhancing transaction transparency. Nevertheless, the nascent nature of smart contracts presents numerous obstacles that impede the various parties involved in its use, including consumers, developers, and the entities that rely on smart contracts as their foundation.

2. REVIEW OF LITERATURE

The blockchain, a decentralised and peer-to-peer network utilising a distributed database, has been in existence for more than ten years as an established method for recording transactions (Taherdoost, 2022). The aforementioned concept can be classified as a model of distributed computing that effectively addresses the issue of trust in a singular entity. Hence, multiple nodes collaborate inside the blockchain network in order to provide the secure and dependable maintenance of a distributed ledger encompassing all historical transactions. Bitcoin was introduced by Satoshi

Nakamoto in 2008 (Nakamoto, 2008) marking the inception of the first proposed cryptocurrency that introduced the concept of blockchain as a decentralised infrastructure platform. The technology let anyone to engage in the transmission and reception of bitcoins, a form of decentralised digital currency, without reliance on a central governing entity. Additional blockchain-based systems have been proposed for use with the aforementioned coin, such as Hyperledger Fabric (Honar et al.,2021) and Ethereum.Unlike Bitcoin, smart contracts can be utilised. Smart contracts have the potential to extend the capabilities of blockchain technology beyond traditional contracts, as they can autonomously execute all aspects of agreements among multiple parties in a decentralised environment, provided that the requisite conditions have been met (Wang et al.,2018).

The increasing popularity of smart contracts has been observed in tandem with the development of blockchain technology (Mohanta et al., 2018). The smart contract(Macrinic et al.,2018) is an advanced technological component that may be employed within a blockchain framework to autonomously facilitate, execute, and uphold the conditions and terms of a contract that is legally binding . Smart contracts offer several advantages over traditional contracts, including reduced risk, cheaper service and administrative costs, and improved business process efficiency (Smith, 2020). Furthermore, it is important to note that smart contracts have the potential to enhance trust in contracting situations when there is a lack of trust between parties (Eenmaa-Dimitrieva, & Schmidt-Kessen, 2019). In this regard, it is anticipated that there would be a significant transformation in conventional business practises.

The ideas of trust, privacy, and transparency are explored in the study literature on blockchain technology (Kingsly 2022; Lemieux, 2016; Beck et al., 2016) and logistics (Léauté and Faltings, 2011; Klein and Rai, 2009). Privacy, specifically information privacy, refers to the ability to exercise control over personal information and its utilisation by external parties without obtaining agreement from the individual (Bélanger and Crossler, 2011). The concept of transparency (Wang, et al.,2023). Rijal, S., & Saranani, F. (2023) presents a more comprehensive interpretation, wherein transparency is characterised as a societal public value that serves as a countermeasure against corruption. This perspective equates transparency with the practise of making decisions openly, both within governmental and non-profit entities.

The concept of transparency, as defined by Do Prado Leite and Cappelli (2010), pertains to the disclosure of information from an information systems perspective. The concepts of confidentiality and transparency in relation to Blockchain technology are closely interconnected due to the fundamental principle of Blockchain being an open system, wherein transactions are both anonymous and accessible to all participants. Nevertheless, it is important to note that Blockchains do not inherently possess an open nature, as there exists a clear differentiation between public and private Blockchains. The phrases 'permissioned' and 'permissionless' are commonly employed in the literature (Verma, 2023; Bezuidenhout, R., Nel, W., & Maritz, J. M. 2023; Llambías, 2023). In a public blockchain, there are no limitations with regards to the players involved in the network, and all transactions can be identified through their public hash value. This hash value plays a crucial role in validating the transaction (Christidis & Devetsikiotis, 2016). In contrast, a private blockchain entails the oversight of both reading and writing permissions in order to limit network access (Pilkington, 2016). The implications arising from the various methodologies suggest that private Blockchains are unable to attain the same degree of decentralisation as public Blockchains. The level of openness within a private Blockchain can be regulated by the implemented user rights management system, since it ensures that users are identifiable rather than anonymous. According to Xu et al. (2016), the participants and their transactions within the public blockchain maintain anonymity, although the transactions themselves remain visible.

3. BLOCKCHAIN TECHNOLOGY AND SMART CONTRACTS

3.1 Blockchain Technology

The technology known as blockchain is sometimes characterised as a publicly accessible ledger that retains data pertaining to all transactions conducted inside a network that is decentralised (Swanson, 2015; Beck and Müller-Bloch, 2017). The name "Blockchain" inherently suggests the interconnectedness of blocks. The concept of a "block" within a Blockchain refers to a fundamental unit of data that contains a collection of transactions. These blocks are interconnected through a process known as "linking" or "chaining." Initially, it is important to note that a block within a Blockchain encompasses pertinent data. The provided information has the potential to be classified into two distinct categories: metadata and content. The material typically pertains to details on a transaction. Metadata is typically kept within the header section. The third block in a blockchain system includes a hash value that is computed using the block's content and a reference to the preceding block (Tama, 2017). The allusion to the preceding block pertains to the computed hash value of the antecedent block (Yadav, Singh & Kushwaha, 2023; Beck et al., 2016).

The consensus mechanism is a crucial idea inside Blockchain technology that addresses the difficulty of achieving agreement on the accuracy of transactions (Chaudhry, & Yousaf, 2018; Crosby et al., 2016). The verification of transaction accuracy is conducted by the utilisation of cryptographic techniques, as discussed by Yli-Huumo et al. (2016). In order to maintain the integrity and consistency of a distributed system, it is imperative to establish a definitive sequence for incorporating

Blocks into the Blockchain. This process is an integral component of consensus discovery, as highlighted by Crosby et al. (2016).

The emergence of blockchain technology can be attributed to its role as the foundational infrastructure of the Bitcoin network. To address the challenges at hand, a consensus mechanism known as "proof-of-work" was implemented (Nakamoto, 2008). The term "proof-of-work" is utilised to describe the process by which a hash code token is generated by the solution of a mathematical problem. This mechanism ensures that the construction of a Block necessitates a specific level of computational effort (Verma, 2022; Crosby et al., 2016). The aforementioned procedure exhibits a notable lack of efficiency and is heavily dependent on costly computational resources, ultimately resulting in the squandering of valuable resources (Yli-Huumo et al., 2016). Nevertheless, the rationale behind the characterization of Blockchain technology as tamper-proof is also rooted in its consensus mechanism.

In the event that an individual endeavours to modify or eliminate a block, it becomes necessary to compute the hash values of all blocks that have been generated subsequently. The achievement of this task is deemed highly challenging in the present era, mostly because to the constraints imposed by the existing computational capabilities (Swanson, 2015; Nakamoto, 2008). As a result of the aforementioned limitations, there is ongoing study into other approaches for achieving consensus. The consensus technique known as Proof-of-Stake does not depend on computer capacity, as discussed by Bentov et al. (2016) and King and Nadal (2012). The allocation of decision-making authority is dispersed among many stakeholders within the system, and the prevention of new block formation follows a deterministic methodology that considers the users' stakes (King & Nadal, 2012). According to Buterin (2014), this methodology results in expedited transactions and reduced energy use. In order for a potential attacker to execute an attack, they would need to possess a substantial stake in the network. However, it is important to note that if the network is subjected to an attack, the value of the stake diminishes, hence reducing the likelihood of an attack (Xu et al., 2016).

3.2 Smart Contract

A smart contract is a programme implemented using blockchain technology, wherein two parties reach a digitally agreed-upon agreement. It replaces the traditional written contract, which involves reaching an agreement in writing form. Ineffectual agreement can lead to errors when one party engages in fraudulent behaviour, so compromising the overall safety and reliability of the agreement. Objects that are susceptible to injury and loss. In contemporary times, there is a growing trend towards the prevalence of industrial operations in several sectors utilising smart contract technology. The term "smart contract" is another reference to the concept of smart contracts, which was previously mentioned.

The concept, initially introduced by Nick Szabo, is designed to facilitate the participation of legal professionals in a particular domain. A contractual agreement was established between the involved parties, with the finding occurring in the year 1994. In the context of blockchain technology, it can be seen that the concept of digital currency, which involves the creation and utilisation of virtual cash, was first introduced in 2008 by an individual named Satoshi Nakamoto. Bitcoin, a decentralised mechanism for transferring information, is a medium of transaction. The transparency of the system enables seamless connectivity among all involved parties, eliminating the need for middlemen.

3.2.1 Sequential Steps in Smart Contract

A smart contract, similar to any conventional contract, represents a mutual agreement between two parties. Smart contracts utilise computer code to harness the advantages offered by blockchain technology, encompassing enhanced efficiency, heightened transparency, and fortified security measures. The outcomes have the potential to be groundbreaking; yet, the utilisation of smart contracts also entails inherent risks.

Smart contracts possess the inherent capability to operate autonomously, owing to their digital nature, which may be achieved through a systematic six-step programming procedure.

- The involved parties mutually consent to the stipulated terms and conditions: The initiation of a smart contract commences with the establishment of a mutually agreed upon arrangement. In order for individuals or entities to engage in the exchange of goods or services, it is imperative that they establish mutual consent to the specific terms and conditions governing the transaction. The stakeholders must also reach a consensus on the operational mechanics of the smart contract, encompassing the requisite circumstances for contract execution and the potential for automated execution.
- Creation of the smart contract: There exist various avenues for the transacting parties to establish a smart contract, encompassing the possibility of self-coding or engaging the services of a smart contract developer. The provisions of the agreement are converted into a computer language in order to generate the smart contract, which delineates regulations and repercussions analogous to those found in a conventional legal contract. The process of developing a smart contract can be straightforward; nonetheless, it is crucial to acknowledge that a smart contract with inadequate design poses a significant security

vulnerability. It is of utmost importance to thoroughly validate the security of the smart contract during this phase.

- The deployment of the smart contract: Once the smart contract has been successfully designed, the next step is to deploy it onto a blockchain network. The smart contract is deployed to the blockchain using a process similar to prior bitcoin transactions. In this process, the code of the smart contract is included within the data field of the transaction. After a transaction is validated, the smart contract becomes active on the blockchain and is unchangeable, indicating that it cannot be revoked or modified.
- The trigger conditions are satisfied: A smart contract operates by keeping an eye out for specific circumstances or triggers on the blockchain or another reliable information source. These triggers can be nearly anything that may be digitally validated, such as the achievement of a deadline, the completion of a payment, the receipt of a monthly bill, or an additional verifiable occurrence. In addition, whenever one or more contract parties carry out a specified action, trigger criteria may also be satisfied.
- The execution of the smart contract: The smart contract comes into action whenever its trigger conditions are met. An autonomously executing smart contract can carry out one or more tasks, like paying a seller money or proving a buyer is the owner of an item.
- The blockchain records the outcome of the contract: The blockchain is instantly informed of the smart contract's execution. The smart contract is verified by the blockchain network, which also logs the execution as a transaction and saves the finished product on the blockchain. Anybody can normally access the smart contract record at any moment for evaluation.

3.3 Integrating Blockchain Technology With Smart Contract

The implementation of blockchain technology facilitates the maintenance of transparency.

The concept of complete traceability refers to the ability to track and document the whole lifecycle of a product or process, from its inception. The transparency of blockchain is regarded as one of its most notable attributes. Blockchain technology demonstrates its transparency through Bitcoin gambling sites, since it enables complete traceability and facilitates easier maintenance. Within the realm of gaming, there exists a widely acknowledged adage that asserts the perpetual triumph of the establishment, sometimes referred to as "the house."

However, this is not applicable to gambling platforms that function using cryptocurrencies such as Bitcoin. Websites such as those offering provably fair games provide users with the ability to verify the server seeds of the game, so ensuring the authenticity and impartiality of the outcomes they receive. This emerging element of internet gaming represents a significant and transformative development. Many casino sites and gaming platforms are actively seeking to include this feature into their systems in order to foster a heightened sense of trust between the platform and its users. The ledger of transactions is designed to be fully auditable and ensure accuracy.

3.4 Leveraging Transparency Through Integrating Smart Contract in Blockchain

Immutable Record-Keeping: The fundamental characteristic of blockchain is its inherent immutability. After data is appended to the blockchain, it acquires immutability, denoting that any modification or deletion of the data would require agreement from the entire network. This particular feature serves to protect the integrity of data, rendering it highly suitable for the recording of vital information such as ownership of properties, academic credentials, and the historical records of items within a supply chain.

Establishing Transparent Audit Trails: The utilisation of blockchain technology enables the creation of transparent and verifiable records. Every transaction is assigned a timestamp and linked to the previous one, creating a continuous sequence of events. The implementation of transparency enhances the ability to monitor the historical records of assets, hence decreasing the likelihood of fraudulent activities and reinforcing the concept of accountability.

Unlocking the Potential of Smart Contracts: Smart contracts are a pivotal advancement within the realm of blockchain technology. These contracts are characterised by their ability to autonomously execute agreements, as the contractual terms are encoded within the underlying code. These actions are executed automatically when predetermined circumstances are met, eliminating the need for intermediaries. Smart contracts enhance transparency by offering a transparent and immutable record of contract execution.

3.5 Leveraging Privacy Through Integrating Smart Contract in Blockchain

Authorised Blockchains: While public blockchains are accessible to all individuals, permissioned blockchains limit access to authorised members. These private or consortium blockchains have been specifically developed to safeguard sensitive data while also leveraging the security features of blockchain technology.

Safeguarding Data via Encryption: Blockchain networks have the capability to implement sophisticated encryption techniques in order to protect the confidentiality of data. The utilisation of blockchain technology allows for the storage of encrypted data, ensuring that unauthorised individuals are unable to access it.

Using Zero-Knowledge Proofs: Using cryptographic techniques, zero-knowledge proofs allow one party to prove the truth of a statement without disclosing the statement's precise specifics. This technology has the potential to be included into blockchain systems in order to authenticate transactions while maintaining transaction confidentiality.

3.6 Smart Contracts in Blockchain Technology

a. Healthcare: The utilisation of blockchain technology is significantly transforming the domain of healthcare records management. Patients have the ability to exert authority over the individuals who are granted access to their data, thereby safeguarding their privacy. Simultaneously, healthcare providers derive advantages from possessing records that are both secure and precise.

b. Supply Chain Management: Blockchain technology is significantly transforming the field of supply chain management by offering comprehensive visibility across the entire process while safeguarding confidential business information. Companies have the capability to track the whole journey of products, thereby ensuring their authenticity and quality.

c. Financial Services: Within the financial services sector, blockchain technology has the potential to optimise transaction processes, mitigate fraudulent activities, and improve transparency. Central banks and financial organisations are currently investigating the potential of utilising blockchain technology to develop digital currencies that can offer secure and efficient payment solutions.

d. Voting Systems: Government entities are now investigating the potential applications of blockchain technology in several areas such as voting systems, property registry management, and public procurement. The objective is to mitigate corruption and foster trust in public institutions by leveraging the secure and transparent nature of blockchain.

4. CHALLENGES IN IMPLEMENTING BLOCKCHAIN AND SMART CONTRACTS

It is imperative for information technology (IT) leaders to possess a comprehensive understanding of the potential hazards associated with the implementation of business blockchain and smart contracts.

- **Monitoring:** At present the regulatory oversight of smart contracts and the underlying blockchain technology has been modest. However, as more businesses adopt blockchain projects, there will be increased scrutiny. Developing business compliance strategies may assist in mitigating losses caused by internal as well as external threats. Blockchain network assaults, cryptojacking, and human incompetence are among the hazards.
- **Data reliability:** Companies with a high volume of transactions may profit from using smart contracts in order to automate data processing. However, the method is still susceptible to erroneous data entry. A bad actor or a not well-trained customer who skips a step may offer dishonest, incorrect, or inaccurate data while still triggering the smart contract. As a result, maintaining the integrity of the incoming data is crucial to preventing errors.
- **Logic exploits:** The use of computational reasoning to transport data between nodes is one of the blockchain technology's capabilities. However, hackers are developing ways to make use of that logic and exploit the software's compatibility. These assaults are most common in cryptocurrency, but smart contracts are not immune. A vulnerable, poorly constructed smart contract could expose a whole corporate blockchain to attackers.
- **Scalability:** It is difficult for the open-source blockchain systems to operate at scale effectively, for example, since the blockchain system is required to be able to support multiple transactions at the same time. Such requirements raise the workload across nodes, necessitating large computer power, electricity, and bandwidth. Sharding, a sort of data division, and the Proof of Stake blockchain consensus methods appear to be promising in alleviating this disadvantage.
- **Safety:** As more businesses incorporate smart contracts into their ecosystems, blockchain technology improves. However, security hazards exist if smart contracts are badly developed or poorly maintained. The critical step of developing a governance model may assist organisations in staying ahead of these difficulties.
- **Requirements:** The fact that only those who have been granted permission will be able to communicate with the data is one advantage of a corporate (private) blockchain over a public blockchain. They may come from outside organisations whose data collecting and processing rules may not translate effectively – if at all – in a business-to-business relationship. A well-coded smart contract can avoid these data inconsistencies, resulting in smooth transactions and improved company communication.
- **Long-term viability:** Although public blockchains have large carbon footprints, corporations are looking for ways to lessen the impact they have on the environment, and innovators who are who are interested in sustainable

may want to be aware of these choices. An business blockchain often consumes a smaller amount of computing power than an open-source blockchain, and proper maintenance can assist avoid this from happening.

- **Ability:** Because of the distributed nature of a shared ledger, different parties can access the data, thus exposing an organisation to fraud and other vulnerabilities. The severity of the threat is usually determined by the permissive level on the blockchain on which the smart contract is stored. Hiring blockchain developers may assist in avoiding potential pitfalls. In-house developers can undertake audits, engage trustworthy third parties to execute penetration testing, and analyse security on a constant basis.

5. STRATEGIES FOR AUGMENTING DATA PRIVACY WITH BLOCKCHAIN TECHNOLOGY

The imperative to solve the issue of data privacy in blockchain technology is of paramount importance in order to guarantee the conscientious and morally upright utilisation of individuals' personal data. The improvement of data privacy in blockchain technology is a multifaceted challenge that necessitates a comprehensive strategy. The following are potential strategies for augmenting data privacy within the context of blockchain technology:

- One potential strategy to address privacy concerns is the application of technologies that improve privacy. Technologies that improve privacy, such as homomorphic encryption, ring signatures, and zero-knowledge proofs, may be able to protect private information during blockchain transactions. These technological advancements have the potential to facilitate the secure sharing of data while also safeguarding data privacy.
- The utilisation of pseudonyms on the blockchain network serves as a means to safeguard the anonymity of users while ensuring their identity verification. Nonetheless, in order to reduce the possibility of pseudonym misuse, identity verification and authentication procedures must be put in place. These precautions include anti-money laundering (AML) and know your customer (KYC) procedures.
- Blockchain technology immutability presents challenges in adhering to Data Privacy laws and regulations, particularly in the areas of data deletion and anonymization. The use of data deletion or anonymization techniques might facilitate compliance with legislation, such as the right to be forgotten as outlined in the General Data Protection Regulation (GDPR).

- Education and awareness initiatives have the potential to enhance knowledge and understanding of the concerns surrounding data privacy in the context of blockchain technology. These programmes aim to provide education to users and developers regarding the significance of Data Privacy and optimal strategies for safeguarding personal data in blockchain transactions.
- The adherence to regulatory requirements is necessary in order to guarantee the responsible and ethical use of personal data within the context of blockchain technology. The establishment of explicit rules and criteria for adherence can contribute to the promotion of blockchain technology's utilisation in a manner that aligns with the requirements and provisions of Data Privacy laws and regulations.

6. CONCLUSION

Blockchain technology has significant potential for business ecosystems in the current technology-driven era. The decentralised ledger structure of this technology guarantees openness, trust, and efficiency. Due to its benefits, this state-of-the-art technology improves accountability and traceability, hence promoting confidence among stakeholders. Moreover, it enhances data confidentiality and integrity, ensures adherence to regulatory standards, and mitigates the risk of counterfeiting. Therefore, leveraging the capabilities of blockchain technology is crucial for organisations to establish and uphold trust within their ecosystems, leading to a heightened level of transparency and security. Although still in its early stages, blockchain technology has the potential to significantly transform corporate operations.

REFERENCES

Akram, A., & Bross, P. (2018). *Trust, privacy and transparency with blockhain technology in logistics*. Academic Press.

Beck, R., Czepluch, J. S., Lollike, N., & Malone, S. (2016). Blockchain–the gateway to trust-free cryptographic transactions. In *Twenty-Fourth European Conference on Information Systems (ECIS),* İstanbul, Turkey, 2016 (pp. 1-14). Springer Publishing Company.

Beck, R., & Müller-Bloch, C. (2017). *Blockchain as radical innovation: a framework for engaging with distributed ledgers as incumbent organization*. Academic Press.

Bentov, I., Gabizon, A., & Mizrahi, A. (2016, February). Cryptocurrencies without proof of work. In *International conference on financial cryptography and data security* (pp. 142-157). Springer Berlin Heidelberg.

Bezuidenhout, R., Nel, W., & Maritz, J. M. (2023). Permissionless blockchain systems as pseudo-random number generators for decentralized consensus. *IEEE Access : Practical Innovations, Open Solutions*, *11*, 14587–14611. doi:10.1109/ACCESS.2023.3244403

Buterin, V. (2014). A next-generation smart contract and decentralized application platform. *White Paper, 3*(37), 2-1.

Chaudhry, N., & Yousaf, M. M. (2018, December). Consensus algorithms in blockchain: Comparative analysis, challenges and opportunities. In *2018 12th International Conference on Open Source Systems and Technologies (ICOSST)* (pp. 54-63). IEEE.

Christidis, K., & Devetsikiotis, M. (2016). Blockchains and smart contracts for the internet of things. *IEEE Access : Practical Innovations, Open Solutions*, *4*, 2292–2303. doi:10.1109/ACCESS.2016.2566339

Crosby, M., Pattanayak, P., Verma, S., & Kalyanaraman, V. (2016). Blockchain technology: Beyond bitcoin. *Applied Innovation*, *2*(6-10), 71.

Do Prado Leite, J. C. S., & Cappelli, C. (2010). Software transparency. *Business & Information Systems Engineering*, *2*(3), 127–139. doi:10.1007/s12599-010-0102-z

Eenmaa-Dimitrieva, H., & Schmidt-Kessen, M. J. (2019). Creating markets in no-trust environments: The law and economics of smart contracts. *Computer Law & Security Report*, *35*(1), 69–88. doi:10.1016/j.clsr.2018.09.003

Honar Pajooh, H., Rashid, M., Alam, F., & Demidenko, S. (2021). Hyperledger fabric blockchain for securing the edge internet of things. *Sensors (Basel)*, *21*(2), 359. doi:10.3390/s21020359 PMID:33430274

King, S., & Nadal, S. (2012). *Ppcoin: Peer-to-peer crypto-currency with proof-of-stake*. Self-Published Paper.

Kingsly, K. M. (2022). *Disruptive Technology: Blockchain: The Crystal Ball: Advancing Financial Trust, Inclusion, and Simplicity Through the Blockchain*. Christian Faith Publishing, Inc.

Klein, R., & Rai, A. (2009). Interfirm strategic information flows in logistics supply chain relationships. *Management Information Systems Quarterly*, *33*(4), 735–762. doi:10.2307/20650325

Kosba, A., Miller, A., Shi, E., Wen, Z., & Papamanthou, C. (2016). Hawk: The blockchain model of cryptography and privacy-preserving smart contracts. *Security and Privacy (SP), 2016 IEEE Symposium on*, 839-858.

Léauté, T., & Faltings, B. (2011). Coordinating logistics operations with privacy guarantees. *IJCAI Proceedings; International Joint Conference on Artificial Intelligence.*

Lemieux, V. L. (2016). Trusting records: Is Blockchain technology the answer? *Records Management Journal*, *26*(2), 110–139. doi:10.1108/RMJ-12-2015-0042

Llambías, G. (2023). *Blockchain Interoperability*. Academic Press.

Macrinici, D., Cartofeanu, C., & Gao, S. (2018). Smart contract applications within blockchain technology: A systematic mapping study. *Telematics and Informatics*, *35*(8), 2337–2354. doi:10.1016/j.tele.2018.10.004

Nakamoto, S. (2008). Bitcoin: A peer-to-peer electronic cash system. *Decentralized Business Review*.

Pilkington, M. (2016). 11 Blockchain technology: principles and applications. *Research handbook on digital transformations*, 225.

Rijal, S., & Saranani, F. (2023). The Role of Blockchain Technology in Increasing Economic Transparency and Public Trust. *Technology and Society Perspectives*, *1*(2), 56–67. doi:10.61100/tacit.v1i2.51

Smith, S. S. (2020). Blockchain, smart contracts and financial audit implications. *IUP Journal of Accounting Research & Audit Practices*, *19*(1), 7–17.

Swanson, T. (2015). *Consensus-as-a-service: A brief report on the emergence of permissioned, distributed ledger systems*. Report.

Taherdoost, H. (2022). A critical review of blockchain acceptance models—Blockchain technology adoption frameworks and applications. *Computers*, *11*(2), 24. doi:10.3390/computers11020024

Tama, B. A., Kweka, B. J., Park, Y., & Rhee, K. H. (2017, August). A critical review of blockchain and its current applications. In *2017 International Conference on Electrical Engineering and Computer Science (ICECOS)* (pp. 109-113). IEEE. 10.1109/ICECOS.2017.8167115

Verma, A., Bhattacharya, P., Madhani, N., Trivedi, C., Bhushan, B., Tanwar, S., Sharma, G., Bokoro, P. N., & Sharma, R. (2022). Blockchain for industry 5.0: Vision, opportunities, key enablers, and future directions. *IEEE Access : Practical Innovations, Open Solutions*, *10*, 69160–69199. doi:10.1109/ACCESS.2022.3186892

Verma, V. (2023). An overview of Blockchain Technology: Past & Future. *Eduzone: International Peer Reviewed/Refereed Multidisciplinary Journal, 12*(1), 100-104.

Wang, R., Bush-Evans, R., Arden-Close, E., Bolat, E., McAlaney, J., Hodge, S., Thomas, S., & Phalp, K. (2023). Transparency in persuasive technology, immersive technology, and online marketing: Facilitating users' informed decision making and practical implications. *Computers in Human Behavior*, *139*, 107545. doi:10.1016/j.chb.2022.107545

Wang, S., Yuan, Y., Wang, X., Li, J., Qin, R., & Wang, F. Y. (2018, June). An overview of smart contract: architecture, applications, and future trends. In *2018 IEEE Intelligent Vehicles Symposium (IV)* (pp. 108-113). IEEE. 10.1109/IVS.2018.8500488

Xu, X., Pautasso, C., Zhu, L., Gramoli, V., Ponomarev, A., Tran, A. B., & Chen, S. (2016). The blockchain as a software connector. *Software Architecture (WICSA), 2016 13th Working IEEE/IFIP Conference on, 2016*, 182-191. 10.1109/WICSA.2016.21

Yadav, A. S., Singh, N., & Kushwaha, D. S. (2023). Evolution of Blockchain and consensus mechanisms & its real-world applications. *Multimedia Tools and Applications*, *82*(22), 1–46. doi:10.1007/s11042-023-14624-6

Yli-Huumo, J., Ko, D., Choi, S., Park, S., & Smolander, K. (2016). Where is current research on blockchain technology?—A systematic review. *PLoS One*, *11*(10), e0163477. doi:10.1371/journal.pone.0163477 PMID:27695049

Chapter 13
Blockchain Health:
Smart Contracts Transforming Healthcare Operations

S. C. Vetrivel
https://orcid.org/0000-0003-3050-8211
Kongu Engineering College, India

K. C. Sowmiya
Sri Vasavi College, India

V. Sabareeshwari
Amrita School of Agricultural Sciences, India

ABSTRACT

Blockchain technology has emerged as a revolutionary force in various industries, and healthcare is no exception. This chapter explores the transformative potential of blockchain-powered smart contracts in healthcare operations. Smart contracts, self-executing agreements with coded rules, offer unprecedented transparency, security, and efficiency in managing healthcare processes. The decentralized and tamper-resistant nature of blockchain ensures the integrity and privacy of health data, addressing concerns related to data breaches and unauthorized access. Smart contracts automate and streamline complex healthcare workflows, reducing administrative overhead and enhancing operational efficiency. Through real-time data synchronization and a distributed ledger, stakeholders across the healthcare ecosystem can access a single version of truth, minimizing discrepancies and improving collaboration.

DOI: 10.4018/979-8-3693-1511-8.ch013

1. INTRODUCTION

1.1. Overview of Blockchain

Blockchain is a revolutionary and decentralized technology that serves as the underlying architecture for digital currencies like Bitcoin, but its applications extend far beyond crypto currencies. At its core, block chain is a distributed and immutable ledger that records transactions across a network of computers in a secure, transparent, and tamper-resistant manner. Unlike traditional centralized systems, where a single authority controls and verifies transactions, block chain operates on a peer-to-peer network, eliminating the need for intermediaries. Each block in the chain contains a cryptographic hash of the previous block, creating a continuous and unchangeable sequence (Linn & Martha, 2016). This ensures the integrity and security of the data stored on the blockchain. Smart contracts, self-executing agreements with the terms of the contract directly written into code, further enhance the capabilities of blockchain by automating and enforcing contractual agreements. The decentralized nature of blockchain not only enhances security but also increases transparency, as every participant in the network has access to the same information (Bocek et al., 2017; Bryatov & Borodinov, 2019). As a result, blockchain technology has found applications in diverse industries, including finance, supply chain, healthcare, and more, offering solutions for issues like fraud prevention, traceability, and data integrity. The potential of blockchain to transform various sectors and redefine how transactions are conducted makes it a key driver of innovation in the digital era.

1.2. Key Principles of Blockchain

Blockchain is a decentralized and distributed ledger technology that underlies cryptocurrencies like Bitcoin, but its applications extend far beyond digital currencies (Decker & Wattenhofer, 2013). Understanding these key principles provides insight into the foundational concepts of blockchain technology and its potential applications across various industries. The key principles of blockchain include:

- **Decentralization:**
    - Blockchain operates on a decentralized network of computers (nodes) that work together to maintain the integrity and security of the system.
    - No single entity has control over the entire blockchain network, making it resistant to censorship and tampering.
- **Distributed Ledger:**

- The ledger or database is distributed across all participating nodes in the network. Each node has a copy of the entire blockchain, ensuring transparency and preventing a single point of failure.
- All participants have access to the same historical records, promoting trust and eliminating the need for intermediaries.

- **Consensus Mechanism:**
  - To validate transactions and add them to the blockchain, nodes must agree on a consensus mechanism. Common consensus mechanisms include Proof of Work (PoW) and Proof of Stake (PoS).
  - Consensus mechanisms ensure that only valid transactions are added to the blockchain, preventing fraud and maintaining the integrity of the ledger.
- **Immutability:**
  - Once a block of transactions is added to the blockchain, it is extremely difficult to alter or delete. Each block contains a cryptographic hash of the previous block, creating a chain of blocks that are linked and secured through cryptography.
  - Immutability enhances the security and reliability of the data stored on the blockchain.
- **Cryptographic Security:**
  - Blockchain uses cryptographic techniques to secure transactions and control access to the network.
  - Public and private key cryptography is commonly employed to verify the identity of participants, secure transactions, and control access to the data on the blockchain.
- **Smart Contracts:**
  - Smart contracts are self-executing contracts with the terms of the agreement directly written into code. They automatically execute and enforce the terms when predefined conditions are met.
  - Smart contracts enable the automation of various processes, reducing the need for intermediaries and increasing efficiency.
- **Permissioned and Permissionless Blockchains:**
  - Permissionless blockchains, like Bitcoin, are open to anyone, and anyone can participate in the validation process.
  - Permissioned blockchains restrict access to certain participants, providing a more controlled environment suitable for specific use cases such as business consortiums.
- **Transparency:**

- All transactions on the blockchain are visible to all participants in the network. While individual identities may be pseudonymous, the transaction history is open and transparent.
  Transparency fosters trust among participants and helps prevent fraud.

1.3. Evolution and Adoption in Various Industries

Blockchain technology has undergone a remarkable journey of evolution and adoption across various industries, transforming traditional paradigms and establishing itself as a disruptive force (Decker & Wattenhofer, 2013). Originating as the underlying technology for cryptocurrencies like Bitcoin, blockchain has evolved beyond its initial use case and found application in diverse sectors. In finance, blockchain has revolutionized the way transactions are conducted, providing secure and transparent ledgers that reduce the need for intermediaries and enhance efficiency. The supply chain industry has embraced blockchain to enhance traceability and transparency, allowing stakeholders to track the journey of products from origin to destination in real-time, reducing fraud and ensuring the authenticity of goods. Healthcare has witnessed the adoption of blockchain for secure and interoperable health records, ensuring data integrity and improving patient care (Dennis & Owen, 2015). Additionally, blockchain has made its mark in the legal and intellectual property sectors by providing immutable records and smart contracts that streamline processes and reduce disputes. The evolution of blockchain technology has been marked by continuous innovation, with the introduction of smart contracts, decentralized finance (DeFi), and non-fungible tokens (NFTs) further expanding its utility. As industries recognize the potential for increased efficiency, security, and transparency, the adoption of blockchain continues to accelerate, paving the way for a decentralized and interconnected future.

2. BLOCKCHAIN IN HEALTHCARE

2.1. Current Challenges in Healthcare Operations

The integration of blockchain technology in healthcare operations has shown promise in addressing various challenges, but it also comes with its own set of hurdles. One significant current challenge is the interoperability of different blockchain platforms and healthcare systems. The lack of standardized protocols and a unified framework makes it difficult for disparate systems to seamlessly communicate and share data (Liang, Zhao, Shetty et al, 2017; Puthal et al., 2018). This interoperability issue hampers the realization of the full potential of blockchain in creating a comprehensive and transparent healthcare ecosystem. Another challenge lies in the scalability of blockchain networks. As healthcare data continues to grow exponentially, blockchain networks must be able to handle increased transaction volumes without compromising speed and efficiency. Additionally, concerns about data privacy and security persist, as sensitive health information stored on a blockchain is only as secure as the underlying technology and the measures in place to protect it. Striking the right balance between transparency and confidentiality is crucial for the successful implementation of blockchain in healthcare (Witchey, 2019; Yue et al., 2016; Zhang, Walker, White et al, 2017). Moreover, regulatory uncertainty and the lack of a standardized legal framework pose challenges in ensuring compliance and gaining widespread acceptance across the healthcare industry. Addressing these challenges requires collaborative efforts from stakeholders, including healthcare providers, technology developers, regulators, and policymakers, to establish common standards, enhance interoperability, and ensure the secure and ethical use of blockchain technology in healthcare operations.

2.2. The Promise of Blockchain in Healthcare

The promise of blockchain in healthcare represents a transformative potential to address critical challenges within the industry. Blockchain technology, with its decentralized and tamper-resistant nature, offers a secure and transparent framework for managing healthcare data. One of the primary advantages is its ability to enhance data interoperability by providing a unified and standardized platform for storing and sharing patient information across disparate healthcare systems (Rabah, 2017). This could streamline processes, reduce administrative overhead, and ensure the accuracy and integrity of medical records. Moreover, blockchain can empower patients by granting them greater control over their own health data, enabling them to share it securely with healthcare providers as needed. The immutability and transparency of blockchain also enhance data security and privacy, mitigating the risk of unauthorized access or data breaches. Smart contracts within blockchain can automate and enforce compliance with healthcare regulations, reducing errors and ensuring adherence to industry standards (Hölbl et al., 2018). Overall, the promise of blockchain in healthcare lies in its potential to revolutionize data management, interoperability, and security, ultimately leading to more efficient and patient-centric healthcare systems.

2.3. Case Studies of Blockchain Implementation in Health Systems

These case studies showcase how blockchain technology can enhance the security, interoperability, and patient empowerment within healthcare systems.

1. Estonia's Electronic Health Records (EHR) System:

Background:

Estonia is known for its advanced digital infrastructure, and in 2002, it initiated a nationwide healthcare project to implement a comprehensive EHR system. The government partnered with Guardtime, a blockchain technology company, to secure and streamline the management of health records.

Blockchain Implementation:

- *Data Security and Integrity:* Blockchain was employed to ensure the security and integrity of patient data. Each entry into the EHR is timestamped and linked to the previous block, creating an immutable chain of health records.
- *Patient Consent:* Smart contracts were utilized to manage patient consent. Patients have control over who can access their health information, and any access requires explicit permission through smart contracts.
- *Interoperability:* Blockchain facilitated interoperability by creating a unified platform where healthcare providers, pharmacies, and other authorized entities could access patient records seamlessly.

Results:

- *Data Accuracy:* The blockchain implementation significantly improved the accuracy and reliability of health data (McGhin et al., 2019). Tampering or unauthorized access became extremely difficult due to the decentralized and cryptographic nature of the technology.
- *Efficiency:* Streamlined access to patient records reduced administrative overhead and enhanced the efficiency of healthcare services. This also resulted in cost savings for the healthcare system.
- *Patient Empowerment:* Patients have more control over their health data, fostering a sense of ownership and empowerment. They can also track who has accessed their information, promoting transparency.

2. MedRec: A Decentralized Medical Record Management System:

Background:

MedRec is a decentralized medical record management system developed by researchers at MIT. It aims to address issues related to data fragmentation and lack of interoperability in the current healthcare systems.

Blockchain Implementation:

- *Interoperability:* MedRec uses blockchain to enable interoperability among different healthcare providers and systems. It creates a shared, decentralized ledger where patient records from various sources can be securely stored and accessed.
- *Patient Ownership:* The system emphasizes patient ownership of data. Patients have control over their medical records and can grant permission for specific healthcare providers to access their information.
- *Data Integrity:* The blockchain's immutability ensures the integrity of medical records. Once a record is added to the blockchain, it cannot be altered, providing a secure and unforgeable history of patient health data.

Results:

- *Improved Data Access:* MedRec facilitates quick and secure access to patient records across different healthcare providers. This can be crucial in emergency situations where timely access to accurate medical information is essential.
- *Reduced Redundancy:* By using a shared blockchain ledger, redundancies in medical data are reduced, leading to a more streamlined and efficient healthcare system.
- *Research Opportunities:* Researchers can access anonymized and aggregated data on the blockchain for medical research, fostering innovation while maintaining patient privacy.

3. SMART CONTRACTS: A FOUNDATION FOR TRANSFORMATION

3.1. Understanding Smart Contracts

Smart contracts are self-executing contracts with the terms of the agreement directly written into code. These programmable contracts operate on blockchain platforms, such as Ethereum, and automatically execute predefined actions when specific conditions are met. The underlying concept of smart contracts is to eliminate the need for intermediaries and establish trust in transactions through transparent, decentralized, and tamper-resistant code execution. Smart contracts are built using programming languages like Solidity and are deployed on blockchain networks, ensuring immutability and security (Engelhardt, 2017; Esposito et al., 2018). They can be employed in various applications, ranging from financial services like decentralized finance (DeFi) to supply chain management and beyond. The key feature of smart contracts is their ability to automate processes, streamline transactions, and enhance efficiency by removing manual intervention and reducing the risk of errors. However, it's crucial to consider the potential challenges, such as code vulnerabilities and legal implications, in the development and deployment of smart contracts to ensure their widespread adoption and successful implementation in diverse industries.

3.2. Features and Benefits

Smart contracts are self-executing contracts with the terms of the agreement directly written into code (Zyskind & Nathan, 2015). They run on blockchain technology, most commonly associated with platforms like Ethereum. Here are some key features and benefits of smart contracts:

Features:

- **Autonomy:** Smart contracts operate without the need for intermediaries, such as banks or legal systems. This reduces the risk of fraud and manipulation.
- **Trust:** The transparent and decentralized nature of blockchain ensures that all parties involved can trust the execution of the contract without relying on a central authority.
- **Security:** Cryptography and consensus mechanisms in blockchain make smart contracts highly secure, protecting them from tampering and unauthorized access.
- **Accuracy:** Automation reduces the chances of human error. Once coded, the smart contract will execute exactly as programmed.
- **Efficiency:** Automated execution eliminates the need for time-consuming manual processes, reducing delays and costs associated with traditional contract execution.
- **Transparency:** All transactions and terms are recorded on the blockchain and are visible to all participants. This transparency enhances accountability and reduces disputes.
- **Cost-Effective:** By eliminating intermediaries and automating processes, smart contracts can significantly reduce transaction costs associated with traditional contracts.

Benefits:

- **Speed:** Smart contracts execute automatically, reducing the time it takes to complete a transaction compared to traditional methods that involve manual processes.
- **Cost Reduction:** The elimination of intermediaries, paperwork, and the need for extensive verification processes results in cost savings.
- **Security:** Cryptography and the decentralized nature of blockchain make smart contracts highly resistant to hacking and fraud, ensuring the integrity of the contract.
- **Trustworthiness:** The transparency of blockchain and the self-executing nature of smart contracts build trust among parties, as they can be certain that the agreed-upon terms will be carried out.
- **Global Reach:** Smart contracts operate on a blockchain, which is accessible globally. This enables parties from different parts of the world to engage in transactions without geographic limitations.
- **Immutable Record:** Once a smart contract is deployed on the blockchain, its code and execution history become part of an immutable ledger, providing a clear and unchangeable record of all transactions.
- **Automation and Accuracy:** Automation reduces the risk of errors and ensures that the terms of the contract are executed precisely as programmed, enhancing overall accuracy.
- **Innovative Applications:** Smart contracts enable the creation of decentralized applications (DApps) and facilitate the development of new, innovative business models in various industries.

3.3. Examples of Smart Contracts in Different Industries

Smart contracts, self-executing contracts with the terms of the agreement directly written into code, have found applications across various industries. Here are some examples of smart contracts in different sectors:

- **Finance and Banking:**
    - **Loan Agreements:** Smart contracts can automate the lending process, defining conditions for loan issuance, interest rates, and repayment schedules. Once predefined conditions are met, the contract can automatically trigger the transfer of funds.
    - **Derivatives and Trading:** Smart contracts facilitate the creation and execution of financial derivatives, ensuring automatic settlement and reducing counterparty risk.

- **Real Estate:**
  - **Property Transactions:** Smart contracts can streamline real estate transactions by automating the transfer of ownership once payment is made. This reduces the need for intermediaries and minimizes the risk of fraud.
- **Supply Chain:**
  - **Provenance Tracking:** Smart contracts can be used to record and track the origin and journey of products in the supply chain. This ensures transparency, reduces fraud, and helps with compliance.
- **Healthcare:**
  - **Patient Data Management:** Smart contracts can manage access to patient data, ensuring that only authorized individuals or systems can retrieve or update specific information, improving data security and privacy.
- **Insurance:**
  - **Automated Claims Processing:** Smart contracts can automatically execute insurance claims based on predefined conditions, reducing processing time and minimizing the risk of fraud.
- **Intellectual Property:**
  - **Royalty Payments:** Smart contracts can automate royalty payments for content creators, ensuring that payments are made in real-time based on predefined criteria such as downloads, views, or usage.
- **Energy:**
  - **Grid Management:** Smart contracts can automate the buying and selling of energy in a decentralized grid, ensuring efficient and transparent transactions between producers and consumers.
- **Legal Industry:**
  - **Escrow Services:** Smart contracts can serve as digital escrow services, holding funds until predefined conditions are met in legal transactions, such as the completion of a service or the delivery of goods.
- **Education:**
  - **Credential Verification:** Smart contracts can be used to verify and authenticate educational credentials, reducing the risk of fraudulent claims on resumes and academic qualifications.
- **Government:**
  - **Voting Systems:** Smart contracts can enhance the security and transparency of voting systems, ensuring that votes are accurately recorded and counted without the risk of manipulation.

4. HEALTHCARE OPERATIONS: A CRITICAL EXAMINATION

4.1. Inefficiencies in Traditional Healthcare Operations

In traditional healthcare operations, various inefficiencies can hinder the delivery of optimal patient care and contribute to increased costs. One prominent inefficiency is the prevalence of paper-based record-keeping systems, which can lead to errors, delays, and difficulties in accessing patient information (Nakamoto, 2008). The manual processing of paperwork not only consumes valuable time but also poses a risk of data inaccuracies, compromising patient safety. Additionally, communication breakdowns among healthcare professionals often occur due to reliance on outdated communication methods, such as phone calls and fax machines, leading to delays in critical decision-making processes. Another notable inefficiency is the lack of interoperability among different healthcare systems and electronic health records (EHRs), making it challenging to seamlessly share patient information across different providers and settings (Curran, 2018). This fragmentation hampers care coordination and can result in redundant tests, unnecessary procedures, and suboptimal outcomes. Moreover, the administrative burden associated with insurance claims processing and billing procedures adds to the complexity, diverting healthcare resources away from direct patient care (Khatoon et al., 2019). These inefficiencies underscore the need for a more integrated and technologically advanced approach to healthcare operations to enhance efficiency, reduce costs, and ultimately improve patient outcomes.

4.2. Data Security and Privacy Concerns

Data security and privacy concerns in traditional healthcare operations have become increasingly prominent with the widespread adoption of electronic health records (EHRs) and other digital technologies. One of the primary issues revolves around the sensitive nature of healthcare data, which includes patients' personal information, medical histories, and treatment plans. Unauthorized access or data breaches can lead to severe consequences, such as identity theft, insurance fraud, or the compromise of patients' medical confidentiality (Academy, 2019). In traditional healthcare settings, where paper records were more prevalent, physical security measures played a crucial role. However, the shift towards digital platforms has introduced new challenges, including the potential for cyberattacks, malware, and ransomware that can compromise the integrity of healthcare systems. Additionally, the interconnected nature of healthcare networks and the sharing of information among various stakeholders, such as hospitals, insurance providers, and government agencies, further complicates data security. The regulatory landscape, including laws like the Health Insurance Portability and Accountability Act (HIPAA) in the

United States, aims to address these concerns by imposing strict guidelines and penalties for non-compliance (Yli-Huumo et al., 2016). However, the evolving nature of technology requires continuous efforts from healthcare organizations to adapt and enhance their security measures to safeguard patient data and uphold privacy standards. As healthcare continues to integrate advanced technologies like telemedicine and Internet of Things (IoT) devices, the need for robust cybersecurity measures and proactive privacy policies becomes even more critical to maintain trust and ensure the confidentiality of patient information in traditional healthcare operations.

4.3. Regulatory Compliance Challenges

Regulatory compliance in traditional healthcare operations poses significant challenges due to the complex and dynamic nature of the healthcare industry. One of the primary obstacles is the ever-evolving landscape of healthcare regulations at both national and international levels. Healthcare providers must navigate a web of rules and standards set by government bodies, such as the Health Insurance Portability and Accountability Act (HIPAA) in the United States or the General Data Protection Regulation (GDPR) in the European Union (James, 2018). The intricate and often ambiguous nature of these regulations can create confusion and make it challenging for healthcare organizations to interpret and implement compliance measures effectively. Additionally, traditional healthcare operations involve a multitude of stakeholders, including healthcare professionals, insurance providers, pharmaceutical companies, and technology vendors. Coordinating and ensuring compliance across these diverse entities can be a formidable task (Beck et al., 2017). The integration of new technologies, such as electronic health records (EHRs) and telemedicine, further complicates the regulatory landscape, requiring organizations to adapt quickly to emerging standards while safeguarding patient privacy and data security. Moreover, the need for interoperability among different systems and platforms poses a constant challenge, as achieving seamless data exchange while adhering to regulatory requirements remains a persistent struggle (Erik et al., 2018). Financial constraints also contribute to compliance challenges, especially for smaller healthcare organizations. The cost of implementing and maintaining compliance measures, such as cybersecurity protocols and staff training programs, can strain limited resources. As regulatory bodies intensify scrutiny and enforcement actions, healthcare providers face increased pressure to allocate resources effectively and stay abreast of regulatory updates (Meng et al., 2018). In conclusion, regulatory compliance challenges in traditional healthcare operations stem from the intricate regulatory landscape, diverse stakeholders, technological advancements, and financial constraints, requiring a concerted effort to navigate and adhere to evolving standards.

5. BLOCKCHAIN SOLUTIONS FOR HEALTHCARE CHALLENGES

Blockchain technology has the potential to address various challenges in the healthcare sector by providing transparency, security, and efficiency. Implementing blockchain solutions in healthcare requires collaboration among stakeholders, adherence to regulatory standards, and overcoming technical challenges (Gipp et al., 2016). However, the potential benefits in terms of data security, interoperability, and transparency make blockchain an increasingly attractive option for addressing healthcare challenges. Here are some key ways in which blockchain solutions can be applied to healthcare challenges:

- Data Security and Integrity:
    - *Problem:* Healthcare systems often face challenges related to the security and integrity of patient data.
    - *Blockchain Solution:* Blockchain ensures secure and tamper-proof storage of health records. Each block in the chain contains a cryptographic hash of the previous block, making it nearly impossible to alter data retroactively. This ensures the integrity of patient information.
- Interoperability:
    - *Problem:* Healthcare data is often scattered across various systems, leading to interoperability issues.
    - *Blockchain Solution:* Blockchain can act as a decentralized ledger that securely stores and shares health data across different entities. Smart contracts can be employed to automate data sharing between healthcare providers, ensuring standardized and seamless interoperability.
- Patient Consent Management:
    - *Problem:* Obtaining and managing patient consent for data sharing is often a complex and time-consuming process.
    - *Blockchain Solution:* Blockchain enables the creation of smart contracts that define and enforce consent rules (Mehdi & Ravaud, 2017). Patients can have more control over who accesses their data, and consent changes can be recorded transparently in the blockchain.
- Drug Traceability:
    - *Problem:* Counterfeit drugs pose a significant threat to patient safety.

    - *Blockchain Solution:* Using blockchain, the entire drug supply chain can be recorded transparently, from manufacturing to distribution to retail. Each step is recorded in a tamper-proof manner, ensuring the authenticity and traceability of pharmaceuticals.
- Streamlining Healthcare Payments:
    - *Problem:* Billing and insurance processes in healthcare are often complex and prone to errors.
    - *Blockchain Solution:* Implementing smart contracts in billing processes can automate and streamline payment procedures. This reduces administrative costs, minimizes fraud, and ensures timely and accurate payments.
- Clinical Trials and Research:
    - *Problem:* Lack of transparency and data sharing in clinical trials can slow down research progress.
    - *Blockchain Solution:* By using blockchain, clinical trial data can be securely shared among stakeholders, including researchers, regulators, and patients. This improves transparency, reduces data silos, and accelerates the research and development process.
- Supply Chain Management:
    - *Problem:* Ensuring the integrity and transparency of the healthcare supply chain is critical.
    - *Blockchain Solution:* Blockchain can be employed to track and authenticate medical supplies and equipment as they move through the supply chain. This enhances traceability, reduces the risk of counterfeit products, and ensures the quality of healthcare materials.
- Identity Management:
    - *Problem:* Patients may have multiple identities in different healthcare systems, leading to identity management challenges.
    - *Blockchain Solution:* Blockchain-based identity management ensures a single, verifiable patient identity across different healthcare providers. This can improve the accuracy of patient records and reduce errors in treatment.

6. IMPLEMENTING SMART CONTRACTS IN HEALTHCARE

6.1. Technical Aspects of Integrating Smart Contracts

Integrating smart contracts into healthcare systems involves a careful consideration of various technical aspects to ensure seamless and secure implementation. Smart contracts, which are self-executing contracts with coded terms, can automate and streamline various processes in healthcare, ranging from patient data management to insurance claims. One critical technical aspect is the choice of blockchain platform, as smart contracts often run on blockchain networks to ensure transparency, immutability, and security (Ahram et al., 2017; Suveen et al., 2017). Ethereum, for instance, is a popular choice due to its robust smart contract capabilities. Smart contracts in healthcare must also adhere to industry standards such as the Health Insurance Portability and Accountability Act (HIPAA) in the United States to ensure the protection of sensitive patient information. Interoperability with existing healthcare IT infrastructure is another crucial consideration, necessitating the use of standards like HL7 (Health Level Seven) for data exchange. Additionally, ensuring data privacy and security through encryption and decentralized storage is paramount (Arati, 2017; Ovais, 2017; Saberi et al., 2019). Smart contracts can be designed to handle various healthcare scenarios, such as insurance claims processing, patient consent management, and supply chain tracking of pharmaceuticals. Continuous monitoring, auditing, and regular updates to smart contract code are essential to adapt to evolving healthcare regulations and technological advancements, ensuring a resilient and efficient integration of smart contracts in the healthcare domain.

6.2. Challenges and Solutions in Implementation

Implementing smart contracts in healthcare presents several challenges and requires careful consideration to ensure successful integration. One primary challenge is the complexity of healthcare data and the need for strict compliance with privacy regulations such as the Health Insurance Portability and Accountability Act (HIPAA). Smart contracts inherently operate on decentralized and transparent platforms, which could potentially compromise patient confidentiality (Chris, 2018). To address this, encryption and permissioned access mechanisms must be incorporated into the smart contracts to safeguard sensitive information. Another hurdle is the interoperability of healthcare systems, as different entities within the healthcare ecosystem may use disparate technologies. Standardization efforts and the development of common data formats are essential to facilitate seamless communication and execution of smart contracts across diverse platforms (Florian, 2017; Lemieux, 2016). Additionally, the integration of smart contracts requires a cultural shift within the healthcare industry, as stakeholders need to adapt to the decentralized nature of these technologies. Education and training programs can play a crucial role in ensuring that healthcare professionals understand and embrace the benefits of smart contracts. Furthermore, scalability issues and the potential for unforeseen technical glitches must be considered, demanding continuous monitoring and refinement of smart contract implementations. Despite these challenges, the potential benefits of increased efficiency, transparency, and reduced administrative overhead make the implementation of smart contracts in healthcare a worthwhile pursuit. Continuous collaboration between technology experts, legal professionals, and healthcare stakeholders is key to overcoming these challenges and ensuring the successful adoption of smart contracts in the healthcare sector.

7. INTEROPERABILITY AND STANDARDIZATION

7.1. Importance of Interoperability in Healthcare

Interoperability in healthcare, particularly under the framework of interoperability and standardization smart contracts, holds paramount importance in revolutionizing the healthcare landscape. Interoperability refers to the seamless exchange and use of health information across various systems, allowing disparate healthcare entities to communicate and share data efficiently. This becomes crucial in ensuring patient-centric care, as it enables healthcare providers to access comprehensive and up-to-date patient information, leading to more informed clinical decisions. Smart contracts, built on standardized protocols, further enhance this interoperability by automating and streamlining processes (Gordon & Catalini, 2018; Weber et al., 2016). This not only expedites data sharing but also ensures the accuracy and security of transactions within the healthcare ecosystem. The significance of interoperability becomes especially pronounced when considering the diverse array of healthcare systems, electronic health records, and medical devices in use today. Standardization through smart contracts facilitates a common language and format for data exchange, reducing errors, enhancing data integrity, and ultimately improving patient outcomes. Furthermore, interoperability supports collaborative research efforts, accelerates innovation, and facilitates the development of personalized and precision medicine. In the context of smart contracts, their automation capabilities not only promote efficiency but also enhance trust and transparency in healthcare transactions (Daisuke et al., 2017). The integration of interoperability and standardization through smart contracts in healthcare lays the foundation for a more connected, efficient, and patient-centric healthcare ecosystem.

7.2. Standardization Initiatives in Blockchain for Healthcare

Standardization initiatives in blockchain for healthcare under interoperability and standardization smart contracts play a crucial role in fostering a transparent, secure, and efficient healthcare ecosystem. Recognizing the potential of blockchain technology in addressing challenges related to data sharing, security, and integrity in healthcare, various organizations and consortia have embarked on initiatives to establish standardized protocols and frameworks (Rouhani et al., 2018; Vazirani et al., 2019). These efforts aim to create a common language for healthcare data exchange and ensure seamless interoperability among diverse systems (Wu & Tsai, 2018). Smart contracts, self-executing agreements with coded business logic, have gained prominence for automating and enforcing terms in healthcare transactions. Standardization initiatives focus on developing interoperable smart contracts that adhere to industry-wide norms, enabling seamless integration across healthcare networks. These efforts encompass defining common data structures, cryptographic standards, and consensus mechanisms to ensure data consistency and integrity (Khezr et al., 2019; Litchfield & Khan, 2019; Shen et al., 2019). These standardized smart contracts not only enhance data sharing and collaboration but also contribute to reducing administrative overhead, minimizing fraud, and ensuring compliance with regulatory requirements (Vora et al., 2018). By promoting uniformity in blockchain implementations and smart contract development, these initiatives pave the way for a more cohesive and trustworthy healthcare infrastructure, ultimately benefiting patients, providers, and other stakeholders.

7.3. Overcoming Interoperability Challenges

Overcoming interoperability challenges in the realm of smart contracts within the healthcare sector necessitates a comprehensive approach that addresses technical, semantic, and organizational barriers (Zhang et al., 2018). Interoperability refers to the seamless exchange and utilization of data across diverse systems, and in the context of healthcare smart contracts, it becomes crucial for ensuring efficient, secure, and standardized transactions (Siyal et al., 2019). Standardization of data formats, communication protocols, and semantic frameworks is a foundational step. Establishing common standards enables different healthcare entities, such as hospitals, insurers, and laboratories, to communicate effectively through smart contracts, fostering a unified and interoperable ecosystem (Jamil et al., 2019). Additionally, the development of standardized smart contract templates tailored to healthcare operations can streamline processes and enhance compatibility. Overcoming technical challenges involves the adoption of widely accepted technologies and protocols, ensuring that smart contracts can execute across various platforms and systems. Moreover, a collaborative and consensus-driven approach among stakeholders is essential to align diverse interests and achieve a shared understanding of interoperability requirements. By addressing these multifaceted challenges, the healthcare industry can leverage smart contracts to improve transparency, reduce administrative overhead, and enhance patient care while ensuring seamless data flow across the healthcare ecosystem.

8. REGULATORY LANDSCAPE AND COMPLIANCE

8.1. Evolving Regulations in Response to Blockchain in Healthcare

The integration of blockchain technology in healthcare has prompted a dynamic shift in regulatory frameworks worldwide, as policymakers grapple with the novel challenges and opportunities presented by this decentralized and transparent system. The fundamental premise of blockchain, with its secure and immutable ledger, has the potential to revolutionize data management, interoperability, and security within the healthcare sector (Agbo et al., 2019; Lee & Yang, 2018). As a result, regulatory bodies are evolving to address the unique features and risks associated with blockchain in healthcare. Concerns such as patient privacy, data ownership, and smart contract enforcement have led to the formulation of guidelines that emphasize the importance of consent, encryption, and secure key management. Governments and regulatory agencies are increasingly recognizing the need for standardized protocols to ensure the ethical and secure deployment of blockchain solutions in healthcare (Azaria et al., 2016). Additionally, the evolving regulatory landscape reflects efforts to strike a balance between fostering innovation and protecting patients' rights, as policymakers work towards creating an environment conducive to the responsible adoption of blockchain technology in the healthcare ecosystem. This ongoing regulatory evolution is vital to establishing trust in blockchain applications, fostering industry-wide collaboration, and ultimately unlocking the full potential of this transformative technology in healthcare.

8.2. Navigating Compliance Challenges

Navigating compliance challenges in the integration of blockchain technology within the healthcare sector demands a nuanced approach due to the intricate regulatory landscape and sensitive nature of patient data. Blockchain's promise of enhancing data integrity, security, and interoperability faces several hurdles, primarily concerning privacy regulations such as the Health Insurance Portability and Accountability Act (HIPAA) in the United States. Implementing decentralized ledger systems requires careful consideration of how to maintain compliance with these stringent regulations while leveraging the benefits of blockchain. Additionally, the cross-border nature of healthcare data exchange necessitates aligning blockchain initiatives with international standards and data protection laws. Transparency and auditability, inherent strengths of blockchain, must be balanced with the need for data anonymization and restricted access to adhere to privacy regulations. Collaborative efforts involving healthcare organizations, technology providers, and regulatory bodies are essential to develop frameworks that accommodate blockchain innovations while safeguarding patient privacy and ensuring adherence to evolving compliance requirements. Continuous monitoring of regulatory updates and proactive engagement with stakeholders will be crucial in successfully navigating compliance challenges in the dynamic intersection of blockchain and healthcare.

9. FUTURE TRENDS AND INNOVATIONS

9.1. Emerging Technologies in Blockchain and Healthcare

Emerging technologies in blockchain and healthcare are revolutionizing the way medical data is managed, shared, and secured. Blockchain, a decentralized and immutable ledger technology, is gaining traction for its ability to enhance data integrity, interoperability, and security in healthcare systems (Kumar et al., 2018; Zhang, White, Schmidt et al, 2017). One notable application is in the management of Electronic Health Records (EHRs), where blockchain ensures the tamper-proof and transparent recording of patient information, enabling seamless sharing of data across healthcare providers while maintaining patient privacy. Additionally, blockchain facilitates efficient and secure management of pharmaceutical supply chains, preventing counterfeiting and ensuring the authenticity of drugs. The technology also supports innovative solutions for clinical trials, enabling transparent and traceable data for drug development (Genestier et al., 2017). Furthermore, smart contracts, self-executing contracts with the terms directly written into code, are being utilized for automating and streamlining various healthcare processes, such as insurance claims and billing. The integration of emerging technologies like blockchain in healthcare not only enhances data security but also fosters trust among stakeholders, reduces administrative overhead, and paves the way for a more patient-centric and efficient healthcare ecosystem (Nofer et al., 2017). As these technologies continue to mature, their widespread adoption holds the promise of transforming the healthcare industry by improving data management, transparency, and ultimately, patient outcomes.

9.2. Predictions for the Future of Healthcare Operations

The integration of blockchain technology into healthcare operations is anticipated to revolutionize the industry, offering increased efficiency, transparency, and security. One prominent prediction for the future of healthcare operations involves the use of blockchain to streamline and secure electronic health records (EHRs). Blockchain's decentralized and tamper-resistant nature can enhance data integrity, ensuring that patient information remains accurate and unaltered (Liang, Shetty, Tosh et al, 2017; Shrier et al., 2016; Stephen & Alex, 2018). This can lead to improved interoperability among different healthcare systems and providers, fostering a more comprehensive and patient-centric approach to care. Additionally, blockchain can facilitate the development of smart contracts, automating various aspects of healthcare operations such as insurance claims processing and billing. This not only reduces administrative burdens but also minimizes the risk of errors and fraud (Mackey et al., 2019). Furthermore, the use of blockchain in the pharmaceutical supply chain is expected to increase, enhancing traceability and authentication of drugs, ultimately combating counterfeit medications. While challenges such as regulatory hurdles and interoperability issues may persist, the ongoing development and adoption of blockchain solutions in healthcare operations hold the promise of transforming the industry into a more efficient, secure, and patient-focused ecosystem.

10. ETHICAL CONSIDERATIONS AND SOCIAL IMPACT

10.1. Ethical Challenges in Blockchain and Healthcare

The intersection of blockchain technology and healthcare presents a myriad of ethical challenges that necessitate careful consideration. One significant concern is the issue of privacy, as blockchain's inherent transparency could potentially compromise sensitive patient data. While the decentralized and tamper-resistant nature of blockchain ensures data integrity, it also poses a challenge in terms of conforming to regulations like the Health Insurance Portability and Accountability Act (HIPAA) in the United States (Carson et al., 2018; Kuo et al., 2017). Striking a balance between transparency and privacy is essential to maintain patient trust and comply with legal frameworks. Another ethical challenge revolves around data ownership and consent. Blockchain's distributed ledger model may complicate the delineation of ownership rights, particularly when patients contribute their health data to decentralized networks (Brennan, 2017; Kshetri, 2018; Randall et al., 2017). Clear mechanisms for obtaining informed consent and ensuring patients have control over their data are crucial to address these concerns. Additionally, issues of inclusivity and accessibility arise, as the adoption of blockchain technology may inadvertently exacerbate existing healthcare disparities, leaving certain populations without access to cutting-edge healthcare solutions (Radanović & Likić, 2018). Tackling these ethical challenges requires a collaborative effort among technologists, healthcare professionals, policymakers, and ethicists to establish guidelines and standards that prioritize both innovation and the well-being of patients.

10.2. Ensuring Equity and Access

Ensuring equity and access within the framework of ethical considerations is a crucial imperative for fostering a just and inclusive society. This multifaceted approach involves addressing disparities in access to resources, opportunities, and services, and requires a commitment to fairness and impartiality. Ethical considerations in this context encompass principles such as justice, beneficence, and non-discrimination. Social impact is a key lens through which the consequences of policies, practices, and innovations must be assessed. By prioritizing equity, decision-makers can mitigate the perpetuation of existing inequalities and promote social cohesion (Dimitrov, 2019). This involves dismantling barriers that hinder marginalized communities' access to education, healthcare, employment, and other essential services. Furthermore, it necessitates recognizing and rectifying historical injustices that have led to systemic disparities. Embracing technology responsibly is also paramount, as it can either exacerbate or alleviate inequities. Striking a balance between innovation and ethical considerations ensures that advancements benefit society as a whole, rather than widening existing gaps. Overall, the pursuit of equity and access under ethical considerations and social impact demands a conscientious, empathetic, and intersectional approach to decision-making and policy implementation.

10.3. Social Impact and Responsiveness

Social impact and responsiveness are crucial aspects within the broader framework of ethical considerations. In the realm of business and technology, companies are increasingly recognizing the importance of not only adhering to ethical principles but also actively contributing to positive social change. Social impact refers to the influence that an organization's actions have on society at large. This can encompass a wide range of factors, including environmental sustainability, diversity and inclusion, community engagement, and philanthropy (Boulos et al., 2018). Responsiveness, on the other hand, involves a company's ability to adapt and address social concerns promptly. Ethical considerations in social impact entail assessing the potential consequences of business decisions on various stakeholders, ensuring fair treatment, and upholding human rights. Companies that prioritize social impact and responsiveness are often more attuned to the needs and concerns of their stakeholders. This approach goes beyond merely complying with regulations; it involves actively seeking ways to make a positive contribution to the community and the world. Ethical considerations in social impact also include transparency and accountability. Companies are expected to communicate openly about their practices, both positive and negative, and take responsibility for any adverse effects they may have on society (Ølnes et al., 2017). Additionally, being socially responsive involves a continuous process of monitoring, evaluating, and adapting strategies to align with changing societal expectations and needs. For example, a tech company committed to ethical considerations might invest in sustainable practices, promote diversity within its workforce, and engage in community initiatives. Such actions not only enhance the company's reputation but also contribute to the betterment of society (Skiba, 2017). Ethical business practices with a focus on social impact and responsiveness are increasingly becoming a key differentiator for companies, influencing consumer preferences and attracting socially conscious investors. As society evolves, the integration of these ethical considerations becomes imperative for sustainable and responsible business practices, fostering a positive and lasting impact on the world.

11. CONCLUSION

In conclusion, the integration of smart contracts into healthcare operations represents a transformative leap forward for the industry. The inherent characteristics of smart contracts, such as transparency, immutability, and automation, address longstanding challenges in healthcare, paving the way for more efficient, secure, and patient-centric processes. The ability of smart contracts to streamline administrative tasks, enhance data accuracy, and facilitate seamless collaboration among stakeholders holds the potential to significantly reduce operational costs and minimize errors. Moreover, the decentralized and tamper-resistant nature of blockchain technology, on which smart contracts are built, ensures the integrity and security of sensitive healthcare data. As we embrace this technological evolution, it is evident that smart contracts not only optimize healthcare operations but also lay the foundation for a more interconnected, interoperable, and patient-focused healthcare ecosystem. The transformative power of smart contracts is poised to redefine the landscape of healthcare, fostering innovation, improving outcomes, and ultimately contributing to the advancement of global health standards.

REFERENCES

Academy, L. (2019). *Consensus Protocols*. Available online: https://lisk.io/academy/blockchain-basics/how-does-blockchain-work/consensus-protocols

Agbo, C. C., Mahmoud, Q. H., & Eklund, J. M. (2019). Blockchain technology in healthcare: A systematic review. *Health Care*, *7*, 56. PMID:30987333

Ahram, T., Sargolzaei, A., Sargolzaei, S., Daniels, J., & Amaba, B. (2017). Blockchain technology innovations. *Proceedings of the 2017 IEEE Technology and Engineering Management Conference (TEMSCON).* 10.1109/TEMSCON.2017.7998367

Arati, B. (2017). *Understanding Blockchain Consensus Models*. Persistent. Available online: https://pdfs.semanticscholar.org/da8a/37b10bc1521a4d3de925d7ebc44bb606d740.pdf

Azaria, A., Ekblaw, A., Vieira, T., & Lippman, A. (2016). Medrec: Using Blockchain for Medical Data Access and Permission Management. *Proceedings of the 2016 2nd International Conference on Open and Big Data (OBD).* 10.1109/OBD.2016.11

Beck, R., Avital, M., Rossi, M., & Thatcher, J. B. (2017). Blockchain technology in business and information systems research. *Business & Information Systems Engineering*, *59*(6), 381–384. doi:10.1007/s12599-017-0505-1

Bocek, T., Rodrigues, B. B., Strasser, T., & Stiller, B. (2017). Blockchains everywhere—A use-case of blockchains in the pharma supply-chain. *Proceedings of the 2017 IFIP/IEEE Symposium on Integrated Network and Service Management (IM).* 10.23919/INM.2017.7987376

Boulos, M. N. K., Wilson, J. T., & Clauson, K. A. (2018). Geospatial blockchain: Promises, challenges, and scenarios in health and healthcare. *International Journal of Health Geographics*, *17*(1), 25. doi:10.1186/s12942-018-0144-x PMID:29973196

Brennan, B. (2017). Blockchain HIE Overview: A Framework for Healthcare Interoperability. *Telehealth and Medicine Today*, *2*, 3.

Bryatov, S. R., & Borodinov, A. A. (2019). Blockchain Technology in the Pharmaceutical Supply Chain: Researching a Business Model Based on Hyperledger Fabric. *International Conference on Information Technology and Nanotechnology (ITNT).* 10.18287/1613-0073-2019-2416-134-140

Carson, B., Romanelli, G., Walsh, P., & Zhumaev, A. (2018). *Blockchain Beyond the Hype: What Is the Strategic Business Value.* McKinsey & Company. Available online: https://www.mckinsey.com/business-functions/mckinsey-digital/our-insights/blockchain-beyond-the-hype-what-is-the-strategic-business-value

Chris, J. (2018). *Blockchain: Background and Policy Issues*. Congressional Research Service. Available online: https://www.hsdl.org/?abstract&did=808684

Curran, B. (2018). *What Are the Trustless Environments and How Cryptocurrencies Create Them?* Blockonomi.com. Available online: https://blockonomi.com/trustless-environments/

Daisuke, I., Kashiyama, M., & Ueno, T. (2017). Tamper-resistant mobile health using blockchain technology. *JMIR mHealth and uHealth*, *5*(7), e111. doi:10.2196/mhealth.7938 PMID:28747296

Decker, C., & Wattenhofer, R. (2013). Information propagation in the bitcoin network. *Proceedings of the IEEE P2P 2013.*

Dennis, R., & Owen, G. (2015). Rep on the block: A next-generation reputation system based on the blockchain. *Proceedings of the 2015 10th International Conference for Internet Technology and Secured Transactions (ICITST)*. 10.1109/ICITST.2015.7412073

Dimitrov, D. V. (2019). Blockchain Applications for Healthcare Data Management. *Healthcare Informatics Research*, *25*(1), 51–56. doi:10.4258/hir.2019.25.1.51 PMID:30788182

Engelhardt, M. A. (2017). Hitching healthcare to the chain: An introduction to blockchain technology in the healthcare sector. *Technology Innovation Management Review*, *7*(10), 22–34. doi:10.22215/timreview/1111

Erik, H., Strewe, U. M., & Bosia, N. (2018). Background III—What Is Blockchain Technology? In *Supply Chain Finance and Blockchain Technology* (pp. 35–49). Springer.

Esposito, C., De Santis, A., Tortora, G., Chang, H., & Choo, K. K. R. (2018). Blockchain: A panacea for healthcare cloud-based data security and privacy? *IEEE Cloud Computing*, *5*(1), 31–37. doi:10.1109/MCC.2018.011791712

Florian, G. (2017). Pervasive Decentralisation of Digital Infrastructures: A Framework for Blockchain Enabled System and Use Case Analysis. *Proceedings of the Hawaii International Conference on System Sciences.*

Genestier, P., Zouarhi, S., Limeux, P., Excoffier, D., Prola, A., Sandon, S., & Temerson, J.M. (2017). Blockchain for consent management in the ehealth environment: A nugget for privacy and security challenges. *Journal of International Society for Telemedicine and eHealth*, *5*, GKR-e24.

Gipp, B., Kosti, J., & Breitinger, C. (2016). Securing Video Integrity Using Decentralized Trusted Timestamping on the Bitcoin Blockchain. *Proceedings of the Mediterranean Conference on Information Systems (MCIS).*

Gordon, W. J., & Catalini, C. (2018). Blockchain technology for healthcare: Facilitating the transition to patient-driven interoperability. *Computational and Structural Biotechnology Journal*, *16*, 224–230. doi:10.1016/j.csbj.2018.06.003 PMID:30069284

Hölbl, M., Kompara, M., Kamisalic, A., & Zlatolas, L. N. (2018). A systematic review of the use of blockchain in healthcare. *Symmetry*, *10*(10), 470. doi:10.3390/sym10100470

James, F. P. (2018). *Blockchain Technology Simplified: The Complete Guide to Blockchain Management, Mining, Trading and Investing Cryptocurrency*. CreateSpace Independent Publishing Platform.

Jamil, F., Hang, L., Kim, K., & Kim, D. (2019). A Novel Medical Blockchain Model for Drug Supply Chain Integrity Management in a Smart Hospital. *Electronics (Basel)*, *8*(5), 505. doi:10.3390/electronics8050505

Khatoon, A., Verma, P., Southernwood, J., Massey, B., & Corcoran, P. (2019). Blockchain in Energy Efficiency: Potential Applications and Benefits. *Energies*, *12*(17), 3317. doi:10.3390/en12173317

Khezr, S., Moniruzzaman, M., Yassine, A., & Benlamri, R. (2019). Blockchain technology in healthcare: A comprehensive review and directions for future research. *Applied Sciences (Basel, Switzerland)*, *9*(9), 1736. doi:10.3390/app9091736

Kshetri, N. (2018). Blockchain and Electronic Healthcare Records. *Computer*, *51*(12), 59–63. doi:10.1109/MC.2018.2880021

Kumar, T., Ramani, V., Ahmad, I., Braeken, A., Harjula, E., & Ylianttila, M. (2018). Blockchain Utilization in Healthcare: Key Requirements and Challenges. *Proceedings of the 2018 IEEE 20th International Conference on e-Health Networking, Applications and Services (Healthcom).*

Kuo, T. T., Kim, H., & Ohno-Machado, L. (2017). Blockchain distributed ledger technologies for biomedical and health care applications. *Journal of the American Medical Informatics Association : JAMIA*, *24*(6), 1211–1220. doi:10.1093/jamia/ocx068 PMID:29016974

Lee, S. H., & Yang, C. S. (2018). Fingernail analysis management system using microscopy sensor and blockchain technology. *International Journal of Distributed Sensor Networks*, *14*(3), 14. doi:10.1177/1550147718767044

Lemieux, V. L. (2016). Trusting records: Is Blockchain technology the answer? *Records Management Journal*, *26*(2), 110–139. doi:10.1108/RMJ-12-2015-0042

Liang, X., Shetty, S., Tosh, D., Kamhoua, C., Kwiat, K., & Njilla, L. (2017). Provchain: A blockchain-based data provenance architecture in cloud environment with enhanced privacy and availability. *Proceedings of the 17th IEEE/ACM International Symposium on Cluster, Cloud and Grid Computing*. 10.1109/CCGRID.2017.8

Liang, X., Zhao, J., Shetty, S., Liu, J., & Li, D. (2017). Integrating blockchain for data sharing and collaboration in mobile healthcare applications. *Proceedings of the 2017 IEEE 28th Annual International Symposium on Personal, Indoor, and Mobile Radio Communications (PIMRC)*. 10.1109/PIMRC.2017.8292361

Linn, L. A., & Martha, B. K. (2016). Blockchain for Health Data and Its Potential Use in Health IT and Health Care Related Research. In *Use of Blockchain for Healthcare and Research Workshop*. ONC/NIST.

Litchfield, A. T., & Khan, A. (2019). *A Review of Issues in Healthcare Information Management Systems and Blockchain Solutions*. CONF-IRM. Available online: https://aisel.aisnet.org/confirm2019/1/

Mackey, T. K., Kuo, T. T., Gummadi, B., Clauson, K. A., Church, G., Grishin, D., Obbad, K., Barkovich, R., & Palombini, M. (2019). 'Fit-for-purpose?'—Challenges and opportunities for applications of blockchain technology in the future of healthcare. *BMC Medicine*, *17*(1), 68. doi:10.1186/s12916-019-1296-7 PMID:30914045

McGhin, T., Choo, K.-K. R., Liu, C. Z., & He, D. (2019). Blockchain in healthcare applications: Research challenges and opportunities. *Journal of Network and Computer Applications*, *135*, 62–75. doi:10.1016/j.jnca.2019.02.027

Mehdi, B., & Ravaud, P. (2017). Blockchain technology for improving clinical research quality. *Trials*, *18*(1), 335. doi:10.1186/s13063-017-2035-z PMID:28724395

Meng, W., Tischhauser, E. W., Wang, Q., Wang, Y., & Han, J. (2018). When intrusion detection meets blockchain technology: A review. *IEEE Access : Practical Innovations, Open Solutions*, *6*, 10179–10188. doi:10.1109/ACCESS.2018.2799854

Nakamoto, S. (2008). *Bitcoin: A Peer-to-Peer Electronic Cash System*. Retrieved from https://www.bitcoin.org

Nofer, M., Gomber, P., Hinz, O., & Schiereck, D. (2017). Blockchain. *Business & Information Systems Engineering*, *59*(3), 183–187. doi:10.1007/s12599-017-0467-3

Ølnes, S., Ubacht, J., & Janssen, M. (2017). Blockchain in government: Benefits and implications of distributed ledger technology for information sharing. *Government Information Quarterly*, *34*(3), 355–364. doi:10.1016/j.giq.2017.09.007

Ovais, A. (2017). *Block Chain Technology: Concept of Digital Economics*. University Library of Munich.

Puthal, D., Malik, N., Mohanty, S. P., Kougianos, E., & Das, G. (2018). Everything you wanted to know about the blockchain: Its promise, components, processes, and problems. *IEEE Consumer Electronics Magazine*, *7*(4), 6–14. doi:10.1109/MCE.2018.2816299

Rabah, K. V. O. (2017). Challenges & opportunities for blockchain-powered healthcare systems: A review. *Mara Research Journal of Medicine and Health Sciences*, *1*, 45–52.

Radanović, I., & Likić, R. (2018). Opportunities for use of blockchain technology in medicine. *Applied Health Economics and Health Policy*, *16*(5), 583–590. doi:10.1007/s40258-018-0412-8 PMID:30022440

Randall, D., Goel, P., & Abujamra, R. (2017). Blockchain applications and use cases in health information technology. *Journal of Health & Medical Informatics*, *8*(3), 2. doi:10.4172/2157-7420.1000276

Rouhani, S., Butterworth, L., Simmons, A. D., Humphery, D. G., & Deters, R. (2018). MediChainTM: A Secure Decentralized Medical Data Asset Management System. *Proceedings of the 2018 IEEE International Conference on Internet of Things (iThings) and IEEE Green Computing and Communications (GreenCom) and IEEE Cyber, Physical and Social Computing (CPSCom) and IEEE Smart Data (SmartData)*. 10.1109/Cybermatics_2018.2018.00258

Saberi, S., Kouhizadeh, M., Sarkis, J., & Shen, L. (2019). Blockchain technology and its relationships to sustainable supply chain management. *International Journal of Production Research*, *57*(7), 2117–2135. doi:10.1080/00207543.2018.1533261

Shen, B., Guo, J., & Yang, Y. (2019). MedChain: Efficient Healthcare Data Sharing via Blockchain. *Applied Sciences (Basel, Switzerland)*, *9*(6), 1207. doi:10.3390/app9061207

Shrier, D., Wu, W., & Pentland, A. (2016). Blockchain & infrastructure (identity, data security). Massachusetts Institute of Technology Connection Science, 1, 1–19.

Siyal, A., Junejo, A., Zawish, M., Ahmed, K., Khalil, A., & Soursou, G. (2019). Applications of Blockchain Technology in Medicine and Healthcare: Challenges and Future Perspectives. *Cryptography*, *3*(1), 3. doi:10.3390/cryptography3010003

Skiba, D. J. (2017). The potential of blockchain in education and health care. *Nursing Education Perspectives*, *38*, 220–221. doi:10.1097/01.NEP.0000000000000190 PMID:28622267

Stephen, R., & Alex, A. (2018). A Review on Blockchain Security. In *Conference Series: Materials Science and Engineering* (Vol. 396, p. 1). IOP Publishing. Available online https://iopscience.iop.org/article/10.1088/1757-899X/396/1/012030/meta

Suveen, A., Krumholz, H. M., & Schulz, W. L. (2017). Blockchain technology: Applications in health care. *Circulation: Cardiovascular Quality and Outcomes*, *10*(9), e003800. doi:10.1161/CIRCOUTCOMES.117.003800 PMID:28912202

Vazirani, A. A., O'Donoghue, O., Brindley, D., & Meinert, E. (2019). Implementing Blockchains for Efficient Health Care: Systematic Review. *Journal of Medical Internet Research*, *21*(2), e12439. doi:10.2196/12439 PMID:30747714

Vora, J., Nayyar, A., Tanwar, S., Tyagi, S., Kumar, N., Obaidat, M. S., & Rodrigues, J. J. (2018). BHEEM: A Blockchain-Based Framework for Securing Electronic Health Records. *Proceedings of the 2018 IEEE Globecom Workshops (GC Wkshps)*. 10.1109/GLOCOMW.2018.8644088

Weber, I., Xu, X., Riveret, R., Governatori, G., Ponomarev, A., & Mendling, J. (2016). Untrusted business process monitoring and execution using blockchain. In *International Conference on Business Process Management*. Springer. 10.1007/978-3-319-45348-4_19

Witchey, N. J. (2019). *Healthcare Transaction Validation via Blockchain, Systems and Methods*. U.S. Patent No. 10,340,038.

Wu, H. T., & Tsai, C. W. (2018). Toward blockchains for health-care systems: Applying the bilinear pairing technology to ensure privacy protection and accuracy in data sharing. *IEEE Consumer Electronics Magazine*, *7*(4), 65–71. doi:10.1109/MCE.2018.2816306

Yli-Huumo, J., Ko, D., Choi, S., Park, S., & Smolander, K. (2016). Where is current research on blockchain technology?—A systematic review. *PLoS One*, *11*(10), e0163477. doi:10.1371/journal.pone.0163477 PMID:27695049

Yue, X., Wang, H., Jin, D., Li, M., & Jiang, W. (2016). Healthcare data gateways: Found healthcare intelligence on blockchain with novel privacy risk control. *Journal of Medical Systems*, *40*(10), 218. doi:10.1007/s10916-016-0574-6 PMID:27565509

Zhang, P., Schmidt, D. C., White, J., & Lenz, G. (2018). Blockchain Technology Use Cases in Healthcare. In *Advances in Computers* (Vol. 111, pp. 1–41). Elsevier.

Zhang, P., Walker, M. A., White, J., Schmidt, D. C., & Lenz, G. (2017). Metrics for assessing blockchain-based healthcare decentralized apps. *Proceedings of the 2017 IEEE 19th International Conference on e-Health Networking, Applications and Services (Healthcom).* 10.1109/HealthCom.2017.8210842

Zhang, P., White, J., Schmidt, D. C., & Lenz, G. (2017). Design of Blockchain-Based Apps Using Familiar Software Patterns to Address Interoperability Challenges in Healthcare. *Proceedings of the PLoP-24th Conference on Pattern Languages of Programs.*

Zyskind, G., & Nathan, O. (2015). Decentralizing privacy: Using blockchain to protect personal data. *Proceedings of the 2015 IEEE Security and Privacy Workshops.* 10.1109/SPW.2015.27

Chapter 14
Applications of Artificial Intelligence Techniques in Modern Banking Sectors

Joel Jebadurai Devapitchai
https://orcid.org/0000-0002-6947-8497
St. Joseph's College of Engineering, Chennai, India

K. Dheenadhayalan
Mepco Schlenk Engineering College, India

L. Rajeshkumar
https://orcid.org/0009-0007-8513-206X
St. Joseph's College of Engineering, Chennai, India

M. Rathi Meena
Dr. Umayal Ramanathan College for Women, India

M. Soundarya
https://orcid.org/0000-0001-7018-7972
Sathyabama Institute of Science and Technology, India

M. S. Sowmiya
Alagappa University, India

K. Udhaya
https://orcid.org/0000-0003-1334-8877
Alagappa University, India

G. Hudson Arul Vethamanikam
Ayya Nadar Janaki Ammal College, India

Thirupathi Manickam
https://orcid.org/0000-0001-7976-6073
Christ University, India

ABSTRACT

AI-powered decision-making instruments are cutting-edge technology that has the potential to displace conventional banking procedures. This chapter emphasizes the critical role artificial intelligence (AI) has played in guiding the banking industry toward expansion. AI techniques including robotics, deep learning, facial recognition, natural language processing, and more are used to achieve this goal. This chapter provides an overview of the use of AI approaches in several banking functional domains, such as loan approval, customer lifecycle management, customer

DOI: 10.4018/979-8-3693-1511-8.ch014

services, alarm systems, and so on. It also highlights the benefits and difficulties that AI-driven financial apps provide. In summary, artificial intelligence (AI) has enormous promise in banking, but it also confronts several obstacles that, if correctly recognized and overcome, might broaden its use. This chapter is an invaluable tool for researchers, lawmakers, and bank officials who want to learn more about the unrealized potential of artificial intelligence in banking.

INTRODUCTION

The banking industry is vital to every individual's existence. A man can't even sleep without making a single transaction with the advent of digital banking. People rely on banking services to carry out all of their daily financial transactions. People are forced to use banking services through financial inclusion and technological transformation. Customers who are tech-savvy and regularly interact with sophisticated technologies anticipate frictionless banking services. To fulfill these demands, banks have branched out into the retail, Information Technology (IT), and telecom sectors to offer services like real-time money transfers, e-banking, and mobile banking (www.forbes.com/). Although these developments have made it possible for clients to access the majority of financial services whenever and wherever they choose, there has been a price for the banking industry. The emergence and the huge number of people's adaptability to banking services compel the banking sector to offer banking services with artificial intelligence techniques. Artificial Intelligence techniques such as Machine Learning (ML), Predictive Analytics (PA), voice recognition, Natural Language Programming (NLP), and chatbots simplify the banking services to the customers and avail all the services in one place 24x7 (www.deloitte.com). AI techniques were applied in the banking sectors to identify various banking frauds, risk modeling, solve customer queries online, and so on.

The use of artificial intelligence in banking will be crucial in the future since it will enable sophisticated data analytics to prevent fraudulent transactions and enhance compliance. An AI program completes anti-money laundering tasks that would often take hours or days in a matter of seconds. Banks can now handle enormous amounts of data at lightning speed thanks to AI and gain insightful knowledge from it. Digital payment advisors, biometric fraud detection systems, and AI bots are features that improve service quality and reach a larger clientele. All of this results in higher sales, lower expenses, and higher profits (Kaya et.al 2019).

This chapter is structured into five parts. The initial section covers the objectives and methodology. The second part delves into AI techniques applied in the banking sector. The third part explores AI techniques as they relate to specific functional aspects of the banking sector. The fourth part addresses both the advantages and hurdles associated with AI in this field. Lastly, the fifth part encompasses case studies, success stories, future trends, and concluding remarks regarding the role of AI in the banking sector.

This chapter comes out with the following objectives. They are.

1. The first objective of this study is to understand AI tools in banking such as machine learning, predictive analytics, voice recognition, natural language techniques, and chatbots
2. The second objective covered the AI applications in various functional areas of banks such as customer lifecycle, loan approval, customer services, alarming systems, cyber security fraud detection, credit risk assessment/credit scoring, management of bad debts, and automation.
3. Benefits, challenges, case studies, and success stories of AI in banking are presented in the third objective.

METHODOLOGY

This book chapter is purely based on secondary data from published articles, case studies, government reports, etc. Secondary data was covered with a focus on AI techniques such as Machine Learning, Chatbots, Deep Learning, Robotics, Voice recognition, Facial recognition, Predictive Analytics, and Natural Language Processing. Also, AI applied functional areas such as customer lifecycle, loan approval, customer services, alarming systems, cyber security fraud detection, credit risk assessment/credit scoring, management of bad debts, and automation. Finally, the benefits and challenges of AI in banking are presented in addition to case studies and success stories.

AI-BASED APPLICATIONS TOOLS IN THE BANKING INDUSTRY

Machine Learning

Machine learning is a branch of Artificial Intelligence (AI) and computer science that focuses on the use of data and algorithms to imitate the way that humans learn, gradually improving its accuracy.

CHATBOTS OR VIRTUAL ASSISTANT

Chatbot is an AI-based machine learning algorithm used by banks to interact with customers autonomously. Also, chatbot technology represents a distinct and compelling form of AI software, engaging customers through preprogrammed queries to ensure polite, efficient communication and immediate issue resolution (www.ibm.com). In banking, chatbot technology not only addresses customer inquiries autonomously but also gathers data on these queries, enabling solutions for future issues. For example, Erica is the virtual assistant used by the Bank of America to provide various services to customers such as reviewing weekly updates, cash flow, balances, transaction history, and upcoming bills. According to the Fintech Times during 2020, Erica assisted over 5 million customers in fulfilling over 75 million requests. Since its launch, Erica has supported 15 million customers, handling over 175 million requests. Daily, Erica engages in around 400,000 interactions (https://thefintechtimes.com).

ROBOTICS

Robots are the newest AI-based digital transformation technology in banking. According to Hitachi Review the largest bank in Japan, Mitsubishi UFJ Financial Group, deployed robot workers, dubbed "Nao," to its Tokyo branches in 2015 (www.hitachi.com). These employees were mobile and could provide customers with advice in a variety of languages. That is the first cooperative robot, or Cabot, working as a bank teller. However, the banking sector has now shifted to using robots that operate virtually in locations where they don't physically exist. The robot responds to client inquiries in a context-appropriate manner by utilizing a variety of gestures and analyzing behavior and facial expressions. The bank has a great chance to increase language coverage should the robot service become popular because it can function in 19 different languages.

According to The Financial Brand Newsletter, Sterling Bank & Trust in California has introduced two robots as greeters at the bank's new locations opening in Cupertino and Alhambra, in the Los Angeles area. As part of their 'training,' the two robots made appearances at the bank's San Francisco branches. It is used to meet and greet customers, answer simple questions in various languages, and free up some of the branch staff's time to work on more value-added services (https://thefinancialbrand.com). High-definition cameras record and match different customers, so identification can begin as soon as the customer enters the branch door.

VOICE RECOGNITION

Artificial intelligence is the foundation of voice technology. It can identify, receive, and comprehend spoken commands much like a digital device, and it can even execute these orders by using sound input as an interface. This voice recognition technology can be used by banks. Voice technology is used in the banking industry for several purposes, including voice remittance, account inquiries, money transactions and expenditures, financial news, and payment processing (www.biometricupdate.com).

According to moneycontrol.com, AI-based voice recognition is used for making the payment process by the customers. The practice of utilizing voice commands to send, receive, and pay money to other people via a speaker or smartphone equipped with artificial intelligence (AI) is known as voice payments. Creating an account for voice payments is quite similar to creating an account for any online wallet. The gadget will acknowledge your request, handle the payment, and reply with confirmation as soon as the payment app is launched. Natural Language Processing (NLP), a subfield of artificial intelligence (AI) that enables computers to learn, comprehend, respond to, and generate material in human languages, is used in this technology, which is a product of advances in artificial intelligence (AI) and Machine Learning (ML). It works closely with voice recognition engines where human speech is converted from analog to digital form which is being used in Google Assistant, Amazon's Alexa, or Apple's Siri.

The usage of voice payments in banking is becoming more common, as seen by the rising popularity of voice assistants like Google Assistant and Amazon Alexa. This ground-breaking innovation in the banking industry provides a smooth and cutting-edge payment experience. According to Yahoo Finance, voice biometrics will have a $3.9 billion worldwide market by 2026, growing at a compound annual growth rate of 22.8% from $1.1 billion in 2020 (https://finance.yahoo.com/).

According to López et.al (2017), 72% of customers claim to have previously used voice search with a personal digital assistant, like Google Assistant, Apple's Siri, or Amazon's Alexa, according to a Microsoft survey.

As per Juniper's projections, the voice commerce industry is anticipated to reach a remarkable $80 billion by 2023, and the transactions via smart home devices are anticipated to soar to $164 billion by 2025.

According to recent Cognizant research titled "The Future of Voice," Indian banking and finance experts were surveyed. In the survey, 94% of respondents indicated they thought the transition toward voice will pick up speed in the future and 72% said voice is critical to the bank's performance going forward.

To improve customer experience and stay up to date with fintech developments, banks employ Siri for voice remittance, account queries, and payments.

Samsung is the primary device that Bixby uses as an assistant. Banks that utilize Bixby for voice payments, account inquiries, expenditure monitoring, and financial news include KEB Hana Bank, Shinhan Bank, and Woori Bank (www.samsung.com).

Tesla is using data-over-voice technology to connect its vehicles to a networked house. Tesla is looking for speech technology solutions for its cars in collaboration with Alexa. Drivers of automobiles will have the ability to pay for petrol at gas stations in the United States using voice assistants thanks to Alexa smart systems. Drivers do not need to swipe their credit cards or log in since the transaction utilizes an Alexa Pay account (www.tesla.com).

DEEP LEARNING

An advanced machine learning (ML) method based on Artificial Neural Network (ANN) algorithms is called Deep Learning (DL). At the moment, DL is widely used in image processing, computer vision, audio-visual recognition, and classification and prediction problems. DL techniques were used in the banking sectors to identify fraud detection, and credit risk analysis and assist the bankers to banks in targeting the "right" customers with the "right" marketing campaign to ensure the effectiveness of its marketing activities. According to (kaggle.com), using Santander's customer data and a Kaggle competition, a deep learning application of convolutional neural networks is used to learn how customers would use bank products.

PREDICTIVE ANALYTICS

Artificial Intelligence (AI) is the area of computer science that seeks to develop systems that are capable of reasoning, learning, and solving problems—tasks that often require human intelligence. The use of Artificial Intelligence (AI) methods to evaluate data and produce predictions includes deep learning, computer vision, natural language processing, and reinforcement learning (Singh 2020). AI is capable of handling enormous and complicated data sets, uncovering hidden patterns and insights, and reacting to input and changing circumstances.

Predictive analytics can benefit from AI in several ways, based on the objectives of the organization and the available data. In banking, predictive analytics refers to the application of computer models that make use of data mining and artificial intelligence to evaluate vast volumes of data and forecast future consumer behavior (Kumar et.al, 2023). AI, for example, can be used to forecast consumer behavior based on interactions, preferences, and feedback, such as churn, retention, lifetime value, and satisfaction. This can provide tailored offers and recommendations in addition to enhancing marketing, sales, and service tactics. According to (mckinsey.com), AI can also be used to forecast price, supply, and demand based on past performance, industry trends, and outside variables. Furthermore, using patterns, rules, and signals, AI-based predictive analytics in banking can be utilized to forecast fraud, risks, and anomalies. This can guarantee regulatory compliance, safeguard assets, and stop losses. Lastly, using models (Logistic Regression), simulations, and optimization, AI can be utilized to forecast events, situations, and behaviors. This can assist in examining choices, testing theories, and coming to well-informed decisions.

FACIAL RECOGNITION

Facial recognition technology, previously only seen in science fiction, has become a reality and altered many aspects of our lives. Early facial recognition algorithms were first tested by researchers in the 1960s (www.nec.co.nz). Through the recording and collection of data from human faces, facial recognition technology facilitates the process of verifying an individual's identity. On the whole, facial recognition involves taking images of a person's face, analyzing it, and comparing the outcomes. Neural networks are used in facial recognition software to implement deep learning techniques. These networks learn from massive volumes of data, frequently in the millions, to understand and draw conclusions (Kabanda, S., & Owusu-Adjei 2019). As a result, the artificial intelligence (AI) model gains the capacity to identify patterns in the encountered data points. This innovative solution offers a smooth, safe, and practical method to conduct financial transactions by combining biometric data with artificial intelligence. Using face recognition technology, users may make payments, access services, and conduct other types of transactions without needing actual payment cards or passwords.

Alibaba's banking section, Ant Banking, was among the first businesses to implement face recognition technology for payment processing. Ant Financial launched "Smile to Pay," a face recognition payment system in 2015, which allowed patrons at certain KFC locations in China to make payments just by smiling at a camera (www.business-standard.com). This move marked a significant turning point in the evolution of face recognition technology for financial applications.

Following Ant Financial's success, other financial institutions and technology giants began investigating similar initiatives. Tencent, a massive Chinese digital company, added facial recognition technology to WeChat Pay, allowing users to approve transactions with just their faces.

Outside of China, other companies have embraced the trend of face recognition payments. With the launch of "Mastercard Identity Check," customers may validate online transactions using facial or fingerprint recognition. Meanwhile, owners of the iPhone X and subsequent models may use their facial biometrics to validate purchases thanks to Apple's Face ID technology, which was introduced in 2017. In January 2023, for example, the Indian government authorized banks to validate individual transactions using face recognition technology to lower the number of fraud cases (https://support.apple.com).

Furthermore, online transactions using Apple Pay, AliPay, and Selfie Pay—which offer face biometric verification in online banking for additional security—can make use of this technology. In 2015, The United Services Automobile Association (USAA) became the first large bank to use face biometrics (www.americanbanker.com). The finance industry is seeing a rise in the use of facial recognition technologies on a variety of platforms. Facial biometric authentication is a useful safeguard in banking since banks are under pressure to make sure that consumer data is kept safe by utilizing cutting-edge technology from reputable suppliers.

NATURAL LANGUAGE PROCESSING

Natural language processing (NLP) is a subfield of Artificial Intelligence (AI) that studies how computers and human language interact. It is an effective technique for processing enormous volumes of textual data because it allows machines to comprehend, interpret, and produce human language. NLP helps bankers do their functions such as document processing, automatic loans, risk management, asset management, sentiment analysis, compliance, and so on. Bankers use the NLP in the tools of translation tools, chatbots, and virtual assistants (https://timesofindia.indiatimes.com).

Founded in 2015, Kasisto is a firm located in New York. The business provides a chatbot named KAI, which it says may assist banks and other financial institutions in creating chatbots that assist their clients with managing their money using Natural Language Processing (NLP), retrieving transactions and account data, and making payments (https://kasisto.com/).

SAS asserts that it assisted the Royal Bank of Scotland (RBS) in assisting its customer service professionals in making their client interactions more personalized (www.sas.com). The bank sought to create an automated system to identify the most common client complaints and concerns based on past customer feedback and conversation data, utilizing SAS data-collecting technologies.

AI APPLICATION AREAS IN THE BANKING INDUSTRY

Customer Life Cycle

In the business realm, customers hold a paramount position. It falls upon bankers to allure customers to initiate their journey with the bank and ensure their retention as long-term patrons. The customer lifecycle spans from acquisition to proficiently servicing their needs. AI-driven technologies assist bankers in comprehending customer lifecycles across multiple dimensions, customer acquisition, credit decisions, monitoring and collections, deepening relations, and smart servicing (www.fintechfutures.com).

Customer Acquisition

The banks' strength is determined by the volume of customers holding accounts, while their profitability relies on analyzing customer databases and the range of banking products utilized. Before AI, acquiring customers was laborious for bankers. However, with AI, customer acquisition has streamlined through digital channels like ATMs, social media links, and bank websites. Bankers leverage AI algorithms such as deep learning and machine learning to comprehend and anticipate customer preferences, enabling tailored offers and recommendations. Additionally, inactive customers receive reminders and are informed about scheme benefits via mobile and email to encourage engagement.

Credit Decisions

Differentiating themselves from regular banks, AI-driven banks have developed quick credit approval turnaround times and streamlined lending procedures. regular banks often require a day or more for credit approvals. These AI-first banks make loan decisions for retail companies, Small and Medium-Sized Enterprises (SMEs), and corporate clients quickly by using a high degree of automation and almost instantaneous consumer data analysis. To do this, a variety of structured and unstructured data sets from more recent sources, such as location data, telecom use records, utility bills, and more, as well as more established ones, such as tax filings, bank transaction histories, credit reports, and credit reports, must be analyzed (Payne et.al 2022). Credit decisions comprised of credit qualifications, limit assessment, pricing, and fraud management.

Logistic regression and linear discriminant analysis stand as the most prevalent models in use. However, they possess certain limitations, such as the assumption of a linear relationship between variables and the need for multivariate normality, which might not align with the reality of nonlinear variables. In contrast, artificial intelligence methods, including decision trees, genetic algorithms, artificial neural networks, and support vector machines, demonstrate superior performance compared to traditional statistical techniques. Three prominent models - support vector machine, neural network, and decision tree - are employed for classification alongside the fuzzy C-Means clustering technique (www.infosys.com). Nevertheless, hybrid approaches have surpassed these specific methods in terms of prediction accuracy. Accurately predicting risk and making informed decisions regarding credit approval is crucial in preventing scenarios such as bankruptcy and fraudulent activities.

Credit qualifications are the primary stage in credit decisions. However, in recent years, both leading banks and fintech lenders have devised intricate models to analyze structured and unstructured data. These models scrutinize numerous data points sourced from social media, browsing habits, telecom usage, and other sources. This entire decision-making process is fully automated, allowing for near-instant completion (Mhlanga 2021). Consequently, banks can predict the probability of default among a substantial and potentially lucrative group consisting of unbanked, underbanked consumers, and SMEs.

Limit assessment is crucial for the banks to decide the loan amount of the customers. Prominent banks are automating the process of figuring out how much a consumer may borrow by utilizing AI/ML models. These loan-approval systems can evaluate a customer's disposable income and ability to make regular loan payments promptly because they use Optical Character Recognition (OCR) to extract data from traditional data sources like utility bills, bank statements, and tax returns (www.accenture.com). Large and varied data sets are also made available by the growth of digital interactions, which are used to power sophisticated machine-learning algorithms. A very accurate estimate of a customer's ability to pay may be produced by banks by creating data sets that incorporate information from both traditional and novel sources.

Pricing refers to fixing the creditworthiness of the customers. In traditional banking, credit worthiness of the customers was done manually. Nowadays, AI and ML models predict the credit score with the creditworthiness of the customers scientifically.

Fraud management is initiated to avoid fraudulent activities in the banks. Frauds can be executed in the banking sectors in various forms such as identity theft, employee fraud, third-party or partner fraud, customer fraud, and payment fraud. To avoid all the aforementioned frauds, bankers frequently update their AI-based models.

Monitoring and Collections

Bankers often find monitoring and collecting sanctioned loans to be a laborious task. AI-enabled models serve as valuable assistance by automatically sending reminders and assessing the default risk of customers before loan approval.

Deepening Relations

Building deeper relationships relies on a bank's precise comprehension of a customer's distinct requirements and anticipations. Through this understanding, a bank can tailor offers to address evolving needs, delivering them at the opportune moment and through suitable channels. This approach showcases the bank's grasp of a customer's present situation and ambitions, enabling it to assist in transitioning customers from their current status to their desired objectives. For instance, by examining browsing history and spending behaviors, a bank could identify a consumer's necessity for credit to facilitate an imminent household appliance purchase. Moreover, scrutinizing internal data on product usage can unveil areas where the bank can enhance its offerings to better align with a customer's immediate needs.

Smart Servicing

Utilizing AI-driven decision-making, banks have the potential to create a highly personalized servicing experience by catering to specific customer microsegments. This approach allows various channels to offer exceptional service, ensuring interactions are quick, straightforward, and user-friendly. By leveraging timely customer insights, banks can empower their relationship managers to provide tailored offers to individual customers. Moreover, they can significantly enhance agent efficiency by providing preapproved products designed to meet the unique needs of each customer. Advanced models that analyze voice and speech patterns can pair agents with customers based on behavioral and psychological profiles. Similarly, analyzing transcripts can predict customer distress and propose solutions to agents, improving overall service resolution (https://internationalbanker.com).

LOAN APPROVAL

Assessing the creditworthiness of a borrower lacking a credit score has posed a significant challenge for banks, resulting in the exclusion of many deserving individuals from accessing credit while causing lenders to miss out on substantial business opportunities. However, AI and Machine Learning (ML) offer a solution to this issue through predictive analytics, intricate algorithms, and diverse data points. Banks can now leverage an applicant's digital footprint, analyzing online shopping patterns, payment histories for utilities and phone bills, and even social media profiles to determine their creditworthiness.

In other perspectives, making loan approvals is a critical decision influencing a bank's profitability and marketing strategies. However, it becomes challenging due to varying lending approaches among competing banks and the frequent shifts in consumer borrowing behavior. Loan applications are generally categorized into two groups: positive credit risk, indicating a high likelihood of loan repayment failure by applicants, and negative credit risk, indicating a low probability of loan repayment failure. Bank managers, dealing with extensive customer data, face the task of appropriately approving applications displaying negative credit risk while rejecting those exhibiting positive credit risk (https://www.bankofbaroda.in). Artificial intelligence has significantly aided managers in making more informed decisions in this regard.

ZestFinance reports that in China, approximately 500 million individuals lack a credit history or credit score (www.latimes.com). However, a significant portion of this population relies on smartphones for their transactions conducted online. As a result, bankers can readily monitor the online activities of potential customers. Instead of relying solely on credit scores and credit histories, bankers are adopting a new metric known as the "social loan quotient" to evaluate loan applicants and gauge their creditworthiness.

CUSTOMER SERVICES

Banks provide a range of services to their customers, who anticipate consistent high-quality standards across all service aspects. To elevate user satisfaction levels and enhance the overall quality of banking services, bankers have integrated AI-enabled technologies across various service offerings. The following services have been augmented with AI-enabled technologies to deliver premium services to customers by every banking entity.

Internet banking is banking services offered by bankers on an online platform with a unique ID and password to their customers. To enhance the user experience and avoid fraudulent activity severe security mechanisms were employed by the banks with AI-enabled technologies such as machine learning and deep learning.

Call center/IVR is an automated phone system called Interactive Voice Response (IVR) that allows callers to communicate with a computer program rather than a live voice assistant. After the procedure, almost all IVR systems provide the ability to route calls to the relevant department or individuals (or a voicemail box). Conventional

IVR systems ask callers to provide basic information by choosing from a list of pre-programmed alternatives, and they provide pre-written replies in response to the prompts they choose. Customer experience (CX) may be revolutionized by conversational AI-powered IVR provided on an omnichannel platform, as these restricted capabilities frequently result in dissatisfied customers.

According to Axis Bank, the third-largest private sector bank in India, the conversational voice BOT powered by artificial intelligence, called Automated Voice Assistant, or "AXAA," was introduced in 2020 (https://www.axisbank.com). The bilingual speech bot AXAA, which speaks Hindi and English, is a product of the future. To help accelerate engagement initiatives, this creative solution makes use of cutting-edge automated speech recognition and natural language understanding technology boosted by artificial intelligence-powered business algorithms.

Smart Wearable Devices Banking refers to the banking services offered by banks through wearable devices like smartphones, wristbands, and watches. The unique services include balance inquiry, cash flow monitoring, alerts, notifications, and offers depending on the geo-locations and other factors.

ALARMING SYSTEM

Artificial intelligence provides a more effective means of enhancing banking system security against bank and ATM robberies than traditional emergency button alarm systems. Three phases comprise this system's operation: To extract characteristics for artificial vision, a picture must first be taken and processed. Using the acquired pattern, an Artificial Neural Network (ANN) categorizes the event and provides the status of the warning signals. The output class is established based on the neural network's categorization. If the output is 1, GSM technology should be used to send a warning message and sound the alarm.

CYBER SECURITY/FRAUD DETECTION

Fraudulent activities within credit card transactions stem from various factors, such as inadequate handling methods for a high volume of transactions, incorrect categorization of transaction costs for different specified amounts, skewed data, and challenges in transforming unlabelled data into labelled data, which is both impractical and time-consuming. To address these issues, the K reverse nearest neighborhood method is utilized to eliminate outliers, and deemed noise labels, after employing stratified random sampling to handle the 20% unbalanced data within the original dataset (Ahmadi 2023).

For classification purposes, an initial step involves reducing dimensionality in the dataset. Subsequently, a specific method called One-Class Support Vector Machine (OCSVM) is employed, differing from the conventional Support Vector Machine (SVM) as it trains using only one class. OCSVM demonstrates significantly enhanced performance in detecting fraudulent claims compared to the Group Method of Data Handling (GMDH) and probabilistic neural network (PNN) when adopting a hybrid under-sampling approach.

CREDIT RISK ASSESSMENT/CREDIT SCORING

Credit risk, or loan risk, is the possibility that a customer won't fulfill their end of the bargain by not paying back credit card debt, loans, or other commitments. This is an expensive problem for banks worldwide. Manually determining a customer's risk profile is a challenging and time-consuming procedure. Despite the introduction of automation in the form of online information verification, this process remains challenging. For this reason, these businesses are now looking for AI solutions to handle this problem on their behalf. Through the use of AI technologies, businesses can classify potential consumers into interest rate bands by determining their credit risk. Through the use of AI technologies, businesses can classify potential consumers into interest rate bands by determining their credit risk. Since there are only two possible outcomes—classes "0 (No Risk)" and "1 (Risk)"—loan risk evaluation is a binary logistics regression classification problem (Ghodselahi & Amirmadhi 2011).

MANAGEMENT OF BAD DEBTS

Bad debts are called Non-Performing Assets in banking terms. Bankers are stunt towards the controlling mechanism of NPA. But after AI NLP and predictive analytics help the bankers to identify and sanction the loans only to the potential customers.

AUTOMATION

Banking institutions are leveraging Robotic Process Automation (RPA), which harnesses AI capabilities, to enhance the customer experience and streamline operations. RPA facilitates the automation of tasks such as data entry, account reconciliation, and regulatory reporting within these institutions. Robotic Process Automation (RPA)

BENEFITS OF AI APPLICATIONS IN THE BANKING INDUSTRY

Boobier 2020 presented the following benefits of AI applications in the banking industry.

Reduce the Operational Costs

AI techniques within the banking sector play a crucial role in pinpointing operational inefficiencies and proposing actionable solutions to alleviate them, ultimately boosting profitability. These AI-driven solutions cut operational costs by automating repetitive tasks, lessening the need for manual intervention across various functions using Chatbots, Machine Learning, and NLP methodologies.

Prediction of Future Trends

AI facilitates predictive analytics in the banking sector, aiding in forecasting customers' credit risk and loan default rates during loan approvals. Additionally, it assists in assessing the current and future standing of banks in a competitive market landscape.

24x7 Banking Services

In traditional banking, customers are confined to receiving services within scheduled banking hours. However, AI-enabled banking services offer round-the-clock access. Through tools like chatbots, virtual assistants, NLP, voice and face recognition, and robo advisors, customers can avail banking services at any hour, enhancing accessibility and convenience.

Increases Return on Investment (ROI)

While the initial investment for integrating AI into banking is substantial, the returns generated by the technology are significant. It diminishes labor expenses and automates repetitive tasks, leading to a subsequent reduction in operating costs.

Enhanced Customer Experiences

The use and implementation of digital financial services in banks are correlated with customer experience and satisfaction. The tastes of customers have shifted significantly over time, and they now want individualized content and fast responses. With the help of AI and machine learning, banks may create personalized strategies for their clients by analyzing and forecasting client behavior and credit scores using an AI-based machine learning algorithm. AI can assist banks in digitizing their operations to satisfy client demands.

Sentiment Analysis

Understanding customer behavioral patterns stands as a pivotal focus for financial institutions in crafting and delivering tailored financial products and services. AI-powered sentiment analysis technology plays a crucial role in forecasting customer emotions, sentiments, and reactions gleaned from emails, social media interactions, and surveys. This innovative technology gathers data to curate and present content that aligns with users' preferences and choices.

Fraud Detection

It's common knowledge that AI excels in managing extensive data and identifying fraud long before humans can. Through the application of diverse algorithms, AI conducts repetitive tasks flawlessly, offering one of the many advantages that the banking industry can leverage due to its data-intensive nature.

CHALLENGES OF AI APPLICATIONS IN THE BANKING INDUSTRY

According to Kaya et.al 2019, the following challenges were faced by AI in the banking industry. They are.

Unemployment

The widespread implementation of AI-driven technologies in banking results in job displacement. Automating repetitive and clerical tasks replaces existing employees engaged in these roles. While technology aims to simplify human tasks, the introduction of AI raises concerns about the job security of employees within the banking sector.

Human Touch and Emotions

In an increasingly automated world, individuals desire empathy and hope for others to comprehend their emotions. AI-driven technologies efficiently accomplish tasks in shorter durations without expressing any emotions or affection, simplifying the workload for people.

Lack of Awareness and Knowledge About AI Technologies

Basic technical skills are necessary for individuals to utilize AI-enabled technologies. Failure of AI in banking often arises due to customers' lack of awareness and understanding regarding technology upgrades. Additionally, customers' fear or reluctance towards technology hinders the adoption of AI-enabled banking technologies.

Privacy Violations Concerns

Most banking AI systems derive their capability from collecting and analyzing extensive amounts of customer data, such as demographics, spending behaviors, contact information, credit and debit card details, social media profiles, and more. Consequently, the use of AI raises concerns about consumer privacy and safety.

Demolish the Creativity and Innovative Skills

Relying excessively on AI for automating decision-making and problem-solving procedures might diminish the creativity and adaptability of employees.

CASE STUDIES AND SUCCESS STORIES

Fluid-AI is utilized by the Barclaycard Technology team located in India. Fluid-AI refers to a platform that leverages machine learning to facilitate decision-making across diverse business functions. To optimize intelligent decision-making, the AI is plug-and-play and connects to hundreds of data sources. There is no need for installation. Fluid.AI also leverages AI to develop advanced virtual customer support for businesses with physical locations. A kiosk's motion-sensitive cameras pick up on users' responses, gestures, and facial expressions whether they apply for a loan, consider credit card alternatives, or check the most recent rates.

Bank of America uses machine learning to detect fraud flagging unusual transactions and alerting customers to potential breaches (https://www.bankofamerica.com).

J.P. Morgan relies on NLP to analyze legal documents in seconds, a process that traditionally took human experts thousands of billed hours (https://www.jpmorgan.com/global) .

Santander was one of the first banks to introduce a blockchain-based money transfer service, allowing customers to make international transfers within a day (https://www.santander.co.uk).

AI TRENDS IN THE BANKING INDUSTRY

The banking sector stands to benefit significantly from the vast potential of Artificial Intelligence (AI). It offers solutions to multiple challenges such as privacy breaches, job displacement, and the crucial need to advance banking services. Despite initial customer reservations stemming from inadequate understanding and education, as well as significant initial expenses, there is a strong likelihood of widespread acceptance of AI technologies in banking. AI possesses the capability to transform banking operations by minimizing reliance on human involvement and efficiently catering to the growing worldwide need for banking services.

As to the 2020 collaborative research performed by Narrative Science and the National Business Research Institute, over 32% of banks are utilizing AI technologies, including speech recognition and predictive analytics, to gain a competitive edge in the market. Furthermore, the market for AI in banking is expected to increase from its estimated \$3.88 billion in 2020 to \$64.03 billion by 2030, with a Compound Annual Growth Rate (CAGR) of 32.6% between 2021 and 2030 (www.iibf.org.in).

CONCLUSION AND FUTURE DIRECTIONS OF RESEARCH

AI is an advanced technology that addresses multiple unaddressed issues within the banking sector, including service disruptions, fraudulent activities, and credit assessments, among others. Consequently, AI has garnered significant attention and traction from diverse stakeholders worldwide involved in the banking industry. It serves as a viable solution to support the expanding financial inclusion and the increased adoption of fintech across global populations. There's a crucial need to investigate different operational domains within banking, such as customer lifecycle management, credit evaluation, fraud prevention, and cybersecurity.

AI is important to the banking industry, even if consumers and bankers may not have completely realized its potential yet. AI is about to become an essential tool and an essential part of the banking sector in very short order. Shortly, AI will surpass all other technologies in popularity and cost for bankers thanks to government efforts and customer technological know-how for AI-based products like chatbots and robotics. Once consumers understand the advantages of AI-based technology, they will also adjust to them. To take the banking industry to the next level, customers needed to be informed and aware of the innovations.

ABBREVIATION

ANN- ARTIFICIAL NEURAL NETWORK
ML-MACHINE LEARNING
PL- PREDICTIVE ANALYTICS
NLP-NATURAL LANGUAGE PROGRAMMING
IT- INFORMATION TECHNOLOGY
AI- ARTIFICIAL INTELLIGENCE
DL- DEEP LEARNING
USAA- UNITED SERVICES AUTOMOBILE ASSOCIATION
RBS-ROYAL BANK OF SCOTLAND
SMES- SMALL AND MEDIUM-SIZED ENTERPRISES
OCR- OPTICAL CHARACTER RECOGNITION
IVR-INTERACTIVE VOICE RESPONSE
OCSVM- ONE-CLASS SUPPORT VECTOR MACHINE
SVM- SUPPORT VECTOR MACHINE
GMDH- GROUP METHOD OF DATA HANDLING
RPA- ROBOTIC PROCESS AUTOMATION
ROI- RETURN ON INVESTMENT

REFERENCES

Ahmadi, S. (2023). Open AI and its Impact on Fraud Detection in Financial Industry. *Journal of Knowledge Learning and Science Technology*.

Boobier, T. (2020). *AI and the Future of Banking*. John Wiley & Sons. doi:10.1002/9781119596165

Effah, E., Kabanda, S., & Owusu-Adjei, E. (2019). Using Motion Detection and Facial Recognition to Secure Places of High Security: A Case Study at Banking Vaults of Ghana. In *Intelligent Systems and Applications: Proceedings of the 2018 Intelligent Systems Conference (IntelliSys)* Volume 1 (pp. 504-520). Springer International Publishing 10.1007/978-3-030-01054-6_36

Ghodselahi, A., & Amirmadhi, A. (2011). Application of artificial intelligence techniques for credit risk evaluation. *International Journal of Modeling and Optimization*, *1*(3), 243–249. doi:10.7763/IJMO.2011.V1.43

Kaya, O., Schildbach, J., AG, D. B., & Schneider, S. (2019). Artificial intelligence in banking. Artificial intelligence.

Kumar, V., Saheb, S. S., Ghayas, A., Kumari, S., Chandel, J. K., Pandey, S. K., & Kumar, S. (2023). AI-based hybrid models for predicting loan risk in the banking sector. *Big Data Mining and Analytics*, *6*(4), 478–490. doi:10.26599/BDMA.2022.9020037

López, G., Quesada, L., & Guerrero, L. (2017). Alexa vs. Siri vs. Cortana vs. Google Assistant: A Comparison of Speech-Based Natural User Interfaces. *8th International Conference on Applied Human Factors and Ergonomics (AFHE),* 241–250.

Manser Payne, E. H., Peltier, J., & Barger, V. A. (2021). Enhancing the value co-creation process: Artificial intelligence and mobile banking service platforms. *Journal of Research in Interactive Marketing*, *15*(1), 68–85. doi:10.1108/JRIM-10-2020-0214

Mhlanga, D. (2021). Financial inclusion in emerging economies: The application of machine learning and artificial intelligence in credit risk assessment. *International Journal of Financial Studies, 9*(3), 39.

Singh, K. (2020). Banks banking on AI. *International Journal of Advanced Research in Management and Social Sciences*, *9*(9), 1–11.

Compilation of References

Abass, M. (2023). Artificial Intelligence Techniques in Egyptian Hotels: Current Status and Prospective. *Egyptian Journal of Tourism and Hospitality*, *30*(1), 1–53. doi:10.21608/ejth.2023.303527

Abbasi, A., Chen, H., & Salem, A. (2008). Sentiment analysis in multiple languages: Feature selection for opinion classification in Web forums. *ACM Transactions on Information Systems*, *26*(3), 1–34. doi:10.1145/1361684.1361685

Abuzayed, B., Al-Fayoumi, N., & Bouri, E. (2022). Hedging UK stock portfolios with gold and oil: The impact of Brexit. *Resources Policy*, *75*, 102434. doi:10.1016/j.resourpol.2021.102434

Academy, L. (2019). *Consensus Protocols*. Available online: https://lisk.io/academy/blockchain-basics/how-does-blockchain-work/consensus-protocols

Ackerman, R. W., & Bauer, R. A. (1976). *Corporate social responsiveness: The modern dilemma.* Reston.

Addeo, F., Delli Paoli, A., Esposito, M., & Ylenia Bolcato, M. (2019). Doing social research on online communities: The benefits of netnography. *Athens Journal of Social Sciences*, *7*(1), 9–38. doi:10.30958/ajss.7-1-1

Adekoya, O. B., Oliyide, J. A., & Oduyemi, G. O. (2021). How COVID-19 upturns the hedging potentials of gold against oil and stock markets risks: Nonlinear evidence through threshold regression and markov-regime-switching models. *Resources Policy*, *70*, 101926. doi:10.1016/j.resourpol.2020.101926

Agathokleous, E., Rillig, M. C., Peñuelas, J., & Yu, Z. (2023). One hundred important questions facing plant science derived using a large language model. *Trends in Plant Science*. doi:10.1016/j.tplants.2023.06.008

Agbo, C. C., Mahmoud, Q. H., & Eklund, J. M. (2019). Blockchain technology in healthcare: A systematic review. *Health Care*, *7*, 56. PMID:30987333

Aggarwal, S. (2023). A Review of ChatGPT and its Impact in Different Domains. *International Journal of Applied Engineering Research: IJAER*, *18*(2), 119–123. doi:10.37622/IJAER/18.2.2023.119-123

Ahmadi, S. (2023). Open AI and its Impact on Fraud Detection in Financial Industry. *Journal of Knowledge Learning and Science Technology*.

Ahram, T., Sargolzaei, A., Sargolzaei, S., Daniels, J., & Amaba, B. (2017). Blockchain technology innovations. *Proceedings of the 2017 IEEE Technology and Engineering Management Conference (TEMSCON)*. 10.1109/TEMSCON.2017.7998367

Ahundjanov, B. B., Akhundjanov, S. B., & Okhunjanov, B. B. (2020). Information search and financial markets under COVID-19. Academic Press. PMID:33286562

Ahundjanov, B. B., Akhundjanov, S. B., & Okhunjanov, B. B. (2020). Information search and financial markets under COVID-19. PMID:33286562

Akhtaruzzaman, M., Banerjee, A. K., Ghardallou, W., & Umar, Z. (2022a). Is greenness an optimal hedge for sectoral stock indices? *Economic Modelling*, *117*, 106030. doi:10.1016/j.econmod.2022.106030

Akhtaruzzaman, M., Boubaker, S., Chiah, M., & Zhong, A. (2021b). COVID– 19 and oil price risk exposure. *Finance Research Letters*, *42*, 101882. doi:10.1016/j.frl.2020.101882 PMID:33312079

Akhtaruzzaman, M., Boubaker, S., Lucey, B. M., & Sensoy, A. (2021a). Is gold a hedge or a safe haven asset in the COVID–19 crisis? *Economic Modelling*, *102*, 105588. doi:10.1016/j.econmod.2021.105588

Akhtaruzzaman, M., Boubaker, S., Nguyen, D. K., & Rahman, M. R. (2022b). Systemic risk-sharing framework of cryptocurrencies in the COVID-19 crisis. *Finance Research Letters*, *47*, 102787. doi:10.1016/j.frl.2022.102787 PMID:35291226

Akhtaruzzaman, M., Boubaker, S., & Sensoy, A. (2021c). Financial contagion during COVID-19 crisis. *Finance Research Letters*, *38*, 101604. doi:10.1016/j.frl.2020.101604 PMID:32837363

Akhtaruzzaman, M., Boubaker, S., & Umar, Z. (2022d). COVID-19 media coverage and ESG leader indices. *Finance Research Letters*, *45*, 102170. doi:10.1016/j.frl.2021.102170 PMID:35221818

Akram, A., & Bross, P. (2018). *Trust, privacy and transparency with blockhain technology in logistics*. Academic Press.

AkulaR.GaribayI. (2021). *Audit and Assurance of AI Algorithms: A framework to ensure ethical algorithmic practices in Artificial Intelligence*. doi:10.48550/ARXIV.2107.14046

Al-Awadhi, Alsaifi, Al-Awadhi, & Alhammadi. (2020). Death and contagious infectious diseases: Impact of the COVID-19 virus on stock market returns. *Journal of Behavioral and Experimental Finance*.

Albulescu, C. T. (2020). COVID-19 and the United States financial markets' volatility. *Finance Research Letters*, 38. PMID:32837380

AlDajani, I. M. (2020). Phronetic Netnography Research Design. In *Internet Communication Technology (ICT) for Reconciliation* (pp. 155–201). Springer. doi:10.1007/978-3-030-41203-6_7

Alkhazali, O. M., & Zoubi, T. A. (2020). Gold and portfolio diversification: A stochastic dominance analysis of the Dow Jones Islamic indices. *Pacific-Basin Finance Journal, 60*, 101264. doi:10.1016/j.pacfin.2020.101264

Alla, L., Bentalha, B., & Bouhtati, N. (2022). Assessing Supply Chain Performance in the Covid 19 Context: A Prospective Model. In *2022 14th International Colloquium of Logistics and Supply Chain Management (LOGISTIQUA)* (pp. 1-6). IEEE.

AllaL.HmiouiA.BentalhaB. (2020). La netnographie dans les recherches marketing: La communauté virtuelle comme consom'acteur vecteur d'efficacité marketing. *Alternatives Managériales et Economiques, 2*(4), 631-652. doi:10.48374/IMIST.PRSM/ame-v2i4.23559

Allam, H., Dempere, J., Akre, V., Parakash, D., Mazher, N., & Ahamed, J. (2023). Artificial Intelligence in Education: An Argument of Chat-GPT Use in Education. *2023 9th International Conference on Information Technology Trends (ITT)*, 151–156. 10.1109/ITT59889.2023.10184267

Alneyadi, S., & Wardat, Y. (2023). ChatGPT: Revolutionizing student achievement in the electronic magnetism unit for eleventh-grade students in Emirates schools. *Contemporary Educational Technology, 15*(4), ep448. doi:10.30935/cedtech/13417

Alsamara, M., Mrabet, Z., Jarallah, S., & Barkat, K. (2019). The switching impact of financial stability and economic growth in Qatar: Evidence from an oil-rich country. *The Quarterly Review of Economics and Finance, 73*, 205–216. doi:10.1016/j.qref.2018.05.008

Al-Towhi, K. (n.d.). *The ideal use of NFT in Metaverse-A Systematic literature review*. Academic Press.

Al-Turkistani, H. F., & AlSa'awi, N. K. (2020, November). Poster: Combination of blockchains to secure smart home internet of things. In *2020 First International Conference of Smart Systems and Emerging Technologies (SMARTTECH)* (pp. 261-262). IEEE. 10.1109/SMART-TECH49988.2020.00069

Alzoubi, H., Alshurideh, M., Kurdi, B. A., Akour, I., & Azi, R. (2022). Does BLE technology contribute towards improving marketing strategies, customers' satisfaction and loyalty? The role of open innovation. *International Journal of Data and Network Science, 6*(2), 449–460. doi:10.5267/j.ijdns.2021.12.009

Ante, L., Fiedler, I., & Strehle, E. (2021). The influence of stablecoin issuances on cryptocurrency markets. *Finance Research Letters, 41*, 101867.

Arati, B. (2017). *Understanding Blockchain Consensus Models*. Persistent. Available online: https://pdfs.semanticscholar.org/da8a/37b10bc1521a4d3de925d7ebc44bb606d740.pdf

Arslan, S. (2023). Exploring the Potential of Chat GPT in Personalized Obesity Treatment. *Annals of Biomedical Engineering, 51*(9), 1887–1888. doi:10.1007/s10439-023-03227-9 PMID:37145177

Ashraf, B. N. (2020). Stock markets' reaction to COVID-19: Cases or fatalities? *Research in International Business and Finance, 54*, 54. doi:10.1016/j.ribaf.2020.101249 PMID:34170989

Association of Chartered Certified Accountants. (2011). *Accountancy futures: The carbon we're not counting: Accounting for scope 3 carbon emissions.* Association of Chartered Certified Accountants. https://www.accaglobal.com/content/dam/acca/global/PDF-technical/climate-change/not_counting.pdf

Atzori, L., Iera, A., & Morabito, G. (2010). The internet of things: A survey. *Computer Networks*, *54*(15), 2787–2805. doi:10.1016/j.comnet.2010.05.010

Azaria, A., Ekblaw, A., Vieira, T., & Lippman, A. (2016). Medrec: Using Blockchain for Medical Data Access and Permission Management. *Proceedings of the 2016 2nd International Conference on Open and Big Data (OBD).* 10.1109/OBD.2016.11

Bahrini, A., Khamoshifar, M., Abbasimehr, H., Riggs, R. J., Esmaeili, M., Majdabadkohne, R. M., & Pasehvar, M. (2023). ChatGPT: Applications, Opportunities, and Threats. *2023 Systems and Information Engineering Design Symposium (SIEDS)*, 274–279. 10.1109/SIEDS58326.2023.10137850

Barauskaite, G., & Streimikiene, D. (2020). Corporate social responsibility and financial performance of companies: The puzzle of concepts, definitions and assessment methods. *Corporate Social Responsibility and Environmental Management*, *28*(1), 1–10. doi:10.1002/csr.2048

Baret, Celner, O'Reilly, & Shilling. (2020). COVID-19 potential implications for the banking and capital markets sector. *Maintaining Business and Operational Resilience.*

Basiago, A. D. (1995). Methods of defining sustainability. *Sustainable Development (Bradford)*, *3*(3), 109–119. doi:10.1002/sd.3460030302

Batuo, M., Mlambo, K., & Asongu, S. (2018). Linkages between financial development, financial instability, financial liberalisation and economic growth in Africa. *Research in International Business and Finance*, *45*, 168–179. doi:10.1016/j.ribaf.2017.07.148

Baucas, M. J., Gadsden, S. A., & Spachos, P. (2021). IoT-based smart home device monitor using private blockchain technology and localization. *IEEE Networking Letters*, *3*(2), 52–55. doi:10.1109/LNET.2021.3070270

Baur, D. G., & Lucey, B. M. (2010). Is gold a hedge or a safe haven? An analysis of stocks, bonds, and gold. *Financial Review*, *45*(2), 217–229. doi:10.1111/j.1540-6288.2010.00244.x

Baur, D. G., & McDermott, T. K. (2010). Is gold a safe haven? International evidence. *Journal of Banking & Finance*, *34*(8), 1886–1898. doi:10.1016/j.jbankfin.2009.12.008

Bayar, Y., Borozan, D., & Gavriletea, M. D. (2021). Banking sector stability and economic growth in post-transition European Union countries. *International Journal of Finance & Economics*, *26*(1), 949–961. doi:10.1002/ijfe.1829

Beardsell, J. (2008, November 21). *The influence of CSR disclosure on corporate governance and company performance* (SMC Working Paper 11/2208 ISSN 1662-761X). Swiss Management Center. doi:10.2139/ssrn.1302314

Becht, M., Bolton, P., & Röell, A. (2003). Corporate governance and control. In G. M. Constantinides, M. Harris, & R. M. Stulz (Eds.), Handbook of the economics of finance (Vol. 1A, pp. 1-109). Elsevier. doi:10.1016/S1574-0102(03)01005-7

Beck, R., & Müller-Bloch, C. (2017). *Blockchain as radical innovation: a framework for engaging with distributed ledgers as incumbent organization*. Academic Press.

Beck, R., Avital, M., Rossi, M., & Thatcher, J. B. (2017). Blockchain technology in business and information systems research. *Business & Information Systems Engineering*, *59*(6), 381–384. doi:10.1007/s12599-017-0505-1

Beck, R., Czepluch, J. S., Lollike, N., & Malone, S. (2016). Blockchain–the gateway to trust-free cryptographic transactions. In *Twenty-Fourth European Conference on Information Systems (ECIS)*, İstanbul, Turkey, 2016 (pp. 1-14). Springer Publishing Company.

Będowska-Sójka, B., & Kliber, A. (2021). Is there one safe haven for various turbulences? The evidence from gold, Bitcoin and Ether. *The North American Journal of Economics and Finance*, *56*, 101390. doi:10.1016/j.najef.2021.101390

Bekiros, S., Boubaker, S., Nguyen, D. K., & Uddin, G. S. (2017). Black swan events and safe havens: The role of gold in globally integrated emerging markets. *Journal of International Money and Finance*, *73*, 317–334. doi:10.1016/j.jimonfin.2017.02.010

Belhassine, O., & Karamti, C. (2021). Contagion and portfolio management in times of COVID-19. *Economic Analysis and Policy*, *72*, 73–86. doi:10.1016/j.eap.2021.07.010 PMID:34518721

Ben Ltaifa, M., & Derbali, A. (2021). Confirmed and death cases of COVID-19: Which is informative in explaining the returns and volatilities of Saudi stock market indices? International Journal of Innovation. *Creativity and Change*, *15*(7), 1000–1029.

Benlagha, N., & El Omari, S. (2021). Connectedness of stock markets with gold and oil: New evidence from COVID-19 pandemic. *Finance Research Letters*, *102373*. Advance online publication. doi:10.1016/j.frl.2021.102373 PMID:35431671

Bentalha, B. (2023). Consumer Perception of Robotic Mobile Fulfillment Systems: A Netnographic Case Study of Amazon. In Innovation, Strategy, and Transformation Frameworks for the Modern Enterprise (pp. 243-264). IGI Global. doi:10.4018/979-8-3693-0458-7.ch010

Bentalha, B., & Hmioui, A. (2021). Smart Service Supply Chain and Just Walk Out Technology: A Netnographic Approach. In *The Proceedings of the International Conference on Smart City Applications* (pp. 223-236). Springer.

Bentalha, B., Hmioui, A., & Alla, L. (2019). The digitalization of the supply chain management of service companies: a prospective approach. In *Proceedings of the 4th International Conference on Smart City Applications* (pp. 1-8). 10.1145/3368756.3369005

Bentalha, B., Hmioui, A., & Alla, L. (2020). Digital service supply chain management: current realities and prospective visions. In *The Proceedings of the Third International Conference on Smart City Applications* (pp. 808-822). Springer. 10.1007/978-3-030-37629-1_58

Bentov, I., Gabizon, A., & Mizrahi, A. (2016, February). Cryptocurrencies without proof of work. In *International conference on financial cryptography and data security* (pp. 142-157). Springer Berlin Heidelberg.

Bezuidenhout, R., Nel, W., & Maritz, J. M. (2023). Permissionless blockchain systems as pseudo-random number generators for decentralized consensus. *IEEE Access : Practical Innovations, Open Solutions*, *11*, 14587–14611. doi:10.1109/ACCESS.2023.3244403

Bhaduri, S. N., & Selarka, E. (2016). *Corporate governance and corporate social responsibility of Indian companies*. Springer. doi:10.1007/978-981-10-0925-9

Bhattacharya, P., Saraswat, D., Savaliya, D., Sanghavi, S., Verma, A., Sakariya, V., Tanwar, S., Sharma, R., Raboaca, M. S., & Manea, D. L. (2023). Towards Future Internet: The Metaverse Perspective for Diverse Industrial Applications. *Mathematics*, *11*(4), 1–41. doi:10.3390/math11040941

Bhuyan, M., Kashihara, S., Fall, D., Taenaka, Y., & Kadobayashi, Y. (2022). A survey on blockchain, SDN and NFV for the smart-home security. *Internet of Things : Engineering Cyber Physical Human Systems*, 100588.

Bin-Hady, W. R. A., Al-Kadi, A., Hazaea, A., & Ali, J. K. M. (2023). Exploring the dimensions of ChatGPT in English language learning: A global perspective. *Library Hi Tech*. Advance online publication. doi:10.1108/LHT-05-2023-0200

Biswas, S. (2023). *Prospective Role of Chat GPT in the Military: According to ChatGPT* [Preprint]. doi:10.32388/8WYYOD

Blanquart, C., Liu, Z., Maudhuit, N., & Zéroual, T. (2019). Les entrepôts du e-commerce: Quelles spécificités? Une étude du cas Amazon. *Logistique & Management*, *27*(1), 44–54. doi:10.1080/12507970.2018.1552088

Bocek, T., Rodrigues, B. B., Strasser, T., & Stiller, B. (2017). Blockchains everywhere—A use-case of blockchains in the pharma supply-chain. *Proceedings of the 2017 IFIP/IEEE Symposium on Integrated Network and Service Management (IM)*. 10.23919/INM.2017.7987376

Bollerslev, T. (1986). Generalized autoregressive conditional heteroskedasticity. *Journal of Econometrics*, *31*(3), 307–327. doi:10.1016/0304-4076(86)90063-1

Bommineni, V. L., Bhagwagar, S., Balcarcel, D., Davatzikos, C., & Boyer, D. (2023). Performance of ChatGPT on the MCAT: The Road to Personalized and Equitable Premedical Learning [Preprint]. *Medical Education*. Advance online publication. doi:10.1101/2023.03.05.23286533

Boobier, T. (2020). *AI and the Future of Banking*. John Wiley & Sons. doi:10.1002/9781119596165

Borgia, E. (2014). The Internet of Things vision: Key features, applications and open issues. *Computer Communications*, *54*, 1–31. doi:10.1016/j.comcom.2014.09.008

Boswijk, A. (2017). Transforming Business Value through Digitalized Networks: A Case Study on the Value Drivers of Airbnb. *Journal of Creating Value*, *3*(1), 104–114. doi:10.1177/2394964317697736

Bouhtati, N., Alla, L., & Bentalha, B. (2023). Marketing Big Data Analytics and Customer Relationship Management: A Fuzzy Approach. In Integrating Intelligence and Sustainability in Supply Chains (pp. 75-86). IGI Global. doi:10.4018/979-8-3693-0225-5.ch004

Boulos, M. N. K., Wilson, J. T., & Clauson, K. A. (2018). Geospatial blockchain: Promises, challenges, and scenarios in health and healthcare. *International Journal of Health Geographics*, *17*(1), 25. doi:10.1186/s12942-018-0144-x PMID:29973196

Bowen, H. R. (2013). *Social responsibilities of the businessman*. University of Iowa Press. doi:10.2307/j.ctt20q1w8f

Bowles, E. (2022). *Economic Opportunities in the Metaverse: A Policy Approach*. Meta. https://about.fb.com/news/2022/12/economic-opportunities-in-the-metaverse/

Brennan, B. (2017). Blockchain HIE Overview: A Framework for Healthcare Interoperability. *Telehealth and Medicine Today*, *2*, 3.

Brown, G. (2003). *2003 Speech at Chatham House* [Speech transcript]. https://www.ukpol.co.uk/gordon-brown-2003-speech-at-chatham-house/

Brusseau, J. (2012). *The business ethics workshop*. Saylor Foundation. https://open.umn.edu/opentextbooks/textbooks/272

Bryatov, S. R., & Borodinov, A. A. (2019). Blockchain Technology in the Pharmaceutical Supply Chain: Researching a Business Model Based on Hyperledger Fabric. *International Conference on Information Technology and Nanotechnology (ITNT)*. 10.18287/1613-0073-2019-2416-134-140

Bugeja, J., Jacobsson, A., & Davidsson, P. (2018). Smart Connected Homes. In Q. F. Hassan (Ed.), *Internet of Things A to Z: Technologies and Applications* (pp. 359–381). Wiley-IEEE Press. doi:10.1002/9781119456735.ch13

Buhalis, D., & Cheng, E. S. Y. (2020). Correction to: Exploring the Use of Chatbots in Hotels: Technology Providers' Perspective. In J. Neidhardt & W. Wörndl (Eds.), *Information and Communication Technologies in Tourism 2020* (pp. C1–C1). Springer International Publishing. doi:10.1007/978-3-030-36737-4_19

Bulchand-Gidumal, J., William Secin, E., O'Connor, P., & Buhalis, D. (2023). Artificial intelligence's impact on hospitality and tourism marketing: Exploring key themes and addressing challenges. *Current Issues in Tourism*, 1–18. doi:10.1080/13683500.2023.2229480

Burch, T. R., Douglas, R. E., & Michael, R. F. (2016). Who Moves Markets in a Sudden Marketwide Crisis? Evidence from 9/11. *Journal of Financial and Quantitative Analysis*, *51*(2), 463–487. doi:10.1017/S0022109016000211

Buterin, V. (2014). A next-generation smart contract and decentralized application platform. *White Paper, 3*(37), 2-1.

Cacioppe, R., Forster, N., & Fox, M. (2008). A survey of managers' perceptions of corporate ethics and social responsibility and actions that may affect companies' success. *Journal of Business Ethics, 82*(3), 681–700. doi:10.1007/s10551-007-9586-y

Camur, D., & Vaizoglu, S. A. (2007). Çevreye ilişkin önemli toplantı ve belgeler [Important meetings and documents concerning environment]. *Turk Silahli Kuvvetleri Koruyucu Hekimlik Bulteni, 6*(4), 297–306. https://search.trdizin.gov.tr/tr/yayin/detay/72082/cevreye-iliskin-onemli-toplanti-ve-belgeler

Canoni-Meynet, L., Verdot, P., Danner, A., Calame, P., & Aubry, S. (2022). Added value of an artificial intelligence solution for fracture detection in the radiologist's daily trauma emergencies workflow. *Diagnostic and Interventional Imaging, 103*(12), 594–600. doi:10.1016/j.diii.2022.06.004 PMID:35780054

Carbon Disclosure Project, Climate Disclosure Standards Board, Global Reporting Initiative, International Integrated Reporting Council, & Sustainability Accounting Standards Board. (2020). *Statement of intent to work together towards comprehensive corporate reporting: Summary of alignment discussions among leading sustainability and integrated reporting organisations CDP, CDSB, GRI, IIRC and SASB* (Impact Management Project). World Economic Forum and Deloitte. https://sasb.org/wp-content/uploads/2023/01/Statement-of-Intent-to-Work-Together-Towards-Comprehensive-Corporate-Reporting.pdf

Carlbring, P., Hadjistavropoulos, H., Kleiboer, A., & Andersson, G. (2023). A new era in Internet interventions: The advent of Chat-GPT and AI-assisted therapist guidance. *Internet Interventions : the Application of Information Technology in Mental and Behavioural Health, 32*, 100621. doi:10.1016/j.invent.2023.100621 PMID:37273936

CarlsonM. A.CorreiaS.LuckS. (2019). The effects of banking competition on growth and financial stability: Evidence from the national banking era. Available at SSRN 3202489.

Carroll, A. B. (1979). A Three-Dimensional Conceptual Model of Corporate Performance. *Academy of Management Review, 4*(4), 497–505. doi:10.2307/257850

Carroll, A. B. (1983, July 15). Corporate Social Responsibility: Will Industry Respond to Cutbacks in Social Program Funding. *Vital Speeches of the Day, 49*(19), 604–608. https://www.researchgate.net/publication/331413180

Carroll, A. B. (1991). The Pyramid of Corporate Social Responsibility: Toward the Moral Management of Organizational Stakeholders. *Business Horizons, 34*(4), 39–48. doi:10.1016/0007-6813(91)90005-G

Carroll, A. B. (1999). Corporate Social Responsibility: Evolution of a Definitional Construct. *Business & Society, 38*(3), 268–295. doi:10.1177/000765039903800303

Carroll, A. B. (2008). A History of Corporate Social Responsibility: Concepts and Practices. In A. Crane, D. Matten, A. McWilliams, J. Moon, & D. S. Siegel (Eds.), *The Oxford Handbook of Corporate Social Responsibility* (pp. 19–46). Oxford University Press. doi:10.1093/oxfordhb/9780199211593.003.0002

Carroll, A. B. (2015). Corporate Social Responsibility: The Centerpiece of Competing and Complementary Frameworks. *Organizational Dynamics*, *44*(2), 87–96. doi:10.1016/j.orgdyn.2015.02.002

Carroll, A. B. (2021). Corporate Social Responsibility: Perspectives on the CSR Construct's Development and Future. *Business & Society*, *60*(6), 1–21. doi:10.1177/00076503211001765

Carson, B., Romanelli, G., Walsh, P., & Zhumaev, A. (2018). *Blockchain Beyond the Hype: What Is the Strategic Business Value.* McKinsey & Company. Available online: https://www.mckinsey.com/business-functions/mckinsey-digital/our-insights/blockchain-beyond-the-hype-what-is-the-strategic-business-value

Carter, D. A., & Betty, J. S. (2004). The Market's Reaction to Unexpected, Catastrophic Events: The Case of Airline Stock Returns and the September 11th Attacks. *The Quarterly Review of Economics and Finance*, *44*(4), 539–558. doi:10.1016/j.qref.2003.10.001

Castelló-Sirvent, F., García Félix, V. E., & Canós-Darós, L. (2023). *AI in higher education: new ethical challenges for students and teachers.* doi:10.21125/edulearn.2023.1172

Celık, S. (2012). The more contagion effect on emerging markets: The evidence of DCC-GARCH model. *Economic Modelling*, *29*(5), 1946–1959. doi:10.1016/j.econmod.2012.06.011

Chakraborty, A., Islam, M., Shahriyar, F., Islam, S., Zaman, H. U., & Hasan, M. (2023). Smart Home System: A Comprehensive Review", 2023. *Journal of Electrical and Computer Engineering*, 7616683.

Chakravorty, A., Wlodarczyk, T., & Rong, C. (2013, May). *Privacy preserving data analytics for smart homes. In 2013 IEEE Security and Privacy Workshops*. IEEE.

Chatterjee, A., & Ahmed, B. S. (2022). IoT anomaly detection methods and applications: A survey. *Internet of Things : Engineering Cyber Physical Human Systems*, *19*, 100568. doi:10.1016/j.iot.2022.100568

Chaudhry, N., & Yousaf, M. M. (2018, December). Consensus algorithms in blockchain: Comparative analysis, challenges and opportunities. In *2018 12th International Conference on Open Source Systems and Technologies (ICOSST)* (pp. 54-63). IEEE.

Chebbi, T., & Derbali, A. (2015). The dynamic correlation between energy commodities and Islamic stock market: Analysis and forecasting. *International Journal of Trade and Global Markets*, *8*(2), 112–126. doi:10.1504/IJTGM.2015.069425

Chebbi, T., & Derbali, A. (2016a). A Dynamic Conditional Correlation between Commodities and the Islamic Stock Market. *Journal of Energy Markets*, *9*(1), 65–90. doi:10.21314/JEM.2016.137

Chebbi, T., & Derbali, A. (2016b). On the role of structural breaks in identifying the dynamic conditional linkages between stock and commodity markets. *Journal of Energy Markets*, *9*(4), 71–81. doi:10.21314/JEM.2016.152

Chemkha, R., BenSaïda, A., Ghorbel, A., & Tayachi, T. (2021). Hedge and safe haven properties during COVID-19: Evidence from Bitcoin and gold. *The Quarterly Review of Economics and Finance*, *82*, 71–85. doi:10.1016/j.qref.2021.07.006 PMID:34898971

Chen, A. H., & Siems, T. F. (2004). The Effects of Terrorism on Global Capital Markets. *European Journal of Political Economy*, *20*(2), 349–366. doi:10.1016/j.ejpoleco.2003.12.005

Chen, M. H., Soo, C. S. J., & Woo, G. K. (2007). The Impact of the SARS Outbreak on Taiwanese Hotel Stock Performance: An Event-study Approach. *International Journal of Hospitality Management*, *26*(1), 200–212. doi:10.1016/j.ijhm.2005.11.004 PMID:32287849

Chkili, W. (2016). Dynamic correlations and hedging effectiveness between gold and stock markets: Evidence for BRICS countries. *Research in International Business and Finance*, *38*, 22–34. doi:10.1016/j.ribaf.2016.03.005

Chkili, W. (2017). Is gold a hedge or safe haven for Islamic stock market movements? A Markov switching approach. *Journal of Multinational Financial Management*, *42*, 152–163. doi:10.1016/j.mulfin.2017.10.001

Chris, J. (2018). *Blockchain: Background and Policy Issues*. Congressional Research Service. Available online: https://www.hsdl.org/?abstract&did=808684

Christidis, K., & Devetsikiotis, M. (2016). Blockchains and smart contracts for the internet of things. *IEEE Access : Practical Innovations, Open Solutions*, *4*, 2292–2303. doi:10.1109/ACCESS.2016.2566339

Clarkson, M. B. (1995). A stakeholder framework for analyzing and evaluating corporate social performance. *Academy of Management Review*, *20*(1), 92–117. doi:10.2307/258888

Climate Disclosure Standards Board. (2019). *CDSB framework for reporting environmental & climate change information: Advancing and aligning disclosure of environmental information in mainstream reports.* Climate Disclosure Standards Board Global. https://www.cdsb.net/sites/default/files/cdsb_climate_change_reporting_framework_edition_1.1.pdf

Coboi, A. E., Tran, T. A., Tran, S. Q., & Nguyen, M. T. (2021). Security Problems in Smart Homes. *ICSES Transactions on Computer Networks and Communications*, *10*, 1–9.

Conlon, T., & Corbet, S. (2023). The Problem with NFTs. SSRN *Electronic Journal*, 1–17. doi:10.2139/ssrn.4640796

Cooke, F. L., Dickmann, M., & Parry, E. (2021). IJHRM after 30 years: Taking stock in times of COVID-19 and looking towards the future of HR research. *International Journal of Human Resource Management*, *32*(1), 1–23. doi:10.1080/09585192.2020.1833070

Costola, M., Nofer, M., Hinz, O., & Pelizzon, L. (2020). *Machine learning sentiment analysis, Covid-19 news and stock market reactions*. econstor.eu

Costola, Nofer, Hinz, & Pelizzon. (2020). *Machine learning sentiment analysis, Covid-19 news and stock market reactions*. econstor.eu

Cotton, D. R. E., Cotton, P. A., & Shipway, J. R. (2023). Chatting and cheating: Ensuring academic integrity in the era of ChatGPT. *Innovations in Education and Teaching International*, 1–12. doi:10.1080/14703297.2023.2190148

Creel, J., Hubert, P., & Labondance, F. (2015). Financial stability and economic performance. *Economic Modelling*, *48*, 25–40. doi:10.1016/j.econmod.2014.10.025

Creti, A., Joëts, M., & Mignon, V. (2013). On the links between stock and commodity markets' volatility. *Energy Economics*, *37*, 16–28. doi:10.1016/j.eneco.2013.01.005

Crosby, M., Pattanayak, P., Verma, S., & Kalyanaraman, V. (2016). Blockchain technology: Beyond bitcoin. *Applied Innovation*, *2*(6-10), 71.

Curran, B. (2018). *What Are the Trustless Environments and How Cryptocurrencies Create Them?* Blockonomi.com. Available online: https://blockonomi.com/trustless-environments/

Daisuke, I., Kashiyama, M., & Ueno, T. (2017). Tamper-resistant mobile health using blockchain technology. *JMIR mHealth and uHealth*, *5*(7), e111. doi:10.2196/mhealth.7938 PMID:28747296

Dalai, S. S. (2022). A study of NFTs (Non-Fungible Tokens). Diagnosis through the lenses of classical Economics. *Digitala Vetenskapliga Arkivet*, (May), 76.

Dang, T. L. N., & Nguyen, M. S. (2018, November). An approach to data privacy in smart home using blockchain technology. In *2018 International Conference on Advanced Computing and Applications (ACOMP)* (pp. 58-64). IEEE. 10.1109/ACOMP.2018.00017

Dapp, M. M. (2021). From fiat to crypto: The present and future of money. *Finance 4.0-Towards a Socio-Ecological Finance System: A Participatory Framework to Promote Sustainability*, 1-25.

Davis, K. (1960). Can business afford to ignore social responsibilities? *California Management Review*, *2*(3), 70–76. doi:10.2307/41166246

Davis, K. (1967). Understanding the social responsibility puzzle: What does the businessman owe to society? *Business Horizons*, *10*(4), 45–50. doi:10.1016/0007-6813(67)90007-9

Davis, K. (1973). The case for and against business assumption of social responsibilities. *Academy of Management Journal*, *16*(2), 312–322. doi:10.2307/255331

Decker, C., & Wattenhofer, R. (2013). Information propagation in the bitcoin network. *Proceedings of the IEEE P2P 2013.*

Dejan, A. J. (2018). *Credit Supply, Price and Financial Stability in Markets and Institutions*. Academic Press.

Delfanti, A., & Frey, B. (2021). Humanly extended automation or the future of work seen through Amazon patents. *Science, Technology & Human Values*, *46*(3), 655–682. doi:10.1177/0162243920943665

Dennis, R., & Owen, G. (2015). Rep on the block: A next-generation reputation system based on the blockchain. *Proceedings of the 2015 10th International Conference for Internet Technology and Secured Transactions (ICITST)*. 10.1109/ICITST.2015.7412073

Dequech, D. (2013). Is money a convention and/or a creature of the state? The convention of acceptability, the state, contracts, and taxes. *Journal of Post Keynesian Economics*, •••, 251–273.

Derbali, A., Chenguel, M. B., Jamel, L., Jouirou, M., & Jouini, F. (2022b). COVID-19 pandemic and co-movement dynamics among American and European stock markets. Financial Transformations beyond the COVID-19 Health Crisis, 309–346.

Derbali, A., Chenguel, M. B., Jamel, L., Jouirou, M., & Jouini, F. (2022b). COVID-19 pandemic and co-movement dynamics among American and European stock markets. Financial Transformations Beyond the COVID-19 Health Crisis, 309–346.

DerbaliA. M. S. (2022). COVID-19 or Russia-Ukraine Conflict: Which Is Informative in Defining the Dynamic Relationship between Bitcoin and Major Energy Commodities? doi:10.2139/ssrn.4280578

Derbali, A., & Bouzgarrou, H. (2020). The dynamic dependence between the major US indices and the meat commodities indices. *PSU Research Review*, *4*(2), 149–168. doi:10.1108/PRR-09-2018-0027

Derbali, A., Jamel, L., Ben Ltaifa, M., Elnagar, A. K., & Lamouchi, A. (2020a). Fed and ECB: Which is informative in determining the DCC between bitcoin and energy commodities? *Journal of Capital Markets Studies*, *4*(1), 77–102. doi:10.1108/JCMS-07-2020-0022

Derbali, A., & Jouini, F. (2019). Analyzing the Dynamic Equicorrelation Between Shanghai Composite (SSEC) and Austral African Stock Market Indices. *Chinese Economy*, *52*(1), 83–106.

Derbali, A., Naoui, K., Ben Sassi, M., & Amiri, M. M. (2021b). Do COVID-19 Epidemic Explains the Dynamic Conditional Correlation between China's Stock Market Index and International Stock Market Indices? *Chinese Economy*, *55*(3), 227–242. doi:10.1080/10971475.2021.1958453

Derbali, A., Naoui, K., & Jamel, L. (2021a). COVID-19 news in USA and in China: Which is suitable in explaining the nexus among Bitcoin and Gold? *Pacific Accounting Review*, *33*(5), 578–595. doi:10.1108/PAR-09-2020-0170

Derbali, A., Naoui, K., & Jamel, L. (2022a). COVID-19 Surprises in China and in the USA: Which Is Useful in Explaining the Dynamic Nexus Among Energy Commodities and Bitcoin? In B. Alareeni & A. Hamdan (Eds.), *Artificial Intelligence and COVID Effect on Accounting. Accounting, Finance, Sustainability, Governance & Fraud: Theory and Application*. Springer. doi:10.1007/978-981-19-1036-4_4

Derbali, A., Wu, S., & Jamel, L. (2020b). OPEC news and predictability of energy futures returns and volatility: Evidence from a conditional quantile regression. *Journal of Economics, Finance and Administrative Science*, *25*(50), 239–25. doi:10.1108/JEFAS-05-2019-0063

Dernbach, J. C. (2012). *The unfinished story of the Rio+20 Conference* (Daily Environment Report, 194 DEN B-1, 10/09/2012, Research Paper No. 12-18). Widener Law School Legal Studies. https://ssrn.com/abstract=2169500

Dev, A., Shaji Gomez, K., & Mathew, S. V. (2022). Non-Fungible Tokens (NFT): New Emerging Digital Asset. *International Journal of Research in Engineering and Science, 10*(4), 1–7. www.ijres.org

Dimitrov, D. V. (2019). Blockchain Applications for Healthcare Data Management. *Healthcare Informatics Research*, *25*(1), 51–56. doi:10.4258/hir.2019.25.1.51 PMID:30788182

Ding, B., Ferràs Hernández, X., & Agell Jané, N. (2023). Combining lean and agile manufacturing competitive advantages through Industry 4.0 technologies: An integrative approach. *Production Planning and Control*, *34*(5), 442–458. doi:10.1080/09537287.2021.1934587

Disli, M., Nagayev, R., Salim, K., Rizkiah, S. K., & Aysan, A. F. (2021). In search of safe haven assets during COVID-19 pandemic: An empirical analysis of different investor types. *Research in International Business and Finance*, *101461*, 101461. Advance online publication. doi:10.1016/j.ribaf.2021.101461 PMID:36540341

Do Prado Leite, J. C. S., & Cappelli, C. (2010). Software transparency. *Business & Information Systems Engineering*, *2*(3), 127–139. doi:10.1007/s12599-010-0102-z

Dorri, A., Kanhere, S. S., Jurdak, R., & Gauravaram, P. (2017, March). *Blockchain for IoT security and privacy: The case study of a smart home. In 2017 IEEE international conference on pervasive computing and communications workshops (PerCom workshops)*. IEEE.

Doshi, R. H., Bajaj, S. S., & Krumholz, H. M. (2023). ChatGPT: Temptations of Progress. *The American Journal of Bioethics*, *23*(4), 6–8. doi:10.1080/15265161.2023.2180110 PMID:36853242

Du, M., Wang, K., Liu, Y., Qian, K., Sun, Y., Xu, W., & Guo, S. (2020). Spacechain: A three-dimensional blockchain architecture for IoT security. *IEEE Wireless Communications*, *27*(3), 38–45. doi:10.1109/MWC.001.1900466

Dwivedi, Y. K., Kshetri, N., Hughes, L., Slade, E. L., Jeyaraj, A., Kar, A. K., Baabdullah, A. M., Koohang, A., Raghavan, V., Ahuja, M., Albanna, H., Albashrawi, M. A., Al-Busaidi, A. S., Balakrishnan, J., Barlette, Y., Basu, S., Bose, I., Brooks, L., Buhalis, D., ... Wright, R. (2023). Opinion Paper: "So what if ChatGPT wrote it?" Multidisciplinary perspectives on opportunities, challenges and implications of generative conversational AI for research, practice and policy. *International Journal of Information Management*, *71*, 102642. doi:10.1016/j.ijinfomgt.2023.102642

Eenmaa-Dimitrieva, H., & Schmidt-Kessen, M. J. (2019). Creating markets in no-trust environments: The law and economics of smart contracts. *Computer Law & Security Report*, *35*(1), 69–88. doi:10.1016/j.clsr.2018.09.003

Effah, E., Kabanda, S., & Owusu-Adjei, E. (2019). Using Motion Detection and Facial Recognition to Secure Places of High Security: A Case Study at Banking Vaults of Ghana. In *Intelligent Systems and Applications: Proceedings of the 2018 Intelligent Systems Conference (IntelliSys)* Volume 1 (pp. 504-520). Springer International Publishing 10.1007/978-3-030-01054-6_36

Ehigiamusoe, K. U., & Samsurijan, M. S. (2020). What matters for finance-growth nexus? A critical survey of macroeconomic stability, institutions, financial and economic development. *International Journal of Finance & Economics.*

Eke, D. O. (2023). ChatGPT and the rise of generative AI: Threat to academic integrity? *Journal of Responsible Technology*, *13*, 100060. doi:10.1016/j.jrt.2023.100060

Elkington, J. (1997). *Cannibals with forks: The triple bottom line of 21st century business.* Capstone Publishing Limited.

Elkington, J. (2004). Enter the triple bottom line. In A. Henriques & J. Richardson (Eds.), *The triple bottom line: Does it all add up?* (pp. 1–16). Earthscan. doi:10.4324/9781849773348

Engelhardt, M. A. (2017). Hitching healthcare to the chain: An introduction to blockchain technology in the healthcare sector. *Technology Innovation Management Review*, *7*(10), 22–34. doi:10.22215/timreview/1111

Engelhardt, N., Krause, M., Neukirchen, D., & Posch, P. N. (2021). Trust and stock market volatility during the COVID-19 crisis. *Finance Research Letters*, *38*, 101873. doi:10.1016/j.frl.2020.101873 PMID:36569649

Engle, R. (2002). Dynamic conditional correlation: A simple class of multivariate generalized autoregressive conditional heteroskedasticity models. *Journal of Business & Economic Statistics*, *20*(3), 339–350. doi:10.1198/073500102288618487

Engle, R. F. (1982). Autoregressive Conditional Heteroskedasticity with Estimates of the Variance of United Kingdom Inflation. *Econometrica*, *50*(4), 987–1007. doi:10.2307/1912773

Epstein, E. M. (1987). The corporate social policy process: Beyond business ethics, corporate social responsibility, and corporate social responsiveness. *California Management Review*, *29*(3), 99–114. doi:10.2307/41165254

Erik, H., Strewe, U. M., & Bosia, N. (2018). Background III—What Is Blockchain Technology? In *Supply Chain Finance and Blockchain Technology* (pp. 35–49). Springer.

Esposito, C., De Santis, A., Tortora, G., Chang, H., & Choo, K. K. R. (2018). Blockchain: A panacea for healthcare cloud-based data security and privacy? *IEEE Cloud Computing*, *5*(1), 31–37. doi:10.1109/MCC.2018.011791712

European Commission. (2011, October 25). *Communication from the Commission to the European Parliament, the Council, the European Economic and Social Committee and the Committee of the Regions: A renewed EU strategy 2011-14 for corporate social responsibility* (COM(2011) 681 final). European Commission. https://www.europarl.europa.eu/meetdocs/2009_2014/documents/com/com_com(2011)0681_/com_com(2011)0681_en.pdf

Farrokhnia, M., Banihashem, S. K., Noroozi, O., & Wals, A. (2023). A SWOT analysis of ChatGPT: Implications for educational practice and research. *Innovations in Education and Teaching International*, 1–15. doi:10.1080/14703297.2023.2195846

Fassin, Y., van Rossem, A., & Buelens, M. (2011). Small-business owner-managers' perceptions of business ethics and CSR-related concepts. *Journal of Business Ethics*, *98*(3), 425–453. doi:10.1007/s10551-010-0586-y

Felse, A., & Kourkine, I. (2014). A Sequence of Technology Commercialization Courses for Science and Engineering. *2014 ASEE Annual Conference & Exposition Proceedings*. 10.18260/1-2--19995

Fernandez-Feijoo, B., Romero, S., & Ruiz, S. (2012). Transparent information system for sustainability: A sectoral analysis. *Procedia Technology*, *5*, 31–39. doi:10.1016/j.protcy.2012.09.004

Firat, M. (2023). *How Chat GPT Can Transform Autodidactic Experiences and Open Education?* [Preprint]. Open Science Framework. doi:10.31219/osf.io/9ge8m

Florian, G. (2017). Pervasive Decentralisation of Digital Infrastructures: A Framework for Blockchain Enabled System and Use Case Analysis. *Proceedings of the Hawaii International Conference on System Sciences*.

Fosso Wamba, S., Queiroz, M. M., Chiappetta Jabbour, C. J., & Shi, C. (2023). Are both generative AI and ChatGPT game changers for 21st-Century operations and supply chain excellence? *International Journal of Production Economics*, *265*, 109015. doi:10.1016/j.ijpe.2023.109015

Frederick, W. C. (1986). Toward CSR3: Why ethical analysis is indispensable and unavoidable in corporate affairs. *California Management Review*, *28*(2), 126–141. doi:10.2307/41165190

Frederick, W. C. (1994). From CSR1 to CSR2: The maturing of business-and-society thought. *Business & Society*, *33*(2), 150–164. doi:10.1177/000765039403300202

Frederick, W. C. (2008). Corporate social responsibility: Deep roots, flourishing growth, promising future. In A. Crane, D. Matten, A. McWilliams, J. Moon, & D. S. Siegel (Eds.), *The Oxford handbook of corporate social responsibility* (pp. 522–531). Oxford University Press. doi:10.1093/oxfordhb/9780199211593.003.0023

Freeman, R. E. (1984). *Strategic management: A stakeholder approach*. Pitman.

Friedman, M. (1970, September 13). A Friedman doctrine -- The social responsibility of business is to increase its profits. *The New York Times*, 17. https://www.nytimes.com/1970/09/13/archives/a-friedman-doctrine-the-social-responsibility-of-business-is-to.html

Friedman, M. (2002). *Capitalism and freedom* (F. A. Edition, Ed.). The University of Chicago Press. doi:10.7208/chicago/9780226264189.001.0001

Frost, J., Shin, H. S., & Wierts, P. (2020). An early stablecoin? The Bank of Amsterdam and the governance of money.

Fuchs, K. (2023). Exploring the opportunities and challenges of NLP models in higher education: Is Chat GPT a blessing or a curse? *Frontiers in Education*, *8*, 1166682. doi:10.3389/feduc.2023.1166682

Fui-Hoon Nah, F., Zheng, R., Cai, J., Siau, K., & Chen, L. (2023). Generative AI and ChatGPT: Applications, challenges, and AI-human collaboration. *Journal of Information Technology Case and Application Research*, *25*(3), 277–304. doi:10.1080/15228053.2023.2233814

Fulton, M., Kahn, B. M., & Sharples, C. (2012, June). *Sustainable investing: Establishing long-term value and performance.* Deutsche Bank Group Climate Change Advisors. https://papers.ssrn.com/sol3/papers.cfm?abstract_id=2222740

Gasmi, R., Hammoudi, S., Lamri, M., & Harous, S. (2023). Recent Reinforcement Learning and Blockchain Based Security Solutions for Internet of Things: Survey. *Wireless Personal Communications*, *132*(2), 1–39. doi:10.1007/s11277-023-10664-1

Genestier, P., Zouarhi, S., Limeux, P., Excoffier, D., Prola, A., Sandon, S., & Temerson, J.M. (2017). Blockchain for consent management in the ehealth environment: A nugget for privacy and security challenges. *Journal of International Society for Telemedicine and eHealth, 5*, GKR-e24.

GeorgeA. S.Hovan GeorgeA. S.Gabrio MartinA. S. (2023). *The Environmental Impact of AI: A Case Study of Water Consumption by Chat GPT.* doi:10.5281/ZENODO.7855594

Gharib, C., Mefteh-Wali, S., & Jabeur, S. B. (2021). The bubble contagion effect of COVID-19 outbreak: Evidence from crude oil and gold markets. *Finance Research Letters*, *38*, 101703. doi:10.1016/j.frl.2020.101703 PMID:32837382

Ghodselahi, A., & Amirmadhi, A. (2011). Application of artificial intelligence techniques for credit risk evaluation. *International Journal of Modeling and Optimization*, *1*(3), 243–249. doi:10.7763/IJMO.2011.V1.43

Ghorbali, B., Naoui, K., & Derbali, A. (2022b). Co-movement Among COVID-19 Pandemic, Crude Oil, Stock Market of US, and Bitcoin: Empirical Evidence from WCA. In B. Alareeni & A. Hamdan (Eds.), *Artificial Intelligence and COVID Effect on Accounting. Accounting, Finance, Sustainability, Governance & Fraud: Theory and Application.* Springer. doi:10.1007/978-981-19-1036-4_3

GhorbaliB.NaouiK.DerbaliA. M. S. (2022a). Does Gold Act as a Safe Haven and Hedge for G7 Stock Markets? A Comparative Assessment between COVID-19 Versus Global Financial Crisis (GFC). doi:10.2139/ssrn.4160586

Gipp, B., Kosti, J., & Breitinger, C. (2016). Securing Video Integrity Using Decentralized Trusted Timestamping on the Bitcoin Blockchain. *Proceedings of the Mediterranean Conference on Information Systems (MCIS).*

Global Reporting Initiative. (n.d.). *Our mission and history: Empowering sustainable decisions for over 25 years.* https://www.globalreporting.org/about-gri/mission-history/

Godelnik, R. (2021). *Rethinking corporate sustainability in the era of climate crisis: A strategic design approach.* Palgrave Macmillan. doi:10.1007/978-3-030-77318-2

Gokten, S., Ozerhan, Y., & Okan Gokten, P. (2020). The historical development of sustainability reporting: A periodic approach. *Zeszyty Teoretyczne Rachunkowości, 107*(163), 99–117. doi:10.5604/01.3001.0014.2466

Golosova, J., & Romanovs, A. (2018, November). The advantages and disadvantages of the blockchain technology. In *2018 IEEE 6th workshop on advances in information, electronic and electrical engineering (AIEEE)* (pp. 1-6). IEEE. 10.1109/AIEEE.2018.8592253

Gomis-Porqueras, P., Shi, S., & Tan, D. (2021). Gold as a financial instrument. *Journal of Commodity Markets*, 100218.

Goodell, J. W. (2020). COVID-19 and finance: Agendas for future research. *Finance Research Letters, 35*, 101512. doi:10.1016/j.frl.2020.101512 PMID:32562472

Gordon, W. J., & Catalini, C. (2018). Blockchain technology for healthcare: Facilitating the transition to patient-driven interoperability. *Computational and Structural Biotechnology Journal, 16*, 224–230. doi:10.1016/j.csbj.2018.06.003 PMID:30069284

Grassini, S. (2023). Shaping the Future of Education: Exploring the Potential and Consequences of AI and ChatGPT in Educational Settings. *Education Sciences, 13*(7), 692. doi:10.3390/educsci13070692

Grinsted, A., Moore, J. C., & Jevrejeva, S. (2004). Application of the cross wavelet transform and wavelet coherence to geophysical time series. *Nonlinear Processes in Geophysics, 11*(5/6), 561–566. doi:10.5194/npg-11-561-2004

Guiolin, M., & La Ferrara, L. (2010). The economic effect of violent conflict: Evidence from asset market reactions. *Journal of Peace Research, 47*(6), 671–684. doi:10.1177/0022343310381853

Gultekin, A. B., Dikmen, C. B., Erciyes, A. H., & Orgu, D. (2018). An examination of sustainability and United Nations sustainable development goals: Turkey case. In S. Firat, J. Kinuthia, & A. Abu-Tair (Eds.), *Proceedings of 3rd International Sustainable Buildings Symposium (ISBS 2017)* (pp. 252-271). Springer International Publishing. 10.1007/978-3-319-64349-6_20

Gupta, B., Mufti, T., Sohail, S. S., & Madsen, D. Ø. (2023). *ChatGPT: A Brief Narrative Review* [Preprint]. Computer Science and Mathematics. https://doi.org/ doi:10.20944/preprints202304.0158.v2

Gursoy, D., Li, Y., & Song, H. (2023). ChatGPT and the hospitality and tourism industry: An overview of current trends and future research directions. *Journal of Hospitality Marketing & Management, 32*(5), 579–592. doi:10.1080/19368623.2023.2211993

Gu, X., Zhang, W., & Cheng, S. (2021). How do investors in Chinese stock marketreact to external uncertainty? An event study to the Sino-US disputes. *Pacific-Basin Finance Journal, 68*(1), 101–614.

Haleem, A., Javaid, M., & Singh, R. P. (2022). An era of ChatGPT as a significant futuristic support tool: A study on features, abilities, and challenges. *BenchCouncil Transactions on Benchmarks. Standards and Evaluations*, *2*(4), 100089. doi:10.1016/j.tbench.2023.100089

Halova, M. W., Kurov, A., & Kucher, O. (2014). Noisy inventory announcements and energy prices. *Journal of Futures Markets*, *34*(10), 911–933. doi:10.1002/fut.21633

Harjoto, M. A., & Jo, H. (2011). Corporate governance and CSR nexus. *Journal of Business Ethics*, *100*(1), 45–67. doi:10.1007/s10551-011-0772-6

Hasan, H. R., Salah, K., Battah, A., Madine, M., Yaqoob, I., Jayaraman, R., & Omar, M. (2022). Incorporating Registration, Reputation, and Incentivization Into the NFT Ecosystem. *IEEE Access : Practical Innovations, Open Solutions*, *10*(June), 76416–76433.. doi:10.1109/ACCESS.2022.3192388

Hasan, M. B., Hassan, M. K., Rashid, M. M., & Alhenawi, Y. (2021). Are safe haven assets really safe during the 2008 global financial crisis and COVID-19 pandemic? *Global Finance Journal*, *50*, 100668. doi:10.1016/j.gfj.2021.100668

Hayes, J. (2018). *The theory and practice of change management* (5th ed.). Macmillan International. doi:10.1057/978-1-352-00132-7

He, Q., Liu, J., Wang, S. & Yu, J. (2020). The impact of COVID-19 on stock markets. *Journal of Economic and Political Studies.* doi:10.1080/20954816.2020.1757570

He, P., Sun, Y., Zhang, Y., & Li, T. (2020). COVID-19's market impact on stock prices across different sectors—An event study based on the Chinese stock. *Emerging Markets Finance and Trade*. PMID:32997308

Hill-Yardin, E. L., Hutchinson, M. R., Laycock, R., & Spencer, S. J. (2023). A Chat(GPT) about the future of scientific publishing. *Brain, Behavior, and Immunity*, *110*, 152–154. doi:10.1016/j.bbi.2023.02.022 PMID:36868432

Hmioui, A., & Bentalha, B. (2020). Service Supply Chain Management et performance commerciale: Esquisse d'une synthèse théorique. *Revue Alternatives Managériales et Economiques*, *2*(1), 1–21. doi:10.48374/IMIST.PRSM/ame-v2i2.20798

Hmioui, A., & Bentalha, B. (2021). Service supply chain management: A literature review. *International Journal of Logistics Systems and Management*, *40*(3), 332–353. doi:10.1504/IJLSM.2021.120253

Hölbl, M., Kompara, M., Kamisalic, A., & Zlatolas, L. N. (2018). A systematic review of the use of blockchain in healthcare. *Symmetry*, *10*(10), 470. doi:10.3390/sym10100470

Holden, E., Linnerud, K., & Banister, D. (2014). Sustainable development: Our common future revisited. *Global Environmental Change*, *26*, 130–139. doi:10.1016/j.gloenvcha.2014.04.006

Honar Pajooh, H., Rashid, M., Alam, F., & Demidenko, S. (2021). Hyperledger fabric blockchain for securing the edge internet of things. *Sensors (Basel), 21*(2), 359. doi:10.3390/s21020359 PMID:33430274

Hudson, R., & Urquhart, A. (2015). War and stock markets: The effect of World War Two on the British stock market. *International Review of Financial Analysis, 40*(1), 166–177. doi:10.1016/j.irfa.2015.05.015

Ijaz, S., Hassan, A., Tarazi, A., & Fraz, A. (2020). Linking bank competition, financial stability, and economic growth. *Journal of Business Economics and Management, 21*(1), 200–221. doi:10.3846/jbem.2020.11761

Iskender, A. (2023). Holy or Unholy? Interview with Open AI's ChatGPT. *European Journal of Tourism Research, 34*, 3414. doi:10.54055/ejtr.v34i.3169

Jamali, D., Safieddine, A. M., & Rabbath, M. (2008). Corporate governance and corporate social responsibility synergies and interrelationships. *Corporate Governance, 16*(5), 443–459. doi:10.1111/j.1467-8683.2008.00702.x

Jameaba, M.-S. (2023). *Digitalization, Emerging Technologies, and Financial Stability: Challenges and Opportunities for the Indonesian Banking Sector and Beyond.* Muyanja Ssenyonga Jameaba. doi:10.32388/CSTTYQ.3

Jamel, L., & Derbali, A. (2019). Damascus Securities Exchange Weighted Index volatilities and Terrorist attacks in Syria. *International Journal of Business and Risk Management, 2*(1), 9–15.

James, F. P. (2018). *Blockchain Technology Simplified: The Complete Guide to Blockchain Management, Mining, Trading and Investing Cryptocurrency.* CreateSpace Independent Publishing Platform.

Jamil, F., Hang, L., Kim, K., & Kim, D. (2019). A Novel Medical Blockchain Model for Drug Supply Chain Integrity Management in a Smart Hospital. *Electronics (Basel), 8*(5), 505. doi:10.3390/electronics8050505

Javaid, M., Haleem, A., & Singh, R. P. (2023). ChatGPT for healthcare services: An emerging stage for an innovative perspective. *BenchCouncil Transactions on Benchmarks. Standards and Evaluations, 3*(1), 100105. doi:10.1016/j.tbench.2023.100105

Jayakumar, M., Pradhan, R. P., Dash, S., Maradana, R. P., & Gaurav, K. (2018). Banking competition, banking stability, and economic growth: Are feedback effects at work? *Journal of Economics and Business, 96*, 15–41. doi:10.1016/j.jeconbus.2017.12.004

Jensen, M. C., & Meckling, W. H. (1976). Theory of the firm: Managerial behavior, agency costs and ownership structure. *Journal of Financial Economics, 3*(4), 305–360. doi:10.1016/0304-405X(76)90026-X

Jiang, Y., Fu, Y., & Ruan, W. (2019). Risk spillovers and portfolio management between precious metal and BRICS stock markets. *Physica A, 534*, 120993. doi:10.1016/j.physa.2019.04.229

Jie, Y., Pei, J. Y., Jun, L., Yun, G., & Wei, X. (2013, June). Smart home system based on iot technologies. In *2013 International conference on computational and information sciences* (pp. 1789-1791). IEEE. 10.1109/ICCIS.2013.468

Ji, Q., Zhang, D., & Zhao, Y. (2020). Searching for safe haven assets during the COVID-19 pandemic. *International Review of Financial Analysis, 71*, 101526. doi:10.1016/j.irfa.2020.101526

Jo, H., & Harjoto, M. A. (2012). The causal effect of corporate governance on corporate social responsibility. *Journal of Business Ethics, 106*(1), 53–72. doi:10.1007/s10551-011-1052-1

Johnson, D., Goodman, R., Patrinely, J., Stone, C., Zimmerman, E., Donald, R., Chang, S., Berkowitz, S., Finn, A., Jahangir, E., Scoville, E., Reese, T., Friedman, D., Bastarache, J., Heijden, Y. V. D., Wright, J., Carter, N., Alexander, M., Choe, J., . . . Wheless, L. (2023). *Assessing the Accuracy and Reliability of AI-Generated Medical Responses: An Evaluation of the Chat-GPT Model* [Preprint]. In Review. doi:10.21203/rs.3.rs-2566942/v1

Jones, T. M. (1980). Corporate social responsibility revisited, redefined. *California Management Review, 22*(3), 59–67. doi:10.2307/41164877

Jong, S. T. (2017). Netnography: Researching Online Populations. In P. Liamputtong (Ed.), *Handbook of Research Methods in Health Social Sciences*. Springer. doi:10.1007/978-981-10-2779-6_17-1

Jouini, F., Ajina, A., & Derbali, A. (2018). Corporate governance and corporate social responsibility. *International Journal of Management and Enterprise Development, 17*(2), 155–167. doi:10.1504/IJMED.2018.090841

Kang, E. S., Pee, S. J., Song, J. G., & Jang, J. W. (2018, April). A blockchain-based energy trading platform for smart homes in a microgrid. In *2018 3rd international conference on computer and communication systems (ICCCS)* (pp. 472-476). IEEE. 10.1109/CCOMS.2018.8463317

Kang, Y.-C. (1995). *Before-profit CSR, stakeholder capitalism and just enterprise system* (UMI No. 9614201) [Doctoral dissertation, University of Pittsburgh]. ProQuest Publishing.

Karugu, C., Achoki, G., & Kiriri, P. (2018). Capital Adequacy Ratios as Predictors of Financial Distress in Kenyan Commercial Banks. *Journal of Financial Risk Management, 7*(03), 278–289. doi:10.4236/jfrm.2018.73018

Kassem, S. (2022). Labour realities at Amazon and COVID-19: Obstacles and collective possibilities for its warehouse workers and MTurk workers. *Global Political Economy, 1*(1), 59–79. doi:10.1332/UVGT2823

Kaur, E. A., Ansari, A., & Kumar, V. (2023). Metaverse Technology. *International Research Journal of Modernization in Engineering Technology and Science, 11*, 308–309. doi:10.56726/IRJMETS45978

Kaya, O., Schildbach, J., AG, D. B., & Schneider, S. (2019). Artificial intelligence in banking. Artificial intelligence.

Kaya, Y., & Utku, M. (2020). Integrated reporting and its application in Turkish banking sector. In Interdisciplinary public finance, business and economics studies (Vol. III, pp. 285-296). Peter Lang GmbH. doi:10.3726/b17540

Kaźmierczak, M. (2022). A literature review on the difference between CSR and ESG. *Zeszyty Naukowe Politechniki Śląskiej. Organizacja i Zarządzanie*, *2022*(162), 275–289. doi:10.29119/1641-3466.2022.162.16

Keiper, M. C. (2023). ChatGPT in practice: Increasing event planning efficiency through artificial intelligence. *Journal of Hospitality, Leisure, Sport and Tourism Education*, *33*, 100454. doi:10.1016/j.jhlste.2023.100454

Khalfaoui, H., & Derbali, A. (2021). Quality of human capital accumulation, higher education graduates and economic growth: A comparative analysis between BRICS, Southeast Asian and MENA countries. *Human Systems Management*, *40*(5), 723–735. doi:10.3233/HSM-190855

Khan, M. A., Abbas, S., Rehman, A., Saeed, Y., Zeb, A., Uddin, M. I., Nasser, N., & Ali, A. (2020). A machine learning approach for blockchain-based smart home networks security. *IEEE Network*, *35*(3), 223–229. doi:10.1109/MNET.011.2000514

Khatoon, A., Verma, P., Southernwood, J., Massey, B., & Corcoran, P. (2019). Blockchain in Energy Efficiency: Potential Applications and Benefits. *Energies*, *12*(17), 3317. doi:10.3390/en12173317

Khezr, S., Moniruzzaman, M., Yassine, A., & Benlamri, R. (2019). Blockchain technology in healthcare: A comprehensive review and directions for future research. *Applied Sciences (Basel, Switzerland)*, *9*(9), 1736. doi:10.3390/app9091736

Kim, J. W. (2020). Blockchain technology and its applications: Case studies. *Journal of System and Management Sciences*, *10*(1), 83–93.

Kim, J., Kim, J. H., Kim, C., & Park, J. (2023). Decisions with ChatGPT: Reexamining choice overload in ChatGPT recommendations. *Journal of Retailing and Consumer Services*, *75*, 103494. doi:10.1016/j.jretconser.2023.103494

King, S. (2013). *Primecoin: Cryptocurrency with prime number proof-of-work*. Academic Press.

King, S., & Nadal, S. (2012). *Ppcoin: Peer-to-peer crypto-currency with proof-of-stake*. Self-Published Paper.

Kingsly, K. M. (2022). *Disruptive Technology: Blockchain: The Crystal Ball: Advancing Financial Trust, Inclusion, and Simplicity Through the Blockchain*. Christian Faith Publishing, Inc.

Kirk-Greene, A. H. (1960). The major currencies in Nigerian history. *Journal of the Historical Society of Nigeria*, *2*(1), 132–150.

Klein, R., & Rai, A. (2009). Interfirm strategic information flows in logistics supply chain relationships. *Management Information Systems Quarterly*, *33*(4), 735–762. doi:10.2307/20650325

Kmenta, J. (1986). *Elements of econometrics* (2nd ed.). Macmillan Publishing Company.

Koc, E., Hatipoglu, S., Kivrak, O., Celik, C., & Koc, K. (2023). Houston, we have a problem!: The use of ChatGPT in responding to customer complaints. *Technology in Society*, *74*, 102333. doi:10.1016/j.techsoc.2023.102333

Kogler, G. (2021). Non Fungible Tokens und Sachenrecht. *Juristische Blätter*, *143*(11), 685. doi:10.33196/jbl202111068501

Kolk, A. (2008). Sustainability, accountability and corporate governance: Exploring multinationals' reporting practices. *Business Strategy and the Environment*, *18*(1), 1–15. doi:10.1002/bse.511

Kollias, C., Efthalia, M., Stephanos, P., & Apostolos, S. (2011). Stock Markets and Terrorist Attacks: Comparative Evidence from a Large and a Small Capitalization Market. *European Journal of Political Economy*, *27*(No. S1), S64–S77. doi:10.1016/j.ejpoleco.2011.05.002

Kosba, A., Miller, A., Shi, E., Wen, Z., & Papamanthou, C. (2016). Hawk: The blockchain model of cryptography and privacy-preserving smart contracts. *Security and Privacy (SP), 2016 IEEE Symposium on*, 839-858.

Kozinets, R. V. (2010). *Netnography. Doing Ethnographic Research Online*. Sage Publications.

Kshetri, N. (2018). Blockchain and Electronic Healthcare Records. *Computer*, *51*(12), 59–63. doi:10.1109/MC.2018.2880021

Kumar, T., Ramani, V., Ahmad, I., Braeken, A., Harjula, E., & Ylianttila, M. (2018). Blockchain Utilization in Healthcare: Key Requirements and Challenges. *Proceedings of the 2018 IEEE 20th International Conference on e-Health Networking, Applications and Services (Healthcom)*.

Kumar, R. L., Khan, F., Kadry, S., & Rho, S. (2022). A survey on blockchain for industrial internet of things. *Alexandria Engineering Journal*, *61*(8), 6001–6022. doi:10.1016/j.aej.2021.11.023

Kumar, R., & Sharma, R. (2022). Leveraging blockchain for ensuring trust in IoT: A survey. *Journal of King Saud University. Computer and Information Sciences*, *34*(10), 8599–8622. doi:10.1016/j.jksuci.2021.09.004

Kumar, V., Saheb, S. S., Ghayas, A., Kumari, S., Chandel, J. K., Pandey, S. K., & Kumar, S. (2023). AI-based hybrid models for predicting loan risk in the banking sector. *Big Data Mining and Analytics*, *6*(4), 478–490. doi:10.26599/BDMA.2022.9020037

Kuo, T. T., Kim, H., & Ohno-Machado, L. (2017). Blockchain distributed ledger technologies for biomedical and health care applications. *Journal of the American Medical Informatics Association : JAMIA*, *24*(6), 1211–1220. doi:10.1093/jamia/ocx068 PMID:29016974

Kuttner, K. N. (2001). Monetary policy surprises and interest rates: Evidence from the fed funds futures market. *Journal of Monetary Economics*, *47*(3), 523–544. doi:10.1016/S0304-3932(01)00055-1

KwonY.KimJ.KimY.SongD. (2021). The trilemma of stablecoin. *Available at* SSRN 3917430.

Laeeq, K., & Sciences, E. (2022). *Metaverse : Why*. How and What. February.

Lamballais, T., Roy, D., & De Koster, M. B. M. (2017). Estimating performance in a robotic mobile fulfillment system. *European Journal of Operational Research*, *256*(3), 976–990. doi:10.1016/j.ejor.2016.06.063

Lamsiah, A., & Bentalha, B. (2023). *2022 Qatar World Cup: A Netnographic Analysis of the Relationship Between Sport, Media and Politic.*Academic Press.

Lantos, G. P. (2001). The boundaries of strategic corporate social responsibility. *Journal of Consumer Marketing*, *18*(7), 595–630. doi:10.1108/07363760110410281

Lau, K. (2020). *Non-Fungible Tokens A Brief Introduction and History*. https://theblockchaintest.com/uploads/resources/Kendrick Lau - Non-Fungible Tokens, A Brief Introduction and History - 2020 Nov.pdf

Léauté, T., & Faltings, B. (2011). Coordinating logistics operations with privacy guarantees. *IJCAI Proceedings; International Joint Conference on Artificial Intelligence.*

Lee, C.-C., Wang, F., & Chang, Y.-F. (2023). Does green finance promote renewable energy? Evidence from China. *Resources Policy*, *82*, 103439. doi:10.1016/j.resourpol.2023.103439

Lee, S. H., & Yang, C. S. (2018). Fingernail analysis management system using microscopy sensor and blockchain technology. *International Journal of Distributed Sensor Networks*, *14*(3), 14. doi:10.1177/1550147718767044

Lee, S. M., & Lee, D. (2021). Opportunities and challenges for contactless healthcare services in the post-COVID-19 Era. *Technological Forecasting and Social Change*, *167*, 120712. doi:10.1016/j.techfore.2021.120712 PMID:33654330

Leff, E. (1997, December 8-12). Environmental education and sustainable development. *International Conference on Environment and Society: Education and Public Awareness for Sustainability.* United Nations Environment Programme. https://www.academia.edu/22269226/Environmental_Education_and_Sustainable_Development

Lemieux, V. L. (2016). Trusting records: Is Blockchain technology the answer? *Records Management Journal*, *26*(2), 110–139. doi:10.1108/RMJ-12-2015-0042

Leopold, A. (1949). *A sand county Almanac and sketches here and there*. Oxford University Press.

Lepetit, L., Strobel, F., & Tran, T. H. (2021). An alternative Z-score measure for downside bank insolvency risk. *Applied Economics Letters*, *28*(2), 137–142. doi:10.1080/13504851.2020.1739222

Leung, X. Y., & Wen, H. (2020). Chatbot usage in restaurant takeout orders: A comparison study of three ordering methods. *Journal of Hospitality and Tourism Management*, *45*, 377–386. doi:10.1016/j.jhtm.2020.09.004

Liang, X., Zhao, J., Shetty, S., Liu, J., & Li, D. (2017). Integrating blockchain for data sharing and collaboration in mobile healthcare applications. *Proceedings of the 2017 IEEE 28th Annual International Symposium on Personal, Indoor, and Mobile Radio Communications (PIMRC).* 10.1109/PIMRC.2017.8292361

Liang, X., Shetty, S., Tosh, D., Kamhoua, C., Kwiat, K., & Njilla, L. (2017). Provchain: A blockchain-based data provenance architecture in cloud environment with enhanced privacy and availability. *Proceedings of the 17th IEEE/ACM International Symposium on Cluster, Cloud and Grid Computing*. 10.1109/CCGRID.2017.8

Lindsay, W. R., Ward, T., Morgan, T., & Wilson, I. (2007). Self-regulation of sex offending, future pathways and the Good Lives Model: Applications and problems. *Journal of Sexual Aggression, 13*(1), 37–50. doi:10.1080/13552600701365613

Linn, L. A., & Martha, B. K. (2016). Blockchain for Health Data and Its Potential Use in Health IT and Health Care Related Research. In *Use of Blockchain for Healthcare and Research Workshop*. ONC/NIST.

Lior, N. (2008). Energy resources and use: The present situation and possible paths to the future☆. *Energy, 33*(6), 842–857. doi:10.1016/j.energy.2007.09.009

Litchfield, A. T., & Khan, A. (2019). *A Review of Issues in Healthcare Information Management Systems and Blockchain Solutions*. CONF-IRM. Available online: https://aisel.aisnet.org/confirm2019/1/

Liu, Wang, & Lee. (2020). Impact of the COVID-19 pandemic on the crude oil and stock markets in the US: A time-varying analysis. *Energy Research Letters, 1*.

Liu, Z., Zheng, S., Zhang, X., & Mo, L. (2023). The Impact of Green Finance on Export Technology Complexity: Evidence from China. *Sustainability (Basel), 15*(3), 2625. doi:10.3390/su15032625

Llambías, G. (2023). *Blockchain Interoperability*. Academic Press.

Logsdon, J. M., & Wood, D. J. (2002). Business citizenship: From domestic to global level of analysis. *Business Ethics Quarterly, 12*(2), 155–187. doi:10.2307/3857809

López, G., Quesada, L., & Guerrero, L. (2017). Alexa vs. Siri vs. Cortana vs. Google Assistant: A Comparison of Speech-Based Natural User Interfaces. *8th International Conference on Applied Human Factors and Ergonomics (AFHE),* 241–250.

Luetkenhorst, W. (2004). Corporate social responsibility and the development agenda: The case for actively involving small and medium enterprises. *Inter Economics, 39*(3), 157–166. doi:10.1007/BF02933583

Lukić, V., Popović, S., & Janković, I. (2019). Nonperforming Loans and Financial Stability–The Case of Serbia. *Facta Universitatis, Series: Economics and Organization*, 349-364.

Lu, W., Chau, K. W., Wang, H., & Pan, W. (2014). A decade's debate on the nexus between corporate social and corporate financial performance: A critical review of empirical studies 2002-2011. *Journal of Cleaner Production*, *79*, 195–206. doi:10.1016/j.jclepro.2014.04.072

Mackey, T. K., Kuo, T. T., Gummadi, B., Clauson, K. A., Church, G., Grishin, D., Obbad, K., Barkovich, R., & Palombini, M. (2019). 'Fit-for-purpose?'—Challenges and opportunities for applications of blockchain technology in the future of healthcare. *BMC Medicine*, *17*(1), 68. doi:10.1186/s12916-019-1296-7 PMID:30914045

MacNeil, I., & Esser, I.-M. (2022). From a financial to an entity model of ESG. *European Business Organization Law Review*, *23*(1), 1–37. doi:10.1007/s40804-021-00234-y

Macrinici, D., Cartofeanu, C., & Gao, S. (2018). Smart contract applications within blockchain technology: A systematic mapping study. *Telematics and Informatics*, *35*(8), 2337–2354. doi:10.1016/j.tele.2018.10.004

Manser Payne, E. H., Peltier, J., & Barger, V. A. (2021). Enhancing the value co-creation process: Artificial intelligence and mobile banking service platforms. *Journal of Research in Interactive Marketing*, *15*(1), 68–85. doi:10.1108/JRIM-10-2020-0214

Marsden, C. (2000). The new corporate citizenship of big business: Part of the solution to sustainability? *Business and Society Review*, *105*(1), 9–25. doi:10.1111/0045-3609.00062

Matten, D., Crane, A., & Chapple, W. (2003). Behind the mask: Revealing the true face of corporate citizenship. *Journal of Business Ethics*, *45*(1/2), 109–120. doi:10.1023/A:1024128730308

McGee, R. W. (2023). Is Chat Gpt Biased Against Conservatives? An Empirical Study. SSRN *Electronic Journal*. doi:10.2139/ssrn.4359405

McGhin, T., Choo, K.-K. R., Liu, C. Z., & He, D. (2019). Blockchain in healthcare applications: Research challenges and opportunities. *Journal of Network and Computer Applications*, *135*, 62–75. doi:10.1016/j.jnca.2019.02.027

McWilliams, A., Siegel, D. S., & Wright, P. M. (2006). Corporate social responsibility: Strategic implications. *Journal of Management Studies*, *43*(1), 1–18. doi:10.1111/j.1467-6486.2006.00580.x

Meadows, D. H., Meadows, D. L., Randers, J., & Behrens, W. W., III. (1972). *The limits to growth*. Universe Books. https://collections.dartmouth.edu/content/deliver/inline/meadows/pdf/meadows_ltg-001.pdf

Mehdi, B., & Ravaud, P. (2017). Blockchain technology for improving clinical research quality. *Trials*, *18*(1), 335. doi:10.1186/s13063-017-2035-z PMID:28724395

Melé, D. (2008). Corporate social responsibility theories. In A. Crane, D. Matten, A. McWilliams, J. Moon, & D. S. Siegel (Eds.), *The Oxford handbook of corporate social responsibility* (pp. 47–82). Oxford University Press. doi:10.1093/oxfordhb/9780199211593.003.0003

Meng, W., Tischhauser, E. W., Wang, Q., Wang, Y., & Han, J. (2018). When intrusion detection meets blockchain technology: A review. *IEEE Access : Practical Innovations, Open Solutions*, *6*, 10179–10188. doi:10.1109/ACCESS.2018.2799854

Mensi, W., Reboredo, J. C., & Ugolini, A. (2021). Price-switching spillovers between gold, oil, and stock markets: Evidence from the USA and China during the COVID-19 pandemic. *Resources Policy*, *73*, 102217. doi:10.1016/j.resourpol.2021.102217 PMID:36567727

Mensi, W., Shafiullah, M., Vo, X. V., & Kang, S. H. (2021). Volatility spillovers between strategic commodity futures and stock markets and portfolio implications: Evidence from developed and emerging economies. *Resources Policy*, *71*, 102002. doi:10.1016/j.resourpol.2021.102002

Mhlanga, D. (2021). Financial inclusion in emerging economies: The application of machine learning and artificial intelligence in credit risk assessment. *International Journal of Financial Studies, 9*(3), 39.

Mill, G. A. (2006). The financial performance of a socially responsible investment over time and a possible link with corporate social responsibility. *Journal of Business Ethics*, *63*(2), 131–148. doi:10.1007/s10551-005-2410-7

Min, F., Wen, F., Xu, J., & Wu, N. (2021). Credit supply, house prices, and financial stability. *International Journal of Finance & Economics*.

Mingxiao, D., Xiaofeng, M., Zhe, Z., Xiangwei, W., & Qijun, C. (2017, October). A review on consensus algorithm of blockchain. In 2017 IEEE international conference on systems, man, and cybernetics (SMC) (pp. 2567-2572). IEEE. doi:10.1109/SMC.2017.8123011

Mitnick, B. M. (1993, March). *Organizing research in corporate social performance: The CSP system as core paradigm* [Paper presentation]. 1993 Annual Meeting of the International Association for Business and Society, San Diego, CA. https://papers.ssrn.com/sol3/papers.cfm?abstract_id=3837714

Mitnick, B. M. (2000). Commitment, revelation, and the testaments of belief: The metrics of measurement of corporate social performance. *Business & Society*, *39*(4), 419–465. doi:10.1177/000765030003900405

Miyazaki, A. D., & Fernandez, A. (2001). Consumer Perceptions of Privacy and Security Risks for Online Shopping. *The Journal of Consumer Affairs*, *35*(1), 27–44. doi:10.1111/j.1745-6606.2001.tb00101.x

Mocrii, D., Chen, Y., & Musilek, P. (2018). IoT-based smart homes: A review of system architecture, software, communications, privacy and security. *Internet of Things : Engineering Cyber Physical Human Systems*, *1*, 81–98. doi:10.1016/j.iot.2018.08.009

Mondal, S., Das, S., & Vrana, V. G. (2023). How to Bell the Cat? A Theoretical Review of Generative Artificial Intelligence towards Digital Disruption in All Walks of Life. *Technologies*, *11*(2), 44. doi:10.3390/technologies11020044

Moniruzzaman, M., Khezr, S., Yassine, A., & Benlamri, R. (2020). Blockchain for smart homes: Review of current trends and research challenges. *Computers & Electrical Engineering, 83*, 106585. doi:10.1016/j.compeleceng.2020.106585

Moon, J. (2007). The contribution of corporate social responsibility to sustainable development. *Sustainable Development (Bradford), 15*(5), 296–306. doi:10.1002/sd.346

Muller, A. R., Pfarrer, M. D., & Little, L. M. (2014). A theory of collective empathy in corporate philanthropy decisions. *Academy of Management Review, 39*(1), 1–21. https://www.jstor.org/stable/43699197. doi:10.5465/amr.2012.0031

Murray, M. D. (2022). NFTs and the Art World – What's Real, and What's Not. *UCLA Entertainment Law Review, 29*(1). Advance online publication. doi:10.5070/LR829158940

Nakamoto, S. (2008). Bitcoin: A peer-to-peer electronic cash system. *Decentralized Business Review.*

Nakamoto, S. (2008). *Bitcoin: A Peer-to-Peer Electronic Cash System.* Retrieved from https://www.bitcoin.org

Nakamoto, S., & Bitcoin, A. (2008). *A peer-to-peer electronic cash system.* https://bitcoin. org/bitcoin. pdf

Narayan, R., Gehlot, A., Singh, R., Akram, S. V., Priyadarshi, N., & Twala, B. (2022). Hospitality Feedback System 4.0: Digitalization of Feedback System with Integration of Industry 4.0 Enabling Technologies. *Sustainability (Basel), 14*(19), 12158. doi:10.3390/su141912158

Nasreen, S., & Anwar, S. (2018). How financial stability affects economic development in south asia: a panel data analysis. *European Online Journal of Natural and Social Sciences, 7*(1), 54.

Nazir, T., Mushhood Ur Rehman, M., Asghar, M. R., & Kalia, J. S. (2022). Artificial intelligence assisted acute patient journey. *Frontiers in Artificial Intelligence, 5*, 962165. doi:10.3389/frai.2022.962165 PMID:36267660

Ng, E. K., & Chan, J. C. (2012). Geophysical applications of partial wavelet coherence and multiple wavelet coherence. *Journal of Atmospheric and Oceanic Technology, 29*(12), 1845–1853. doi:10.1175/JTECH-D-12-00056.1

Ngun. (2016). *Gold price and stock markets nexus under mixed-copulas.* Academic Press.

Nikkinen, J., Mohammad, M. O., Petri, S., & Janne, A. (2008). Stock Returns and Volatility Following the September 11 Attacks: Evidence from 53 Equity Markets. *International Review of Financial Analysis, 17*(1), 27–46. doi:10.1016/j.irfa.2006.12.002

Nippani, S., & Washer, K. M. (2004). SARS: A Non-event for Affected Countries' Stock Markets? *Applied Financial Economics, 14*(15), 1105–1110. doi:10.1080/0960310042000310579

Njang, I. I., Omini, E. E., Bekun, F. V., & Adedoyin, F. F. (2020). *Financial System Stability and Economic Growth in Nigeria.* Academic Press.

Nofer, M., Gomber, P., Hinz, O., & Schiereck, D. (2017). Blockchain. *Business & Information Systems Engineering*, *59*(3), 183–187. doi:10.1007/s12599-017-0467-3

Oh, W.-Y., Chang, Y. K., & Kim, T.-Y. (2018). Complementary or substitutive effects?: Corporate governance mechanisms and corporate social responsibility. *Journal of Management*, *44*(7), 2716–2739. doi:10.1177/0149206316653804

Oliver, N. (2021). When philanthropy meets data science: A framework for governance to achieve data-driven decision-making for public good. In Data science for social good: Philanthropy and social impact in a complex world (pp. 55-68). Springer. doi:10.1007/978-3-030-78985-5_5

Ølnes, S., Ubacht, J., & Janssen, M. (2017). Blockchain in government: Benefits and implications of distributed ledger technology for information sharing. *Government Information Quarterly*, *34*(3), 355–364. doi:10.1016/j.giq.2017.09.007

Olson, E. (2013, February 5). *BSR and the state of CSR: What we mean when we say 'CSR': What is CSR?* https://www.bsr.org/en/our-insights/blog-view/bsr-and-the-state-of-csr-what-we-mean-when-we-say-csr

Öresland, S., Määttä, S., Norberg, A., Jörgensen, M. W., & Lützén, K. (2008). Nurses as Guests or Professionals in Home Health Care. *Nursing Ethics*, *15*(3), 371–383. doi:10.1177/0969733007088361 PMID:18388171

Orlitzky, M. (2005). Payoffs to social and environmental performance. *Journal of Investing*, *48-52*(3), 48–52. Advance online publication. doi:10.3905/joi.2005.580548

Othman, A. H. A., Musa Alhabshi, S., Kassim, S., Abdullah, A., & Haron, R. (2020). The impact of monetary systems on income inequity and wealth distribution: A case study of cryptocurrencies, fiat money and gold standard. *International Journal of Emerging Markets*, *15*(6), 1161–1183.

Ovais, A. (2017). *Block Chain Technology: Concept of Digital Economics*. University Library of Munich.

Ozili, P. K. (2018). Banking stability determinants in Africa. *International Journal of Managerial Finance*, *14*(4), 462–483. doi:10.1108/IJMF-01-2018-0007

OziliP. K.ArunT. (2020). *Spillover of COVID-19: impact on the Global Economy*. doi:10.2139/ssrn.3562570

Ozili, P. K., & Iorember, P. T. (2023). Financial stability and sustainable development. *International Journal of Finance & Economics*, ijfe.2803. doi:10.1002/ijfe.2803

Panapanaan, V. M., Linnanen, L., Karvonen, M.-M., & Phan, V. T. (2003). Roadmapping corporate social responsibility in Finnish companies. *Journal of Business Ethics*, *44*(2), 133–148. doi:10.1023/A:1023391530903

Papakyriakou, P., Athanasios, S., & Zenon, T. (2019). The Impact of Terrorist Attacks in G7 Countries on International Stock Markets and the Role of Investor Sentiment. *Journal of International Financial Markets, Institutions and Money*, *6*, 143–160. doi:10.1016/j.intfin.2019.03.001

Parker, S. K., & Grote, G. (2020). Automation, algorithms, and beyond: Why work design matters more than ever in a digital world. *Applied Psychology*. Advance online publication. doi:10.1111/apps.12241

Patel, K. (2022, August 5). Blockchain Technology as a Foundation of the Metaverse. *Tech Insights*. https://www.techinsights.com/blockchain-technology-metaverse

Paul, J., Ueno, A., & Dennis, C. (2023). ChatGPT and consumers: Benefits, Pitfalls and Future Research Agenda. *International Journal of Consumer Studies*, *47*(4), 1213–1225. doi:10.1111/ijcs.12928

Peng, X. (2020). Do precious metals act as hedges or safe havens for China's financial markets? *Finance Research Letters*, *37*, 101353. doi:10.1016/j.frl.2019.101353

Phan, D. H. B., & Narayan, P. K. (2020). Country responses and the reaction of the stock market to COVID-19—A preliminary exposition. *Emerging Markets Finance & Trade*, *56*(10), 2138–2150. doi:10.1080/1540496X.2020.1784719

Pilkington, M. (2016). 11 Blockchain technology: principles and applications. *Research handbook on digital transformations*, 225.

Platform, M. V. O. (2012). *CSR: Frame of reference 2012*. MVO Platform. https://www.mvoplatform.nl/en/csr-frame-of-reference-2012/

Porisky, A., & Glas, A. (2023). Insiders, Outsiders, and Credible Visitors in Research. *PS, Political Science & Politics*, *56*(1), 51–55. doi:10.1017/S1049096522001172

Porter, M. E. (2003, May 14). *Corporate philanthropy: Taking the high ground* [Paper presentation]. A gathering of corporate philanthropy leaders sponsored by the Foundation Strategy Group & the Center for Corporate Citizenship, New York City, NY.

Post, J. E., & Berman, S. L. (2001). Global corporate citizenship in a dot.com world: The role of organisational identity. In J. Andriof & M. McIntosh (Eds.), *Perspectives on corporate citizenship* (pp. 66–82). Greenleaf Publishing Limited. doi:10.9774/GLEAF.978-1-909493-19-3_6

Pradana, M., Elisa, H. P., & Syarifuddin, S. (2023). Discussing ChatGPT in education: A literature review and bibliometric analysis. *Cogent Education*, *10*(2), 2243134. doi:10.1080/2331186X.2023.2243134

Prentice, C., Dominique Lopes, S., & Wang, X. (2020). Emotional intelligence or artificial intelligence– an employee perspective. *Journal of Hospitality Marketing & Management*, *29*(4), 377–403. doi:10.1080/19368623.2019.1647124

Prochniak, M., & Wasiak, K. (2017). The impact of the financial system on economic growth in the context of the global crisis: Empirical evidence for the EU and OECD countries. *Empirica*, *44*(2), 295–337. doi:10.1007/s10663-016-9323-9

Puthal, D., Malik, N., Mohanty, S. P., Kougianos, E., & Das, G. (2018). Everything you wanted to know about the blockchain: Its promise, components, processes, and problems. *IEEE Consumer Electronics Magazine*, *7*(4), 6–14. doi:10.1109/MCE.2018.2816299

J. Quarrie (Ed.). (1992). Earth Summit 1992*: The United Nations Conference on Environment and Development.* Regency Press.

Rabah, K. V. O. (2017). Challenges & opportunities for blockchain-powered healthcare systems: A review. *Mara Research Journal of Medicine and Health Sciences*, *1*, 45–52.

Radanović, I., & Likić, R. (2018). Opportunities for use of blockchain technology in medicine. *Applied Health Economics and Health Policy*, *16*(5), 583–590. doi:10.1007/s40258-018-0412-8 PMID:30022440

Randall, D., Goel, P., & Abujamra, R. (2017). Blockchain applications and use cases in health information technology. *Journal of Health & Medical Informatics*, *8*(3), 2. doi:10.4172/2157-7420.1000276

Rediker, K. J., & Seth, A. (1995). Boards of directors and substitution effects of alternative governance mechanisms. *Strategic Management Journal*, *16*(2), 85–99. doi:10.1002/smj.4250160202

Rehman, W., Zainab, H. e., Imran, J., & Bawany, N. Z. (2021). NFTs: Applications and Challenges. *2021 22nd International Arab Conference on Information Technology (ACIT)*, 1-7. 10.1109/ACIT53391.2021.9677260

RemountakisM.KotisK.KourtzisB.TsekourasG. E. (2023). *ChatGPT and Persuasive Technologies for the Management and Delivery of Personalized Recommendations in Hotel Hospitality.* doi:10.48550/ARXIV.2307.14298

Report. (2020). *Cisco Annual Internet Report (2018-2023).* https://www.cisco.com/c/en/us/solutions/collateral/executive-perspectives/annual-internet-report/white-paper-c11-741490.html

Report. (2021). *Cellular IoT & LPWA Market Tracker (Q3 2021).* https://iot-analytics.com/

Report. (2022). *Blockchain Distributed Ledger Market by Component, Type, Enterprise Size, Application and End User: Opportunity Analysis and Industry Forecast, 2020–2027.* Allied Market Research.

Report. (2023). *Gartner.* https://www.gartner.com/

Rese, A., & Tränkner, P. (2024). Perceived conversational ability of task-based chatbots – Which conversational elements influence the success of text-based dialogues? *International Journal of Information Management*, *74*, 102699. doi:10.1016/j.ijinfomgt.2023.102699

Rijal, S., & Saranani, F. (2023). The Role of Blockchain Technology in Increasing Economic Transparency and Public Trust. *Technology and Society Perspectives*, *1*(2), 56–67. doi:10.61100/tacit.v1i2.51

Robinson, J. (2022). *Exploring the metaverse and the digital future*. GSMA Asia Pacific. doi:10.4018/978-1-7998-5839-3.ch005

Roman, R., Zhou, J., & Lopez, J. (2013). On the features and challenges of security and privacy in distributed internet of things. *Computer Networks*, *57*(10), 2266–2279. doi:10.1016/j.comnet.2012.12.018

Rouhani, S., Butterworth, L., Simmons, A. D., Humphery, D. G., & Deters, R. (2018). MediChainTM: A Secure Decentralized Medical Data Asset Management System. *Proceedings of the 2018 IEEE International Conference on Internet of Things (iThings) and IEEE Green Computing and Communications (GreenCom) and IEEE Cyber, Physical and Social Computing (CPSCom) and IEEE Smart Data (SmartData)*. 10.1109/Cybermatics_2018.2018.00258

Saberi, S., Kouhizadeh, M., Sarkis, J., & Shen, L. (2019). Blockchain technology and its relationships to sustainable supply chain management. *International Journal of Production Research*, *57*(7), 2117–2135. doi:10.1080/00207543.2018.1533261

SalahM.AlhalbusiH.IsmailM. M.AbdelfattahF. (2023). Chatting with ChatGPT: Decoding the Mind of Chatbot Users and Unveiling the Intricate Connections between User Perception, Trust and Stereotype Perception on Self-Esteem and Psychological Well-being [Preprint]. doi:10.21203/rs.3.rs-2610655/v2

Şalçini, S., & Yerlikaya, T. (2022). Metaverse: Technology of the Future. *Prizren Social Science Journal*, *6*(3), 55–63. doi:10.32936/pssj.v6i3.332

Salisu, A. A., Raheem, I. D., & Vo, X. V. (2021). Assessing the safe haven property of the gold market during the COVID-19 pandemic. *International Review of Financial Analysis*, *74*, 101666. doi:10.1016/j.irfa.2021.101666 PMID:36531084

Sankar, J. G., & David, A. (2023). Measuring the Service Quality of Artificial Intelligence in the Tourism and Hospitality Industry. In G. P. Fernandes & A. S. Melo (Eds.), *Advances in Hospitality, Tourism, and the Services Industry* (pp. 133–155). IGI Global. doi:10.4018/978-1-6684-6985-9.ch007

Sansa, N. A. (2020). The Impact of the COVID - 19 on the Financial Markets: Evidence from China and USA. *Electronic Research Journal of Social Sciences and Humanities*, *2*(2), 29–39.

Sansa, N. A. (2020). *The Impact of the COVID-19 on the Financial Markets: Evidence from China and USA*. Electronic Research Journal of Social Sciences and Humanities.

Schanzenbach, M. M., & Sitkoff, R. H. (2020). Reconciling fiduciary duty and social conscience: The law and economics of ESG investing by a trustee. *Stanford Law Review*, *72*(2), 381–454. https://review.law.stanford.edu/wp-content/uploads/sites/3/2020/02/Schanzenbach-Sitkoff-72-Stan.-L.-Rev.-381.pdf

Scholtens, B., & Sievänen, R. (2013). Drivers of socially responsible investing: A case study of four Nordic countries. *Journal of Business Ethics*, *115*(3), 605–616. doi:10.1007/s10551-012-1410-7

Schwab, K. (2008, January/February). Global corporate citizenship: Working with governments and civil society. *Foreign Affairs*, *87*(1), 107–118. https://www.jstor.org/stable/20020271

Sethi, S. P. (1975). Dimensions of corporate social performance: An analytical framework. *California Management Review*, *17*(3), 58–64. doi:10.2307/41162149

Shafeeg, A., Shazhaev, I., Mihaylov, D., Tularov, A., & Shazhaev, I. (2023). Voice Assistant Integrated with Chat GPT. *Indonesian Journal of Computer Science*, *12*(1). Advance online publication. doi:10.33022/ijcs.v12i1.3146

Shahzad, S. J. H., Mensi, W., Hammoudeh, S., Sohail, A., & Al-Yahyaee, K. H. (2019). Does gold act as a hedge against different nuances of inflation? Evidence from Quantile-on-Quantile and causality-in-quantiles approaches. *Resources Policy*, *62*, 602–615. doi:10.1016/j.resourpol.2018.11.008

Shaik, M. (2023). Impact of artificial intelligence on marketing. *East Asian Journal of Multidisciplinary Research*, *2*(3), 993–1004. doi:10.55927/eajmr.v2i3.3112

Sharif, Aloui, & Yarovaya. (2020). COVID-19 pandemic, oil prices, stock market, geopolitical risk and policy uncertainty nexus in the US economy: Fresh evidence from the wavelet-based approach. *International Review of Financial Analysis*, 70.

Shehzad, K., Bilgili, F., Zaman, U., Kocak, E., & Kuskaya, S. (2021). Is gold favorable to bitcoin during the COVID-19 outbreak? Comparative analysis through wavelet approach. *Resources Policy*, *102163*, 102163. Advance online publication. doi:10.1016/j.resourpol.2021.102163 PMID:34121797

Sheikholeslami, M., & Jafaryar, M. (2023). Performance of energy storage unit equipped with vase-shaped fins including nanoparticle enhanced paraffin. *Journal of Energy Storage*, *58*, 106416. doi:10.1016/j.est.2022.106416

Shen, B., Guo, J., & Yang, Y. (2019). MedChain: Efficient Healthcare Data Sharing via Blockchain. *Applied Sciences (Basel, Switzerland)*, *9*(6), 1207. doi:10.3390/app9061207

Shrier, D., Wu, W., & Pentland, A. (2016). Blockchain & infrastructure (identity, data security). Massachusetts Institute of Technology Connection Science, 1, 1–19.

Sicari, S., Rizzardi, A., Grieco, L. A., & Coen-Porisini, A. (2015). Security, privacy and trust in Internet of Things: The road ahead. *Computer Networks*, *76*, 146–164. doi:10.1016/j.comnet.2014.11.008

Singh, K. (2020). Banks banking on AI. *International Journal of Advanced Research in Management and Social Sciences*, *9*(9), 1–11.

Siyal, A., Junejo, A., Zawish, M., Ahmed, K., Khalil, A., & Soursou, G. (2019). Applications of Blockchain Technology in Medicine and Healthcare: Challenges and Future Perspectives. *Cryptography*, *3*(1), 3. doi:10.3390/cryptography3010003

Skiba, D. J. (2017). The potential of blockchain in education and health care. *Nursing Education Perspectives*, *38*, 220–221. doi:10.1097/01.NEP.0000000000000190 PMID:28622267

Skjuve, M., Følstad, A., & Brandtzaeg, P. B. (2023). The User Experience of ChatGPT: Findings from a Questionnaire Study of Early Users. *Proceedings of the 5th International Conference on Conversational User Interfaces*, 1–10. 10.1145/3571884.3597144

Smids, J., Nyholm, S., & Berkers, H. (2019). Robots in the workplace: A threat to – or opportunity for – meaningful work? *Philosophy & Technology*, *33*(3), 503–522. doi:10.1007/s13347-019-00377-4

Smith, S. S. (2020). Blockchain, smart contracts and financial audit implications. *IUP Journal of Accounting Research & Audit Practices*, *19*(1), 7–17.

Sohail, S. S., Farhat, F., Himeur, Y., Nadeem, M., Madsen, D. Ø., Singh, Y., Atalla, S., & Mansoor, W. (2023). The Future of GPT: A Taxonomy of Existing ChatGPT Research, Current Challenges, and Possible Future Directions. SSRN *Electronic Journal*. doi:10.2139/ssrn.4413921

Solouki, M., & Bamakan, S. M. H. (2022). An In-depth Insight at Digital Ownership Through Dynamic NFTs. *Procedia Computer Science*, *214*(C), 875–882. doi:10.1016/j.procs.2022.11.254

Soni, S., & Bhushan, B. (2019, July). A comprehensive survey on blockchain: Working, security analysis, privacy threats and potential applications. In *2019 2nd international conference on intelligent computing, instrumentation and control technologies (ICICICT)* (pp. 922-926). IEEE.

Sotiropoulou, T., Giakoumatos, S. G., & Petropoulos, D. P. (2019). Financial development, financial stability, and economic growth in European Union: A panel data approach. *Advances in Management and Applied Economics*, *9*(3), 55–69.

Sparkes, R. (2002). *Socially responsible investment: A global revolution* (J. Goodchild & C. Callow, Eds.). John Wiley & Sons Ltd.

Spindler, E. A. (2013). The history of sustainability: The origins and effects of a popular concept. In I. Jenkins & R. Schröder (Eds.), *Sustainability in tourism: A multidisciplinary approach* (pp. 9–31). Springer Gabler. doi:10.1007/978-3-8349-7043-5_1

Stahlke WallS. (2014). Focused Ethnography: A Methodological Adaptation for Social Research in Emerging Contexts. *Forum Qualitative Sozialforschung / Forum: Qualitative Social Research*, *16*(1). doi:10.17169/FQS-16.1.2182

Stephen, R., & Alex, A. (2018). A Review on Blockchain Security. In *Conference Series: Materials Science and Engineering* (Vol. 396, p. 1). IOP Publishing. Available online https://iopscience.iop.org/article/10.1088/1757-899X/396/1/012030/meta

Stewart, R., Chowdhury, M., & Arjoon, V. (2020). Bank stability and economic growth: Trade-offs or opportunities? *Empirical Economics*, 1–27.

StrachanJ.AlbergoD.BorghiniG.PansardiO.ScalitiE.RufoA.ManziG.GrazianoM.BecchioC. (2023). Testing Theory of Mind in GPT Models and Humans [Preprint]. doi:10.21203/rs.3.rs-3262385/v1

Strategic Organizing Center. (2019). *Primed for Pain: Amazon's Epidemic of Workplace Injuries*. https://thesoc.org/amazon-primed-for-pain/

Strzelecki, A. (2023). To use or not to use ChatGPT in higher education? A study of students' acceptance and use of technology. *Interactive Learning Environments*, 1–14. doi:10.1080/10494820.2023.2209881

Sudirjo, F., Diawati, P., Riady, Y., Almaududi Ausat, A. M., & Suherlan, S. (2023). The Role of ChatGPT in Enhancing the Information Search and Decision-Making Process of Travellers. *Jurnal Minfo Polgan*, *12*(1), 500–507. doi:10.33395/jmp.v12i1.12443

Sukoharsono, E. (2019). Sustaining a sustainability Report by modifying triple bottom line to pentaple bottom line: An imaginary research dialogue. *The International Journal of Accounting and Business Society*, *27*(1), 119–127. doi:10.21776/ub.ijabs.2019.27.1.7

Sun, Y., Zhang, J., Xiong, Y., & Zhu, G. (2014). Data Security and Privacy in Cloud Computing. *International Journal of Distributed Sensor Networks*, *10*(7), 190903. doi:10.1155/2014/190903

Surameery, N. M. S., & Shakor, M. Y. (2023). Use Chat GPT to Solve Programming Bugs. *International Journal of Information Technology and Computer Engineering*, *31*(31), 17–22. doi:10.55529/ijitc.31.17.22

Suveen, A., Krumholz, H. M., & Schulz, W. L. (2017). Blockchain technology: Applications in health care. *Circulation: Cardiovascular Quality and Outcomes*, *10*(9), e003800. doi:10.1161/CIRCOUTCOMES.117.003800 PMID:28912202

Swanson, T. (2015). *Consensus-as-a-service: A brief report on the emergence of permissioned, distributed ledger systems*. Report.

Swanson, D. L. (2008). Top managers as drivers for corporate social responsibility. In A. Crane, A. McWilliams, D. Matten, J. Moon, & D. S. Siegel (Eds.), *The Oxford handbook of corporate social responsibility* (pp. 227–248). Oxford University Press. doi:10.1093/oxfordhb/9780199211593.003.0010

Swart, R. J., Raskin, P., & Robinson, J. (2004). The problem of the future: Sustainability science and scenario analysis. *Global Environmental Change*, *14*(2), 137–146. doi:10.1016/j.gloenvcha.2003.10.002

Taherdoost, H. (2022). A critical review of blockchain acceptance models—Blockchain technology adoption frameworks and applications. *Computers*, *11*(2), 24. doi:10.3390/computers11020024

Talukder, M. B. (2021). An assessment of the roles of the social network in the development of the Tourism Industry in Bangladesh. *International Journal of Business, Law, and Education*, *2*(3), 85–93. doi:10.56442/ijble.v2i3.21

Tama, B. A., Kweka, B. J., Park, Y., & Rhee, K. H. (2017, August). A critical review of blockchain and its current applications. In *2017 International Conference on Electrical Engineering and Computer Science (ICECOS)* (pp. 109-113). IEEE. 10.1109/ICECOS.2017.8167115

Tantidham, T., & Aung, Y. N. (2019, March). Emergency service for smart home system using ethereum blockchain: System and architecture. In 2019 IEEE international conference on pervasive computing and communications workshops (PerCom Workshops) (pp. 888-893). IEEE.

Ten PierickE.BeekmanV.van der WeeleC. N.MeeusenM. J.de GraaffR. P. (2004). *A framework for analysing corporate social performance: Beyond the Wood model.* Agricultural Economics Research Institute. doi:10.22004/AG.ECON.29081

Thakor, A. V. (2018). Post-crisis regulatory reform in banking: Address insolvency risk, not illiquidity. *Journal of Financial Stability*, *37*, 107–111. doi:10.1016/j.jfs.2018.03.009

The European Union Blockchain Observatory & Forum. (2018). *Demystifying Non- Fungible Tokens (NFTs).* Author.

Thielen, P. (2005). *Good corporate citizenship: A Delphi study defining the key aspects according to the business and academic communities* (UMI No. 3160519) [Doctoral Dissertation, Fielding Graduate University]. ProQuest Publishing.

Torrence, C., & Compo, G. P. (1998). A practical guide to wavelet analysis. *Bulletin of the American Meteorological Society*, *79*(1), 61–78. doi:10.1175/1520-0477(1998)079<0061:APGTWA>2.0.CO;2

Torrence, C., & Webster, P. J. (1999). Interdecadal changes in the ENSO–monsoon system. *Journal of Climate*, *12*(8), 2679–2690. doi:10.1175/1520-0442(1999)012<2679:ICITEM>2.0.CO;2

Tosunoglu, B. T. (2018, June). Relationship Between Financial Stability and Economic Growth in Turkey (2002-2017). In *Proceedings of International Academic Conferences* (No. 6409266). International Institute of Social and Economic Sciences.

Trabelsi, N., Gozgor, G., Tiwari, A. K., & Hammoudeh, S. (2021). Effects of Price of Gold on Bombay Stock Exchange Sectoral Indices: New Evidence for Portfolio Risk Management. *Research in International Business and Finance*, *55*, 101316. doi:10.1016/j.ribaf.2020.101316 PMID:34173411

United Nations Environment Programme. (1992, June). *Convention on Biological Diversity* (Na. 92-8314). UNEP Environmental Law and Institutions Programme Activity Centre. https://wedocs.unep.org/bitstream/handle/20.500.11822/29146/COB.pdf?sequence=1&isAllowed=y

United Nations Environment Programme. (n.d.). *Stockholm+50: A Healthy Planet for the Prosperity of All – Our Responsibility, Our Opportunity.* https://www.stockholm50.global

United Nations General Assembly. (1987). *Development and international economic co-operation: Environment, Report of the World Commission on Environment and Development, Note by the Secretary-General* (A/42/427). New York: United Nations. https://digitallibrary.un.org/record/139811?ln=en

United Nations General Assembly. (1992). *Report of the United Nation Conference on Environment and Development: Rio Declaration on Environment and Development* (A/CONF.151/26) (Vol. I). Rio de Janeiro: United Nations. https://www.un.org/en/development/desa/population/migration/generalassembly/docs/globalcompact/A_CONF.151_26_Vol.I_Declaration.pdf

United Nations General Assembly. (1997). *Resolution adopted by the General Assembly: Programme for the further implementation of Agenda 21* (A/RES/S-19/2). New York: United Nations. https://digitallibrary.un.org/record/244113

United Nations General Assembly. (2012). *Resolution adopted by the General Assembly, The future we want* (A/RES/66/288). Rio de Janeiro: Rio+20 United Nations General Assembly. https://documents-dds-ny.un.org/doc/UNDOC/GEN/N11/476/10/PDF/N1147610.pdf

United Nations General Assembly. (2015). *Resolution adopted by the General Assembly on 29 September 2015: Transforming our world: The 2030 Agenda for Sustainable Development* (A/RES/70/1). New York: United Nations. https://documents-dds-ny.un.org/doc/UNDOC/GEN/N15/291/89/PDF/N1529189.pdf?OpenElement

United Nations General Assembly. (2017). *Implementation of the Outcomes of the United Nations Conferences on Human Settlements and on Housing and Sustainable Urban Development and strengthening of the United Nations Human Settlements Programme (UN-Habitat), New Urban Agenda: Draft resolution / submitted by the President of the General Assembly* (A/71/L.23). New York: United Nations. https://digitallibrary.un.org/record/850965?ln=en

United Nations. (1976). *Report of Habitat: United Nations Conference on Human Settlements, Vancouver, 31 May - 11 June 1976* (A/CONF.70.15). New York: United Nations Publication. https://digitallibrary.un.org/record/793768

United Nations. (1992a). *United Nations Conference on Environment and Development, Non-legally binding authoritative statement of principles for a global consensus on the management, conservation and sustainable development of all types of forests, Rio de Janeiro, 3-14 June 1992* (A/CONF.151/6). New York: United Nations Publication. https://digitallibrary.un.org/record/144461

United Nations. (1992b). *United Nations Framework Convention on Climate Change* (FCCC/INFORMAL/84 GE.05-62220 (E) 200705). New York: United Nations Publications. https://unfccc.int/resource/docs/convkp/conveng.pdf

United Nations. (1994). *United Nations Convention to Combat Desertification in those Countries Experiencing Serious Drought and / or Desertification, Particularly in Africa.* Paris: United Nations. https://catalogue.unccd.int/936_UNCCD_Convention_ENG.pdf

United Nations. (1996). *Report of the United Nations Conference on Human Settlements (Habitat II), Istanbul, 3-14 June 1996* (A/CONF.165/14 GE.96-02500 (E)). Istanbul: United Nations. New York: United Nations Publication. https://documents-dds-ny.un.org/doc/UNDOC/GEN/G96/025/00/PDF/G9602500.pdf?OpenElement

United Nations. (2002). *Report of the World Summit on Sustainable Development, Johannesburg, South Africa, 26 August - 4 September 2002* (A/CONF.199/20). New York: United Nations Publication. https://digitallibrary.un.org/record/478154

United Nations. (2022). *Stockholm+50: A healthy planet for the prosperity of all - Our responsibility, our opportunity, Stockholm, 2 and 3 June 2022* (A/CONF.238/9). Estonia: United Nations. https://documents-dds-ny.un.org/doc/UNDOC/GEN/K22/117/97/PDF/K2211797.pdf?OpenElement

United Nations. (n.d.-a). *United Nations Conference on Human Settlements - Habitat I Vancouver, Canada, 31 May-11 June 1976: Adequate shelter as a basic human right*. https://www.un.org/en/conferences/habitat/vancouver1976

United Nations. (n.d.-b). *United Nations Conference on Human Settlements: Habitat II: Urban Exodus*. https://www.un.org/en/conferences/habitat/istanbul1996

United Nations. (n.d.-c). *Special Session of the General Assembly on Habitat: Istanbul+5: 6-8 June 2001, New York: A Five-Year Review*. https://www.un.org/en/conferences/habitat/newyork2001

United Nations. (n.d.-d). *UN Conference on Housing and Sustainable Urban Development: Habitat III 17-20 October 2016, Quito, Ecuador: The Potential of Cities*. https://www.un.org/en/conferences/habitat/quito2016

Van Marrewijk, M. (2003). Concepts and definitions of CSR and corporate sustainability: Between agency and communion. *Journal of Business Ethics*, *44*(2), 95–105. doi:10.1023/A:1023331212247

Van Nooten, J., & Daelemans, W. (2023). Improving Dutch Vaccine Hesitancy Monitoring via Multi-Label Data Augmentation with GPT-3.5. *Proceedings of the 13th Workshop on Computational Approaches to Subjectivity, Sentiment, & Social Media Analysis*, 251–270. 10.18653/v1/2023.wassa-1.23

Vazirani, A. A., O'Donoghue, O., Brindley, D., & Meinert, E. (2019). Implementing Blockchains for Efficient Health Care: Systematic Review. *Journal of Medical Internet Research, 21*(2), e12439. doi:10.2196/12439 PMID:30747714

Vázquez-Cano, E., Ramírez-Hurtado, J. M., Sáez-López, J. M., & López-Meneses, E. (2023). ChatGPT: The brightest student in the class. *Thinking Skills and Creativity*, *49*, 101380. doi:10.1016/j.tsc.2023.101380

Verma, V. (2023). An overview of Blockchain Technology: Past & Future. *Eduzone: International Peer Reviewed/Refereed Multidisciplinary Journal, 12*(1), 100-104.

Verma, A., Bhattacharya, P., Madhani, N., Trivedi, C., Bhushan, B., Tanwar, S., Sharma, G., Bokoro, P. N., & Sharma, R. (2022). Blockchain for industry 5.0: Vision, opportunities, key enablers, and future directions. *IEEE Access : Practical Innovations, Open Solutions*, *10*, 69160–69199. doi:10.1109/ACCESS.2022.3186892

Vora, J., Nayyar, A., Tanwar, S., Tyagi, S., Kumar, N., Obaidat, M. S., & Rodrigues, J. J. (2018). BHEEM: A Blockchain-Based Framework for Securing Electronic Health Records. *Proceedings of the 2018 IEEE Globecom Workshops (GC Wkshps)*. 10.1109/GLOCOMW.2018.8644088

Wagner, A. F. (2020). What the stock market tells us about the post-COVID-19 world. *Nature Human Behaviour*, *4*(5), 440. doi:10.1038/s41562-020-0869-y PMID:32242087

Walid, Sensoy, Vo, & Kang. (2020). *Impact of COVID-19 outbreak on asymmetric multifractality of gold and oil prices*. doi:10.1016/j.resourpol.2020.101829

Wan, D., Xue, R., Linnenluecke, M., Tian, J., & Shan, Y. (2021). The impact of investor attention during COVID-19 on investment in clean energy versus fossil fuel firms. *Finance Research Letters*, *101955*. Advance online publication. doi:10.1016/j.frl.2021.101955 PMID:36406287

Wang, R., Bush-Evans, R., Arden-Close, E., Bolat, E., McAlaney, J., Hodge, S., Thomas, S., & Phalp, K. (2023). Transparency in persuasive technology, immersive technology, and online marketing: Facilitating users' informed decision making and practical implications. *Computers in Human Behavior*, *139*, 107545. doi:10.1016/j.chb.2022.107545

Wang, S. (2015). *Chinese strategic decision-making on CSR* (S. O. Idowu & R. Schmidpeter, Eds.). Springer. doi:10.1007/978-3-662-44997-4

Wang, S., Yuan, Y., Wang, X., Li, J., Qin, R., & Wang, F. Y. (2018, June). An overview of smart contract: architecture, applications, and future trends. In *2018 IEEE Intelligent Vehicles Symposium (IV)* (pp. 108-113). IEEE. 10.1109/IVS.2018.8500488

Wartick, S. L., & Cochran, P. L. (1985). The evolution of the corporate social performance model. *Academy of Management Review*, *10*(4), 758–769. doi:10.2307/258044

Weber, I., Xu, X., Riveret, R., Governatori, G., Ponomarev, A., & Mendling, J. (2016). Untrusted business process monitoring and execution using blockchain. In *International Conference on Business Process Management*. Springer. 10.1007/978-3-319-45348-4_19

Weber, M. (2008). The business case for corporate social responsibility: A company-level measurement approach for CSR. *European Management Journal*, *26*(4), 247–261. doi:10.1016/j.emj.2008.01.006

Weller, A. (2020). Exploring practitioners' meaning of "ethics", "compliance", and "corporate social responsibility" practices: A communities of practice perspective. *Business & Society*, *59*(3), 518–544. doi:10.1177/0007650317719263

Wiens, J. A. (2013). Is landscape sustainability a useful concept in a changing world? *Landscape Ecology*, *28*(6), 1047–1052. doi:10.1007/s10980-012-9801-9

Wilkinson, A., Hill, M., & Gollan, P. (2001). The sustainability debate. *International Journal of Operations & Production Management*, *21*(12), 1492–1502. doi:10.1108/01443570110410865

Witchey, N. J. (2019). *Healthcare Transaction Validation via Blockchain, Systems and Methods.* U.S. Patent No. 10,340,038.

Wong, I. A., Lian, Q. L., & Sun, D. (2023). Autonomous travel decision-making: An early glimpse into ChatGPT and generative AI. *Journal of Hospitality and Tourism Management*, *56*, 253–263. doi:10.1016/j.jhtm.2023.06.022

Wood, D. A. (2011). Back to 3BL basics. *Petroleum Review, 30*, 32. https://knowledge.energyinst.org/search/record?id=76840

Wood, D. J. (1991). Corporate social performance revisited. *Academy of Management Review, 16*(4), 691–718. doi:10.2307/258977

Wood, D. J. (2010). Measuring corporate social performance: A review. *International Journal of Management Reviews, 12*(1), 50–84. doi:10.1111/j.1468-2370.2009.00274.x

Wood, D. J., & Jones, R. E. (1995). Stakeholder mismatching: A theoretical problem in empirical research on corporate social performance. *The International Journal of Organizational Analysis, 3*(3), 229–267. doi:10.1108/eb028831

Wu, H. T., & Tsai, C. W. (2018). Toward blockchains for health-care systems: Applying the bilinear pairing technology to ensure privacy protection and accuracy in data sharing. *IEEE Consumer Electronics Magazine, 7*(4), 65–71. doi:10.1109/MCE.2018.2816306

Xu, X., Pautasso, C., Zhu, L., Gramoli, V., Ponomarev, A., Tran, A. B., & Chen, S. (2016). The blockchain as a software connector. *Software Architecture (WICSA), 2016 13th Working IEEE/IFIP Conference on, 2016*, 182-191. 10.1109/WICSA.2016.21

Yadav, A. S., Singh, N., & Kushwaha, D. S. (2023). Evolution of Blockchain and consensus mechanisms & its real-world applications. *Multimedia Tools and Applications, 82*(22), 1–46. doi:10.1007/s11042-023-14624-6

Yang, L., Liu, X. Y., & Gong, W. (2020, July). Secure smart home systems: A blockchain perspective. In *IEEE INFOCOM 2020-IEEE Conference on Computer Communications Workshops (INFOCOM WKSHPS)* (pp. 1003-1008). IEEE. 10.1109/INFOCOMWKSHPS50562.2020.9162648

Yan, Q., Lin, H., Zhang, M., Ai, X., Gejirifu, D., & Li, J. (2022). Two-stage flexible power sales optimization for electricity retailers considering demand response strategies of multi-type users. *International Journal of Electrical Power & Energy Systems, 137*, 107031. doi:10.1016/j.ijepes.2021.107031

Yeo-Teh, N. S. L., & Tang, B. L. (2023). Letter to editor: NLP systems such as ChatGPT cannot be listed as an author because these cannot fulfill widely adopted authorship criteria. Accountability in Research, 1–3. doi:10.1080/08989621.2023.2177160

Ye, S., & Karali, B. (2016). The informational content of inventory announcements: Intraday evidence from crude oil futures market. *Energy Economics, 59*, 349–364. doi:10.1016/j.eneco.2016.08.011

Yli-Huumo, J., Ko, D., Choi, S., Park, S., & Smolander, K. (2016). Where is current research on blockchain technology?—A systematic review. *PLoS One, 11*(10), e0163477. doi:10.1371/journal.pone.0163477 PMID:27695049

Younsi, M., & Nafla, A. (2019). Financial stability, monetary policy, and economic growth: Panel data evidence from developed and developing countries. *Journal of the Knowledge Economy, 10*(1), 238–260. doi:10.1007/s13132-017-0453-5

Youssef, M., Mokni, K., & Ajmi, A. N. (2021). Dynamic connectedness between stock markets in the presence of the COVID-19 pandemic: Does economic policy uncertainty matter? *Financial Innovation*, *7*(1), 13. doi:10.1186/s40854-021-00227-3 PMID:35024274

Yudiansyah, A., Keke, Y., & Veronica, V. (2020). Can the mobile robot be a future order-picking solution? A case study at Amazon fulfillment center. *Advances in Transportation and Logistics Research*, *3*(1), 800–806.

Yue, X., Wang, H., Jin, D., Li, M., & Jiang, W. (2016). Healthcare data gateways: Found healthcare intelligence on blockchain with novel privacy risk control. *Journal of Medical Systems*, *40*(10), 218. doi:10.1007/s10916-016-0574-6 PMID:27565509

Yu, H. (2023). Reflection on whether Chat GPT should be banned by academia from the perspective of education and teaching. *Frontiers in Psychology*, *14*, 1181712. doi:10.3389/fpsyg.2023.1181712 PMID:37325766

Zaremba, A., Kizys, R., Aharon, D. Y., & Demir, E. (2020). Infected markets: Novel coronavirus, government interventions, and stock return volatility around the globe. *Finance Research Letters*, *35*(101597), 101597. doi:10.1016/j.frl.2020.101597 PMID:32550842

Zezulka, F., Marcon, P., Vesely, I., & Sajdl, O. (2016). Industry 4.0 – An Introduction in the phenomenon. *IFAC-PapersOnLine*, *49*(25), 8–12. doi:10.1016/j.ifacol.2016.12.002

Zhang, P., Walker, M. A., White, J., Schmidt, D. C., & Lenz, G. (2017). Metrics for assessing blockchain-based healthcare decentralized apps. *Proceedings of the 2017 IEEE 19th International Conference on e-Health Networking, Applications and Services (Healthcom)*. 10.1109/HealthCom.2017.8210842

Zhang, P., White, J., Schmidt, D. C., & Lenz, G. (2017). Design of Blockchain-Based Apps Using Familiar Software Patterns to Address Interoperability Challenges in Healthcare. *Proceedings of the PLoP-24th Conference on Pattern Languages of Programs*.

Zhanga, Hua, & Jibc. (2020). Financial markets under the global pandemic of COVID-19. *Finance Research Letters*, 36. PMID:32837360

ZhangC.ZhangC.LiC.QiaoY.ZhengS.DamS. K.ZhangM.KimJ. U.KimS. T.ChoiJ.ParkG.-M. BaeS.-H.LeeL.-H.HuiP.KweonI. S.HongC. S. (2023). *One Small Step for Generative AI, One Giant Leap for AGI: A Complete Survey on ChatGPT in AIGC Era*. doi:10.48550/ARXIV.2304.06488

Zhang, P., Schmidt, D. C., White, J., & Lenz, G. (2018). Blockchain Technology Use Cases in Healthcare. In *Advances in Computers* (Vol. 111, pp. 1–41). Elsevier.

Zohuri, B., Nguyen, H. T., & Moghaddam, M. (2022). What is the Cryptocurrency. *Is it a Threat to Our National Security, Domestically and Globally*, 1-14.

Zyskind, G., & Nathan, O. (2015). Decentralizing privacy: Using blockchain to protect personal data. *Proceedings of the 2015 IEEE Security and Privacy Workshops*. 10.1109/SPW.2015.27

About the Contributors

* * *

Maithili Vijay Arjunwadkar received her doctorate from Symbiosis International University. She is currently working as a Director in PES Modern Institute of Business Studies, affiliated to Savitribai Phule Pune University, Maharashtra. She has more than 20 years of teaching and 3 years of industry experience. She has published more than 20 research papers in journals and international conferences. Her current research interest includes Data Security, Stenography, Cryptography, Block Chain Technology and Big data Analytics.

V. R. Balasaraswathi works as an Assistant Professor in the School of Computer Science and Engineering, Vellore Institute of Technology, Chennai, India. She received her Bachelor's degree in Computer Science and Engineering from Madras University in 2002 and a Master's in Computer Science and Engineering from Anna University in 2008. She completed her doctorate in Computer Science and Engineering in the year 2020.Her area of interest includes Machine Learning, Data Mining, and Artificial intelligence.

Badr Bentalha teaches Supply Chain and Operations Management at National School Of Business and Management – Fez, Sidi Mohamed Ben Abdellah University – Morocco. Dr. Bentalha investigates the structural dynamics and control of complex networks, applying his findings to supply chain management, Industry 4.0, risk analysis, and digital supply chains. Dr. Bentalha's academic background includes management and economics, operations research, and supply chain management. He studied management operations and supply chain management, graduating with honors. He earned PhD degrees and completed an aggregation in economics and management. Before entering academia, he primarily worked in industry and consulting, focusing on process optimization in manufacturing, logistics, and ERP systems. His practical experience includes numerous operations research and process optimization projects for operations design, logistics, scheduling, and supply chain management. Before joining the Fez National School of Business and Management, he was a professor of economics and management preparatory classes since 2009. Dr. Bentalha's influential research is cited in supply chain management and logistics. His publication record includes over 60 papers in prestigious academic journals such as the International Journal of Logistics Systems and Management, International Journal of Business Performance Management, International Journal of Business and Technology Studies, Journal of Environmental Issues and Climate Change, and Economical Managerial Alternatives. He is also the author of three books: Netnography: Principles, Method, and Ethics, Internal Audit of Treasury and Cash Management: Report on the Audit of Treasury and Integrating Intelligence and Sustainability in Supply Chains. Professor Bentalha specializes in supply chain and operations management, operations research, and service management. He is passionate about integrating knowledge across disciplines to solve real-world problems. He has delivered numerous invited plenary talks, keynotes, and panel discussions at conferences and global webinars. He serves as Associate Editor of the Economical Managerial Alternatives journal and is on the editorial boards and advisory committees of several other publications. He regularly presents his research and has chaired organized program committees, and served on advisory boards for over 60 international conferences.

Joel Jebadurai Devapitchai currently working as a Assistant Professor in Department of MBA St. Joseph's college of Engineering OMR Chennai. He has published two books and 50 research articles in various peer reviewed journals. For his research excellence, he has been rewarded the Major Research Projects by Indian Council of Social Science Research, New Delhi India.

Gokcen Evci received her BA in Business Administration from Marmara University and MSc in Accounting and Finance from the University of Leicester in 2014. She received a She has been awarded the Turkish Ministry of National Education Scholarship, and thus, in 2014 she was hired as a research assistant by the Yalova University (where she still works). She successfully passed the PhD Qualification Exam and continues her PhD studies in Finance at Istanbul University under the supervision of Istanbul University faculty member Professor Bengu Vuran. Her research interests are corporate finance, financial economics, corporate social responsibility, mergers and acquisitions, and econometrics, and financial mathematics.

Arnav Garg is a Student of BBA Fintech at Christ (Deemed to be University), Delhi, NCR.

Lamia Jamel is a PhD in Economics at the Faculty of Economic Sciences and Management of Sousse in University of Sousse, Tunisia. His research interests include Economic analysis, financial economics, quantitative finance, financial development, and energy commodities.

Babita Jha is working as an Associate Professor in Christ (Deemed to be University), Delhi-NCR.

Deepak Jha is an Assistant Professor in Christ (Deemed to be University).

Samay Jolly is a student of BBA Fintech at Christ (Deemed to be University).

Dheenadhayalan K., MBA, M.Com, M.Phil, is currently working as an Assistant Professor in Mepco School of Management Studies, Mepco Schlenk Engineering College, Sivakasi.

Sowmiya K. C., an accomplished Ph.D. scholar at Sri Vasavi College in Erode, emerges as a dynamic and vibrant researcher with a rich educational background. Having laid the foundation with a B.Ed. degree and furthered her academic pursuits with post-graduation at PSGR Krishnammal College for Women, she has adeptly positioned herself at the forefront of scholarly exploration. Her commitment to advancing knowledge is exemplified through her proactive involvement in two conferences in 2023, where she not only showcased her research prowess but also actively engaged with peers and experts, fostering meaningful discussions. Notably, the recognition garnered from presenting her research findings at these conferences has resulted in the acceptance of her journal article for publication later this year. This noteworthy achievement not only underscores Sowmiya's dedication to the academic realm but also highlights her impactful contributions to the scholarly discourse. As a Ph.D. scholar, she stands as a vibrant and influential contributor to the ever-evolving landscape of research and academic exploration, leaving an indelible mark on her field.

Sanjeev Kumar is an accomplished expert in Food and Beverage. He currently holds the positions of Professor at the Lovely Professional University, Punjab, India. With over a decade of experience in the field, food Service Industry, his research focuses on Alcoholic beverages, Event management and Sustainable Management Practices, Metaverse and Artificial Intelligence. He has published more than 35 research papers, articles, and chapters in Scopus Indexed, UGC Approved and peer reviewed Journals and books. Dr. Sanjeev Kumar participated and acted as resource person in various National and International conferences, seminars, research workshops and industry talks and his work has been widely cited.

Rajesh Kumar L. is an Assistant Professor in the Department of MBA. He has graduated BBA from Aditanar College of Arts and Sciences, MBA, and M.Phil from Manonmaniam Sundarnar University in Tirunelveli. In December 2012, he qualified for the UGC-NET examination. Then 2018, he received his Ph.D with a marketing specialization especially in FMCG. He started his career at Manonmaniam Sundaranar University College, Govindaperi, in September, 2012. After that, he moved to DMI. St. Eugune University, Zambia, for one year in the 2014–15 academic year. In 2015, he began his Ph.D. studies at Manonmaniam Sundarnar University in Tirunelveli. In July 2018, he submitted his thesis and started his journey at the Aarupadai Veedu Institute of Technology, Chennai, in February 2018. Then, in February 2020, he shifted his work to TNJFU - Fisheries Business School, Tamilnadu Dr.J. Jayalalithaa Fisheries University, OMR Campus, Chennai. After that, in October 2022, he joined as an assistant professor in the department of MBA at St.Joseph's College of Engineering, Chennai. Overall, he has 11 years of experience, including 3 years of research and 8 years of teaching. He has specialized in Marketing.

Rathi Meena M. has been rich experience in the field of research and teaching

Soundarya M. M. acted as an assistant professor in the School of management studies Sathyabama Institute of science and Technology. She has a lot of research papers to her credit.

Thirupathi Manickam, M.Com, M.Phil, B.Ed, TN-SET, KSET, Ph.D., works as an Assistant professor in the Department of Professional Studies at CHRIST (Deemed To Be University), Bangalore. It is one of the leading institutions in Bangalore, Karnataka, and the institution is Accredited by NIRF, NBA and NAAC Accredited university. He has more than seven years of teaching and Research experience. He has 68 citations and four h-Index. He has published 25 research papers in Scopus, Web of Science, UGC-CARE, and UGC-approved and leading international journals, and 14 presented papers at national and international conferences. He has also participated in over 40 seminars, conferences, FDP & workshops at the National and International Levels. His areas of expertise are Financial Accounting, Corporate Accounting, Financial Management, Management Accounting, Taxation, Digital Marketing and Technology Management.

L. Mary Shamala is currently working as an Assistant Professor in the School of Computer Science and Engineering, Vellore Institute of Technology, Chennai,

India. She received her Bachelor of Engineering Degree with distinction in Information Technology from Manonmanium Sundaranar University, Tirunelveli, India. She pursued her M.Tech and Ph.D. in Computer Science and Engineering from Pondicherry University, Puducherry, India. She has more than 12 years of teaching experience at undergraduate and postgraduate levels. Her areas of interest include Internet of Things Cryptography, Network and Information Security, Blockchain technologies, and Privacy in Online Social Networks.

Sabyasachi Pramanik is a professional IEEE member. He obtained a PhD in Computer Science and Engineering from Sri Satya Sai University of Technology and Medical Sciences, Bhopal, India. Presently, he is an Associate Professor, Department of Computer Science and Engineering, Haldia Institute of Technology, India. He has many publications in various reputed international conferences, journals, and book chapters (Indexed by SCIE, Scopus, ESCI, etc). He is doing research in the fields of Artificial Intelligence, Data Privacy, Cybersecurity, Network Security, and Machine Learning. He also serves on the editorial boards of several international journals. He is a reviewer of journal articles from IEEE, Springer, Elsevier, Inderscience, IET and IGI Global. He has reviewed many conference papers, has been a keynote speaker, session chair, and technical program committee member at many international conferences. He has authored a book on Wireless Sensor Network. He has edited 8 books from IGI Global, CRC Press, Springer and Wiley Publications.

Vetrivel S. C. is a faculty member in the Department of Management Studies, Kongu Engineering College (Autonomous), Perundurai, Erode Dt. Having experience in Industry 20 years and Teaching 16 years. Awarded with Doctoral Degree in Management Sciences in Anna University, Chennai. He has organized various workshops and Faculty Development Programmes. He is actively involved in research and consultancy works. He acted as a resource person to FDPs & MDPs to various industries like, SPB ltd, Tamilnadu Police, DIET, Rotary school and many. His areas of interest include Entrepreneurship, Business Law, Marketing and Case writing. Articles published more than 100 International and National Journals. Presented papers in more than 30 National and International conferences including IIM Bangalore, IIM Kozhikode, IIM Kashipur and IIM Indore. He was a Chief Co-ordinator of Entrepreneurship and Management Development Centre (EMDC) of Kongu Engineering College, he was instrumental in organizing various Awareness Camps, FDP, and TEDPs to aspiring entrepreneurs which was funded by NSTEDB – DST/GoI.

Anushka Sharma is a Post Graduate student in the School of Computer Science and Engineering, Vellore Institute of Technology, Chennai, India.

Raajvunsh Singh is a student of BBA Fintech at Christ (Deemed to be University), Delhi, NCR.

Mohammad Badruddoza Talukder is an Assistant Professor & Head of the Department, Department of Tourism and Hospitality Management, Daffodil Institute of Information Technology (at the National University), Dhaka, Bangladesh. Presently, he is pursuing PhD in Hotel Management, School of Hotel Management and Tourism, Lovely Professional University, India. He holds a bachelor's and a master's degree in Hotel Management from India. He has been teaching various courses in the Department of Tourism and Hospitality at various universities in Bangladesh since 2008. His research areas include tourism management, hotel management, hospitality management, food & beverage management, and accommodation management, where he has published research papers in well-known journals in Bangladesh and abroad. Mr. Talukder is one of the executive members of the Tourism Educators Association of Bangladesh. He has led training and consulting for a wide range of hospitality organizations in Bangladesh. He just became an honorary facilitator at the Bangladesh Tourism Board's Bangabandhu international tourism and hospitality training institute.

Sabareeshwari V. currently serves as Assistant Professor in Department of Soil Science, Amrita School of Agricultural Sciences, Coimbatore. Having more than 5 years of research experience and more than 2 years of teaching experience. She got 7 awards in the field of agriculture. Her field of expertise are soil genesis, soil pedological studies as well as soil fertility mapping using advanced software like Arc GIS. She had published 22 research papers and more than 10 book chapters and books in high- impact reputed journals. She has actively participated and presented her papers in more than 20 conferences and seminars. She not only restrict her contribution only in the academic and research part, she had extension experience at farm level (lab to land) with varied crop research.

Hudson Arul Vethamanikam G. works as Assistant Professor at Ayya Nadar Janaki Ammal College, Sivakasi, Tamil Nadu. His Educational Qualifications are M.B.A., M.Com., MHRM., M.Phil., and Ph.D., in Management. His specialization is in Accounting and Finance. He published 03 books such as Financial Management, Production and Operations Management, Principles of Management. He has over 37 National and International publications to his credit and has Membership in 16 National, International, Professional and Academic bodies. He has received 15 honours or awards from Professional bodies, Universities across the global, including Academic Professional Award, Dubai in 2019 and Excellent Professional Achievement [Business Management] Award, Malaysia in 2018. He has been the editor of several National and International Journals. His academic research includes 61 research paper presentations in different conferences and seminars across the globe. He has organized eight programs like FDPs, seminars, conferences and workshops. He has attended 45 Faculty Development Programme organized by different reputed institutes, colleges and universities.

Bengu Vuran (Professor) received her BA and her Master's degree in Business Administration from Istanbul University. She has successfully completed her PhD degree in Finance from Istanbul University. The title of her PhD dissertation was "Model Studies Related to Firm Failure Prediction: An Application in Turkey". Currently, she is a Professor of Finance at the same university. The courses she teaches include International Finance, Financial Management, Business Finance, Financial Statement Analysis, Risk Management and Financial Instruments, and Strategic Finance Decisions. Her research interests are financial markets and investment management, financial statement analysis, accounting, corporate finance, corporate governance, and strategic finance decisions.

Index

T

V

W

www.ingramcontent.com/pod-product-compliance
Lightning Source LLC
LaVergne TN
LVHW080635011026
849160LV00014B/1220